Entrepreneurship and Development in South Asia: Longitudinal Narratives

Series Editor

Jay Mitra, Essex Business School, University of Essex, Colchester Campus, UK

The series aims to provide a unique new insight into entrepreneurship and development in South Asia, using a longitudinal narrative approach based on qualitative empirical analysis of actual developments on the ground. The focus is on new business and social enterprise creation and their impact on opportunity creation, job creation, contribution to local GDP, resolution of regional economic and social issues, the environment, and social attitudes towards entrepreneurship and innovation in all their forms (i.e. business and social). It especially examines the relationship between policy and practice and the mediating effects of context and institutions on this relationship. The series will cover policy issues concerning entrepreneurship, innovation and economic development as they affect people, organisations and the environment in specific regions in South Asia.

Omar Javaid

Socioeconomic Sustainability Through Moral and Social Capital

A Tale of Three Enterprising Communities

Springer

Omar Javaid
Department of Entrepreneurship
Institute of Business Management
Karachi, Pakistan

ISSN 2367-2722 ISSN 2367-2730 (electronic)
Entrepreneurship and Development in South Asia: Longitudinal Narratives
ISBN 978-981-96-8133-4 ISBN 978-981-96-8134-1 (eBook)
https://doi.org/10.1007/978-981-96-8134-1

This Springer imprint is published by the registered company Springer Nature Singapore Pte Ltd.
The registered company address is: 152 Beach Road, #21-01/04 Gateway East, Singapore 189721, Singapore

Dedicated to Sadia

Ahmed, and

Ayesha

Preface

Almost two decades ago, when I first formally studied unemployment and inflation as externalities of economic policies, I was told that during economic growth, the poor were affected by inflation, while during the recession, it was unemployment. I was dumbfounded and could not help but ask where relief was for the poor. This apparent weakness of the macroeconomic strategies I learned in my MBA course got me interested in poverty alleviation programs. The microfinance approach, like the one initiated by Dr. Yunus in Bangladesh, appealed to me the most. I then became a voluntary member of a non-profit initiative in the city that provided interest-free microfinance to the poor to start small businesses. In the universities I taught at, I also supervised many projects where students would identify a poor, unemployed fellow and help them start a business with donations raised from their network. While I was engaged in such projects, something struck me. It was not just the lack of finance, but the lack of moral support that also appeared critically important for the poor. The poor folk did not just lack financial capital, but they also felt isolated, and the idea that someone cared for them and was willing to offer support till they stood on their feet appeared to have greatly impacted their morale. In this process, I heard many stories of how the poor became poor. Many of them had better financial status earlier, but a tragedy took their livelihood away. But this was not the end of the story. All of them said something similar, that the people in their network or neighborhood did not step up to help them out of their crisis. It did not appear to be a purely economic problem in all cases, but a social one as well. These individuals were excluded from their social networks. They suffered alienation.

In contrast, there were stories about rags to riches. Stories of people who were poor or came from humble backgrounds but, in a few decades, were able to erect business empires. Looking closely at the story of such entrepreneurs reveals that they often belong to some communities known for their entrepreneurial orientation. Among many such communities in the country, Memon, Delhiwala, and Chinioti were the leading ones. When I looked up the academic literature on the socioeconomic dynamics of these communities, I could not find much. I thus got motivated to explore the particularities of these communities in my doctoral thesis. The communities appeared to remain socially cohesive while thriving economically. My primary interest in my doctoral research was how the community members evaded the socially disintegrating effects of economic activity, which is a typical side effect of neoliberal-style capitalism. On the flip side, the emotional aspect of social relationships is often also seen as an impediment to economic activity. So, I wanted to explore how the community members kept the social and economic prevailing side by side, without one harming the other. My exploration for my doctoral research also supported my earlier understanding of poverty. That is, the absence of social support isolates people in crisis, worsening their condition and keeping them trapped there. However, a supporting community that would not alienate but would come forward to help and uplift a struggling person can be seen as a potent antidote to poverty.

The book, therefore, attempts to show how the communities in focus have been maintaining their social support for each other while thriving economically. It explores the social and moral angles of the problem while also attempting to understand why social disintegration, poverty, and alienation emerged in the modern market society, particularly when it operates on neoliberal lines. The book's first four chapters discuss the theoretical aspects of the problem and the solution. Chapters 5–7 discuss the particularities of the communities I studied; however, I have attempted to evaluate the findings within these chapters, particularly in Chap. 8, in light of the literature from other places to improve the relevance for international readers.

The approach taken in this book has been multidisciplinary as it evaluates the problems in focus and their possible solutions from multiple angles. The book looks at the historical and cultural particularity of modern markets from a post-colonial studies perspective. The book also looks at the genealogical foundations of the market institutions that legitimize their socially disintegrating character. It will dwell on the psychology of human relations, which affects one's moral behavior, and how it is shaped inside a family environment. The literature on family business and literature on contemporary and pre-modern community-based economic activity also enriches the discussion in the book. The question of morality is likewise evaluated from historical, philosophical, psychological, and theological lenses. It cannot be claimed, of course, that the book covers the entirety of the issue in focus, and is free from errors and bias. The research was done in a social constructivist research paradigm, which suggests that it is impossible for any research, even in physical sciences, to be free from bias. Social reality is complex and multi-layered, so it cannot be ruled out that some aspects of the problem could have been overlooked. So, readers are requested to provide constructive feedback and ask necessary questions to probe the issues further from angles that may require further exploration in future work.

The journey taken to write this book could not have been completed without the immense support from several individuals. Their direct and often indirect support and guidance helped in the stages of data collection and analysis, and the conceptual understanding that then guides the conclusion drawn from the data and relevant literature. Dr. Irfan Hyder's mentorship and special interest in fine-tuning my doctoral thesis cannot be overstated in this sense. Dr. Hyder went the extra mile, even inviting me to his home on weekends to improve the thesis after Dr. Keith Thomas from Victoria University, Australia (one of the external reviewers of my doctoral thesis) rejected my thesis during the review process. Special thanks to Dr. Thomas as well, as without the crisis he put me through, I would not have given it the extra effort needed to refine the work. Dr. Amir Feroz Shamsi, who formally supervised my doctoral thesis, was the one who found Dr. Thomas to review my thesis and did all in his capacity to keep my morale high in the process. The entire process, however, still became too stressful and traumatizing, keeping me from wanting to work in the same domain for a long time. This is where the help of my wife, Sadia, deserves a special mention. Further, Psychologist Syeda Fatima Zehra's advice and guidance became critical in my recovery, which later allowed me to revive my interest in the subject and find the motivation to write this book. The readers would notice that at various places in the book, I have included the psychological perspective to explain certain details about human relationships and moral behavior. This was possible because of my interest in the domain of psychology, which was reignited by Ms. Fatima while she helped me gain perspective on the psychological trauma I developed in the process of completing my thesis. The philosophical angle that enriches the discussion in the book is credited to two more of my informal teachers. One of them is Dr. Wahab Suri, Chairman Philosophy Department at Karachi University, who has always been kind enough to provide me guidance whenever I have made a request. The other is Dr. Asad Zaman, former Vice Chancellor of Pakistan Institute of Developmental Economics, who introduced me to the work of Karl Polanyi and many other notable thinkers that enrich the discussion in this book. The students in the classes I have taught have frequently shared their feedback when I discuss my findings and interpretations with them, so I am also grateful for their input. I would like to extend special gratitude to MPhil students of 2016 batch, namely: Muhammad Adeel Hanif, Abdul Wahid, Sadia Umar, Muneshia Maheshwari, Aqsa Sikandar, Kamran Nawaz, Falak Shad Memon, Saniya Mehboob, and Zain Zeeshan helped me in the process of identifying, interviewing the respondents and transcribing the interviews. I am also thankful to Mr. Noman Mehmood, my colleague, for his authentic feedback, which helped in improving the quality of the output of this dissertation. I am also indebted to Dr. Shahid Qureshi, currently Rector at GIFT University, Gujranwala Campus, who guided me to improve the basic idea of my doctoral thesis during the very early stages of my work. My parents' and ancestors' experiences also played a significant role in shaping my understanding of the significance of the problems addressed in this book. Finally, all praise to God for bringing these amazing individuals to guide me along the process.

I hope the book will allow readers to see the source and solution to problems in question from a multidisciplinary angle, as viewing a problem and its solution from the vantage point of a single academic lens often misses out on many critical components. A multidisciplinary perspective therefore would offer a more informed view to understand and address a problem of a socioeconomic nature, which is also in its essence a moral problem.

Karachi, Pakistan — Omar Javaid

Contents

List of Figures

List of Tables

Chapter 1
Introduction

Every year, almost a million people die from suicide worldwide, and many others seek relief from various addictive substances, some of which are also legally available, such as sugar, alcohol, or nicotine. Suicide and addiction abuse are two of the leading causes of death among the younger population (WHO, 2023), particularly in high-income countries (Ishimo et al., 2021). The experts identify several interconnected causes, like a prevailing sense of isolation, individualistic culture, lack of meaningful connections with a collective, poverty caused by social and economic exclusion, social disintegration, greater feelings of deprivation due to inequalities, and class consciousness (Baudelot & Establet, 2008). Inequality, poverty, exclusion, and social disintegration make many see themselves as not good enough in comparison to a few who enjoy wealth and social status. The teenagers hooked to social media also feel likewise when they compare themselves to others in the digital world. Haidt (2023), for example, argues that this sense of worthlessness among teenagers caused by online comparisons has likely contributed to a rise in self-harm and suicidal ideation among teenage girls in particular. The rate of suicide and suicidal ideation is intriguingly higher on average in high-income countries despite greater support available for mental health as compared to low-income countries (WHO, 2019). The health care system typically attempts to treat the condition with psychiatric drugs, which, as per Storr (2018), if they become unavailable, the number of people who would want to end their lives, or who would attempt to do so, would rise many times. Now, if I extend Storr's hypothesis and imagine that alcohol also disappears along with narcotic drugs, online gaming, junk food, and anything that generates a temporary pleasure-inducing or pain-numbing neurochemical activity, then the number may go even higher, perhaps making suicide among the top causes of death in some high-income countries. So, the idea that 'I am not good enough' when exacerbated beyond a certain limit may turn into a severe existential crisis, which can push a person toward addiction, or even suicidal ideation, eventually, when distractions prove to be ineffective.

O. Javaid, *Socioeconomic Sustainability Through Moral and Social Capital*,
Entrepreneurship and Development in South Asia: Longitudinal Narratives,
https://doi.org/10.1007/978-981-96-8134-1_1

This sense of worthlessness is often socially constructed, as individuals can likely assume so or otherwise based on their interaction with others (Bandura, 1972; Blumer, 1986). So, when individuals with the agency and skills to make themselves useful also have the opportunities to prove their usefulness, which is also appreciated by others, like their family or community, are unlikely to develop a sense of unworthiness (Rosenberg, 1979). Even in the case of some disability, it is entirely possible that others around can help the disabled to be of use. In the case of children (Harter, 1999) or the elderly, who cannot always prove their usefulness, more care and compassion are needed to communicate their worthiness (Rowe & Kahn, 1997). Being among supportive people who compassionately help the vulnerable is unlikely to develop a sense of inadequacy, even for the disabled or vulnerable (Holt-Lunstad et al., 2010). The absence of such support would lead to what Durkheim (2005) referred to as 'anomie' for an individual, which, according to Durkheim, is a major reason why people may want to commit suicide in the modern world. Marx (2012) also acknowledged the problem of alienation that emerges from social disintegration when a traditional society is turned into a market society as per the logic of capitalism's production apparatus. This apparatus attempts to disintegrate everything it engages into bits, from social order to nature, even the individual's psyche, to selectively use the bits for its goals. Erich Fromm has also acknowledged that labor in the industrial world feels like an insignificant, dispensable part of a giant machine, the entirety of which is beyond the grasp of an individual working in a minuscule corner of the whole (Fromm, 2017). Fromm contrasts this with the traditional society where the laborers would directly experience the output of their efforts, which had meaning within their sociocultural premise, giving the laborers a sense of relevance. Such a sociocultural order reportedly has been facing disintegration due to the spread of modern markets organized on neoliberal lines (Jaffe & Quark, 2006).

To prove their worth, individuals resort to consumption in the contemporary market society. To feel socially accepted, one ought to be driving a certain car, living in a certain locality, and wearing clothes and accessories of certain brands (Bauer et al., 2012; Harvey, 2005). Many who are unable to do so feel left behind. Their existential crisis deepens, often pushing them toward suicidal ideation. However, for those who can afford much of the stuff the market has to offer, at the end of the day, their feeling of not being good enough does not necessarily disappear (Han, 2015) unless they seek fulfillment in meaningful relationships (Waldinger & Schulz, 2023). A person who is content with what they have and does not feel the need to prove their worth, who belongs to a community that reinforces their self-worth, would perhaps be seen as a bad consumer in the world of capitalism. A good consumer is perhaps an addicted consumer (Courtwright, 2021), and a consumer who feels alienated has a greater propensity to become addicted to the stuff available in the market. Johann Hari, for example, has also connected the problem of addiction with alienation (Hari & Corballis, 2019). Alexander (2010) and Maté (2013) also suggest that mass addiction caused by a feeling of alienation, rejection, and a sense of unworthiness has become a driver of excessive consumption, and thus excessive production. Woodman (1993) would also agree.

It appears that the population with addictive tendencies cannot get enough of it, consequently, the production apparatus produces a lot more than needed, leading to a variety of problems, such as damage to the ecosystem and unequal distribution of all resources, including food. The dots, perhaps, are not too hard to connect. Those with higher purchasing power often get stuck in a vicious cycle of buying more and more as much as their purchasing power allows, leading to a colossal amount of waste as well. Processed food, for example, is addictive as it is designed to engage the dopamine receptors through sugar and other ingredients. The population with enough purchasing power buys and consumes more than necessary in the USA, for example. Obesity and food waste then become huge problems. In the USA 1/3rd of the population is overweight and every 2 in 5 people are obese (Fryar et al., 2020), while 66 million tons of food (that is around 140 billion meals) is wasted in the US every year (EPA, 2020), and yet at the same time, 40 million people in the US face hunger (USDA, 2023). Globally, 9 million people die of hunger every year, as per the UN (2008). Food and other stuff, it appears, go to those who can pay more, even if they waste much of it, while those who are in desperate need often starve to death. Starvation is not always caused by the supply chain of global capitalism, but more than often it contributes to exacerbating global inequalities by either exploiting the local population in the global south or pushing them into economic activity, often forcefully, that benefits the capitalist economy while not allowing enough space for indigenous solutions to spring up (Escobar, 2012). Subsequent resource deprivation thus forces many to migrate, disintegrating their communities, and furthering dislocation and alienation (Sachs, 2010). Therefore, it can be said that the sense of alienation of a class of people on one side of the world indirectly contributes to the alienation of another class on another side of the planet (Harvey, 2005).

1.1 Alienation as a Factor of Production

Alienation can happen more in crowded places, as the feeling of loneliness is more significant when a person has to put up a performance much of the time in public. Fromm (2017) calls it 'moral loneliness'. Putting up a fake smile when feeling sad, frustrated, angry, or scared can be painful and traumatizing (Gabor Maté, 2013). Employees are expected to put up a performance and perform as expected by their employers. Because if they do not, someone else may outperform and take their position. It can get exhausting and draining, sparking a need for stimulants that generate a continuous supply of dopamine to keep them from losing motivation (Volkow & Boyle, 2018). Maté (2012) talks about the Buddhist idea of hungry ghosts in this context. Furthering the thought, one may ask, how many sandwiches are needed to quench thirst? This question may sound ridiculous, as it seems to presume an absurdity, but unfortunately, it's a common phenomenon in the modern world. For example, when stressed out, destressing is needed, like spending time with loved ones and being authentic in a safe space to unwind; however, many choose to consume carbs or sugary stuff while watching movies. They therefore get hooked on junk food, social media, shopping, and a variety of stuff offered by the market today that claims to come to our rescue (Courtwright, 2021). Lambke (2021) suggests that the excess dopamine that is produced by our brains in this cycle of consumption tips off our homeostasis, eventually making us depressed. The worsened physical and psychological health of affected people becomes another profit-making opportunity for the medical-industrial complex. Capitalism wins again. Capitalism, it appears, has an autonomic propensity to create a problem, like a sense of being not good enough, and then introduce profit-focused symptomatic treatments (like consumerism), never focusing on the root cause (Beck & Ritter, 1992). Dopamine, therefore, has become the most prized neurochemical for the capitalist world, manipulation of which is so common that David Cockwright called it "limbic capitalism", as it is the limbic system of the brain that experiences the dopamine-related neural activity (Courtwright, 2021).

Alienation, therefore, can be seen as an indirect factor of production, but a direct factor of consumption, a lot of which may not happen if a healthy social environment is available. A Harvard study, spanning four generations, identifies what keeps us healthy and happy, and it is not the stuff sold by 'limbic capitalism' today; it is rather healthy relationships with family and friends (Waldinger & Schulz, 2023). A social environment where individuals are supported during moments of emotional vulnerability, are accepted unconditionally, and are cared for when they are sick. It's a place where people do not have to constantly put up a performance, and also offer the same support to others when needed, as it gives life a sense of purpose. Since known history, homo sapiens have survived via such social environments (Diamond, 2012). Could the modern market society provide us with it instead of manipulating and eventually exploiting us due to the vulnerabilities created by the absence of such an environment? The answer is perhaps no, as in capitalism, it is argued, problems are typically not solved but used as profit-making opportunities (Beck & Ritter, 1992).

Liang (1999) suggests that the problem of alienation and a sense of unworthiness makes a modern subject haunted by their existence. Polanyi (2001) describes that the sense of unworthiness and alienation was reinforced by the experience of being dislocated during the early stages of capitalism. People had to leave their families behind to make a living, to avoid the risk of starvation. The forced dislocation during the enclosure movement in Europe is a notable historical episode in this context (Thompson, 2016). During the colonial periods, the indigenous people in the Americas, Africa, and Australia were also brutally exploited and dislocated (Dunbar-Ortiz, 2023; Zinn, 2003). The exploitation of the same regions in the south, now more systemic, is still a distinct feature of capitalism today as well (Escobar, 2012; Harvey, 2005; Sachs, 2010). The fear of exclusion and starvation still keeps people clinging to exploitative structures in many countries. In places that have excelled economically in this global order, the common folk may not fear starvation, but the fear of being left behind in the race for material consumption haunts commoners, often leading them to 'burnout', in the words of Han (2015). The race never stops, as there is always another level that promises more than the current status, making satiation unlikely. In urban areas, the fear would push people to work multiple jobs, barely giving them enough time to reflect on what they need, and even if they do realize it, there is not enough time to be with friends and family. More materialism, wealth, and subsequent hollower relationships sustain the feeling of alienation and unworthiness, thus endlessly pushing those caught up in this vicious cycle to keep finding a symptomatic quick fix. Alienation and the addictive tendency it generates, therefore, can be said to be a key driver of consumption, as it fuels a multi-trillion-dollar industry (Courtwright, 2021). Many now also die of overconsumption, whether it be an overdose of an illegal substance, a legal substance like sugar (leading to obesity), or alcohol.

1.2 Antidote to Alienation

Capitalism's antagonism with nature is no secret, hence the concept of sustainability. When the term sustainability is mentioned, it generally refers to the sustainability of the ecosystem and the biosphere. What is discussed less often, it seems, is the sustainability of the organic form of the human family, comprised of a mother and father, their children, and their children, and so on, forming tribes, or kinship networks. A social environment that would naturally give an individual a sense of worthiness and belongingness; an environment that has existed since the beginning of history (Diamond, 2012; Fromm, 2017). Extended families, which often turn into large tribes that eventually grow into major ethnic groups in a society, having a distinct sociocultural environment, often provide a sense of belonging to their members. Survival of such environments has increasingly been threatened by neoliberal-style Capitalism. Such tribes or communities used to be part of the biosphere, living close to nature while holding great reverence for it. Their deep respect for nature and ways to mutually co-exist with it has been an integral part of their sociocultural imagination (Maffi, 2018). The idea of sustainability, therefore, should also include the sustenance of the social organization of human life, which naturally sprang from the process of organizing family life in its very organic sense. Many now acknowledge the fact that sustaining the natural social order is also critical for the survival of nature as a whole as well, and it is the way of life of the traditional societies; their ways involving sharing and caring can offer a guide for the rest of the world particularly when it comes to taking care of biosphere (Caputi, 2020; Jackson, 2011; Maffi, 2018; Shiva, 2016). A balance is thus needed in how humans organize their collective affairs with what exists naturally, as our survival as a species requires such a balance.

This balance has been lost particularly in the contemporary world, where the norms of capitalism dominate, the market colonizes the family, the natural social life suffers from the tyranny of the public or private institutional order, while individuals are allowed to act freely in the market but only as consumers, where freedom comes in proportion to their purchasing power, but within the range of options presented to them by the market (Sandel, 2012). The primary aim of the order of the market or the state in the capitalist world is, of course, to maximize returns or GDP, while individuals are pushed to maximize their consumption (Curtis, 2011). The economy sustains, but at the cost of social and environmental sustainability, eventually causing many of the modern problems, which then become key concerns behind each of the

SDGs advocated by the United Nations. However, it appears that the treatment of these problems in SDGs discourse is merely symptomatic (Raworth, 2017; Sachs, 2010). The underlying systemic causes are overlooked, such as the tyrannical dominance of economic structures over the natural order, social order in particular. This book attempts to contribute to the discourse that explains the causes behind such dominance, its eventual consequences on our collective and individual lives, and how to organize economic and social life in harmony. In complex societies, markets become indispensable because of the division of labor. The division then necessitates the phenomenon of exchange, which makes it essential that a corresponding parallel order is sustained where sharing and caring happen more unconditionally, as humans are often vulnerable and not always in a position to sell their labor or produce. The two need to go together, so the question is how we can learn to create and maintain this balance wherever needed. To find an answer to this question, we can perhaps look at the enterprising communities around the world that have been relatively successful in doing so.

We, however, need to do so with caution, as the social environment of any community can also become unhealthy and unsustainable for reasons other than the dominance of the market itself. The environment of tribes or communities, for example, may suffocate individuals of their authenticity, creating theproblem of moral loneliness as described by Erich Fromm. That is why the emphasis on the health of the community is essential, which implies that there is a balance between the needs of the collective and the needs of the individuals, which, if not maintained, takes a culture either toward being too tyrannical or too chaotic. This may happen because of too much stagnation or adherence to certain cultural norms that do not allow change even when the norms no longer serve the needs of the members. No community or society can be deemed as perfect, so any human organization needs to keep improving to meet the unmet needs and adapt to external circumstances beyond its control. The inability to adapt, therefore, can weaken the ability of a community to sustain itself as well (Diamond, 2013). Such tendencies also require a cure, and should not be blamed on the market itself. So, there is also a need to explore the causes of such rigidity and how to remain flexible to sustain socially. A key challenge in this context can be the conflict between individual needs and the need to maintain a collective order for social stability. Leaning toward the former can cause chaos, instability, and insecurity, while leaning toward the latter can be tyrannical and suffocating for an individual's creative potential (Peterson, 2002). How then to maintain this balance between order and chaos, 'mimesis' of a culture, and 'poiesis' of an individual (Trueman & Dreher, 2020)? This has been noted as a key challenge throughout history (Fukuyama, 2011; Peterson, 2002). This book also explores how this internal balance within the organic social environments could be possible, as any imbalance will weaken the position of organic social environments in opposition to capitalism. This imbalance may allow the capitalist markets to take advantage of insecure or desperate individuals belonging to unhealthy communities.

To present its argument, the book dwells on how this balance is maintained in some communities in South Asia, currently in the Pakistan region, which have kept their organic social environment alive for many centuries while also thriving economically. While discussing three specific communities in detail, the book attempts to compare their particularities with other examples across the region and the world to establish that their story is not unique, but is shared to an extent by other communities in the world today, historically as well. There are many communities around the world today, referred to as enterprising communities (Dana et al., 2007; Ojo, 2019), or ethnic entrepreneurial communities (Adendorff & Halkias, 2014; Aldrich & Waldinger, 1990; Ramadani et al., 2019; Volery, 2007), which share comparable characteristics, that are described at appropriate places where necessary. The flow of discussion, however, follows the findings from the country's three most prominent communities, referred to as Memon, Delhiwala, and Chinioti. These findings are based on the data collected by the author in his doctoral research, which was analyzed and processed as per Eisenhardt's case-based method of theory development within a social constructivist paradigm. The details of the research process have been published in an open-access paper(See: Javaid & Hyder, 2018).

1.3 Key Concepts

The book uses certain terms to refer to the nature of economic and social entities that have the potential to get into an unhealthy conflict with each other, leading to imbalance. Below are some definitions of these terms, which may appear reductionist and oversimplifying; however, they may be sufficient to identify their contrast despite their low resolution. In the context of the original thesis of this book, markets and their institutions are referred to be primarily 'rational' in nature, organic family and community or tribe have an 'emotional' and 'social' foundation, and thus also have a 'cultural' component which binds them together, individuals, on the other hand, can be 'creative' and have the potential to act 'morally', both of which can go against the cultural norms or rational objectives of the market.

The term 'rational' is used in a Weberian sense to refer to the techniques to improve efficiency and effectiveness (Weber & Tribe, 2019) in the process of generating some quantifiable results independent of human bias, like a firm's profit (Friedman, 2007). The idea of prioritizing profits, for example, may not be rational in its own right;however, methods employed within the firm and the market environment can be. The rational primarily focuses on the 'how' (Podvoyskiy, 2022). The institutional design of a modern firm, for example, or the overall nature of the modern market or state institutions are rational in this sense (Brouwer, 2002; Metcalf et al., 2019). Contractual relationships that are legally enforceable are also referred to as rational. Formal, therefore, is rational (Diefenbach & Sillince, 2011).

'Emotional' refers to purely relational matters in contrast to rational, where the relationships are non-contractual and informal, and their presence within a rational enterprise is seen as nepotism, like hiring someone based on familial or tribal relationships, not based on merit (Dyer, 2006). Relationships inside the family are primarily emotional, like the relationship between parents and children, between siblings, between extended family, and between a pet and its owner (Tata & Prasad, 2015). In emotional relationships, the expectation is to be accepted with all imperfections, or disabilities, which could be temporary or permanent. Violation of expectations, however, doesn't typically lead to legal action, but can be hurtful. Emotional relationships can be reciprocal; however, if a disability does not allow the beneficiary to return the favor, the giver does not claim compensation (Holt-Lunstad et al., 2010).

A human organization where relations are primarily emotional is referred to as 'social'. In this context, an organic family, a tribe (which is mainly a large extended family), or an organic community are social organizations of humans. Modern communities can also be inorganic, while the term family can be used by a group of friends with no blood relationship or legal commitment (Aldrich et al., 2021) and therefore may not be as stable as the organic ones (more discussion on this in Chapter 3). 'Socioemotional' has also been used in the literature, that is, the environment within a family, between families, or in a tribe (Gomez-Mejia et al., 2011). It is presumed here that rational, emotional (one-on-one relationships), and socioemotional (relationships with or between organic groups) in this sense have their place in our lives, but can lead to very distinct and opposing outcomes. Rational, as described above, is often present within an organic family or tribe, but it may not be its dominant characteristic, at least in ordinary circumstances. For example, tribes may need to act rationally while using a critical resource that is short in supply so they have to act efficiently to minimize wastage; or a group of tribes may join hands to fight against a common threat they may require each person to not prioritize their family or tribe over others while utilizing resources for the defense of the collective (Fukuyama, 2011).

The term 'cultural' is used to refer to collective norms of any social unit, like a family, tribe, or community. It provides an informal structure to sustain by creating a sense of unity and similarity among individuals belonging to the collective. It could be shared norms, rituals, festivals, language, specific terminologies, food, tastes, conflict mediation protocols, matrimonial norms, set of values, worldview, meta-history, or mythology, which create a shared sense of experience for the members of a collective (Afghan & Wiqar, 2007; Gharipour, 2012). Since culture is expected to bond people together, therefore, a culture may provide a means for the emotions of individuals to be expressed and understood within the collective. Culture, therefore, needs to evolve as the tastes of individuals may change over the generations, and their emotional state may also shift either naturally or due to exposure to phenomena beyond the control of the collective. The inability of a culture to adapt to internal transitions or external challenges may cause the culture to become redundant or lose its effectiveness in keeping the collective united (Diamond, 2013). Traditional markets may also possess a culture (Gharipour, 2012; Yi, 2004). Culture, in this sense, is an informal framework to unite, synchronize emotions, and survive collectively; thus can be considered both rational (Taleb, 2018) and socioemotional. However, the values of traditional cultures may not align with the capitalist values. Also, traditional cultures can turn into a framework of tyranny to ensure survival against a real or perceived threat (Peterson, 2002).

Human-to-human engagement, whether social or economic, or human engagement with nature, necessitates a moral framework. This is particularly important in situations where there is a possibility of conflict or exploitation, especially when a power differential exists between the engaged parties. 'Moral', therefore, in a Hobbesian sense, refers to a set of ideas that help avoid and mediate conflicts between people in a variety of contexts (Hobbes & Missner, 2016). Confucius seems to have advocated for a similar idea of morality that emphasizes maintaining social harmony much earlier than Hobbes (Confucius, 2014). In a more Kantian sense, the moral framework may also encourage sacrifice for some greater good, or others, and also provide a rationale for the sacrifice (Stratton-Lake, 2005). It may encourage individuals to look beyond their self-interest and prioritize the interests of others by turning the sacrifice into a win–win scenario. If we introduce a utilitarian angle, the moral framework would answer the question 'What's in it for me' when there is nothing at least in the material sense, especially when there is no apparent cost or penalty attached to prioritizing self-interest even if it causes harm to others or society (Perry, 2014). Bringing in Giddens' (2013) perspective on human agency would imply that the idea of the moral would not be enforced; rather, it is exercised voluntarily, depending on the strength of an individual's conscience. Sen (2017) has emphasized the use of human agency for moral action as well. From the perspective of MacIntyre (2013), morality would be something beyond emotivism, as the exercise of morality may still be necessary when there are no emotions in a relationship, even when emotions encourage one to look the other way.

Likewise, emotionally driven altruistic action may not be considered moral, due to its dependence on emotion, which, if we're not there, would not have instigated the act. Like in the case of a mother who sacrifices for the well-being of her children because of her affection is not referred to as moral here. A healthy and sane mother would be naturally compelled to take care of their children while sacrificing her needs. However, if there is no affection at play in a relationship, how will one act to benefit others and sacrifice their self-interest? There are examples when mothers project their insecurities onto their child, turning the relationship psychologically, if not physically, harmful for the child. Here, moral is not emotive, nor it is driven by aesthetic standards in the context of MacIntyre's (2013) critique of contemporary morality (killing a cockroach is good, killing a butterfly is bad). It is something beyond our emotions or feelings; it is rather intuitive (Haidt & Graham, 2007).

The emotional bond between two strangers may emerge after one helps the other for no tangible or intangible benefit, except for the satisfaction of one's conscience. The understanding of harm or benefit to others may be subjective; however, there can be an honest intent as per the best of one's understanding about the potential benefit and harm that may be caused to the other. The opposite of moral action would be a purely self-interested action, irrespective of the consequences to others. An individual who has no regard for how their action affects others is deemed as sociopathic, psychopathic, or narcissistic (Babiak & Hare, 2006; Fuchs & Lingnau, 2024). An immoral person will find it alright to take advantage of the needs of others, even if it causes great harm to them. Institutions in this context are not moral or immoral entities, they are rather amoral, they are like machines designed to achieve an aim (Greenwood et al., 2017; Mander, 1991), which over time may shift to institutions' survival for the sake of it (Dari-Mattiacci & Fabbri, 2023). Chapter 4 goes into further detail on the question of morality.

The terms described above are used to understand the conflict between the capitalist market, family, tribe, culture, and individual needs. For example, overdominance of the market is the overdominance of the rational over the socioemotional bonds of the organic family and community. The phenomenon has been referred to as McDonaldization by Ritzer (2016), where the market logic of efficiency, rationalization, quantification, predictability, and control penetrates the non-market spheres of society. Morality is then also exclusively defined in utilitarian terms. The end justifies the means. The cultural, socioemotional, creative, and moral are all expected to serve the ends of the capitalist market, which is to perpetually maximize profits, for its own sake. Any cultural, socioemotional, creative, or moral manifestation that does not serve the ends of the market faces the risk of being canceled out. The instrumentalization of the socioemotional and the creative, referred to as 'repressive desublimation' by Marcuse (2013), also produces alienation, as people are no longer there for each other, but only if their presence is mutually beneficial for them in economic terms. And if there is a difference of power between the two, the possibility of exploitation and manipulation remains in the absence of any socioemotional or moral framework that transcends the economic nature of their relationship.

The conflict between the modern market and the organic family can therefore be seen as a conflict between various institutional manifestations of rational forces of our time and socioemotional forces of the organic social environment. The book first explores how the dominance of the rational took place in the world, and what price the world is paying as a result. This is done in Chapter 2. Chapter 3 describes the particularities of the organic social environments that need to be sustained. Chapter 4 then discusses the significance of the moral for balancing the social with the economic. In Chapter 5, findings from the data and examples from extant literature are shared, which explain how the rational and the emotional, the social and the economic, can be balanced with the help of the moral. The literature on family business also offers insight into how to balance the rational and the socioemotional. My doctoral research specifically focused on three such communities in Pakistan: Memon, Delhiwala, and Chinioti. There are other communities also in Pakistan which have been scarcely studied, like Bohri and Ismaili. Chapter 6 describes the socioemotional dynamics within the families of the respective communities. Chapter 7 outlines how the social relationships facilitate the economic activity organized by the communities in focus. Chapter 8 analyzes the findings described in earlier chapters to explain how the social, the economic, and the moral interact with each other, and how other supporting factors like culture, religion, and formalization facilitate the process of sustaining the communities in focus. Chapter 9 concludes with a discussion on policy implications, limitations, and possibilities of future research.

References

Adendorff, C., & Halkias, D. (2014). Leveraging ethnic entrepreneurship, culture, and family dynamics to enhance good governance and sustainability in the immigrant family business. *Journal of Developmental Entrepreneurship, 19*(02), 1450008. https://doi.org/10.1142/S1084946714500083

Afghan, N., & Wiqar, T. (2007). Succession in family businesses of Pakistan: Kinship culture and Islamic inheritance law. In *CMER working paper no. 07-54.*

Aldrich, H. E., Brumana, M., Campopiano, G., & Minola, T. (2021). Embedded but not asleep: Entrepreneurship and family business research in the 21st century. *Journal of Family Business Strategy, 12*(1), Article 100390. https://doi.org/10.1016/j.jfbs.2020.100390

Aldrich, H. E., & Waldinger, R. (1990). Ethnicity and entrepreneurship. *Annual Review of Sociology, 16*(1), 111–135.

Alexander, B. (2010). *The globalization of addiction: A study in poverty of the spirit.* Oxford: OUP.

Babiak, P., & Hare, R. D. (2006). Snakes in suits: When psychopaths go to work. *Applied Psychology, 44*(2006), 171–188.

Bandura, A. (1972). *Self-efficacy: The exercise of control.* Freeman.

Baudelot, C., & Establet, R. (2008). *Suicide: The hidden side of modernity.* London: Polity Press.

Bauer, M. A., Wilkie, J. E. B., Kim, J. K., & Bodenhausen, G. V. (2012). Cuing consumerism: Situational materialism undermines personal and social well-being. *Psychological Science, 23*(5), 517–523.

Beck, U., & Ritter, M. (1992). *Risk society: Towards a new modernity.* London: SAGE Publications Inc.

Blumer, H. (1986). *Symbolic interactionism: Perspective and method.* London: University of California Press.

Brouwer, M. T. (2002). Weber, Schumpeter and Knight on entrepreneurship and economic development. *Journal of Evolutionary Economics, 12*(1–2), 83–105.

Caputi, J. (2020). *Call your "Mutha": A deliberately dirty-minded manifesto for the earth mother in the anthropocene.* Oxford University Press.

Confucius. (2014). *The analects (norton critical editions)* (M. Nylan (ed.)). W.W Norton & Company.

Courtwright, D. T. (2021). *The age of addiction: How bad habits became big business.* London: Harvard University Press.

Curtis, A. (2011). *All watched over by machines of loving grace (documentary).* London: BBC.

Dana, L. P. (2007). A humility-based enterprising community: The Amish people in Lancaster County. *Journal of Enterprising Communities: People and Places in the Global Economy, 1*(2), 142–154.

Dari-Mattiacci, G., & Fabbri, M. (2023). How institutions shape morality. *The Journal of Law, Economics, and Organization, 39*(1), 160–198. https://doi.org/10.1093/jleo/ewab016

Diamond, J. (2012). *The world until yesterday: What can we learn from traditional societies?* Viking.

Diamond, J. (2013). *Collapse: How societies choose to fail or survive.* Penguin Books Limited.

Diefenbach, T., & Sillince, J. A. A. (2011). Formal and informal hierarchy in different types of organization. *Organization Studies, 32*(11), 1515–1537.

Dunbar-Ortiz, R. (2023). *An indigenous peoples' history of the United States.* London: Beacon Press.

Durkheim, E. (2005). *Suicide: A study in sociology.* London: Taylor & Francis.

Dyer, J. W. G. (2006). Examining the family effect on firm performance. *Family Business Review, 19*(4), 253–273.

EPA. (2020). *Food: Material-specific data.* https://www.epa.gov/facts-and-figures-about-materials-waste-and-recycling/food-material-specific-data

Escobar, A. (2012). *Encountering development: The making and unmaking of the third world.* Princeton: Princeton University Press.

Friedman, M. (2007). The social responsibility of business is to increase its profits. In W. C. Zimmerli, M. Holzinger, & K. Richter (Eds.), *Corporate ethics and corporate governance* (Vol. 32, pp. 173–178). London: Springer.

Fromm, E. (2017). *The sane society* (L. A. Anderson (ed.)). Taylor & Francis.

Fryar, C. D., Carroll, M. D., & Afful, J. (2020). *Prevalence of overweight, obesity, and severe obesity among adults aged 20 and over: United States, 1960–1962 through 2017–2018. NCHS Health E-Stats*. Centers for Disease Control and Prevention; NHANES. https://www.cdc.gov/nchs/products/index.htm

Fuchs, F., & Lingnau, V. (2024). The homo economicus as a prototype of a psychopath? A conceptual analysis and implications for business research and teaching. *Journal of Business Ethics*. https://doi.org/10.1007/s10551-024-05638-7

Fukuyama, F. (2011). *The origins of political order: From prehuman times to the French revolution*. Profile Books Ltd.

Gabor Maté. (2012). *The power of addiction and the addiction of power: Gabor Maté at TEDxRio+20—YouTube*. https://www.youtube.com/watch?v=66cYcSak6nE

Gharipour, M. (2012). The culture and politics of commerce: Bazaars in the Islamic world. In M. Gharipour (Ed.), *The bazaar in the Islamic City: Design, culture and history*. London: The American University in Cairo Press.

Giddens, A. (2013). *The constitution of society: Outline of the theory of structuration*. New York: Polity Press.

Gomez-Mejia, L. R., Cruz, C., Berrone, P., & De Castro, J. (2011). The bind that ties: Socioemotional wealth preservation in family firms. *The Academy of Management Annals, 5*(1), 653–707.

Greenwood, R., Oliver, C., Lawrence, T. B., & Meyer, R. E. (2017). *The SAGE handbook of organizational institutionalism*. London: SAGE Publications.

Haidt, J. (2023). Devices and desires: Social media is the major cause of the mental illness epidemic among young women. *New Statesman, 152*(5710–5711), 29.

Haidt, J., & Graham, J. (2007). When morality opposes justice: Conservatives have moral intuitions that liberals may not recognize. *Social Justice Research, 20*(1), 98–116.

Han, B. C. (2015). *The Burnout society*. Stanford University Press.

Hari, J., & Corballis, A. (2019). Johann Hari discusses the opioid crisis and ways of responding to anxiety and depression | International Journal of Narrative Therapy and Community Work. *International Journal of Narrative Therapy and Community Work, 4*, 61–69.

Harter, S. (1999). *The construction of the self: A developmental perspective*. London: Guilford Publications.

Harvey, D. (2005). *A brief history of neoliberalism*. Oxford University Press.

Hobbes, T., & Missner, M. (2016). *Thomas Hobbes: Leviathan (longman library of primary sources in philosophy)*. Berlin: Taylor & Francis.

Holt-Lunstad, J., Smith, T. B., & Layton, J. B. (2010). Social relationships and mortality risk: A meta-analytic review. *PLoS Medicine, 7*(7), 1–20.

Ishimo, M.-C., Sampasa-Kanyinga, H., Olibris, B., Chawla, M., Berfeld, N., Prince, S. A., Kaplan, M. S., Orpana, H., & Lang, J. J. (2021). Universal interventions for suicide prevention in high-income Organisation for Economic Co-operation and Development (OECD) member countries: A systematic review. *Injury Prevention, 27*(2), 184 LP – 193.

Jackson, T. (2011). *Prosperity without growth: Economics for a finite planet*. London: Earthscan.

Jaffe, J., & Quark, A. A. (2006). Social cohesion, neoliberalism, and the entrepreneurial community in rural Saskatchewan. *American Behavioral Scientist, 50*(2), 206–225.

Javaid, O., & Hyder, I. (2018). Using Eisenhardt's method to study ethnic entrepreneurial communities. *South Asian Journal of Management Sciences, 12*(1), 25–45.

Laing, R. D. (1999). *The divided self: An existential study in sanity and madness*. Berlin: Routledge.

Lembke, A. (2021). *Dopamine nation: Finding balance in the age of indulgence*. New York: Penguin Publishing Group.

MacIntyre, A. (2013). *After virtue: A study in moral theory* (3rd ed.). London: Bloomsbury Publishing.

Maffi, L. (2018). Biocultural diversity. In *The international encyclopedia of anthropology* (pp. 1–14). https://doi.org/10.1002/9781118924396.wbiea1797

Mander, J. (1991). *In the absence of the sacred: The failure of technology and the survival of the Indian Nations*. London: Sierra Club Books.

Marcuse, H. (2013). *One-dimensional man: Studies in the ideology of advanced industrial society*. Berlin: Taylor & Fancis.

Marx, K. (2012). *Economic and philosophic manuscripts of 1844*. Berlin: Dover Publications.

Maté, G. (2013). Addiction: Childhood trauma, stress and the biology of addiction. *Journal of Restorative Medicine, 1*(1), 56–63.

Metcalf, J., Moss, E., & Boyd, D. (2019). Owning ethics: Corporate logics, silicon valley, and the institutionalization of ethics. *Social Research: An International Quarterly, 82*(2), 449–476. https://muse.jhu.edu/article/732185

Ojo, S. (2019). Navigating ethnic entrepreneurship in religion and culture meld. *Journal of Enterprising Communities, 13*(5), 625–646.

Perry, J. (2014). *God, the good, and utilitarianism: Perspectives on peter singer*. Cambridge: Cambridge University Press.

Peterson, J. B. (2002). *Maps of meaning: The architecture of belief*. London: Taylor & Francis.

Podvoyskiy, D. G. (2022). "Dangerous modernity!", or the shadow play of modernity and its characters: Instrumental rationality-money-technology (Part 2). *RUDN Journal of Sociology, 22*(1), 40–57.

Polanyi, K. (2001). *The great transformation: The political and economic origins of our time*. Berlin: Beacon Press.

Ramadani, V., Dana, L.-P., Ratten, V., & Bexheti, A. (Eds.). (2019). *Informal ethnic entrepreneurship: Future research paradigms for creating innovative business activity*. London: Springer.

Raworth, K. (2017). Why it's time for doughnut economics. *IPPR Progressive Review, 24*(3), 216–222. https://doi.org/10.1111/newe.12058

Ritzer, G. (2016). The mcdonaldization of society. In E. Mofield & T. Stambaugh (Eds.), *In the mind's eye* (1st ed.). London: Routledge.

Rosenberg, M. (1979). *Conceiving the self*. Basic Books.

Rowe, J. W., & Kahn, R. L. (1997). Successful aging. *The Gerontologist, 37*(4), 433–440.

Sachs, W. (2010). *The development dictionary: A guide to knowledge as power* (W. Sachs (Ed.); 2nd ed.). Zed Books.

Sandel, M. J. (2012). *What money can't buy: The moral limits of markets*. London: Allen Lane.

Sen, A. (2017). *Development as freedom*. Berlin: Macat Library.

Shiva, V. (2016). *Staying alive: Women, ecology, and development*. Berlin: North Atlantic Books.

Storr, W. (2018). *Selfie: How the west become self-obsessed*. London: Pan Macmillan.

Stratton-Lake, P. (2005). *Kant*. Taylor & Francis.

Taleb, N. N. (2018). *Skin in the game: Hidden asymmetries in daily life*. London: Random House Publishing Group.

Tata, J., & Prasad, S. (2015). Immigrant family businesses: Social capital, network benefits and business performance. *International Journal of Entrepreneurial Behavior and Research, 21*(6), 842–866.

Thompson, E. P. (2016). *The making of the English working class*. New York: Open Road Media.

Trueman, C. R., & Dreher, R. (2020). *The rise and triumph of the modern self: Cultural amnesia, expressive individualism, and the road to sexual revolution*. New York: Crossway.

UN. (2008). *Losing 25,000 to hunger every day*. https://www.un.org/en/chronicle/article/losing-25000-hunger-every-day

USDA. (2023). *Food security in the U.S.* https://www.ers.usda.gov/topics/food-nutrition-assistance/food-security-in-the-u-s/key-statistics-graphics/#foodsecure

Volery, T. (2007). Ethnic entrepreneurship: A theoretical framework. In L. P. Dana (Ed.), *Handbook of research on ethnic minority entrepreneurship: A co-evolutionary view on resource management* (pp. 30–41). London: Edward Elgar Publishing Limited.

Volkow, N. D., & Boyle, M. (2018). Neuroscience of addiction: Relevance to prevention and treatment. *American Journal of Psychiatry, 175*(8), 729–740.
Waldinger, R., & Schulz, M. (2023). *The good life: Lessons from the world's longest scientific study of happiness*. Berlin: Simon & Schuster.
Weber, M., & Tribe, K. (2019). *Economy and society: A new translation*. Harvard: Harvard University Press.
WHO. (2019). *Suicide: One person dies every 40 seconds*. https://www.who.int/news/item/09-09-2019-suicide-one-person-dies-every-40-seconds
WHO. (2023). *Suicide*. https://www.who.int/news-room/fact-sheets/detail/suicide
Woodman, M. (1993). Conscious femininity: Interviews with marion woodman. In *Studies in jungian psychology by jungian analysts*. Inner City Books.
Yi, E. (2004). Guild dynamics in seventeenth-century Istanbul: Fluidity and leverage. In *The Ottoman empire and its heritage* (Issue 27). Brill Publishers.
Zinn, H. (2003). *A people's history of the United States: 1492–present*. HarperCollins.

Chapter 2
Genealogical Background of Socioeconomic Imbalance in Neoliberal Capitalism

This chapter discusses how the imbalance occurred between the economic world of the modern neoliberal markets and the social reality of the organic family, and how the former begins to dominate and disintegrate the latter. For that matter, a genealogical perspective is taken to see how the ideological shift in post-fourteenth-century Europe eventually caused this imbalance, which was ultimately exported to the rest of the world during colonization. This imbalance continues even in the post-colonial world. It appears to be deeply rooted, as there is an inherent bias in favor of certain forms of human experience and potentialities in modern society. Consider the list of some contrasting potentialities in Table 2.1:

Ancient Chinese would call them the yin and yang of our life experiences. If I ask the reader to identify which of the two sets appears to be more prevalent in the modern market society or its institutions in comparison to the organic family or tribal environments, it would not be too difficult to guess. This chapter traces the source of this imbalance, how it structures the activity in the modern market environment, and the consequences it potentially has for our social lives. However, before doing so, the chapter establishes the significance of the balance and how fundamental it is to the fabric of the physical reality.

2.1 The Dance of the Opposites

If we take a broader look, we can see that the balance between two opposing elements is a fundamental property of the universe around us, and it is fundamental to our survival. Everywhere, from the subatomic world to the structure of the galaxies, some forces oppose each other, and unless these contradicting forces dance in balance, nothing will exist. Inside the very atom, electromagnetism is balanced by the weak force and the strong force (Shankar, 2007). On an interstellar level, we have the gravity of objects like the sun or black holes and the inertia of rotating planets or

O. Javaid, *Socioeconomic Sustainability Through Moral and Social Capital*,
Entrepreneurship and Development in South Asia: Longitudinal Narratives,
https://doi.org/10.1007/978-981-96-8134-1_2

Table 2.1 Examples of contrasting potentialities and experiences of life in general

Set 1	Set 2
Rational	Emotional
Objective	Subjective
Scientific	Intuitive
Quantitative	Qualitative
Impersonal	Personal
Formal	Informal
Contractual	Voluntary
Individualistic	Collectivistic
Artificial	Natural
Material	Spiritual
Disintegration	Integration
Standardization	Creativity
Becoming	Being
Fatherly	Motherly

other objects balancing out each other. If the gravity to too strong, the rotating objects will fall into the star or black hole in the center, if their inertia is too much, they will leave the orbit. The gravity and inertia of the circulating objects thus need to balance out each other to form a stable orbit (Binney & Tremaine, 2011). Balance is not just found in the inanimate world, but also in the living world around us. If we assume the ecosystem to be a living system, we see a balance being maintained on many different levels. Like the proportion of various gasses in the air, to the temperature range of the plant, all is maintained in the state of equilibrium by numerous living (except most modern humans, of course) and non-living components of the ecosystem operating in sync with each other (Campbell, 2023). If we zoom in on living organisms to their cellular levels, again, we see an intricate balance being maintained between ion concentration, pH levels, and nutrients inside the human cell. The double helix of DNA is a profound example of symmetry and balance (Nelson & Cox, 2017). Zooming out a little, we find various symmetries and balancing acts happening within our bodies, also. Our endocrine system tries to maintain homeostasis, while our nervous system strives for what is referred to as an autonomic balance between sympathetic and parasympathetic sides (Berntson et al., 1991). If these balances are disturbed, they pose a threat to our well-being. In extreme cases, this imbalance can be lethal, so there is an autonomic system within our bodies dedicated to maintaining this balance in response to the stressors from the external environment (McEwen, 2007). Zooming out further, the male and female ratio among all types of species is yet another profound example surrounded with mystery as to exactly how this balance is maintained, but it is indeed maintained (Hamilton, 1967). Nature, it seems, attempts to maintain homeostasis, not just within our bodies, but on every level of our existence.

The requirement of balance does not diminish in human systems. However, the job which is performed by nature elegantly from the subatomic to the galactic level, from the physical to the biological world, is often performed imperfectly by homo sapiens, more so—as it appears—if they are the denizens of the modern world. On a behavioral level, we act in contradictory ways because of the antagonistic nature of our needs. From being to becoming, from the need to be authentic to the need to connect with others for survival, from being rational to emotional, while seeking security and yet craving for exploration out of curiosity, we are a package of opposing psychological forces (just like everything else in nature). The challenge—that we experience because of the antagonistic needs pushing us in the opposite direction—is there perhaps because we have been bestowed with the burden of making a choice. Thankfully, this choice we make is in the context of a very narrow set of our needs, as many of the critical functions in our bodies operate without our conscious will. Imagine the mess we would have created if we also had to decide which cells need to be replicated, or how much of a particular hormone or protein needs to be produced. We have a very limited ability to make choices, but is often denied by some neurologists these days (Sapolsky, 2024; Wegner & Gilbert, 2017). However, if we did not have free will, our ability to maintain a balance between ourselves and nature perhaps would not be in such a deplorable state, as no other species turns against their nature as humans do. We frequently get confused and make mistakes, stumble, and then try again, often giving up altogether, which is perhaps a sign that we do have the freedom to make some choices if not all. Our blunders often hurt others, and our urge to avoid them points toward our ability to make moral choices, which, as per Immanuel Kant, very much exists, as otherwise, the discussion about morals would be meaningless (Kant et al., 2019).

It gets complicated with the number of engagements with other humans in our lives, as everyone has multiple needs that often contradict our needs as well. When we engage with others, we often suppress our authentic expression in case it threatens our connection with others around us, particularly when our survival depends on this connection. We may learn to do so from the very early stages of our lives, depending on what our parents or other elders, on whom our survival is dependent, can tolerate, depending on their own set of needs. A healthy family environment would thus maintain a balance between the needs of the child and the needs of caretakers, often sacrificing the latter for the former. If the environment is too suppressive for the child or poses no restriction on any harmful behavior that the child may indulge in, it can lead to adverse consequences. If you have little children in your home who have learned to walk around, you will agree how necessary it is to keep an eye on them. One can often find them inserting something inside an electrical socket or grabbing a knife to play with, and not letting go. Constant supervision is needed; however, if the behavior of adults becomes too constraining for children because adults are anxious about the mess they would make, it can again harm their psychological and mental growth.

Too much order and too much chaos are therefore considered unhealthy (Peterson, 2002). The orderly side has been referred to as the domain of the fatherly instinct (which the mothers can also possess), while the accommodating side comes under the domain of the motherly instinct (which the father can also possess). The motherly side of parents is believed to facilitate children in being who they are. The motherly side sees and acknowledges children's creativity while accepting them despite their messy side. Conversely, the fatherly side may help them 'become' capable of surviving the social reality that surrounds them (Milevsky et al., 2007). An intricate balance between the two, therefore, is needed. As an often-cited African proverb suggests, it takes a village to raise a child; so the fatherly and motherly character is not exclusive to the biological mother and the father, but the entire extended family which engages with the child in the process of their upbringing need to possess and demonstrate such characteristics (Benson et al., 2012). Today, it is increasingly being recognized that the healthiest environment for a child to grow is similar to that available in hunter-gatherer bands, comprising multiple individuals, including multiple children (Diamond, 2012; Hewlett, 2005; Lancy, 2022). Often, when the parents are not available, someone else may take care of the child in an extended family environment. Studies are showing that in contemporary nuclear families where parents are busy doing multiple jobs and children are taken care of by nannies or staff at the daycare center can lead to psychological issues in children as they grow up (Belsky, 2001).

Several millennia ago, when society grew more complex from the hunter-gatherers (where everyone from the same generation is related to others as a first or second cousin) to larger communities comprising hundreds, even thousands of individuals, more people around would become distant relatives in comparison to the number of close relatives. A respondent I interviewed for my doctoral thesis, who belonged to a community with tens of thousands of members, said, "All of us have the same grandmother". If a tribe expands to this size, antagonism between the need to connect with the tribe and the specific needs of the family may emerge. For example, if there are limited resources available to the entire tribe, the two heads of the family with a different number of dependents may want to negotiate the quantity of share both will take; imagine how justice will be ensured while a critical yet scarce resources is shared among hundreds if not thousands of families with distinct needs. This problem, as I discovered while collecting primary data for my doctoral research, can arise even in a family firm where two brothers working together may get into a conflict with each other if they want to draw a different sum from the firm's income because of the different number of their children, how old they are, or any other unique need of their respective families. The needs can sometimes vary due to the presence of a disabled or sick member within a family. There can be other differences between families, also, like kids in one family may be too chaotic, but not so in others. So, if several families are living nearby, then the parents of the naughty little humans may need to tame their offspring so that they do not cause trouble to the rest. More examples can be mentioned, the point being that to be part of a collective, different families need a formal or informal mechanism to manage or normalize their differences, and even offer support to each other whenever needed. A culture, therefore, can be relatively more fatherly and less motherly in this context, in comparison to the environment inside a healthy family. The specific mechanism for sharing resources may therefore be different from culture to culture. It could be voluntary, done in a very decentralized way by each individual, or it could be managed by a centralized authority, or it could be a mixture of both. The communities I studied had a very decentralized and informal mechanism for that matter (more detail in Chapter 5 and onwards).

A culture in tribes emerges to keep the families bonded together, minimizing their differences, while maintaining an order between distantly related families, and accommodating their character. An ideal culture in this sense would assume the dual character of being fatherly and motherly at the same time, as it provides certain standards for everyone to follow to minimize their differences, and yet provides means to accommodate the distinct needs and creative output of each family or individual. Things are not so ideal, as more often than not, a culture assumes an extra fatherly character, imposing too much order, while violators of the code are penalized harshly. In rural areas in the Asian subcontinent, there are examples of women who decide to marry someone they like are often murdered by their family members. The community to which the family belongs also does not negatively see this act of brutal violence referred to as 'honor killings' (Solotaroff et al., 2014). The so-called Dark Ages in Europe also exemplify another example of too much order, which eventually gave rise to individualistic tendencies (Fromm, 1994).

Too much order, it is said, creates an imbalance, increasing the likelihood of chaos erupting in retaliation for the tyranny. Societies that become too insecure, typically due to an external or natural threat, or uncertainty, may want to cling to any set of practices that unites the people, minimizes variation, ensures predictability of behavior, and creates a sense of certainty and sameness. One generation may do so due to a genuine threat; however, the coming generation may just follow the precedent set by their elders. Adherence to norms set by ancestors rises to religious significance, violation of which can be declared a punishable crime by any cultural authority. Culture, therefore, turns into a tyranny, suppressing any necessary change (Campbell et al., 1991). The resulting rigidity may even ignore the necessary changes that may be crucial for survival, thus often causing harm to the members of the community (Diamond, 2013; Tainter, 1988). Since any manmade culture cannot be considered perfect, implying that some human needs are ignored, often because the focus could have been on some pressing needs at the time of cultural formation. Changing times may change the shift of the needs of some or all members of the community, creating desperation elsewhere. Any basic need ignored for too long can create desperation.

If the culture adapts to the changing needs, then it may be deemed as healthy, but if it does not, then desperation may build around the ignored needs. Now, if cultural tyranny—referred to as the terrible father by Campbell (1991), for example—takes a community to this point, it may eventually brew the material for violent revolutionary change, leading to chaos or anarchy, referred to as the terrible mother. Contrarily, a culture depicting a good father in this sense would facilitate the motherly character of the culture; however, a terrible father would turn the mother revengeful, also making her children rebel against the tyranny of the father. This phenomenon can manifest on the level of the family, on the level of a larger community or tribe, and even on the level of the entire civilization (Neumann, 2015). If people are lucky, something new may emerge from the chaos, like in the case of the French Revolution; however, often vultures and hyenas come forward to take full advantage of the anarchy. The uncertainty and subsequent sense of insecurity caused by anarchic times may also open an opportunity for dictatorial forces to impose tyranny, which people may also accept for the sake of security.

The fact that this oscillation between too much order to too much chaos in the collective context has been a subject of ancient mythologies, as per the concerned experts like Joseph Campbell, Mircea Eliade, Eric Neuman, and more recently Jordan Peterson. These experts (Campbell et al., 1991; Eliade, 1963; Neumann, 2015; Peterson, 2002) point toward the fact that the said imbalance has been problematized since the beginning of known history, as it has been a subject of ancient mythologies. These experts suggest that god figures in ancient mythologies symbolize certain individual or collective behaviors that often manifest instinctively, without conscious choice of individuals. Since they are instinctive, therefore, they are considered forces of nature operating through humans. Their interaction has been described in different sets of stories that form the mythology of ancient cultures. This depicts that the understanding of the imbalance, and the kind of reactions it unleashes in the form of individual or collective behavior, has been a subject of analysis during ancient times also. These mythologies also offer various recommendations to avoid the imbalance, hence, the mythological figures depicting a good father and a good mother are presented as role models, while the figures depicting the role of terrible mothers and terrible fathers are described to exemplify a set of behaviors that need to be avoided.

2.2 From Too Much Order to Too Much Chaos and Back

The terrible father is terrible because he imposes a strict adherence to past patterns of collective behavior, even when some change becomes essential. However, there are circumstances when the very order that appears tyrannical is necessary for the survival of the community. War, for example, is a kind of scenario where order—strict discipline—becomes critical for survival. If a tribe comprising several families, or a larger society comprising several tribes, faces a common threat, then they may have to pool their resources and utilize them in the most efficient and unbiased manner. If the combatants favor their tribes or families, it may put the survival of the collective at stake. Even when not at war, a human may take charge of a collective, and he or she may favor his family and tribe. That's how dynasties emerge. A particular family keeps promoting its heirs unless they grow too corrupt or incompetent so that society no longer has a reliable center of gravity, which often leads to anarchy. So, the need for institutions that operate in an unbiased, rational manner is even felt during peacetime in a complex society. Although modern forms of bureaucratic institutions are roughly 200 years old, the idea of such a rational institution is roughly 2000 years old. Bureaucracy is exactly the kind of invention that has been designed to eliminate the inclination of individuals toward their blood relations and rather channel their energies toward a collective goal. Bureaucracies were originally meant to manage the military during war times and use the tax revenue during peacetime in an unbiased manner. However, bureaucracies also possess the potential to become corrupt and turn into a self-perpetuating machine, similar to a culture turning into a terrible father, acting like a parasite attached to the body of the collective, enforcing a status quo for its advantage.

It is pertinent to discuss the creation of bureaucracy in the context of the discussion here, as modern market institutions like the corporate world, financial sector, large industry, and the regulatory body of the state if there is one, operate largely on bureaucratic logic, and due to their dominance eventually influence the non-market segments including the organic social structures. The characteristics of these sets of institutions can be said to exemplify the concept of a terrible father who then also exerts their influence on those segments of society where the motherly side is more prominent. As a result, segments with a motherly nature find it hard to sustain themselves. The sharing-collective nature takes a shift toward a competitive-individualistic-rationalistic orientation under the influence of these institutions. Fukuyama (2011) explains that "Individualism seems today like a solid core of our economic and political behavior, [it] is [so] only because we have developed institutions that override our more natural communal instincts" (Page 29).

Modern institutions, as per Fukuyama, attempt to disconnect individuals from their patrimonial instinct, reconnect them rationally and contractually, and constrain them in a system of reward and punishment. Every relationship of an individual becomes conditional, unlike familial relationships, where the unconditional character is often more prominent than conditional ones. It's not difficult to imagine how people spending most of their lives in such environments would not feel lonely. One has to maintain their utility for the system to survive, or risk being replaced by someone else. This rarely happens in a healthy environment of collective families (or other environments with a good motherly character), where the disabled members are also taken care of unconditionally. The idea of usefulness has penetrated the individualistic cultures of modern society to the extent that there are frequent examples of children being abandoned by their parents not because of some financial difficulty but because the child is suffering from some terminal illness, like cancer, or some disability (Lemmon, 2017). Fevre (2000) notes that some American mothers were found calculating whether it is cost-effective to spend time with children, in comparison to spending time on their careers. If someone is not useful in a material or economic sense, like children, sick children in particular, or the sick elderly, they face the risk of being excluded, canceled, ignored, or abandoned. In case there is some emotional attachment, the care of such vulnerable individuals is often outsourced to daycare centers or hospices, as the highly competitive environment of the modern markets does not give enough time to their family members to take care of them.

The cold, calculating, depersonalized, individualizing, and rational nature of modern market culture is hard to ignore, which primarily aims at efficiently and effectively achieving its quantifiable targets. It therefore encourages goal orientation, forms contractual relations, encourages formalism, incentivizes every initiative, sees nature as a resource, and relationships as a means to an end. Since early education, citizens of modern societies are trained to be a part of such a culture or institutional environments, often making them less capable of sustaining their organic social relations with family and community. Formal education, writes Fukuyama (2011), was first invented by the Chinese to depersonalize students so that they work efficiently for the state bureaucracy. The European education system also trained individuals precisely to become a replaceable component of Victorian bureaucracy (Mitra, 2015). Modern educated Individuals, after spending much of their lives in institutional environments, often bring the same attitude or mindset of efficiency, calculability, utilitarianism, and rationality to their families and communities. The phenomenon has been referred to as McDonaldization by Ritzer (2016).

Bureaucracies in Europe were a product of war (Tilly, 2015); however, their legacy is believed to have been set by the institution of the church itself (Weber & Tribe, 2019). The institution of the church perhaps killed the possibility of nepotism from the very bud by prohibiting its members from even getting married. The fatherly persona of the church was unmistakable; however, the church also provided care to the poor, the social outcast, and the diseased, by taking care of them in a very motherly fashion. However, eventually, the institution, which started in service to religious ideals, began to use the same ideals to maintain power; the good father turned into a terrible one, which eventually pushed people like Martin Luther to take a stand. The Protestant Revolution led to wars, which are said to be motivated by a struggle between countries to gain control over resources (Armstrong, 2014; Cavanaugh, 2009). When people lose trust in power, or rather see it as a self-serving apparatus, imposing tyranny to maintain power, distrust, resistance to power is a likely outcome. Too much chaos, however, culminated in another class of order, which emerged as a result of the scientific, institutional, financial, and industrial revolutions, all complementing each other to create a new form of society that eventually spread to the entire world, often ruthlessly by force.

2.3 The Tyranny of Science

When religion was turned into an instrument to legitimize unjust power in Europe, it lost its significance. A further blow was created by Greek philosophy introduced to Europe by Muslim philosophers like Ibn-e-Rushd (Davidson, 2023). The intellectuals in Europe, after being influenced by Greek philosophy, raised questions that religious scholarship could not sufficiently answer. René Descartes, who also studied Greek Philosophy, introduced the idea of Cartesian Dualism, which considers our thinking minds to be superior, existing independently of the body (Dika, 2020). This idea was perhaps taken by Bacon to redefine the relationship traditional cultures had with nature (Hickel, 2020). Nature was traditionally seen as alive, and having a motherly character, while humans were supposed to take care of it with a sense of respect and reverence (Shiva, 2016). Bacon, however, proposed a scientific, soulless view of nature and saw it as a mere material resource to be utilized for ends like making profits (Horkheimer et al., 2002). The scientific method was applied to study nature for the very purpose of exploitation (Sachs, 2010). The man-nature bond was broken; now the man was supposed to be a master of nature, and nature his slave.

Anthropocentrism was thus born (Caputi, 2020). The relationship turned exploitative, the very opposite of what it used to be. Those who saw nature in such a way were considered rational, worthy of owning the land and resources (Rand & Peikoff, 1984), while those who wanted to adhere to the traditional notion of nature were deemed as irrational, deserving to be civilized even ruled by the rational ones, even against their own will (Graeber & Wengrow, 2023). The land was thus taken away from the irrational people, not just in Europe, but also in Africa, Australia, and the Americas, so that it could be better used by the rational man of Europe. The (sic) irrational people of the colonies or the resources they possessed were deemed worthy of exploitation for rational ends (Said, 1993). The idea that rational Europeans were better qualified to rule the rest became part of the 'social imaginary' of the West. Winston Churchill is reported to have said:

> I do not admit, for instance, that a great wrong has been done to the Red Indians of America or the black people of Australia. I do not admit that a wrong has been done to these people by the fact that a stronger race, a higher-grade race, a more worldly wise race, to put it that way, has come in and taken their place. (Bartal, 2017)

This "higher-grade race, a more worldly wise" was rational in their approach, whose superiority was established earlier by Cartesian Dualism, as opposed to those who involved emotions and intuition in their engagement with nature and others around them. The homo-economicus was born, who would act with cold logic, calculating in all his approach, yet devoid of emotions or empathy, like a machine. Today, psychologists refer to them as psychopaths or those having psychopathic tendencies (Fuchs & Lingnau, 2024). McGilchrist (2019) notes that such a tendency is caused by the left side of the brain dominating due to some damage in the right hemisphere, making such individuals incapable of exercising empathy and compassion. It has been noted that contemporary market institutions, like corporations and the banking system, have a propensity to prioritize the inclusion of such individuals in their top hierarchies (Babiak & Hare, 2006; Brooks & Fritzon, 2016). The state of neurological imbalance of such individuals would also make them feel superior as compared to the rest, as their imbalanced minds would even offer moral justifications for their exploitative designs.

A person who is devoid of empathy, capable of making cold rational decisions, does not feel guilt or remorse, someone who demonstrates psychopathic tendencies, with high levels of intelligence and ambition, are more likely to reach the top in market institutions like corporations in capitalism, as compared to those who are more empathetic in their decisions. René Descartes, the father of rationalism, is known to have cut open animals alive under the belief that they don't feel any pain. How heartless one has to be to ignore the screams of the animals while cutting them open. Francis Bacon, the father of the scientific method, is also known to have invented torture techniques that would be applied to the local population who would rebel during the enclosure movement. The system that emerged from the rationalistic and scientific revolution of Descartes and Bacon does not act with such brutality so explicitly, but numerous examples show that the system does cause harm to people, communities, all sentient or non-sentient life, which reminds us of its potential psychopathic nature. The top command of the system, however, is often found denying the damage it has been causing to the entire planet (Bakan, 2020; Hickel, 2020).

Such a sense of denial, a characteristic of the left brain as per McGilchrist (2019), coupled with a sense of superiority and technological advancements launched the greatest spree of violence and theft of land and resources that mankind has ever witnessed (Diamond, 2017; Zinn, 2003). The resources are then said to be utilized rationally as compared to their alleged irrational use by indigenous inhabitants. Here, the rational implies quantitative ends like capital accumulation (Cheung & King, 2004; Reisman, 1998). Prominent thinkers from the eighteenth century onwards have been justifying this theft and subsequent displacement of the indigenous population (Graeber & Wengrow, 2023; Rand & Peikoff, 1984). The displacement also disintegrated the organic social reality of the affected population. This also happened in Europe during the enclosure movement, where the peasants were forced to work as laborers in industries to survive (Brouwer, 2002; Thompson, 2016). The labor class would live near the factories while leaving their families in the suburbs. Hickel (2020) notes that poverty was deliberately manufactured by the industrial class and shamelessly justified by the elite to keep the workers desperate and dependent on the employer. Disconnection from their organic family and subsequent poverty thus also created the problem of alienation.

The above may imply that the idea of alienating the body from the rational mind, and subsequent undermining of the emotional in the paradigm of Cartesian Dualism, eventually led to the formation of a society where emotional bonds, like those that exist within organic social environments, were considered a sign of inefficiency. The emotional nature of man did not disappear, but was seen as an exploitable resource for those in power. For this purpose, the scientific method was employed to study human psychology to find ways to manipulate the emotional nature of man to enhance productivity and competitiveness in the modern market, or to be used as a source to encourage consumers to spend on stuff they do not essentially require (Curtis, 2002, 2007; Manicas, 1987; Marcuse, 2013). The emotional side could only survive if it serves as a handmaiden to the rational side. Those who would understand and manipulate their own emotions were deemed as emotionally intelligent (Goleman, 2012). Modern humans, therefore, do not only experience the possibility of alienation externally but internally as well (Hochschild, 2012), as they attempt to survive in the scientifically driven, rational environment of modern market society while being at odds with their nature (Fromm, 2017; Jung, 2006).

Scientific enterprise was thus initiated to understand anything natural, which includes human emotions and social bonds, to be utilized for the goals of the rational man. From the cultures of indigenous populations to the structure of the atom, everything is studied for the sake of exploitation (Denzin & Lincoln, 2005; Smith, 2016). The scientific method breaks down any object of study into its sub-components to the tiniest bits possible. The components deemed useful for the process of production and accumulation of capital are identified, while the rest are discarded or thrown away. The organic thus finds it difficult to survive intact. The same happens with organic social networks, like family and tribe, the same happens to plants, and the rest of the living world. The process of disintegration, insolation, extraction, and exclusion appears to be in the very nature of the capitalist machine, and the scientific method is its very instrument. Nature cannot use its ingredients as efficiently as the industry would do, it is believed, so nature will be dismembered to extract useful elements to be utilized in the production process. From the subatomic particles to the various phytochemicals, to various capacities humans possess (Sachs, 2010; Shiva, 2016).

This dismemberment so thus happens within each individual also, for the labor class, their muscle is of use for the production, while their capacity to be curious, and ask questions about the very purpose of the production process isn't (Orr, 2004), is their socioemotional capacity to bond with other humans including their family (Fukuyama, 2011). Likewise, for a white-collar worker, a clerk, or a manager, their rational faculty is needed in the administration process, not their ability to ask 'why' except in case to improve the processes they are a part of, but not when they become curious about where it all ultimately leads to, or how it may be affecting the natural environment (Podvoyskiy, 2022). The muscular capacity of the white-collar worker is, however, not of much use, nor is their conscience, nor their socioemotional capacity, which may likely bring nepotism in the organization. When the same worker wears the cap of a consumer in the market, the dopamine-releasing limbic system of their brains becomes significant for the capitalist machine to get them addicted to anything they consume (Courtwright, 2021; Lembke, 2021). The useful bit in the human workforce is only required while the rest is to be suppressed, unless there is a use for the process of capital accumulation. The scientific method is again utilized to isolate the psychological from the physiological to manipulate either for enhanced productivity.

2.4 Capitalism, Bureaucracy, and the Scientific Establishment

The idea of enhancing productivity for the sake of capital accumulation, which ultimately became the very purpose of existence of a modern human, is said to have emerged from the Protestant Revolution. Protestant beliefs advocated for working hard for the love of God, who would reward the hardworking with riches in the world. The rich were declared to be closer to God, while the poor were believed to be experiencing God's punishment (Brouwer, 2002; Munro, 2010; Weber & Tribe, 2019). The aristocratic class in Europe typically liked the idea. As the minds turned scientific and hearts capitalistic, the concept of God in heaven appeared too restrictive for the sake of enhancing their worldly riches (Weber & Kalberg, 2013). Cartesian Dualism and later Nietzsche's Übermensch turned the rational brains of the modern subject into the ultimate arbitrators of the truth, replacing God (Nietzsche & Parkes, 2008). The elite generally adopted a rational mind that saw their efforts being the source of their riches, not some old man in the sky. They were now the gods; however, acting like gods wasn't entirely their innovation, perhaps, as they were only following the corrupted legacy of the church, perhaps, but much more bluntly. The human authority in the Church, who had earlier assumed the responsibility to bring the word of God to the masses, led the way toward the abuse of authority and religion for selfish ends (Ogden, 2017). Instead of connecting the people to God, the Church authorities acted like gods, yet claimed to do otherwise. The elite followed. In a society where many would want to describe truth as it suits them individually, chaos would likely ensue. The emerging scenario was the very opposite of the traditional religious-inspired culture, where individuals would typically bow down to a single God. As per Fromm (2017), the traditional culture at least provided individuals with stability via a structured plan for their entire life. The plan decided what role they would perform, how would they perform, which careers they may choose, who would they marry, how would they raise their children, which lines must not be crossed, what is truth, what is falsehood, what is the meaning of existence and the very purpose of everything else that exists in the universe. The way of seeing and living life was well-defined and structured, giving individuals a sense of security. The ideological revolution that spread in Europe and then the rest of the world promoted self-determined, rationalistic individualism, shook the very foundation of the traditional culture (Horkheimer et al., 2002).

The religious and cultural disintegration, along with physical dislocation that started with the enclosure movement, did not make people homeless physically, but ideologically as well, furthering their sense of insecurity. The world around an ordinary person did not just become unfamiliar in an objective sense, but also the subjective understanding of the nature of reality shifted, as religion was no longer considered a source of truth. Everyone was entitled to their truth, but only if they followed a scientific approach. Science, however, could not offer a meaningful alternative to the answers to the perennial questions, and the new breed of philosophers also never agreed on any single understanding. The scientific method bred positivism, which encouraged people to follow the norms and focus on means, but for what meaning or end?, asks Harari (2015). The (sic) freedom from religion and tradition brought too much insecurity, eventually creating a strong yearning for something stable and secure. The commoners in Europe, as described by Fromm (2017), literally craved to 'escape' from the so-called freedom they found themselves in and even accepted the reign of brutal dictators in Europe, as well as in colonies. The suffocating order of the church, it may be argued, first led to the chaos of rationalistic individualism, and eventually created an impetus for dictators to again suffocate and cause havoc in Europe and around the world. Too much order (of the Church) led to too much chaos (individualism), which eventually led to too much order (Dictatorships).

The reign of these brutal dictators was short-lived; however, what was more pervasive and long-lasting was the spread of institutionalism in the world (Weber & Tribe, 2019), as the need for stability or structure prevailed in an individualistic society, a vacuum created due to the absence of religion and tradition. The rational state was now the new god (Freud, 2022; Hallaq, 2013). The insecurity that naturally emerges in a non-religious, pro-scientific individualistic society breeds more individualism, as insecurity triggers the primal instinct of self-preservation (Bauman,

2013a; Neumann, 2015). Such individuals, if left to their vices, would eventually create chaos, often in a mob-like manner, thus creating the need for some structure to maintain order. Therefore, the bureaucratic design of institutions came in handy to fulfill this need in a rationalistic society that could no longer use religion to enforce order. This was perhaps truer for colonies during the colonial period. The bureaucratic approach has been designed to constrain the chaos of instinctual individuals, including their patrimonial instinct, by putting them into compartments and binding them by a set of rules that would reward and punish them into submission for their institutional role meant to serve some scientifically[1] warranted end (Weber & Tribe, 2019). Ironically, the institutional framework that is designed to counter the externalities of individualism tends to produce more individualism (Fukuyama, 2011).

As mentioned earlier, the Church originally set the precedent to remove the possibility of the primal instinct of humans to favor one's biological family. Later, the wars in Europe in the sixteenth and seventeenth centuries, made it necessary to manage military resources efficiently, hence the bureaucratic approach was adopted. The colonial era also further refined the bureaucratic system, as the Victorian empire, which spread across the world, it is said, had to be managed efficiently while taming the nepotistic tendencies and the rebellious nature of the local population in the colonies (Mitra, 2015). The education system was thus created to tame the local population into submission to institutional authority and filter out those who were untamable (Orr, 2004). The bureaucracy and the corresponding education system continued even during peacetime, not just in Europe but also in many places in the colonial world. The same system was then adopted by the capitalist industry, which first emerged to fulfill the need for mass manufacturing of uniforms and arsenal for the military. The system is also said to have been perfected during the world wars (Ferguson, 2012). The military administration, therefore, likely inspired the institutional design of a capitalist industry (Javaid & Suri, 2016), which also came in handy when the typical family enterprise in Europe expanded beyond the capacity of a single family to manage (Colli, 2003). The bureaucratic system was employed to manage the factors of production in the most efficient and unbiased manner, in a rational way that is, which even became more refined later with the advent of scientific management by Friedrich Taylor in the Americas at the start of the twentieth century, the very epoch of rationalistic approach to production (Mcdonald, 2017). This was, it has been described, precisely needed by the capitalist class to constrain the atomized individuals—emotional beings—to use them for capitalist ends (Curtis, 2007).

The bureaucratic machine, it can be argued, requires humans as raw materials, who must be trained to prioritize the interest of the machinery over their patrimonial commitments (Fukuyama, 2011). In contrast, Ritzer (2016) would perhaps agree that the role of the family in the McDonaldized society is to produce new workers,

[1] Here the term is used in a broader context, it implies the goals that make rational sense and can be empirically verified as per some quantitative criteria, focusing toward efficiency of resource utilization or growth of some quantitative outcome, see for example Gilmartin (2014).

and also provide a place to refresh and recharge every day so that the employee can function without wearing out and losing their sanity. However, the increasing cost of living has threatened the survival of a large family. To have a family has even become an economic decision for many. One may want to go for it only if it is cost-effective to have one. Otherwise, one's institutional career takes precedence (Fevre, 2000). In the name of career, becoming an instrument of the bureaucratic machine in a McDonaldized society has adversely impacted the overall well-being of the modern man. The loss of meaning in one's life, and the feeling of alienation, along with the constant fear of being replaced by someone else in the market, keep the modern worker under constant stress (Marx, 2012; Maté & Maté, 2024). The experience of factory workers has been agonizing since the beginning, and it even provided fuel for the communist revolution (Polanyi, 2001). Today, however, individuals are now encouraged to become self-employed, start their businesses, become entrepreneurs, and become masters of their destiny. But to what end? To replicate the same order in another form? (Örtenblad, 2020).

Atomize individuals, without any structure to channel their energies, are an embodiment of chaos. Traditional societies had religion and culture; modern society thus relies more on bureaucratic institutions for that purpose. Earlier, religion and culture formed around religious ideas provided a transcendental meaning for individuals to surrender or channel their emotional energies. Capitalist structures put the capital in the place of God (Heilbroner, 1994), mimicking the transcendence of earlier traditions, not fully catching up, though, as religions first accepted people for who they were, with all their imperfections, in exchange for their surrender to the Divine. Capitalism, on the other extreme, cannot accept people for who they are; rather, it keeps telling them what they must become and cancels those who cannot comply. Capitalism, it can be argued, is an enterprise of becoming, but at the expense of being. However, the family, traditional culture, and religion first attempted to accept individuals in their state of being before they were encouraged to become something they ought to be. In contrast, modern entrepreneurs, operating in the neoliberal paradigm of modern market society, are exclusive agents of becoming. They cannot accept the natural state of being. What they then create is preserved by the modern institutional order (Javaid, 2022). This has profound implications for the modern concepts of morality, which are discussed in Chapter 4.

2.5 Entrepreneurship as Disintegration, Isolation, Extraction, and Exploitation

Entrepreneurship is famously referred to as a process of creative destruction, a term coined by Schumpeter (2024). But what is created and what is destroyed? Particularly in a society where capitalism has just begun? As mentioned earlier, the scientific wing of capitalism provides the blueprint to disintegrate what naturally exists; the scientific gaze bifurcates every living or non-living thing into its smallest bits to identify what can be sold in the market at a profit. Then it outlines the process of extraction of what is sellable. An entrepreneur can be referred to as a person who executes this process. A modern entrepreneur would thus disintegrate and extract what can be sold or would combine the extracted bits into a new complex whole to sell, like an automobile or a cell phone. Nature is thus disintegrated into bits, which are then joined together into something artificial like junk food, viewed as rational by modern economists, as it has turned into something profitable. The very process of creative destruction. It is best executed by psychopathic types as one has to turn a blind eye to any environmental or social consequences (Örtenblad, 2020). This entrepreneurial process typically has side effects known as externalities, as when the natural is mixed with artificial, it often has unexpected results, like destabilization of the natural order.

The scientific gaze is microscopic; it focuses on bits, and bits are territorialized by those who discover and study them for utilization in the process of production. They are known as specialists, those who colonize nature, and are typically only aware of the developments of their disciplines (Spectre, 2019). Nature is first 'deterritorialized' and then 'reterritorialized' in Deleuzian terms (Deleuze et al., 2013). Reterritorialized in the context of the market potential of what lies within the territory, a conceptual boundary that separates disciplines. Hayek (1945) proposed that capitalism encourages specializations as it enhances the profit-maximizing opportunity, as specialists are in short supply and likely to be in high demand. Specialists trying to be the first in the race do not have enough time, resources, or interest to study the wider implications of their inventions. They would create a solution before someone else would, even when the pros turn out to be less than the cons in the long run in social or environmental terms. The tangible or intangible damage or side effects to the society or the environment are known as externalities, which are seen as an acceptable outcome of an invention as there are profits to be made (Beck & Ritter, 1992; Curtis, 2002). The Frankensteinian solutions to the problems created by extant inventions, as per Beck (1992), create more externalities, which thus create more opportunities to create more solutions and then make more money. The process keeps happening until it is not possible to escape the externalities. Like the innocent victims of wars waged to keep the military-industrial complex running (A. Loewenstein, 2023). That is where perhaps the market of illusions steps in, the entertainment industry, which attempts to keep the common man distracted, while nature (from our bodies, our souls, to organic communities, to the nature outside) is polluted and obliterated (Herman & Chomsky, 2002; Postman, 2006). David Abram counters:

> A civilization that relentlessly destroys the living … is not well acquainted with truth, regardless of how many supported facts it has amassed regarding the calculable properties of its world. (Abram, 2012)

Specialists, for example, would bifurcate and territorialize a land based on its unique productive capacity. Can it grow cash crops, can it be used for constructing a housing scheme, it is asked, or maybe there are some oil or minerals underneath? If the land is fertile, the planets whose yield can be efficiently utilized in the production processes are chosen to grow. A natural forest is often seen as unproductive by an entrepreneurial mind, so the wood is chopped and sold, or the forest is burnt down so that a cash crop like palm can grow in its place, which then is generally used to manufacture junk food, which when consumed by the modern consumer cause diseases like obesity and diabetes that eventually creates opportunities for the pharma industry to sell synthetic chemicals, called drugs, to manage the symptoms while causing some other side effects, thus creating more opportunities (Bakan, 2020; Norberg-Hodge & Davis, 2023; Sbert, 2010). At every stage of the process, something is thrown out of balance, let it be the natural ecosystem, the homeostasis of the human body, the livelihood of the communities, or the income or resource distribution in the economy. In this process of creative destruction, what is created is artificial, and what is destroyed is natural. The natural is expected to be forgotten, artificial is then presented as original, a 'simulation' as per Baudrillard (1994). The specialists also see human society in a disintegrating manner, divide humans into the role of the consumer and the worker, the consumers are then segmented demographically or psychographically, while the blue- or white-collar workers are filtered through the process of training or education to identify the employable from the unemployable. Those who can be competitive, are skillful but devoid of wisdom, those who focus on the 'how' irrespective of the 'why', 'instrumentally rational' as per Weber (2019), obedient to the authority, are filtered out to perform in the system, while the rest are left at their vices (Giroux, 2012; Orr, 2004). Those who do not choose to transform themselves into productive labor, like those women who willingly choose to take care of the home, are seen as lost potential (Pilling, 2019).

The human body is also segmented; the womb of a skillful woman comes into competition with her mental skills, which are required by her employer. Often, women employees are paid to freeze their eggs to avoid pregnancy so they can continue to work (Mertes, 2015). Transhumanism, a new niche explored by Silicon Valley entrepreneurs, now even allows the integration of devices inside a human body, to make humans more productive (Harari, 2017), which would bypass key autonomic functions to make the person comfortable in psychologically toxic or often meaningless environments of corporate capitalism. One doesn't have to imagine Sisyphus happy anymore (Camus et al., 2015), as he now can purchase a brain-hacking device to make him feel happy. On a consumer level, humans can order designer babies with genetically enhanced features like higher IQs and better looks that are expected to help them excel in the techno-capitalist machine (Klitzman, 2019). Genes are fragmented to identify the genes that produce desirable traits, or avoid undesirable ones in babies. Such an idea of fragmenting and manipulating the body to enhance its productive capacity, either as a worker or a consumer, however, is not new. What is now being sought genetically or by manipulating our nervous system has already been done via manipulating our neurochemistry for a long time. Caffeine, nicotine, sugar, and alcohol, for example, are already used extensively for this purpose. A while back, heroin was also legally available as an OTC product (Hosztafi, 2001). Today, our limbic systems are hacked to make us dependent, even addicted to dopamine, thus making us addicted to the products or services so that, as consumers, we find it impossible to stop. Social media, digital gaming, and the junk food industry use it so extensively that their market value totals trillions of dollars. Here, the human limbic system is isolated and exploited by contemporary entrepreneurs and big business (Courtwright, 2021).

The rational phenomenon of disintegrating, isolating, and exploiting extends to many levels. For example, the land and its people are also seen as two distinct entities that need to be separated from each other to be exploited separately if needed. If the land could be used productively, and the people who live there are turning out to be a barrier in the process, they are asked to leave (Hickel, 2020). On the flip side, the European entrepreneurs who mastered the art of human trafficking on an industrial scale a few centuries ago would distinguish productive Africans from unproductive ones (Zinn, 2003). The productive ones were transported to the Americas or Europe, while the rest were left behind, even if they belonged to the same family. This, of course, does not happen nowadays legally. Today, people in general have internalized leaving their families behind for the sake of making enough money to enhance their consumption patterns (Bauman, 2013a, 2013b; Putnam, 2020). Many in poor countries do so due to fear of poverty and starvation, while people in richer countries face burnout when they cannot get enough to satisfy their insatiable desires (Han, 2015). The African proverb foretold the problem long before, as it says, 'If you want to go fast, go alone, if you want to go far, go together'. In modern market society today, fewer and fewer people want to go far, but many want to go fast, like entrepreneurs, thus they are often willing to leave others behind while chasing an illusion that with more money they can fill in the vacuum in their lives (Christensen, 2010; Örtenblad, 2020).

2.5.1 Opportunity in Externalities

I asked this question earlier as well: how many sandwiches would you consume to quench your thirst? When confused about the answer, a person may keep consuming sandwiches as the thirst does not go away. The excess consumption of what is wanted (while genuine human needs like that of authentic companionship are misunderstood as something else) thus causes burnout in terms of Han (2015), which modern consumers try to overcome with more material access without realizing what exactly is keeping them from satiation. The excess of dopamine generated through the excess consumption disturbs our homeostasis, explains Lembke (2021). The excess on one side triggers our endocrine system to push on the other side, causing depression to balance out the excess pleasure created, which then the modern consumer desperately tries to overcome with more consumption, getting stuck in a vicious cycle that keeps their inner physiological and psychological balance off. Many even try to overcome the need for serotonin and oxytocin, which is rather produced in a healthy interaction of caring family and friends, who are already left behind in pursuit of more money to buy stuff, which causes an imbalance in our bodies and psyches. The unawareness of the masses about what they need has perhaps turned into a gold mine for modern entrepreneurs, as they rake in billions as the masses overindulge themselves with things they have falsely believed they need in the modern society where all kinds of imbalances and disintegrations are normalized. Psychological trauma faced by economically deprived workers and psycho-spiritually deprived consumers has perhaps become another factor of production in capitalism (Han & Butler, 2017; Maté & Maté, 2024).

Such restructuring of our lives, our bodies, our communities, societies, and nature as a whole, while tipping off its critical balancing mechanisms, is said to be inspired by the obsession of the modern man for goals like unprecedented amounts of capital accumulation. The restructuring and subsequent instability create a void within, which is again seen as an opportunity by entrepreneurs to sell something new, which then is extracted through a process that yet causes more instability to the natural systems. In the context of the thesis of the book, the modern entrepreneurial phenomenon also restructures, even disintegrates, organic social networks directly or indirectly (Jaffe & Quark, 2006). Directly by taking away their lands, or indirectly by outcompeting local businesses by selling cheaper products subsidized by either taxpayers' or investors' money (Lanier, 2014; O'Reilly, 2017). Local business is often destroyed as a result, people are forced to flee, often turning themselves in as employees to the factories set up by entrepreneurs. From, the enclosure movement (Polanyi, 2001), the slave trade and land confiscation by the Europeans during the colonial era (Diamond, 2017; Zinn, 2003), the wars that are manufactured for profits (Klein & Smith, 2008), the deforestation of the Amazon or other forests in the contemporary world (Javaid, 2021), or the relocation of manufacturing from one country to another to reduce costs and increase profits (Harvey, 2005), has been dislocating and disintegrating families and communities everywhere in the world since the start of the industrial revolution (Norberg-Hodge & Davis, 2023; Polanyi, 2001; Sachs, 2010). In traditional societies, business was meant to provide sustenance to the family, where members of the immediate or extended family would often work together, to sustain the family not just economically but socially also. The markets in traditional communities would perform the same function of sustaining the community socially and economically (Landes et al., 2010; Polanyi, 2001). Even today, economic activity in not-so-modern places, or places not yet touched by globalization, is carried out similarly (Javaid et al., 2020; Norberg-Hodge & Davis, 2023).

Modern entrepreneurs, however, operate with a different aim, which is to help investors generate the highest return; for that purpose, they need to keep shifting stakeholders, which include employees, locations, suppliers, and customers. The idea of loyalty between the firm and stakeholders now becomes even more comical as the world moves toward the gig economy. The geographical distance between entrepreneurs and the people they hire or sell their products to makes it easier to end contractual relationships whenever a better worker, customer, or employer is found online. The market space in the gig economy appears to operate like the musical chair game , which keeps excluding less competitive players while perpetually raising the bar higher and higher (Herrmann & Jayne, 2019). AI has now jumped into the competition, which may outcompete humans as well, shifting the jobs to the companies that own AI (Harari, 2017; Tagmark, 2018). AI is yet another symptomatic treatment of the problem. Instead of fixing the root, it is like something new that is being added by technology entrepreneurs, which is likely to have externalities that will outcompete all other inventions (Crawford, 2021; Tagmark, 2018). The problems AI seems to address are the productivity issues caused by the vulnerabilities of human labor and their inseparable emotional nature (Goleman, 2012). So, AI offers a promising alternative for the employer, the entrepreneur, who no longer has to deal with the untamable side of human nature. A problem, caused by the dominance of the rational over the emotional, is being addressed ironically with more rationality, but this time by inventing an entity that can only mimic human rational faculty but is completely devoid of any emotional or moral instincts (Vogl et al., 2019), a mistake foresaw by Fromm (2017) many decades ago.

2.5.2 *Birthing an Alienating Machine*

In smaller organizations, where employees directly report to the entrepreneur, a one-on-one relationship, a degree of personalization exists, with a lesser possibility for the workforce to feel alienated (Schumacher, 2010). More so if the entrepreneurs and the workers belong to the same community and also know each other and their customers outside the context of their professional engagement (Javaid et al., 2020). However, as an organization grows in capitalism, the distance between the owners and the workers increases, as the owners cannot deal directly with thousands of workers. When the firm goes for IPO, now being owned by shareholders, the role of the founding entrepreneur is minimized further (Jensen & Meckling, 1976), who can even be fired by the board. This happened with Steve Jobs once, for example. A public limited company is legally required to ensure sustained returns on the money invested by the shareholders, so it has to employ a rationalizing system, also known as bureaucracy, that turns workers, even middle management, into replaceable components (Weber & Tribe, 2019). The environment becomes depersonalized, even if someone proves their capacity to facilitate the corporation toward its primary aim. An employee can keep their job as long as they can keep demonstrating their productive capacity, while any hint of non-performance can risk exclusion (Marx, 2012).

The policy decision to optimize factors of production, like hiring better workers or deploying AI, is typically a responsibility of the top management of a corporate entity. The factors of production are then handed over to the middle management, who would then also treat the workforce like replaceable machine components. The primary aim of the middle manager is to save their jobs and get promoted, which is possible if they make sure that the targets assigned are met, so a non-performing worker is often replaced, irrespective of the cause of non-performance. The work environment may become more and more depersonalized and mechanical with an increasing number of managerial levels between the top management and the lowest level of the workforce. It is not hard to imagine why a person would feel alienated while working at such a workplace, perpetually fearing the possibility of exclusion.

The inclusion and exclusion of what is deemed useful in the capitalist machine can be seen at every stage of the supply chain. From selecting the raw material of a product or service to identifying the appropriate customer segments, to identifying employees; the fittest survive, turning capitalist processes into a tasteless parody of the evolutionary processes as seen in nature. Something referred to as Social Darwinism (Boltanski & Chiapello, 2007; Hofstadter, 2017). In most human cultures, the social environment has been largely inclusive for the non-performing members of the community, at least (with some exceptions), and some communities offer a good example of inclusion, which are discussed in Chapters 5 and 7. Here, the focus is on the exclusionary nature of modern markets, from the entrepreneurial processes to the market institutions, which typically engage the factors of production, including human beings, as per a stringent criterion of artificial selection (Schumacher, 2010).

In this heartless disintegration, isolation, extraction, and exploitation of the useful bits extracted from everything natural, from people to communities, and declaring the rest of the whole useless presumes that there is no connection between the two while ignoring the fact that such severance would cause pain and suffering. This hints toward the archetypical significance of Descartes's legacy within the blueprint which inspires the methods employed by entrepreneurs at every level of the market economy. The severance of the mind–body connection as envisioned in Cartesian Dualism has also severed one's connection with the moral intuition as it emerges in the human heart. In the absence of moral intuition, what is left is the cold, rational logic of the human brain, which ends up chasing the chaotic forces of lust and power. The chaos manifesting within the entrepreneurial process is then followed by the bureaucratic structures erected to maintain what's created. McGilchrist (2019) explains:

> At present, the domain – our civilization – finds itself in the hands of the vizier, who, however gifted, is effectively an ambitious regional bureaucrat with his interests … Meanwhile the Master [right brain with its empathic character], the one whose wisdom gave the people peace and security, is led away in chains. The Master is betrayed by his emissary. (p. 31)

The society that emerges subsequently under the influence of this bureaucratic manager has been regarded as imbalanced, that is, overly rational, so much so that it no longer recognizes being reasonable. Yet, it keeps attempting to be objective through the scientific gaze, declaring anything beyond the objective as irrelevant (Fromm, 2017). Such a society is contractual and individualistic, where relationships become increasingly soulless (Podvoyskiy, 2022). The natural is disintegrated into bits and reorganized to create artificial whole, which is then replicated through institutions resembling more like machines, less like humans, where identical output is produced under the tyranny of rules and standards. A world where the father turns terrible and tyrannical, the good mother cannot survive, as her nurturing nature rather requires a protective and caring environment. The environment is rather exploitative, which also brings out her terrible side, which is branded as disruptive, as it seamlessly performs acts of creative destruction. Too much order on one side, too much chaos on the other, eventually creating conditions for too much order, different in form, similar in substance, causing destabilization of natural balances and homeostasis within the living beings, communities, and the ecosystem of the planet (Javaid, 2021).

2.6 Modern Market Versus the Family

The destabilizing impact of the modern capitalist market on the organic family has been extensively discussed in the literature. The organic family and community face disintegration everywhere the capitalist market has established itself. Many scholars have highlighted the dislocation and disintegration of traditional communities or tribes all over the world from the start of the colonial period. It is indeed true that such dislocation and disintegration had happened earlier also because of several reasons like climate change, depletion of resources, or invasion by another larger tribe or empire. However, it can be argued in the light of historical accounts that the degree of dislocation and disintegration since the enclosure movement and then during the colonial era, and its continuation even in the post-World War era, dwarfs what happened earlier in terms of magnitude and brutality (Harvey, 2005; Hickel, 2020; Zinn, 2003). Organic communities or tribes have been living on a particular piece of land, all over the world, for numerous generations, often for thousands of years, but had to move because their livelihood was no longer secure due to the encroachment by a public or private entity (Norberg, 2016), a literal manifestation of the terrible father (Peterson, 2002). The entire colonial episode can be mentioned as an example in this context (Fanon et al., 2007). The process did not discontinue in the post-colonial era, rather, it is being pushed by institutions like the World Bank and IMF in the name of development, or other corporate entities operating on a global scale (López-Castellano et al., 2022; Stiglitz, 2015). In more recent times, third-world countries have been pushed into borrowing money that they cannot return, and eventually have to grow or make stuff for exporting so that foreign exchange is earned to pay back international lenders like the IMF (Vreeland, 2003). Subjecting vulnerable economies to the ruthless forces of the international market came at a price. When third-world countries were unable to compete in terms of quality or price, or there was a fluctuation in international demand, the export-dependent local population suffered, which was already under pressure due to IMF conditions of high tax rates and removal of subsidies (Bello, 2009; Chang, 2021; Kentikelenis et al., 2016). Often, corrupt regimes are supported by international forces as well, who keep producing or extracting raw materials on terms of international buyers, often at the expense of the local population (Cockcroft, 2012; Nordstrom, 2007). The resulting poverty pushes many to leave their families or force entire families to leave their land or community in search of a livelihood, leading to social disintegration (Sachs, 2010).

A small elite minority in debt-ridden third-world countries can reap some benefit from such economic arrangements. They are tempted to adopt a foreign lifestyle that can only be sustained through imported items, and thus bring in the Western consumer culture that is built around individualistic values. The consumer culture also introduces processed food among the locals, bringing in modern illnesses as well, writes Diamond (2012), which would create the demand for imported medicine and modern healthcare facilities, eventually increasing the dependence of the locals on the international markets. The lack of availability of modern health care facilities in rural areas also becomes a reason for many to relocate to urban centers if processed food reaches such places before the health care facilities. With the arrival of consumer culture, electronic goods also include television. The television, describes Norberg (1995), continuously tells the locals that the modern consumerist lifestyle is better and that the traditional methods of ancestors are backward, instilling a sense of inferiority among the local population, eventually creating a desire to have enough money to maintain the modern lifestyle. Many from traditional societies then follow the lead, without realizing the indirect cost that they may pay eventually.

The parents in such communities would push their children to acquire modern education, which is believed to give them a ticket to the market or state institutions where they can earn enough to maintain the imported lifestyle. This contributes to the rural-to-urban migration or migration to more advanced countries where they can continue their education, get high-paying jobs to earn enough money to send back home so that their family can keep following the latest consumer trends (Narayan & Kankanhalli, 2021; Ofori-Appiah et al., 2024). Migrations are often done illegally as well, which itself requires paying massive fees to agents, to seek employment in the informal sector in a foreign country where the currency has a higher purchasing power. Savings are then sent back to the family to increase the standard of living (Garha, 2020; Rajan, 2020). Many who can take their immediate family with them do so as well. Since not everyone can modernize their life equally because of varying, often unavoidable circumstances, inequality emerges, and subsequent class consciousness and a sense of deprivation that comes along make it difficult to maintain a peaceful environment as well. Places where violence and crime were unthinkable, explains Norberg (2016), where the people traditionally would not consider themselves poor but rather rich, as their natural environment provided them everything they needed, experienced a sense of deprivation and scarcity after adopting a consumerist lifestyle. The resulting frustration also bred a tendency for violence (Goldsmith et al., 1995). Crime and poverty emerge, forcing more people to relocate themselves and their families to places that appear safe in the media.

Once families migrate to urban centers, various factors such as rising living costs, particularly property prices, make it increasingly difficult for extended families to remain together, particularly in the second and third generations. The children and grandchildren, who get educated in modern schools in urban areas, become accustomed to serving the rational environment of modern institutions, while their skills to navigate the socioemotional environment of the organic family remain unpolished. So, when they grow up, they are less likely to work hard to keep the extended family intact and make decisions more in the context of how to survive in an environment where the cost of living keeps going up (Appadurai, 1996). In many countries, a single member of the family cannot earn and feed all family members, so the idea of a corporate family is no longer financially feasible, so both the mother and the father work, while the children are left with daycare centers. The next generation is even further away from entertaining the idea of having a family (Kornbluth et al., 2013). Subsequently, divorce rates also increase in modern society due to several reasons, which also include the limited time husband and wife spend with each other, and how skilled they are in dealing with the socioemotional dynamics of their relationships.

The increased possibility of divorce and eventual consequences of the breakdown of the family also discourage many from even getting married in the first place (Cherlin, 2014). All these dynamics have even changed the very concept of the family itself. Now, even two consenting individuals, of any gender, living together without signing even the contract of marriage, also refer to themselves as family (Aldrich et al., 2021). The idea of the family thus turns increasingly comical. It appears to follow the typical path described by Baudrillard (1994), that is, the original is replaced with the artificial, or a simulation of the original, the original becomes irrelevant and so disappears, the simulation is now referred to as the original.

The critical significance of the organic family becomes more obvious when the nurturing needs of children are realized. Adults who have received the necessary care in their early childhood may survive in the absence of a healthy social environment later in life (despite its need do not disappear entirely), but the case of children is different. Children are particularly vulnerable. A village-like environment that offers care, unconditional support, and acceptance, and a sense of safety when the child is young, is needed at least until the child reaches puberty. If it is not available, it can cause a variety of developmental issues among children, which can adversely affect the emerging personality even during adulthood, often negatively affecting the relationships that the adults may form to survive economically or socially. The deteriorating healthy family environment in modern market society, therefore, has long-term social consequences, and like any other problem, they are again treated symptomatically. To feel a sense of belongingness to a social group, various forms of artificial social entities have emerged in the modern market society after industrialization. From socialist movements to unionization, to the birth of the co-ops (cooperatives), to the creation of civil society, non-profit initiatives, to volunteering organizations, clubs, and even social media, all attempting to offer a sense of belonging to their participants. In the words of Polanyi, "Laissez-faire was planned, planning was not" (p. 147), implying that all forms of socialist initiatives were created when the traditional forms of social reality generally disintegrated in Europe.

The traditional forms of social reality have survived, however, in several locations globally. Many of these traditional collectivist cultures, or ethnic groups in various Asian or African regions, including the West, possess a strong entrepreneurial orientation as well. Such communities are typically referred to as ethnic entrepreneurial communities. The phenomenon of ethnic or minority entrepreneurship is extensively studied, as it contributes to GDP, creates employment, and keeps community members busy in productive activities (Ojo, 2019; Volery, 2007; Waldinger et al., 2000). Often, the members of such communities migrate to other regions to search for better opportunities, and once a few of them succeed in financially establishing themselves, they facilitate others in the process of migration and starting a venture. This form of entrepreneurship is studied under the category of migrant entrepreneurship (Dana & Morris, 2007; Tata & Prasad, 2015). If one generation of migrant entrepreneurs can grow and establish themselves financially, it often creates a stepping stone for the next generation to move forward, who may join the family business or go for higher education to get better-paying jobs. Most migrant entrepreneurship, however, remains in the micro or small category (Trehan et al., 2020). The demonstration of the fatherly or motherly character on the healthier side, however, is not uncommon among migrants from any ethnic or religious background. Mutual support and cooperation, maintaining ties with the people in their organic tribe, is necessary for their survival, as it is hard to get support from any other source in a foreign land (Flap et al., 2000; Zimmer & Aldrich, 1987).

The phenomenon of ethnic entrepreneurship, which is also referred to as community-based entrepreneurship (Peredo, 2014; Peredo & Chrisman, 2006), appears to have a long history in Asia in particular (Javaid, 2015; Javaid et al., 2020). Organic social networks were already prevalent in the Asian regions, where the society grew complex, while the economy and markets also relatively developed as compared to the rest of the world. In the Ottoman, Safavid, and Mughal Empires for example, the organic social reality did not experience a similar invasion by the so-called Robber Barons as it did in Europe, until the colonial era. The markets there appear to evolve through the social, not despite. The family, business, community, and market remained highly interlinked, overlapping in general. The environment in the market can be said to be a mixture of motherly and fatherly traits. A balance between the social and the economic could be observed, as both were considered necessary for the well-being within the ideological framework that dominated the region. Maintaining ties with the family and the community was important, and so was the exchange process necessitated by the division of labor (Gharipour, 2012; Yi, 2004).

Such markets were also present in European society as well before the Industrial Revolution, though relatively primitive in comparison to the markets in the Ottoman, Safavids, and Mughal Empires, as the society there had grown significantly complex (Braudel & Reynold, 1992; Chaudhuri, 1985; Mikhail, 2021). Polanyi (2001) described economic activity as embedded in the social fabric of societies that prevailed in the pre-industrial era. Such societies have developed thriving markets that would not just sell the local produce, but the traders would travel the world to import and export products via various land and sea routes. Despite extensive economic activity the economy did not seem too dominant and disintegrated the social, in fact, the organic social life also thrived. The economy was balanced with the social, rather often led by the social. The market did not suffocate the social, but rather served it, often under a transcendental moral framework. The motherly was thus sustained often through the fatherly character of the community.

In the contemporary world, such examples can be found, not always in the form of entire societies, but more so in the form of ethnic cultures prevailing within larger societies. These ethnic cultures, like the ones explored in the later chapters of this book, can offer insight into how to balance the economic with the social, and thus maintain a healthier environment for its members to fulfill both economic and socioemotional needs. What exactly are those socioemotional needs, and how the market can facilitate in achieving those needs directly or indirectly by not interfering in the social reality, by remaining embedded into the social fabric of society, is a topic of the coming chapters. The next chapter in particular contrasts the organic social with an artificial version of it that emerged as a counter-reaction but on the same blueprint of the modern market, creating a simulation, in the Baudrillardian sense. It is arguably necessary to do so as the socioemotional needs of people may only be fulfilled genuinely in a healthy organic social reality, not with artificial simulations. The idea of sustainability of the social should therefore include the former, while the artificial versions may only be seen as a means to sustain the organic social reality.

References

Abram, D. (2012). *The Spell of the Sensuous: Perception and Language in a More-Than-Human World*. Knopf Doubleday Publishing Group.

Aldrich, H. E., Brumana, M., Campopiano, G., & Minola, T. (2021). Embedded but not asleep: Entrepreneurship and family business research in the 21st century. *Journal of Family Business Strategy, 12*(1), Article 100390. https://doi.org/10.1016/j.jfbs.2020.100390

Appadurai, A. (1996). *Modernity at large: Cultural dimensions of globalization*. University of Minnesota Press.

Armstrong, K. (2014). *Fields of blood: Religion and the history of violence*. Random House LLC.

Babiak, P., & Hare, R. D. (2006). Snakes in suits: When psychopaths go to work. *Applied Psychology, 44*(2006), 171–188.

Bakan, J. (2020). *The new corporation how "good" corporations are bad for democracy*. Penguin Canada.

Bartal, S. (2017). The Peel Commission Report of 1937 and the Origins of the Partition Concept. *Jewish Political Studies Review, 28*(1/2), 51–70. http://www.jstor.org/stable/44510475

Baudrillard, J., Glaser, S. F., & Press, U. of M. (1994). *Simulacra and simulation*. University of Michigan Press.

Bauman, Z. (2013a). *Liquid modernity*. Polity Press.

Bauman, Z. (2013b). *The individualized society*. Polity Press.

Beck, U., & Ritter, M. (1992). *Risk society: Towards a new modernity*. SAGE Publications, Inc.

Bello, W. (2009). *The food wars*. Verso Books.

Belsky, J. (2001). Emanuel Miller lecture developmental risks (still) associated with early child care. *Journal of Child Psychology and Psychiatry, 42*(7), 845–859.

Benson, P., Leffert, N., Scales, P. C., & Blyth, D. A. (2012). Beyond the "village" rhetoric: Creating healthy communities for children and adolescents. *Applied Developmental Science, 16*(1), 3–23.

Berntson, G. G., Cacioppo, J. T., & Quigley, K. S. (1991). Autonomic determinism: The modes of autonomic control, the doctrine of autonomic space, and the laws of autonomic constraint. *Psychological Review, 98*(4), 459–487. https://doi.org/10.1037/0033-295x.98.4.459

Binney, J., & Tremaine, S. (2011). *Galactic dynamics: Second edition*. Princeton University Press.

Boltanski, L., & Chiapello, E. (2007). *The new spirit of capitalism*. Verso.

Braudel, F., & Reynold, S. (1992). *Civilization and capitalism, 15th–18th century, vol. I: The structure of everyday life*. University of California Press.

Brooks, N., & Fritzon, K. (2016). Psychopathic personality characteristics amongst high functioning populations. *Crime Psychology Review, 2*(1), 22–44.

Brouwer, M. T. (2002). Weber, Schumpeter and Knight on entrepreneurship and economic development. *Journal of Evolutionary Economics, 12*(1–2), 83–105.

Campbell, J., Moyers, B., & Flowers, B. S. (1991). *The power of myth*. Knopf Doubleday Publishing Group.

Campbell, M. O. (2023). *Biogeochemistry and the Environment*. Springer.

Camus, A., ́Brien, J. O., & Martinez, J. (2015). *The myth of sisyphus*. CreateSpace Independent Publishing Platform.

Caputi, J. (2020). *Call your "Mutha": A deliberately dirty-minded manifesto for the earth mother in the anthropocene*. Oxford University Press.

Cavanaugh, W. T. (2009). *The myth of religious violence: secular ideology and the roots of modern conflict*. Oxford University Press.
Chang, H. J. (2021). *Kicking away the ladder*. Anthem Press.
Chaudhuri, K. N. (1985). *Trade and civilisation in the Indian Ocean: An economic history from the rise of Islam to 1750*. Cambridge University Press.
Cherlin, A. J. (2014). *Labor's love lost: The rise and fall of the working-class family in America*. Russell Sage Foundation.
Cheung, T. S., & King, A. Y. (2004). Righteousness and profitableness: The moral choices of contemporary Confucian entrepreneurs. *Journal of Business Ethics, 54*(1), 245–260.
Christensen, C. M. (2010). *How will you measure your life? Create a strategy for your life*. Harvard Business Review.
Cockcroft, L. (2012). *Global corruption: Money, power and ethics in the modern world*. I.B. Tauris.
Colli, A. (2003). *The history of family business, 1850–2000*. Cambridge University Press.
Courtwright, D. T. (2021). *The age of addiction: How bad habits became big business*. Harvard University Press.
Crawford, K. (2021). *The atlas of AI: Power, politics, and the planetary costs of artificial intelligence*. Yale University Press.
Curtis, A. (2002). *The century of self (documentary)*. BBC Two.
Curtis, A. (2007). The trap: What happened to our dream of freedom? *BBC Newsnight*.
Dana, L. P., & Morris, M. (2007). Towards a synthesis: A model of immigrant and ethnic entrepreneurship. In L.-P. Dana (Ed.), *Handbook of research on ethnic minority entrepreneurship: A co-evolutionary view on resource management* (pp. 803–812). Edward Elgar Publishing Limited.
Davidson, H. A. (2023). *Alfarabi, Avicenna, and Averroes on intellect: Their cosmologies, theories of the active intellect, and theories of human intellect*. Oxford University Press.
Deleuze, G., Guattari, F., Hurley, R., Seem, M., & Lane, H. R. (2013). *Anti-oedipus: Capitalism and schizophrenia*. Bloomsbury Publishing.
Denzin, N. K., & Lincoln, Y. S. (2005). *The Sage handbook of qualitative rresearch*. SAGE Publications, Inc.
Diamond, J. (2012). *The world until yesterday: What can we learn from traditional societies?* Viking.
Diamond, J. (2013). *Collapse: How societies choose to fail or survive*. Penguin Books Limited.
Diamond, J. (2017). *Guns, germs, and steel: The fates of human societies* (20th Anniversary). Norton.
Dika, T. R. (2020). The origins of Cartesian dualism. *Journal of the American Philosophical Association, 6*(3), 335–352.
Eliade, M. (1963). *Myth and reality*. Harper & Row.
Fanon, F., West, C., Philcox, R., Bhabha, H. K., & Sartre, J. P. (2007). *The wretched of the earth*. Grove Atlantic.
Ferguson, N. (2012). *Civilization: The west and the rest*. Penguin Books.
Fevre, R. (2000). *The demoralization of western culture: Social theory and the dilemmas of modern living*. Continuum.
Flap, H., Kumcu, A., & Bulder, B. (2000). The social capital of ethnic entrepreneurs and their business success. In J. Rath (Ed.), *Immigrant businesses the economic, political and social environment* (pp. 142–161). Macmillan Press Ltd.
Freud, S. (2022). *The future of an illusion (deluxe library edition)*. Repro India Limited.
Fromm, E. (1994). *Escape from freedom*. Henry Holt and Company.
Fromm, E. (2017). *The sane society* (L. A. Anderson (Ed.)). Taylor & Francis.
Fuchs, F., & Lingnau, V. (2024). The homo economicus as a prototype of a psychopath? A conceptual analysis and implications for business research and teaching. *Journal of Business Ethics*. https://doi.org/10.1007/s10551-024-05638-7
Fukuyama, F. (2011). *The origins of political order: From prehuman times to the French revolution*. Profile Books Ltd.

Garha, N. S. (2020). Punjabi irregular immigration to Italy and Spain: Causes and consequences. *South Asian Diaspora, 12*(2), 195–211. https://doi.org/10.1080/19438192.2020.1793449

Gharipour, M. (2012). The culture and politics of commerce: Bazaars in the Islamic world. In M. Gharipour (Ed.), *The Bazaar in the Islamic City: Design, culture and history*. The American University in Cairo Press.

Gilmartin, D. (2014). *Civilization and modernity: Narrating the creation of Pakistan*. 312.

Giroux, H. A. (2012). *Education and the crisis of public values: Challenging the assault on teachers, students, & public education*. Peter Lang.

Goldsmith, E., Khor, M., Norberg-Hodge, H., & Shiva, V. (1995). *The future of progress: Reflections on environment and development*. Green Books, Ltd.

Goleman, D. (2012). *Emotional intelligence: Why it can matter more than IQ*. Random House Publishing Group.

Graeber, D., & Wengrow, D. (2023). *The dawn of everything: A new history of humanity*. Picador.

Hallaq, W. B. (2013). *The impossible state: Islam, politics, and modernity's moral predicament (Reprint)*. Columbia University Press.

Hamilton, W. D. (1967). Extraordinary sex ratios. *Science, 156*(3774), 477–488.

Han, B. C., & Butler, E. (2017). *Psychopolitics: Neoliberalism and new technologies of power*. Verso.

Han, B. C. (2015). *The burnout society*. Stanford University Press.

Harari, Y. N. (2015). *Sapiens: A brief history of humankind*. Harper.

Harari, Y. N. (2017). *Homo deus: A brief history of tomorrow*. Vintage.

Harvey, D. (2005). *A brief history of neoliberalism*. Oxford University Press.

Hayek, F. A. (1945). The use of knowledge in society. *The American Economic Review, 35*(4), 519–530.

Heilbroner, R. L. (1994). *Twenty first century capitalism*. W.W Norton & Company.

Herman, E. S., & Chomsky, N. (2002). *Manufacturing consent: The political economy of the mass media*. Knopf Doubleday Publishing Group.

Herrmann, K., & Jayne, K. (2019). *Animal experimentation: Working towards a paradigm change*. Brill.

Hewlett, B. S. (2005). *Hunter-gatherer childhoods: Evolutionary, developmental, and cultural perspectives* (1st ed.). Routledge.

Hickel, J. (2020). *Less is more: How degrowth will save the world*. Penguin Random House.

Hochschild, A. R. (2012). *The managed heart: Commercialization of human feeling*. University of California Press.

Hofstadter, R. (2017). *Social Darwinism in American thought, 1860–1915*. University of Pennsylvania Press.

Horkheimer, M., Adorno, T. W., & Noeri, G. (2002). *Dialectic of enlightenment*. Stanford University Press.

Hosztafi, S. (2001). The history of heroin. *Acta Pharmaceutica Hungarica, 71*(2), 233–242.

Jaffe, J., & Quark, A. A. (2006). Social cohesion, neoliberalism, and the entrepreneurial community in rural Saskatchewan. *American Behavioral Scientist, 50*(2), 206–225.

Javaid, Omar. (2021). A multi-layer analysis and solution for climate crisis: From the restructuring of production to restructuring of knowledge. In S. N. Ali & Z. H. Jumat (Eds.), *Islamic finance and circular economy: Challenges and opportunities*. Springer.

Javaid, O. (2015). The original socio-cultural and economic context for practicing shirkat-ul-aqd. *International Journal of Pluralism and Economics Education, 6*(4), 371.

Javaid, O. (2022). An Islamic vision and approach for entrepreneurship: Developing through a multi-stage comparative analysis of systems, ideologies and code of ethics. *International Journal of Ethics and Systems, 38*(1), 125–146.

Javaid, O., Shamsi, A. F., & Hyder, I. (2020). Religious entrepreneurial communities as a solution for socioeconomic injustice. *Journal of Enterprising Communities: People and Places in the Global Economy, 14*(3), 415–446.

Javaid, O., & Suri, A. W. (2016). Bureaucratic system of management in Islamic financial institutions: Implications and alternatives for social inclusion. *Journal of Islamic Business and Management, 6*(2), 89–114.

Jensen, M. C., & Meckling, W. H. (1976). Theory of the firm: Managerial behavior, agency costs and ownership structure. *Journal of Financial Economics, 3*(4), 305–360.

Jung, C. (2006). *The undiscovered self (reprint)*. New American Liberary.

Kant, I., Bennett, C., & Stern, R. (2019). *Groundwork for the metaphysics of morals*. Oxford University Press.

Kentikelenis, A. E., Stubbs, T. H., & King, L. P. (2016). IMF conditionality and development policy space, 1985–2014. *Review of International Political Economy, 23*(4), 543–582.

Klein, N., & Smith, N. (2008). The shock doctrine: A discussion. *Environment and Planning D: Society and Space, 26*(4), 582–595.

Klitzman, R. (2019). *Designing babies: How technology is changing the ways we create children*. Oxford University Press.

Kornbluth, J., Chaiken, J., Dungan, S., Reich, R. B., Cvetko, S., Krauss, D., & D'Ambrosio, M. (2013). *Inequality for all*.

Lancy, D. F. (2022). *The anthropology of childhood: Cherubs, chattel, changelings* (3rd ed.). Cambridge University Press. https://doi.org/10.1017/9781108943000

Landes, D. S., Mokyr, J., & Baumol, W. J. (2010). *The invention of enterprise: Entrepreneurship from ancient mesopotamia to modern times*. Princeton University Press.

Lanier, J. (2014). *Who owns the future*. Penguin Books.

Lembke, A. (2021). *Dopamine nation: Finding balance in the age of indulgence*. Penguin Publishing Group.

Lemmon, G. T. (2017). *The foster father who cares when terminally ill kids have no one*. PBS. https://www.pbs.org/newshour/show/foster-father-cares-terminally-ill-kids-no-one

Loewenstein, A. (2023). *The palestine laboratory: How Israel exports the technology of occupation around the world*. Verso.

López-Castellano, F., Lizárraga, C., & Manzanera-Ruiz, R. (2022). Neoliberalism and unequal development. *Routledge*. https://doi.org/10.4324/9781003153306

Manicas, P. T. (1987). *A history and philosophy of the social sciences*. Basil Blackwell.

Marcuse, H. (2013). *One-dimensional man: Studies in the ideology of advanced industrial society*. Taylor & Fancis.

Marx, K. (2012). *Economic and philosophic manuscripts of 1844*. Dover Publications.

Maté, G., & Maté, D. (2024). *The myth of normal: Trauma, illness, and healing in a toxic culture*. Ebury Publishing.

Mcdonald, D. (2017). *The golden passport: Harvard business school, the limits of capitalism, and the moral failure of the MBA elite*. HarperCollins.

McEwen, B. S. (2007). Physiology and neurobiology of stress and adaptation: Central role of the brain. *Physiological Reviews, 87*(3), 873–904.

McGilchrist, I. (2019). *The master and his emissary: The divided brain and the making of the western world, second edition*. Yale University Press.

Mertes, H. (2015). Does company-sponsored egg freezing promote or confine women's reproductive autonomy? *Journal of Assisted Reproduction and Genetics, 32*(8), 1205–1209. https://doi.org/10.1007/s10815-015-0500-8

Mikhail, A. (2021). *God's shadow: Sultan Selim, his Ottoman empire, and the making of the modern world*. Liveright Publishing Corporation.

Milevsky, A., Schlechter, M., Netter, S., & Keehn, D. (2007). Maternal and paternal parenting styles in adolescents: Associations with self-esteem, depression and life-satisfaction. *Journal of Child and Family Studies, 16*(1), 39–47.

Mitra, S. (2015). From hole in the wall to school in the cloud. In P. Dixon, S. Humble, & C. Counihan (Eds.), *Handbook of international development and education* (pp. 368–376). Edward Elgar Publishing Ltd.

Munro, J. (2010). Tawney's century, 1540–1640: The roots of modern capitalist entrepreneurship. In D. S. Landes, J. Mokyr, & W. J. Baumol (Eds.), *The invention of enterprise: Entrepreneurship from ancient Mesopotamia to modern times* (pp. 107–155). Princeton University Press.
Narayan, V., & Kankanhalli, S. (2021). The economic and social impacts of migration on brand expenditure: Evidence from rural India. *Journal of Marketing, 85*(6), 63–82.
Nelson, D. L., & Cox, M. M. (2017). *Lehninger principles of biochemistry*. Freeman.
Neumann, E. (2015). *The origins and history of consciousness*. Taylor & Francis.
Nietzsche, F., & Parkes, G. (2008). *Thus spoke zarathustra: A book for everyone and nobody*. OUP Oxford.
Norberg, H. (1995). The pressure to modernise. In *The future of progress: Reflections on environment and development* (pp. 91–108). Green Books, Ltd.
Norberg, H. (2016). *Ancient futures*. Local Futures.
Norberg-Hodge, H., & Davis, R. (2023). *Local is our future*. Author's Republic.
Nordstrom, C. (2007). *Global outlaws: Crime, money, and power in the contemporary world*. University of California Press.
O'Reilly, T. (2017). *What's the future and why its up to us* (Penguin Ra).
Ofori-Appiah, E. D., Dwumor Kessey, K., & Oduro-Ofori, E. (2024). Expenditure decisions on international remittances received by households in Ghana. *Cogent Social Sciences, 10*(1), 2302800. https://doi.org/10.1080/23311886.2024.2302800
Ogden, S. G. (2017). *The church, authority, and foucault: Imagining the church as an open space of freedom*. Taylor & Francis.
Ojo, S. (2019). Navigating ethnic entrepreneurship in religion and culture meld. *Journal of Enterprising Communities, 13*(5), 625–646.
Orr, D. W. (2004). *Earth in mind: On education, environment and the human prospect*. Island Press.
Örtenblad, A. (2020). *Against entrepreneurship: A critical examination*. Springer.
Peredo, A. M. (2014). Poverty, reciprocity and community-based entrepreneurship. In T. Baker & F. Welter (Eds.), *The routledge companion to entrepreneurship* (pp. 263–280). Routledge.
Peredo, A. M., & Chrisman, J. J. (2006). Toward a theory of community-based enterprise. *The Academy of Management Review, 31*(2), 309–328.
Peterson, J. B. (2002). *Maps of meaning: The architecture of belief*. Taylor & Francis.
Pilling, D. (2019). *The growth delusion: The wealth and well-being of nations*. Bloomsbury Publishing Plc.
Podvoyskiy, D. G. (2022). "Dangerous modernity!", or the shadow play of modernity and its characters: Instrumental rationality-money-technology (Part 2). *RUDN Journal of Sociology, 22*(1), 40–57.
Polanyi, K. (2001). *The great transformation: The political and economic origins of our time*. Beacon Press.
Postman, N. (2006). *Amusing ourselves to death: Public discourse in the age of show business*. Penguin Books.
Putnam, R. D. (2020). *Bowling alone: Revised and updated: The collapse and revival of American community*. Simon & Schuster.
Rajan, S. I. (2020). Governance and labour migration. *Routledge India*. https://doi.org/10.4324/978 1003157175
Rand, A., & Peikoff, L. (1984). *Philosophy: Who needs it*. Penguin Publishing Group.
Reisman, G. (1998). *Capitalism*. Jameson Books.
Ritzer, G. (2016). The mcdonaldization of society. In E. Mofield & T. Stambaugh (Eds.), *In the mind's eye* (1st ed.). Routledge.
Sachs, W. (2010). *The development dictionary: A guide to knowledge as power* (W. Sachs (Ed.); 2nd ed.). Zed Books.
Said, E. W. (1993). *Culture and imperialism*. Vintage Books.
Sapolsky, R. M. (2024). *Determined: The science of life without free will*. Tbs-Penguin Random House Wholesale.

Sbert, J. M. (2010). Progress. In W. Sachs (Ed.), *The development dictionary: A guide to knowledge as power* (pp. 212–227). Zed Books.
Schumacher, E. F. (2010). *Small is beautiful: Economics as if people mattered*. HarperCollins.
Schumpeter, J. A. (2024). *Capitalism, socialism, and democracy* (2nd ed.). London: National Book Network.
Shankar, R. (2007). *Principles of quantum mechanics* (2nd ed.). London: Springer.
Shiva, V. (2016). *Staying alive: Women, ecology, and development*. North Atlantic Books.
Smith, L. T. (2016). *Decolonizing methodologies: Research and indigenous peoples*. Bloomsbury Publishing.
Solotaroff, J. L., Pande, R. P., & Bank, W. (2014). *Violence against women and girls: Lessons from South Asia*. World Bank Publications.
Spectre, L. (2019). Compartmentalized knowledge. *Philosophical Studies, 176*(10), 2785–2805.
Stiglitz, J. (2015). *Globalization and its discontents*. Penguin Books Limited.
Tagmark, M. (2018). *Life 3.0: Being human in the age of artificial intelligence*. Penguin Books.
Tainter, J. A. (1988). *The collapse of complex societies*. Cambridge University Press.
Tata, J., & Prasad, S. (2015). Immigrant family businesses: Social capital, network benefits and business performance. *International Journal of Entrepreneurial Behavior and Research, 21*(6), 842–866.
Thompson, E. P. (2016). *The making of the english working class*. Open Road Media.
Tilly, C. (2015). *Coercion, capital, and European states, AD 990–1992*. Blackwell.
Trehan, K., Vedi, P., & Kevill, A. (2020). Against entrepreneurship: Unveiling social inequalities for minority entrepreneurship. In A. Örtenblad (Ed.), *Against entrepreneurship* (pp. 111–131). Cham: Springer. https://doi.org/10.1007/978-3-030-47937-4_7
Vogl, T. M., Seidelin, C., Ganesh, B., & Bright, J. (2019). Algorithmic bureaucracy: Managing competence, complexity, and problem solving in the age of artificial intelligence. *SSRN Electronic Journal, 2019*, 148–153.
Volery, T. (2007). Ethnic entrepreneurship: A theoretical framework. In L. P. Dana (Ed.), *Handbook of research on ethnic minority entrepreneurship: A co-evolutionary view on resource management* (pp. 30–41). Edward Elgar Publishing Limited.
Vreeland, J. R. (2003). *The IMF and economic development*. Cambridge University Press.
Waldinger, R., Aldrich, H. E., & Ward, R. (2000). Ethnic entrepreneurs. *Entrepreneurship a Social Science View, 2000*, 356–388.
Weber, M., & Tribe, K. (2019). *Economy and society: A new translation*. Harvard University Press.
Weber, M., & Kalberg, S. (2013). *The protestant ethic and the spirit of capitalism*. Taylor & Francis.
Wegner, D. M., & Gilbert, D. (2017). *The illusion of conscious will, new edition*. MIT Press.
Yi, E. (2004). Guild dynamics in seventeenth-century Istanbul: Fluidity and leverage. In *The ottoman empire and its heritage* (Vol. 27). Brill Publishers.
Zimmer, C., & Aldrich, H. (1987). Resource mobilization through ethnic networks. Kinship and friendship ties of shopkeepers in England. *Sociological Perspectives, 30*(4), 422–445.
Zinn, H. (2003). *A people's history of the United States: 1492–present*. HarperCollins.

Chapter 3
The Question of Social in the Socioeconomic, What is to Be Balanced with the Economic?

It is pertinent to spend time describing the term 'social' while contrasting it with 'economic' so that it is established what needs to be balanced and sustained with the economic. Today, there is no confusion about what an economic activity is; however, the term social has taken a variety of forms. Some are natural, but some are artificial, constructed within and on the blueprints of modern market society. Civil society is one, digital social networks are another, voluntary organizations of individuals for a specific cause, or people living together calling themselves a family despite no bond of marriage, irrespective of gender, cooperatives, are some examples out of many. Escobar (2012) argues that the idea of an artificial form of social came into vogue when poverty was created after the enclosure movement. After the Industrial Revolution, when the poor were disconnected from their community of origin and unaccustomed to ways considered productive by capitalism, the 'social' was invented "not only to create consumers but to transform society by turning the poor into objects of knowledge and management" (Escobar, 2012, p. 23). The disintegration of the organic family and community happened not just in rural areas, but everywhere, somewhere directly through brute force, while somewhere indirectly, thanks to the changing social imaginary, economic pressures, and the push created by the new market norms. The disintegration eventually pushed individuals to respond to newly created problems like poverty, isolation, inequality, disease, and pollution, either reactively or proactively, but while not directly getting into conflict with the techno-scientific complex of industrial capitalism (Escobar, 2012; Harvey, 2005; Polanyi, 2001). Reactively by responding after a crisis, like helping the poor, or cleaning the beaches, or proactively by advocating the industry in the public or private sector to minimize their negative impact, or by insisting the public offices to create policies or laws to regulate the private sector, often unsuccessfully (Bourdieu & Nice, 1998).

These alternative forms of social activity and organization may offer value to the people engaged with them or their beneficiaries; however, it is critical to identify that these artificial constructs may not be equal to the organic form of the social that naturally exists. The positivist-desacralized gaze of social sciences may rather

O. Javaid, *Socioeconomic Sustainability Through Moral and Social Capital*, Entrepreneurship and Development in South Asia: Longitudinal Narratives,
https://doi.org/10.1007/978-981-96-8134-1_3

consider the artificial and the natural morally comparable or rank them as per some rational measure of the contemporary socioeconomic discourse (Denzin & Lincoln, 2005). Modern market society tends to create an artificial, Frankensteinian version of literally everything natural. From artificial food to artificial trees to artificial intelligence, to artificial humans (sex robots are in the making as I write this book), to artificial relations, to virtual reality, are created and presented as a better alternative for capital gain (Baudrillard et al., 1994; Swyngedouw, 2010). However, the artificial construction of the social may appear to fill in the gaps within the modern market society or its institutions, typically in response to its social externalities, but often inadvertently, follow the same rationalistic, individualistic spirit of the system they appear to oppose (Horkheimer et al., 2002). The literature on social sustainability barely mentions the social as organic family and community, let alone anything on their sustainability. The description of the social typically remains abstract that does not appear to contrast organic from the artificial in much of the literature (Eizenberg & Jabareen, 2017; Wang & Ke, 2024). The claim for social sustainability, under a tendency to blur the difference between the natural and the artificial, raises the question about the nature of the social being sustained. If it remains predominantly artificial, then the modern initiatives for socioeconomic sustainability in modern market society attempt to balance one form of the economic or the rational with another of its forms being disguised as the social (Escobar, 2012). If so, then the sustainability discourse perhaps touches the social, or the environmental, only in form, not in substance, as economic sustainability or the sustainability of the rational institutions or the market society takes precedence in practice, if not always in theory (Scott, 2020; Swyngedouw, 2010).

When Baudrillard (1994) said socialism emerges "from the death of the social" (p. 26), he perhaps suggested that the original or natural form of social relationship, which is being mentioned here as organic, has been murdered (systemically or directly) in the modern world, and just like anything else, is also replaced with something artificial. Organic social constructs, from traditional communities to their culture, to their traditional institutions, are obliterated, disintegrated, deterritorialized, then reterritorialized (Deleuze et al., 2013), and eventually offered an alternative blueprint to reorganize by the private or public setups under the rational direction of social or economic policy. The top-down approach replaces the organic forms of social with the artificial. But that's not the end of the story, as per Baudrillard. The artificial is then assumed as natural, original, eternal, even, while natural is hidden or wiped out of existence, even forgotten. The artificial, directly or indirectly, then facilitates the functioning of the neoliberal modern market society (Escobar, 2012; Sbert, 2010; Shiva, 2016). Some forms of artificial constructions fill in the gaps created by the market, like social media, while other forms offer symptomatic treatment of social externalities. However, they do not challenge the systemic designs or the imbalances at the very ideological core of modern market society, like the one that is ingrained in the idea of Cartesian Dualism, as discussed in Chapter 2. Escobar explains:

> As a domain of knowledge and intervention, the social became prominent in the nineteenth century ... Not only poverty but health, education, hygiene, employment, and the poor quality of life in towns and cities were constructed as social problems ... Yet the most significant aspect of this phenomenon was the setting into place of apparatuses of knowledge and power that took it upon themselves to optimize life by producing it under modern, "scientific" conditions. (Escobar, 2012, p. 23)

These alternative forms of relationships or engagements are social in appearance but often function on the episteme of the techno-scientific industrial complex. The rational dimension operates in the background, while emotional appearance provides the cover for the rational nature of the relationships (Hochschild, 2013). Like the relationship between a customer service representative and a customer (Hochschild, 2012; Ritzer, 2016). The original socioemotional energy is subjected to "repressive desublimation" and used for rational ends if we borrow from Marcuse (2013). The rational, the fatherly, dominates; it turns terrible, as it manipulates and exploits the emotional, the motherly, for rational ends. The relationship between the rational and emotional, therefore, emulates a toxic version of patriarchy, contrary to a healthy relationship between the fatherly and motherly. When the emotional is turned into a parody, to ensure the dominance of the rational, it would thus also turn the idea of balance between the economic and the social into a parody as well. However, it is argued in this book that to have a healthy society, the rational and the emotional, the social and the economic, are rather required to operate in a balance, facilitating each other as and when needed. This can happen when they both evolve in parallel while being in a supporting relationship. In fact, in the sequence of their evolution, as is evident from historical evidence, the organic social comes first, then it gives birth to the economic for its needs. However, to understand and appreciate the *pas de deux* between the two, the organic form of social needs to be first clearly defined in contrast with the economic.

A key distinction between the social and the economic is perhaps the degree of conditionality. In any market transaction, the conditionality is standardized, and a price measured in monetary terms must be offered, in unhealthy social relations; however, conditionality emerges when a particular behavior is desired before something essential is offered. In this sense, can some claim to be your friend if you must put up a certain artificial performance to receive their attention, or worse, if you must pay money for them to spend time with you? Sandel (2012) has made this argument in his book What Money Cannot Buy, intending to explain the 'moral limits' of the market. Sandel explains that the conceptual limit of the market ends at a point where the sphere of the moral and social begins. A key point to identify is that the complementary spheres of the social and the moral are there to fulfill some of our individual and collective needs, which, if we attempt to address by involving the logic of the market, we end up more deprived than before. For example, the need for genuine acceptance and companionship, a sense of purpose in a relationship, clarity of conscience, or to instill trust in a relationship, are some needs where the involvement of money is the negation of the very idea of fulfillment. The antidote to alienation, for example, in this context cannot come through the logic of the market, but in having genuinely accepting relationships, which naturally are found in healthy families, the prevalence of which has reduced significantly in capitalism.

In this context, it becomes critical to acknowledge the fundamental human nature and identify the entire range of our needs, as some of these can only be fulfilled in healthy social environments, while some would indeed require a market. It is through this identification and understanding of what it takes to fulfill those needs that the significance of the social can be appreciated in contrast with the economic, which is rather needed for another set of needs. An understanding of our needs will also set the healthy limits of the market beyond which its role becomes unhealthy, so that the sanctity of a healthy social environment remains intact, and the balance between social and economic is sustained. Markets in capitalism, directly or indirectly, disintegrate the social and then encroach into the domains of the social by offering artificial alternatives to the deprivation felt by the people. Modern victims of Cartesian Dualism, disconnected from their socioemotional and moral needs, eventually become active recipients of the illusions sold by the market in place of a healthy social environment. Knowledge of what we need as humans, therefore, can limit the encroachment of the market and encourage individuals to seek what it takes to fulfill their needs, socioemotional and moral needs in particular, eventually preventing alienation as well.

3.1 The Natural Origins of the Social

Development in neuroscience has debunked the notion that humans are primarily rational beings (Barrett, 2020). Neuroscience now establishes that humans are primarily emotional before they are rational (Ledoux, 2015). Humans are born in their pure instinctual and emotional states, while their rational brains develop much later (Giedd et al., 1999). So, the first relationships we form with others around us, adults in particular, can be said to be primarily emotional (Bowlby, 2012b). Emotions here imply the instinctual energy that emerges in our relationship with another subject, which could be a human, animal, or object. This energy either bonds us or pushes us away from a particular subject or object, for no material reason. Two individuals spending time with each other only for the pleasure of each other's company point toward a healthy emotional bond (Ledoux, 2015). There is also an element of mutual care not conditioned upon what is received from the other side, while the other side also gives when needed, again unconditionally, a phenomenon referred to as 'reciprocity' (Bubolz, 2001). However, purely economic relations as envisioned by classical or neoclassical economists, formed by homo-economicus types, are devoid of such emotional attachments, a view that is now being challenged by behavioral economists. Such relations are purely conditional, impersonal, and rational, implying that the focus on both sides is on a tangible outcome[1] (Becker, 2013). So, if economic relationships are rational predominantly, then, in contrast, social relations would have

[1] A socioeconomic bond is also possible, but more on it later.

a predominant emotional component while the rational side aims at emotional ends. Socioemotional is a term often used in family business literature to describe the nature of relationships among family members, as the emotional dimension of the relationship becomes obvious in comparison to the rational nature of the engagement of the family members in a family firm (Gomez-Mejia et al., 2011; Sarasvathy et al., 2016). Such relationships are personal and unconditional as they create an 'affect' that is not always dependent on the ability of the other person to return the favor. As in the case of a child-parent relationship, the child may be affected badly because of dependency if the parent is unable to pay attention to their needs. Reciprocity may exist if the bond is between two adults; however, the flow of care can be quite unequal as well due to certain disabilities or incapacities. Like the relationship with one's elderly parent, as they may not be capable anymore of offering anything back. Classical economists, from their disenchanted gaze, see such engagements as irrational, as altruism is typically puzzling for them (Fehr & Fischbacher, 2003; Gintis, 2000; Henrich et al., 2001). However, we experience such engagement at first with our mothers if they are fully available physically and psychologically, like not lost in the state of post-partum depression (Morris & Williamson, 2019).

We also meet our mothers before our fathers. Rather, we meet our mothers before we are born, as children begin to experience the world from the womb, so the first thing they experience is their mother. A newborn gets attached to a mother, whose emotional presence is critical for the survival of the newborn (Bowlby, 2012b). A healthy mother then does everything in her capacity for the well-being of the child, despite the child causing all sorts of disturbances in her life. In case the biological mother is not available, the motherly presence of other adults becomes critically necessary (Perry & Szalavitz, 2006). Children have various needs that they cannot yet fulfill on their own. Some needs can never be fulfilled alone, no matter what the age, like the need to speak one's heart out to a compassionate listener (Waldinger & Schulz, 2023). However, children also need to be fed, cleaned, held, soothed, and protected from any harm. A critical need is to be seen by others, who mirror the child's expressions and emotions, as that provides critical information to their autonomic nervous system that they are not alone (Zeanah, 2018). This requires emotionally available caretakers, mothers in particular, who try to understand and respond to the child's emotional reactions. Children learn to trust their instincts and creative impulses depending on the corresponding reaction given by adults around them. If they are discouraged, or the caretakers have their attention elsewhere often, then children do not get sufficient feedback to make sense of their intuitive or creative instincts or emotional reactions (Maté & Maté, 2024). A healthy family, therefore, offers a space where children learn how to engage with their emotional selves and learn ways to get their message across to other humans. In an unhealthy upbringing environment, children may learn to hide or suppress their emotions, and other instincts also, as they fear unpleasant responses from the elders around them. Strict toilet training, for example, can have adverse effects on children's perception of themselves and others, likely sowing the seeds of how they would include or exclude others (Robinson et al., 2016).

The need to be seen, appreciated, and mirrored does not disappear as children grow up; a need for respect also emerges as they develop their ego. To feel a sense of belonging, children eventually learn to mirror what others do around them. From speaking the same language to following the same clothing sense to etiquettes about expressing emotions, or not expressing them at all (which leaves a critical need unfulfilled), to following the discipline of the community, or to qualify to the cultural standard which helps them find a spouse eventually at the right age (Tomasello, 2015). A healthy family would offer a motherly environment that offers acceptance to the raw emotional and instinctual self, while also fulfilling basic physiological needs. The motherly is balanced with the fatherly, as the family also equips a child with the tools to engage with the larger community so that the child is not left alone and excluded while growing up (Bronfenbrenner, 2009). Ideally, the inclusion of a person in the community need not be at the expense of their emotional side, the emotional requires expression in culturally acceptable ways, otherwise, it leads to a problem described by Fromm (2017) as 'moral loneliness'. A culture that may discourage the expression of some or all emotions, or instrumentalize them for some rational ends, eventually creates the problem of isolation (Susan Harter, 2002). A healthy family and community environment, therefore, would need to do otherwise, that is, help individuals be themselves emotionally and yet be connected with others also, a dichotomy that is often hard to balance. The relationship with others in the family, extended family, and community, if they fulfill the emotional and social needs, thus can be referred to as socioemotional.

A healthy family environment, particularly for the children, must possess an element of unconditionality (Rogers & Webb, 2013). This implies that the individuals who bond healthily do not have to put up a performance to gain something from the other. If receiving from the other is conditioned to a performance one has to put up, then the relationship becomes transactional rather. The socioemotional is there only in its form, but lacking substance. Children can learn to put up a performance at a very young age when parents make their love conditional, contingent upon the demonstration of some desired behavior, which may go against the natural inclination of the child. Children, when they grow up, may also offer their support to others, again conditionally, continuing the legacy of their parental figures (Maté & Maté, 2024; Rohner & Britner, 2002). The performative culture that emerges becomes transactional, as unconditional support without putting up a performance is absent. Showing one's authentic side—that includes the feelings of joy, hurt, fear, distastefulness, or resentment—may come at a cost, often leaving the person unheard or unseen, which if becomes chronic can keep a person in search of a place where they can be genuinely seen and heard (Susan Harter, 2002; Kernis & Goldman, 2006). However, being authentic doesn't imply that one becomes inconsiderate to others while being who they are, especially when one holds some authority over others, as it may suppress the desire of others to express their authenticity as well. So, a mutual, reciprocal acceptance of authentic expression from two or more people engaged with each other may balance the natural state of being of each individual, while offering acceptance to others' natural states as well. A healthy social environment would contain a balance between 'personal autonomy' and 'connectedness' (Susan Harter,

2002). In a child-parent relationship, if children see their parents showing unconditional acceptance of their authenticity, they may also learn to show similar acceptance to others' genuine expression (excluding anything immoral or unjust, of course) as they grow up. Individuals who demonstrate inclusive behavior toward others despite differences may have a more accepting childhood as compared to those who demonstrate a more exclusionary attitude (Goldstein & Michaels, 2023; Hoffman, 2001; Zhuravlova et al., 2021).

Such a parenting experience may sound too idealistic, as in real life, we more than often encounter a scenario where, to create space for others to be themselves, we hold our own need for authentic expression. A healthy relationship, therefore, becomes a mixture of authentic expression, sacrifice, understanding, and mutual respect. If, to create space for the other, one person has to hold themselves back most of the time, then an imbalance has ensued, and the relationship may not survive, or continue in an imbalanced way if the survival of one is dependent on the other (Susan Harter, 2002). The dominant person, demonstrating the behavior of the terrible father, may also be devoid of empathy and may be consciously or unconsciously exploiting the dependent one, for the ends they may seek. This may happen when the dominant one is a parent, and the dependent one is a child or two partners in a co-dependent relationship (Neumann, 2015; Peterson, 2002). The devouring mother complex, where the mother keeps the children dependent on her even when they grow up, is an example (Lawson, 2002). On the other extreme, the parents may inadvertently react to the presence of the children as if they are a burden. The same behavior may be replicated by the children once they grow up and form relationships outside their family as well (Bowlby, 2012a). If such unhealthy dynamics are present in the upbringing environment of a family, they also likely sow the seed of later disintegration of the family, particularly in response to challenges offered by the external world. The children once grown up may use external challenges, even minor, as an excuse to leave the family and their birthplace to find opportunities elsewhere in the contemporary world (Rohner & Britner, 2002) or may search for a connection in the artificial social constructs presented by the modern market society (Baudrillard, 2016).

3.2 The Natural Origin of the Socioeconomic

In a healthy relationship, there is a receiving end, and there is a giving end. The receiver can receive without giving, while the giver can give without receiving, before the receiver becomes the giver and vice versa—a non-transactional yet reciprocal relationship, in other words. Or one remains in the position of a receiver or a giver indefinitely if the circumstances demand, like in the case of a disabled child, or an elderly parent with dementia who receives from their caretakers. However, conflict can ensue if both want to receive something, without the urge to give. The refusal to give what the other needs can create a sense of deprivation, which may be perceived as a threat. The resulting fear can generate an unpleasant or even aggressive response. The very opposite of a healthy, caring emotional bond, yet still emotional. The emotions are now showing their destructive side, which can even start a fight. A conflict in this context can emerge between children, grown-ups, or between social groups and tribes. Such conflicts can also turn violent, as documented numerous times in human history. From tribes to empires, humans have sacrificed themselves for their own family or tribal members and killed others for the sake of their own (Diamond, 2012). Raw emotions, when accumulated, explode, causing a great amount of damage, therefore, a healthy presence of the rational is needed to balance the emotional side. A sense of morality also becomes necessary, particularly when one side is too powerful while the other is not, as it may discourage the powerful from committing an atrocity on the weaker despite the emotional push and no rational reason to stop (more discussion on this in Chapter 4). However, if the two sides in a conflict are of comparable strength, like in tribal cultures, their feuds often end with an exchange of gifts. Exchanging gifts has been a means to maintain relationships between tribes who may otherwise be at each other's throats. Within tribes, a gift economy is often found, where members of the tribe make, grow, and share what they have in excess based on their unique capacities. The exchange of gifts within and between tribes eventually results in mutual solidarity and the maintenance of peace. Mauss (2015) notes:

> Societies have progressed in so far as they, their subgroups, and lastly, the individuals in them, have succeeded in stabilizing relationships, giving, receiving, and finally, giving in return. To trade, the first condition was to be able to lay aside the spear. From then onwards they succeeded in exchanging goods and persons, no longer only between clans, but between tribes and nations, and, above all, between individuals. (pp. 105–6)

The culture of reciprocal gift exchange eventually evolved into a culture of exchange against a monetary unit. The use of monetary units implies that the exchange is now not out of generosity but is based on the mutual need of the individuals buying or selling an item. The individuals are not closely related, as otherwise they would likely be mutually sharing what they have. Their personal or family needs are a priority over the needs of the person selling them something; however, they are not interested in stealing, either, implying an urge to maintain some degree of relationship with the seller or maintain peace. There may be a fear that the seller may not give what's due. So, to ensure justice, the idea of measuring the quantity and the value per unit against some standard was born, even in the earliest cultures in known history, explains Graeber (2001). The monetary unit thus measures the value, while weight or length is measured as per some other standard. Standardization, particularly the use of a monetary unit as a standard to measure value, perhaps has been one of the greatest social inventions that allowed complex societies to function, without breaking down into anarchy, more so than language itself (Simmel, 2004). A society where division of labor has been achieved, where people exchange goods they grow or produce, and to exchange, they also use a monetary unit to measure the value, is a society where the market has been established, which is essentially an embodiment of the rational. A healthy social order would also grow a healthy market to sustain itself (Landes et al., 2010). The rational, therefore, emerges to balance out the emotional, ensuring the sustainability of the society as a whole. Manifestation of the good father on the cultural scale.

The gift economy also runs parallel within close or distant relatives in complex societies where the organic family has not disintegrated. However, a healthy gift economy is more a manifestation of the good mother, as the quantity and quality of gifts are not typically compared between individuals or families sharing gifts. Sharing of gifts does not turn into a competition to match quality and quantity; different members with different capacities are accommodated, even if someone remains on the receiving end indefinitely due to their lack of capacity. Behind the motherly or fatherly form of exchange is the idea of mutual interdependence, which once established, links the well-being of individuals, individual families, or individual tribes, with that of others who need something that others can produce, while others also have something that they need (Greaber, 2001; Mauss, 2015; Polanyi, 2001). The mutual interdependence, therefore, eventually tames down the emotional chaos that can disrupt one's relationship with those on whom one's survival is dependent. However, in case of an unequal relationship, where one has an upper hand and is not dependent on the other for survival, there no reciprocal or economic relationship is possible. If there is no emotional bond as well, like with a distant family member, who is only a recipient and cannot give in return, necessary resources may flow voluntarily only when there is a sense of morality that shimmers in the heart of the resourceful. When there is no socioemotional or economic motivation to facilitate someone, the moral would need to step in. The question of morality is discussed in Chapter 4. Here, the primary focus is on the social, which is essentially emotional at its core, but in the light of known history, we can say it creates rational structures, including a market and an exchange culture to neutralize the chaotic side of emotional energy, eventually giving birth to the socioeconomic.

The markets that emerge out of the social (a healthy one) are also said to possess a social character. The buyers and sellers do not exclusively behave in a purely rational self-interested manner, but also with kindness as and when needed, especially in transactions involving debt, due to the nature of the relationship that develops after frequent interactions (Javaid et al., 2020). The motherly and the fatherly character may be present simultaneously. There is a rational component to the support offered as well, as the customer or seller who is facilitated will likely come back to do more business in the future. Often, the debtor is unable to pay the amount due when promised but is given more time in kind. Likewise, sometimes the buyer does not have cash, so the seller asks the buyer to take the goods and pay them back later. Often, struggling businesses are supported by the stakeholders depending on their capacity, like their customers (particularly in a B2B context) may pay in advance, or the suppliers may offer supplies on extra credit with relaxed payback time. New ventures are supported likewise by suppliers and customers based on the goodwill of the family to which the budding entrepreneurs belong (Javaid, 2024). A purely rational view of the situation, as typically taken by classical economists, is, however, reductionist, as it doesn't include the socioemotional and moral dimension of the support. This rationalistic view discards the role of our emotional nature and moral capacity, putting it all under the category of the irrational, eventually seeding an imbalance on every scale. Such a view may undermine those societies or communities where the rational and socioemotional are balanced, as they do not appear to let the rational dominate. Often, the rational is directed by the socioemotional or the moral (Gharipour, 2012; Hallaq, 2013).

In traditional societies, often the market had (has) a social character, unlike the modern market society, where the social predominantly has market-like character. The markets or economic relationships in the pre-industrial world, and those parts of the world today that have not been deeply influenced by the spirit of capitalism, are often deeply embedded in social relations, as described by Polanyi (2001) and others. The formation of relationships in the market, therefore, in traditional societies occurred (also occurs) on top of prior social relationships, characterized by kindness, emotional sensitivity, and trust, a decline of which leads to the disintegration of such societies. Modern authors use the term 'social capital' to describe this trust and cohesion that exists between people (Carradore, 2022). The term social capital, when used in a capitalist context, implies its instrumental value for economic ends, which indeed exists (DeFilippis, 2001). However, the social relationships in traditional societies may not only exist because they lead to certain rational ends, but they are often ends in themselves, reinforced by the cultural norms or religious beliefs (Candland, 2001; Javaid et al., 2020).

3.3 The Socioemotional and the Economic

In traditional societies in particular, it may be argued in the light of available evidence that it is difficult to isolate the socioemotional from the economic or isolate the organic community from the market, as the two are deeply interwoven with one another. Often, business partners are family members or establish family ties by encouraging their children to marry each other (Afghan & Wiqar, 2007; Gharipour, 2012; Papanek, 1972). The entire market typically appears like an extended family, more like a tribe. The first customers, investors, employees, and advisors come from the kinship networks. Someone from the immediate and extended family often becomes a supplier or vendor for a particular business (Danes et al., 2009). I also found in my doctoral research that such businesses often employ those who would be declared unemployable in the modern capitalist world (Javaid et al., 2018). They are hired with a motherly intent, as they are assigned a task and a salary as per their potential, but the primary aim is to keep them from feeling useless or drowning in an existential crisis. Such a function is typically outsourced in capitalist economies to the state, which has been quite ineffective in eliminating the subsequent problem of alienation (Harvey, 2005; Krier & Worrell, 2016). However, this problem is unlikely to emerge in closely-knit enterprising communities. More details of how members of such communities offer support to each other are discussed in Chapters 5 and 7. In this part of the chapter, the focus is more on describing the conceptual significance of the social, its emotional and moral nature, and how it is balanced by the rational within the context of the family firm.

The support mindset can also be lethal for the business, as the support that is offered to people and the community can sometimes exceed the capacity of the business to bear (DeFilippis, 2001). The emotional in such cases perhaps dominates the rational, eventually threatening the survival of the business. The use of rational faculty would rather imply knowing the limits to support and often saying no, which can negatively influence the socioemotional nature of the relationships with the community members. However, to economically sustain, one has to balance the emotional side while being rational (Gintis, 2000). Motherly character needs to be balanced with the fatherly character. Another problem that may emerge among the employees is the feeling of being treated unfairly by employing the unemployable and giving them a share, especially when the business is sailing through rough waters (Barnett & Kellermanns, 2006).

Business, since the earliest known human history, has been a family enterprise. So, often employees, particularly in smaller ventures, were (are) all family members, siblings, parents, and cousins working together under the same roof. This has been reported to be the case for thousands of years until the Industrial Revolution in Europe gave birth to the joint stock company, which necessitated rationalization by employing bureaucratic machinery to run the operations (Colli & Rose, 2007; Landes et al., 2010). However, family businesses of all sizes still exist in large numbers where their survival depends on their ambidexterity between the rational and socioemotional nature of their engagement, particularly when the family members are involved in the operational level management (Caputo et al., 2018). Often, the rational goals of the business come into conflict with the socioemotional aims of the relationships between family members, who constantly have to negotiate their way between the two extremes. The entire act of sustaining the firm while engaging the members of the organic family and community may thus become an act of maintaining a fine balance between the rational and the socioemotional (Berrone et al., 2012; Chrisman et al., 2012).

The difficulty involved in this complex jugglery comes with various benefits as well. The trust among family members reduces the agency cost (Karra et al., 2006). Family members often work on a significantly lesser amount, especially when the venture is new, or if facing financial challenges. The support and commitment from family members, if persistent, can help the business withstand the pressures offered by economic recession. This is valid in small businesses in particular, where the family members are the only ones employed. In larger firms, family members head key operations and often hold positions related to finance and accounts (Le Breton-Miller & Miller, 2006). However, if family members remain unwilling to trust people from outside the family for key positions, the prospects of the business to grow beyond the managing capacity of the family remain limited (Dyer, 2006; Javaid et al., 2020). Nevertheless, some of the oldest businesses in the world are family enterprises, as a few of them are still run by the same family even after centuries of their inception (Birdthistle & Hales, 2023). One can argue that they are mere exceptions, as it is also true that a significant number of family ventures do not survive after the second generation, while most disintegrate when transitioning to the third (Caputo et al.,

2017; Chang et al., 2020) unless key measures are taken to prevent the disintegration. These measures are discussed in Chapters 5 and 7.

3.4 The Disintegration

If the family environment is not been able to meet the needs of the new generation, which includes the physiological, emotional, social, economic, and moral needs, for any reason, the next generation is less likely to stay with the family. For example, external uncertainties, like the market going through a recession, may steal the focus of the parents to ensure the economic survival of the family, while socioemotional issues of the family members may appear more like a distraction. The rational thus suffocates the socioemotional during times of uncertainty. The existential threat posed by the external challenges also makes the natural chaos of the family with young children appear like a nuisance. If this scenario continues for a long period, it may deprive the children of the due emotional attention they require, leaving them on their own, and planting the very belief in their minds that their parents cannot truly see them for who they are. The family's incapacity to meet the expectations of the children may also be due to anticipated threats, not actual ones. Like fear of unemployment, or fear of not being able to sustain the family business. Further, the uncertainties that are big enough for the adults to get stressed and remain distracted for long durations, but complex enough for children to understand, that why their parents are not paying attention to their needs, may take their toll (Evans et al., 2013; Le Breton-Miller & Miller, 2006; Masarik & Conger, 2017; Prime et al., 2020).

The frustrations while dealing with external threats that the adults may experience may often leak onto the children as well. Such parents may shame some or all of their children for their mistakes, leaving a moral trauma (Griffin et al., 2019). Often, parents compare siblings depending on who causes them more or less distraction, eventually making them feel guilty for being authentic, affecting their self-image for life (Hashim et al., 2017). The treatment can also become discriminatory depending on the specific needs of siblings, creating a sense of resentment among them. Often, children are too immature to understand even if there is a genuine reason for paying more attention to a particular sibling, subsequently making them feel treated unfairly or unjustly (Kowal et al., 2004). It may also be because of the degree of distraction a particular child may offer while the parents focus on the external world. This may likely affect the degree of their self-confidence while growing up, which may also influence their ability to honor commitments and thus prove their trustworthiness (Buist et al., 2013; Kowal et al., 2004). The external chaos of the market can resurrect the terrible father (not literally, of course), whose shadow eventually intensifies the chaos within the family. The resulting discord between children and parents may also make them reluctant to join the family business, particularly when the business may not offer the future they desire (Avloniti et al., 2014). These are some examples of reasons that may make children reluctant to rely on the family to meet their needs as they grow up. All of this may give the children reasons to look elsewhere to satisfy their needs, which may include finding economic opportunities elsewhere. The financial challenges may also push the parents to motivate the children to relocate for a better economic future.

In such a scenario, any external blow can disintegrate the family whose internal cohesion has been weakened significantly. The external blow may come when some key resource on which the survival of the family is dependent, like land, gets depleted due to natural causes (Barrios et al., 2006) or is taken away by those in power (Robbins, 2019). Or it could be systemic (Cernea, 2000), like cost inflation that reduces their profit margins, too much competition in the market, or a key material or human resource now being supplied to another geographical location due to higher demand, creating a shortage, making it difficult for the family maintain their source of livelihood (Harvey, 2005). Consumerist pressures, nowadays, also include the fear of missing out (also referred to as FOMO) on the latest trends of consumer culture, or how hopeful the next generation is on the future economic outlook. If they are not hopeful, they are likely to relocate to places that allow them to enjoy the latest modern amenities (Benson & O'Reilly, 2009, 2016). Consumer culture, I found in my doctoral thesis, can also create tension between brothers, often causing cracks within family cohesion. The persistent threat perhaps affects everyone on the scale of the community, potentially suppressing their motherly instinct also, the community members may care less for others and more about increasing their consumption standards (Javaid et al., 2018).

Due to these external pressures and declining support from the community, a family if already struggling internally may not be able to stay together, as the family members may find an excuse to migrate to other locations to try their luck. This if happens may imply that the interdependence between family or community members is no longer sufficient, the emotions are rather pushing people apart, or at least not strong enough to pull them together, the moral values that insist on maintaining the bonds despite lack of emotional connection or material benefit are not taken seriously as such (Swartz, 2009). However, the extended family and community may respond differently to threats that are not vague but too obvious, big, and urgent. Their bonds may strengthen as a result, as if they are like a non-Newtonian fluid, their cohesion may become stronger when the impact is powerful and obvious (Hogg, 2007). But, gradually rising pressures shrouded in perpetual uncertainty may be more likely to disintegrate them if the internal bonds are already weakened (Lockwood, 1999). Like a frog, whose natural defenses may immediately respond when it is thrown in boiling water, but it may not react if it is placed in water at room temperature, and the temperature is then raised gradually to the boiling point. However, if a community's internal cohesion has already been weakened, the homeostasis is already disturbed, the individuals are already finding an opportunity to escape, the cracks have penetrated deep; a sudden blow may be the final blow to the community as a whole (Norris et al., 2008).

3.5 Collective Homeostasis

Like any living organism, an organic social entity like a family or a community will have ways to keep itself together, alive, and self-replicating. It will have defense mechanisms, which can be strengthened and weakened, mechanisms to maintain internal homeostasis between the fatherly and motherly, the emotional and the rational, the order and the chaos, and not let them manifest their terrible side. However, like any living organism, they will also have natural limits to external stressors, and they may also stumble upon pressures beyond a certain limit. What keeps the family bonding together in an extended sense despite external pressures would perhaps keep the community socially sustainable as well (Wellman & Wortley, 1990). The bonds with the extended family members are typically weaker in comparison with the immediate family. However, if these weaker bonds survive the external pressure, the community also may survive (Emery & Flora, 2006; Granovetter, 1973; Magis, 2010; Norris et al., 2008).

To understand this, the relationship between the family, extended family, and the community needs to be visualized. It is possible to distinctly identify a single organic family that is comprised of parents and their children. The boundary between nuclear families is, therefore, clear. However, the boundaries between the extended families are not, unless the two have grown in two geographically distant locations and turned into separate clans or tribes. Though within a large tribe, ethnic group, or an organic community, the lines between extended family are blurred, due to marital bonds that are formed outside the circle of cousins (Levi-Strauss, 2016). Memon community, for example, whose dynamics I explored in my doctoral thesis, is comprised of various sub-clans, who often interbreed with each other, eventually forming a larger community, connected via marital bonds. Different clans, who have chosen to live together, also eventually form marital bonds and may become related to each other (Javaid et al., 2018). Many extended families form a community, and when communities grow large enough, they form the whole society. Many societies in the world, like Pakistan and India, are a heterogeneous mixture of communities of multiple ethnic backgrounds, living together due to shared cultural and religious values (Bose & Jalal, 2004; Gilmartin, 2014).

There have been many examples of communities that have shown resilience to external pressures, eventually surviving the rainy days through mutual support for multiple generations. Such communities also eventually thrive much better economically when the rainy days are over. Puritans in early Europe are an example who experienced a similar scenario when they were cornered by the ruling authorities and had to develop alternative venues for their socioeconomic survival. Massive flooding in November 1170 forced Dutch peasants to the cities from the countryside, where they reorganized for their socioeconomic survival (Baumol & Storm, 2010). The migration to the cities also freed the Dutch peasants from monarchic authorities, which also played a role in their subsequent prosperity. Their spirit of cooperation and mutual support also protected the community from any unprecedented events. Baumol and Storm (2010) identify more examples:

> … the Spanish victory brought an exodus of enterprising Calvinist refugees, fleeing Spanish oppression. These refugees joined others, such as the Jews who had fled from Spain, in bolstering Amsterdam's entrepreneurial activity. This expulsion of talent to other countries can, of course, be seen many times in history, from Louis XIV's expulsion of the Huguenots from France, to Hitler's expulsion of the Jews, to the exodus of members of the middle class from Castro's Cuba. (p. 484)

Memon and Chinioti communities are two examples that I studied in my doctoral thesis that remained resilient to external threats for several generations after their inception. The Delhiwala community, which I also studied, has a slightly different story. However, they also rose to prominence in an environment where they faced competition from another more dominating community and later survived the brutal tyranny of the colonial empire that confiscated their source of livelihood. Bohri and Ismaili communities in Pakistan are two more such communities, which, despite the perpetual economic uncertainties, have remained integrated, which I could not include in my doctoral research because of delimitations. Today, it would not be incorrect to state that many other communities that have been resilient for many centuries are now facing a breakdown due to external stressors. In the contemporary world, these stressors are often manmade. They are being exerted by the economic activity, which is often aided by the system of power. Some stressors induce fear of scarcity among the members of the community, pushing them into survival mode, which eventually disrupts their internal homeostasis. However, there are incentives also for members to care less about their organic family or community. The psychological pressures created by consumerism, the fear of missing out, such as the technological advancements that allow easy mobility but trap you financially, or the illusion of digital connectivity that blurs the need to reengage the organic social community. The fear of scarcity is now being replaced by the fear of burnout caused by the race toward overconsumption, where nothing is enough in the modern consumer culture (Han, 2015). Both can be said to disturb the homeostasis of the individual, the organic family, and the community.

Organic communities, especially the ones with an entrepreneurial orientation that also have stayed together for generations, thus can offer some insight. As they have remained both socially and economically sustainable, that is, the organic family and community have not disintegrated, while economically they have also thrived. This implies that they have to withstand external pressures while also sufficiently fulfilling the socioemotional and economic needs of their members. In other words, the socioeconomic interdependence of the community members on each other has kept the community sustaining itself generation after generation. The key question here is how community members do not lose trust in each other, and sustain their bonds from one generation to the next. The trust and cohesion among a group of people have been referred to as social capital, which cannot be produced and reproduced without another quality referred to as moral capital, as it is through the perpetual demonstration of moral behavior, trust is maintained and inculcated. This chapter started with the description of the organic form of the social in contrast to how the economic can also originate organically. This description begins with early childhood experiences, which, if devoid of fairness, kindness, acceptance, and justice, can turn siblings into rivals. This hints toward the source of social capital within the bounds of the family, which then also manifests in the patterns of behavior toward others that the child demonstrates after growing up. A key job of the family is also to inculcate the necessary moral character, which, if absent, can potentially turn social capital into something unhealthy as well. However, if used judiciously, it can subsequently be beneficial for the community and the society in which the community exists. This necessitates discussion on the concept of social capital, how it emerges, how it may potentially turn toxic, and what can be done to keep it from turning detrimental for the members of the community.

3.6 Social Capital

Cooperation, trust, support, and reciprocity that can exist in human communities are typically referred to as social capital. Oxoby (2009) defines social capital as "an individual's sacrifices (time, effort, consumption) made to promote cooperation with others [in the community]" (p. 1136). For Bourdieu (Pierre Bourdieu, 2011), social capital is "the aggregate of the actual or potential resources which are linked to possession of a durable network of more or less institutionalized relationships of mutual acquaintance and recognition" (p. 246). In Coleman's view "social capital is productive, making possible the achievement of certain ends that would not be attainable in its absence … a group whose members manifest trustworthiness and place extensive trust in one another will be able to accomplish much more than a comparable group lacking that trustworthiness and trust" (Coleman, 1994). As per DeFilippis (2001) "social capital is meant to be a means to the end of economic security and development, not an end in and of itself" (p. 798). This can indeed be true within the confines of modern market society, where economic ends are prioritized over social goals. However, in societies that have not bought into the metaphysics of capitalism, social capital can be an end in itself, or a means to achieve something sacred if the society has a predominant religious character (Candland, 2001).

Two complementary dimensions of social capital have been discussed in relevant literature: (1) structural or bridging social capital, and (2) relational or bonding social capital (Pearson et al., 2008; Tata & Prasad, 2015). Structural social capital refers to the "pattern and strength of ties" (Pearson et al., 2008, p. 957) among the members of a social group. It also refers to the quantity, density, and degree of reusability of social relations or how the social ties from one social group are easily transferred to another group. It is not just the stronger ties within one's family network that can be beneficial, but also the weaker ones, like with acquaintances, which can connect people with opportunities not inside but nearby their immediate network (Granovetter, 1973). These weaker ties are also referred to as 'bridging social capital', "which provides a kind of social 'lubricant', important for 'getting ahead' economically and socially for both individuals and communities" (Evans & Syrett, 2007, p. 58). Relational social capital, on the other hand, refers to the quality of relationships expressed in the form of trust, norms of reciprocity and cooperation, obligation to well-being, and a sense of belongingness to the group strengthened by emotions, intimacy, and shared morality. The stronger ties or the 'bonding social capital', on the other hand, are considered beneficial for moral and financial support (Evans & Syrett, 2007; Putnam, 2020).

3.6.1 Generating Social Capital Through Economic Activity

The social ties, either weak or strong, contribute to the economic activity initiated by members of a community, which in turn strengthens the bonds as well (Peredo & Chrisman, 2006). The economic and social capital, therefore, can both reproduce each other if the economic activity remains "embedded" in the social relationships (Granovetter, 1973; Olofsson, 1999; Polanyi, 2001; Woolcock, 1998). A wide range of literature surveyed by Rothausen (2009) suggests that members of the same family or community working together offer social and economic benefits to all working together if their goals align as well. These benefits may include skill enhancement, increased personal satisfaction and mood, increased level of support in life, and "personal fulfillment and success that" (Rothausen, 2009, p. 224) may increase the well-being of all stakeholders involved in the economic activity. Conflicts nevertheless happen when the personal, social, and economic interests of individuals collide in the short run. However, in the long run, the positive reinforcements may predominate in socioeconomic relationships (Rothausen, 2009). The goal is also "… the preservation of socioemotional wealth … [as] an end in and of itself, strongly influencing strategic decisions and sometimes even conflicting with economic objectives. This is not to say that family firms sacrifice or ignore financial goals. (Gomez-Mejia et al., 2011, p. 694). Gomez-Mejia, et al. (2011) further suggest that future research should give equal weight to the goals of the family firms, for example, "stable employment, harmony among kin, and long-term survival" (p. 694) along with economic goals. Other authors have also acknowledged that businesses backed by family and community may be considered as a medium of producing and sustaining social capital when the financial benefits of the business are justly shared with all participating members (Aldrich & Cliff, 2003; Arregle et al., 2007).

In this context, the role of small and medium businesses in producing social capital and generating employment for marginalized communities may be acknowledged. Businesses can help poor communities to break away from the vicious circle of "losing people, wealth, services, employment opportunities, and business investment" (Peattie, 2007, p. 173), more so if the entrepreneurs belong to the same community (Javaid et al., 2020). Social capital can be developed through inclusion when businesses are encouraged by policymakers to "generate employment opportunities" and facilitate the development of trust, reciprocity, and cooperative behavior among the stakeholders through their inclusive approach (Peattie, 2007). Joseph (2000) has also noted that in the UK, several SME (Small and Medium Enterprise) size businesses are consciously including members of marginalized groups to generate employment and subsequently contribute to their socioemotional well-being (Labonte, 2004) as employment closer to their home keep them connected to their organic family and community.

Moon (2001) also acknowledged the contribution of large businesses in the development of social capital at the community level in his study on the social responsibility of businesses in Australia. He notes that "community involvement can be incorporated into company strategy as opposed to being detached from the core market activities" (p. 41). Contrary to Friedman's (2007) advice of making profit maximization the primary social responsibility of corporations, the evidence suggests that "development of norms of reciprocity and networks of civic engagement" (Moon, 2001, p. 44) is possible. Social capital development can be achieved through community development initiatives if done with pure intention. Businesses can initiate a "multiplier effect" of the development of social capital via frequent "acts of social cooperation" leading to the development of "norms of reciprocity within networks of civic engagement" (Moon, 2001, p. 44). However, the role of larger businesses in the process of keeping the communities together should be appraised with caution. As large corporations often use impersonal bureaucratic design, thus prioritizing rational over socioemotional (Allan & Ritzer, 1999; Astrachan, 1988; Hales, 2002). They thus promote and capitalize on an individualistic-consumerist culture (Barber, 1992). They also have a propensity to automate and relocate jobs to other places to minimize cost (Boltanski & Chiapello, 2007), which destroys the employment opportunities they first created, forcing people to relocate and disconnect from their organic family and community, as mentioned earlier as well. However, small and medium-sized businesses established and driven by community members utilizing the social capital that exists within the community, who shares the economic benefit with the community, are likely to do a better job in reproducing social capital in this context (Rothausen, 2009).

3.6.2 Generating Social Capital Through the Entrepreneur's Family and Community

The institution of the family is considered to be a primary producer of social capital (Crosnoe, 2004; Parcel & Menaghan, 1994; Portes, 1998). We saw earlier in Sect. 3.4 that unhealthy family environments can produce antisocial tendencies in children as they grow up. On the flip side, as per Bubolz (2001), a healthy family nurtures a safe and accepting environment for their offspring from the very beginning, where the children learn to trust others and also demonstrate trustworthy behavior. This happens when the elders can provide physiological and psychological security to the young. When a family fails to do so, as explained in Sect. 3.4, a feeling of mistrust may develop among the children, which, if perpetual, may shape their perception of the people outside the family, also undermining their capacity to form healthy relationships with others as they grow up (Bubolz, 2001). This may also adversely affect their capacity for moral conduct (Lockwood, 1999; Stolle, 2003). So, the capacity to avoid and resolve conflicts is also developed, as when "a basic sense of trust has been established, betrayal and disappointment can be easier to deal with" (Bubolz, 2001, p. 129). The elders in the family, therefore, can create the appropriate environment, and teach the young how to establish trust with people outside the family via engaging in various cultural, religious, economic, and civic activities. "This type of infrastructure is essential for the development and flow of social capital. The family is an integral player in such an interdependent system for creating and using social capital [in business]" Explains Bubloz (p. 131). Artificial social formations, from clubs to voluntary organizations, may reproduce the social capital. However, they typically would use and reproduce what is already produced within the new generation by their caretakers. If antisocial behavior has been inculcated due to the negligent behavior of parents or their absence, which could very likely be due to the disintegrating influence of market forces, the hope of recovery is not entirely lost, though, it would depend on the kind of exposure the person may receive, like that of some religious organization or some rehabilitation program. Due to the limited availability relative to the need for such interventions in modern society, many do not receive any transformative exposure to recover from their antisocial behavior for their entire lives. In this context, the significance of the healthy organic family environment remains profound, which cannot be expected to be effectively replaced by any artificial social formation later in life.

The family can also teach reciprocity. For example, in traditional families, often there is an understanding between parents and children that when the parents grow old, the children will take care of the parents as the children were taken care of during their childhood. Within the context of many traditional families, one is expected to reciprocate any favors done by other family members. The return can also be an expression of gratitude, appreciation, and respect, which often makes the process of giving and receiving unconditional in purely economic terms. On a community level, such a culture often suppresses exploitative behavior while creating a healthy atmosphere for organized action against any emerging challenges faced by the community as a whole. When members of a community feel confident that their vulnerabilities will not be exploited by other members, then cooperation is more likely (Putnam, 1993a). If such families form communities, then the principles of trust and reciprocity may be reproduced on a cultural level within the larger structure of the community through "generalized reciprocity" (Putnam, 1993a, p. 172). Trust reinforced through reciprocity also facilitates the resolution of various disputes without involving any legal action, as the contracts are believed to be embedded within a system of reciprocal and fluid relationships, maintenance of which is also seen as an end in itself (Granovetter, 1985). Economic activity within such an environment over a long period also reproduces social capital, which includes norms of reciprocity, trust, and spirit of cooperation, a publicly owned 'moral resource'. This resource tends "to be self-reinforcing and cumulative … [its] supply increases rather than decreases through use [and is] … depleted if not used" (Putnam, 1993b). Evans and Syrett (2007) also note that "Social capital is generated through regular exchanges within such networks, it becomes appropriable, or re-usable, by those parties with access to such networks … Economic development is, therefore, expedited by the presence of networks exhibiting such characteristics of social capital as trust and reciprocity" (p. 59).

3.6.3 The Dark Side of Social Capital

The bonding relationships within the family can insist on abiding by some norms damaging to the business. Poutzioris et al. (2004) suggest that nepotism, lack of meritocracy and professionalism, conservative and introverted approach, inflexibility, lack of formal communication, and family disputes are some of the ways bonding social capital within the family can negatively affect the family business.. Mutual care and trust can make it easy to engage "in moral hazard, … shirk, free ride, and consume perks" (Karra et al., 2006, p. 874), implying the absence of a healthy father's character. However, a moral resource can be used for unproductive ends when the moral framework has blind spots or is not strong enough to tame the emotional or motherly side of the relationship. Table 3.1 provides a summary of this section.

Excessive drawing by family members or extra urges from the community to support the needy can financially burden the business, converting them into welfare agencies and also leading to their bankruptcies in worst-case scenarios (Levitte, 2004). Bonding with elders in the family in an evolving market and political economy can also hinder the growth of the business. The elders, who have worked with a set of old public institutions and inside the markets that no longer exist, can impose their experience on the juniors, a clear manifestation of the characteristic of the terrible father. Arregle et al. (2015) notes:

> … business advice that family members can provide to entrepreneurs in these emerging countries is probably of lower value or quality, as they usually have little expertise or lack

Table 3.1 Possible downsides of high bonding social capital

Examples of possible downsides	
Nepotism and disputes among family members[11]	
Inefficiency in financial and operational management[7, 8, 11]	
Demands for community support can lead to bankruptcy for businesses[8]	
Lack of updated and fresh insight, due to lack of outside exposure, particularly of elders[1]	
Exclusion of outsiders, excess claims on community members[2, 9, 10]	
Restrictions on individual freedoms and downward leveling norm[9, 12]	
Prevailing social ills due to restricted outside intervention[3, 4, 9]	
A resource-rich community with high bonding capital may avoid sharing its resources with impoverished communities[2, 5, 6]	

References: 1. Arregle et al. (2015); 2. DeFilippis (2001); 3. DeKeseredy and Schwartz (2010); 4. Evans (2016); 5. Evans and Syrett (2007); 6. Higuchi (2014); 7. Karra et al. (2006); 8. Levitte (2004); 9. Portes (1998); 10. Portes and Sensenbrenner (1993); 11. Poutziouris et al. (2004); 12. Woolcock (1998)

> an understanding of business development or competition. Although some family members may have experience or knowledge acquired before these economic changes, their knowledge may be of lower relevance to entrepreneurs in the new institutional and economic setting. (pp. 334–5)

The terrible father can manifest in more ways, as the strength of ties within a community can sometimes cut both ways. Portes (1998) has reviewed at least four negative consequences of strong relations among ethnic communities: "exclusion of outsiders, excess claims on group members, restrictions on individual freedoms, and downward leveling norms" (p. 15). The bounded solidarity can restrict the inclusion of outsiders, subsequently confining the economic benefits of social capital within an entrepreneurial community. DeFilippis (2001) argues that such exclusionary nature of some ethnic communities "completely closes off the market, and access to the market, to anyone who is not part of the ethnic group creating the enclave" (p. 792). Woolcock (1998) refers to it as a lack of linkage with extra-community networks and argues that such a lack of autonomy can also restrict the individual members of the community from engaging with business opportunities outside the network. However, in his view, if the autonomy for individuals within a community is high, yet the social cohesion within the community is low, then the community can eventually face the problem of Anomie (a distrustful and hostile environment). On the other hand, if the cohesion is high yet outside linkage with others is restricted, then the community can remain stuck in a vicious circle of poverty and other social ills that Portes and Sensenbrenner (1993) refer to as the 'downward leveling norm'.

A high degree of individual freedom to engage with economic opportunities outside the community and a high degree of social integration within the community are often desirable (Portes & Sensenbrenner, 1993). Portes (1998) also acknowledged the problem of restrictions on individual freedom typically caused by excessive group loyalty with community members. As a consequence, the community can suffer from the downward leveling norm, where the living standards can also remain stagnant, particularly in economically marginalized communities. For the sake of loyalty to the group, the community members can be discouraged from economically engaging with extra-community networks, which may offer opportunities for economic prosperity for individual members. Such restrictions can add to the vicious circle also particularly when the community culture allows free riding, converting businesses into charity organizations, subsequently leading to their collapse.

Binding social capital can also be a breeding ground for social ills and venues of unproductive entrepreneurship like that of "mafia families, prostitution and gambling rings, and youth gangs" (Baumol & Storm, 2010) where even unwilling members can be stuck in the vicious circle only because they do not have anywhere else to go. Others can also avoid accepting members from such groups because of their background (M. Evans, 2016). These examples often display "the characteristics of social capital—symbolized identities, tight networks, and the requisite displays of trust" (Evans, 2016, p. 53). Such restrictions imply that "embeddedness in [certain] social structures can be turned to less than socially desirable ends" (Portes, 1998, p. 19). This exemplifies the complete absence of the moral from the picture. The power system can also influence the flow of resources from the privileged to the marginalized end. If those who control the resources restrict the free flow of physical capital, then the idea of having good, trustworthy relationships with community members becomes meaningless, at least in an economic sense (DeFilippis, 2001). "It is, therefore, a vertical dimension of social capital", suggests Evans and Syrett (2007), "which may permit the less powerful to leverage resources, ideas and information from more formal institutions beyond their 'community'" (p. 59).

This can be claimed for the atmosphere within the community and also between different communities. A privileged community, in control of material resources, might restrict its distribution to the marginalized ones where it is more needed, another display of the character of the terrible father. In this context, binding social capital (intra-community bonding) in the absence of bridging social capital (extra-community bonding) can create problems by excluding those who are less privileged and less powerful (DeFilippis, 2001; Higuchi, 2014). According to DeFilippis (2001):

> Simply put, certain social networks are in greater positions of power than others, and they can therefore yield much more substantial returns to their members when those networks are engaged in social or political conflict. (p. 791)

In a market society, class conflict is said to be a default phenomenon, which paradoxically instrumentalizes the existence of social capital within some networks or communities. In other words, privileged access to social capital within networks in a market society can make those networks valuable. Such networks may not be open for everyone in society due to the "competitive nature of capitalism" (DeFilippis, 2001, p. 793). In a free market context, social capital can become a means to economic capital, a state of imbalance in favor of the economy. Social capital, as per DeFilippis (2001), "must therefore be premised on the ability of certain people to realize it at the expense of others" (p. 793) in the modern free market. The economically marginalized and politically disempowered communities in a market society can also become morally corrupt while instrumentalizing their social capital for socially destructive ends (DeKeseredy & Schwartz, 2010; Evans, 2016; Portes, 1998).

DeFilippis (2001) argues that the existence of social capital might also take a community away from economic prosperity. It is also possible that "economic growth and development might promote the destruction of trust-based noncommodified relationships" (DeFilippis, 2001, p. 797). Colonization of the social sphere by the neoliberal market can also immerse the communities "in the commodity relations central to the capitalist economy" (DeFilippis, 2001, p. 797), leading to the dissolution of social capital. Hence, there is not enough evidence to assume a positive economic influence of social capital in the context of unique power dynamics and the competitive atmosphere of a modern free market. A balance, therefore, is critical, which necessitates the need for a moral framework that transcends both the social and the economic, which would guide both the rational and the emotional forces at play within the socioeconomic realms of the community and the market. The next chapter will attempt to delve into the significance, particularities, and challenges of developing such a moral framework.

References

Afghan, N., & Wiqar, T. (2007). Succession in family businesses of Pakistan: Kinship culture and Islamic inheritance law. In *CMER working paper no. 07-54*.

Aldrich, H. E., & Cliff, J. E. (2003). The pervasive effects of family on entrepreneurship: Toward a family embeddedness perspective. *Journal of Business Venturing, 18*(5), 573–596.

Allan, K., & Ritzer, G. (1999). The McDonaldization thesis: Explorations and extensions. *Contemporary Sociology, 28*, 200.

Arregle, J. L., Batjargal, B., Hitt, M. A., Webb, J. W., Miller, T., & Tsui, A. S. (2015). Family ties in entrepreneurs' social networks and new venture growth. *Entrepreneurship: Theory and Practice, 39*(2), 313–344.

Arregle, J., Hitt, M. A., Sirmon, D., & Very, P. (2007). The development of organizational social capital: Attributes of family firms. *Journal of Management Studies, 44*(1), 73–95.

Astrachan, J. H. (1988). Family firm and community culture. *Family Business Review, 1*(2), 165–189.

Avloniti, A., Iatridou, A., Kaloupsis, I., & Vozikis, G. S. (2014). Sibling rivalry: Implications for the family business succession process. *International Entrepreneurship and Management Journal, 10*(4), 661–678. https://doi.org/10.1007/s11365-013-0271-6

Barber, B. R. (1992). *Jihad vs. how globalization and tribalism are reshaping the world*. Ballantine Books, London.

Barnett, T., & Kellermanns, F. W. (2006). Are we family and are we treated as family? Nonfamily employees' perceptions of justice in the family firm. *Entrepreneurship Theory and Practice, 30*(6), 837–854. https://doi.org/10.1111/j.1540-6520.2006.00155.x

Barrett, L. F. (2020). *How emotions are made: The secret life of the brain*. Pan Macmillan.

Barrios, S., Bertinelli, L., & Strobl, E. (2006). Climate change and rural–urban migration: The case of sub-Saharan Africa. *Journal of Urban Economics, 60*(3), 357–371. https://doi.org/10.1016/j.jue.2006.04.005

Baudrillard, J. (2016). *The consumer society: Myths and structures*. SAGE Publications.

Baudrillard, J., Glaser, S. F., Press, U. of M. (1994). *Simulacra and simulation*. University of Michigan Press.

Baumol, W. J., & Storm, R. J. (2010). "Useful knowledge" of entrepreneurship: Some implications of the history. In D. S. Landes, J. Mokyr, & W. J. Baumol (Eds.), *The invention of enterprise: Entrepreneurship from ancient Mesopotamia to modern times* (pp. 527–542). Princeton University Press.

Becker, G. S. (2013). *The economic approach to human behavior*. University of Chicago Press.

Benson, M., & O'Reilly, K. (2009). Migration and the search for a better way of life: A critical exploration of lifestyle migration. *The Sociological Review, 57*(4), 608–625. https://doi.org/10.1111/j.1467-954X.2009.01864.x

Benson, M., & O'Reilly, K. (2016). From lifestyle migration to lifestyle in migration: Categories, concepts and ways of thinking. *Migration Studies, 4*(1), 20–37. https://doi.org/10.1093/migration/mnv015

Berrone, P., Cruz, C., & Gomez-Mejia, L. R. (2012). Socioemotional wealth in family firms: Theoretical dimensions, assessment approaches, and agenda for future research. *Family Business Review, 25*(3), 258–279. https://doi.org/10.1177/0894486511435355

Birdthistle, N., & Hales, R. (2023). The meaning of being a family business in the 21st century. In N. Birdthistle & R. Hales (Eds.), *Attaining the 2030 sustainable development goal of responsible consumption and production* (pp. 11–20). Emerald Publishing Limited. https://doi.org/10.1108/978-1-80455-840-920231002

Boltanski, L., & Chiapello, E. (2007). *The new spirit of capitalism*. Verso.

Bose, S., & Jalal, A. (2004). *Modern south Asia: History, culture, political economy*. Routledge.

Bourdieu, P. (2011). The forms of capital (1986). *Cultural Theory: An Anthology, 1*(81–93), 949.

Bourdieu, P., & Nice, R. (1998). *Acts of resistance: Against the tyranny of the market*. New Press.

Bowlby, J. (2012a). *A secure base*. Taylor & Francis.

Bowlby, J. (2012b). *The making and breaking of affectional bonds*. Taylor & Francis.

Bronfenbrenner, U. (2009). *The ecology of human development*. Harvard University Press.
Bubolz, M. M. (2001). Family as source, user, and builder of social capital. *The Journal of Socio-Economics, 30*, 129–131.
Buist, K. L., Deković, M., & Prinzie, P. (2013). Sibling relationship quality and psychopathology of children and adolescents: A meta-analysis. *Clinical Psychology Review, 33*(1), 97–106. https://doi.org/10.1016/j.cpr.2012.10.007
Candland, C. (2001). Faith as social capital: Religion and community development in Southern Asia. In J. D. Montgomery & A. Inkeles (Eds.), *Social capital as a policy resource* (pp. 355–374). Springer.
Caputo, A., Marzi, G., Pellegrini, M. M., & Rialti, R. (2018). Conflict management in family businesses: A bibliometric analysis and systematic literature review. *International Journal of Conflict Management, 29*(4), 519–542. https://doi.org/10.1108/IJCMA-02-2018-0027
Caputo, A., Pellegrini, M., Valenza, G., & Zarone, V. (2017). Conflict management and negotiation in family business succession: Critical literature review and research Agenda. *European Academy of Management, 29*(4), 519–542.
Carradore, M. (2022). Academic research output on social capital: A bibliometric and visualization analysis. *International Journal of Sociology and Social Policy, 42*(13/14), 113–134. https://doi.org/10.1108/ijssp-11-2022-0281
Cernea, M. M. (2000). Risks, safeguards and reconstruction: A model for population displacement and resettlement. *Economic and Political Weekly, 35*(41), 3659–3678. http://www.jstor.org/stable/4409836
Chang, A. A. R., Mubarik, M. S., & Naghavi, N. (2020). Passing on the legacy: Exploring the dynamics of succession in family businesses in Pakistan. *Journal of Family Business Management, 11*(2), 161–184.
Chrisman, J. J., Chua, J. H., Pearson, A. W., & Barnett, T. (2012). Family involvement, family influence, and family-centered non-economic goals in small firms. *Entrepreneurship Theory and Practice, 36*(2), 267–293. https://doi.org/10.1111/j.1540-6520.2010.00407.x
Coleman, J. S. (1994). *Foundations of social theory*. Belknap Press of Harvard University.
Colli, A., & Rose, M. (2007). Family business. *The Oxford Handbook Business History, 2007*, 194–217.
Crosnoe, R. (2004). Social capital and the interplay of families and schools. *Journal of Marriage and Family, 66*(2), 267–280.
Danes, S. M., Stafford, K., Haynes, G., & Amarapurkar, S. S. (2009). Family capital of family firms: Bridging human, social, and financial capital. *Family Business Review, 22*(3), 199–215.
DeFilippis, J. (2001). The myth of social capital in community development. *Housing Policy Debate, 12*(4), 781–806.
DeKeseredy, W. S., & Schwartz, M. D. (2010). Friedman economic policies, social exclusion, and crime: Toward a gendered left realist subcultural theory. *Crime, Law and Social Change, 54*(2), 159–170.
Deleuze, G., Guattari, F., Hurley, R., Seem, M., & Lane, H. R. (2013). *Anti-oedipus: Capitalism and schizophrenia*. Bloomsbury Publishing.
Denzin, N. K., & Lincoln, Y. S. (2005). *The Sage handbook of qualitative research*. SAGE Publications Inc.
Diamond, J. (2012). *The world until yesterday: What can we learn from traditional societies?* Viking.
Dyer, J. W. G. (2006). Examining the family effect on firm performance. *Family Business Review, 19*(4), 253–273.
Eizenberg, E., & Jabareen, Y. (2017). Social sustainability: A new conceptual framework. *Sustainability, 9*(1), 1.
Emery, M., & Flora, C. (2006). Spiraling-up: Mapping community transformation with community capital framework. *Community Development, 37*(1), 19–35.
Escobar, A. (2012). *Encountering development: The making and unmaking of the third world*. Princeton University Press.

Evans, G. W., Li, D., & Whipple, S. S. (2013). Cumulative risk and child development. *Psychological Bulletin, 139*(6), 1342–1396. https://doi.org/10.1037/a0031808

Evans, M. (2016). Social capital and the shadow economy. *Journal of Economic Issues (m.e. Sharpe Inc.), 50*(1), 43–58.

Evans, M., & Syrett, S. (2007). Generating social capital? *European Urban and Regional Studies, 14*(1), 55–74.

Fehr, E., & Fischbacher, U. (2003). The nature of human altruism. *Nature, 425*(6960), 785–791. https://doi.org/10.1038/nature02043

Friedman, M. (2007). The social responsibility of business is to increase its profits. In W. C. Zimmerli, M. Holzinger, & K. Richter (Eds.), *Corporate ethics and corporate governance* (Vol. 32, pp. 173–178). London: Springer.

Fromm, E. (2017). *The sane society* (L. A. Anderson (Ed.)). Taylor & Francis.

Gharipour, M. (2012). The culture and politics of commerce: Bazaars in the Islamic world. In M. Gharipour (Ed.), *The Bazaar in the Islamic City: Design, culture and history.* London: The American University in Cairo Press.

Giedd, J. N., Blumenthal, J., Jeffries, N. O., Castellanos, F. X., Liu, H., Zijdenbos, A., Paus, T., Evans, A. C., & Rapoport, J. L. (1999). Brain development during childhood and adolescence: A longitudinal MRI study. *Nature Neuroscience, 2*(10), 861–863. https://doi.org/10.1038/13158

Gilmartin, D. (2014). *Civilization and modernity: Narrating the creation of Pakistan.* 312.

Gintis, H. (2000). Beyond homo economicus: Evidence from experimental economics. *Ecological Economics, 35*(3), 311–322. https://doi.org/10.1016/S0921-8009(00)00216-0

Goldstein, A. P., & Michaels, G. Y. (2023). *Empathy: Development, training, and consequences.* Taylor & Francis Limited.

Gomez-Mejia, L. R., Cruz, C., Berrone, P., & De Castro, J. (2011). The bind that ties: Socioemotional wealth preservation in family firms. *The Academy of Management Annals, 5*(1), 653–707.

Granovetter, M. (1973). The strength of weak ties. *The American Journal of Sociology, 78*, 1360–1380.

Granovetter, M. (1985). Economic action and social structure: The problem of embeddedness. *American Journal of Sociology, 3*, 481–510.

Greaber, D. (2001). *Debt: The first 5000 years.* Mellville House.

Griffin, B. J., Purcell, N., Burkman, K., Litz, B. T., Bryan, C. J., Schmitz, M., Villierme, C., Walsh, J., & Maguen, S. (2019). Moral injury: An integrative review. *Journal of Traumatic Stress, 32*(3), 350–362. https://doi.org/10.1002/jts.22362

Hales, C. (2002). 'Bureaucracy-lite' and continuities in managerial work. *British Journal of Management, 13*(1), 51–66.

Hallaq, W. B. (2013). *The impossible state: Islam, politics, and modernity's moral predicament (Reprint).* Columbia University Press.

Han, B. C. (2015). *The burnout society.* Stanford University Press.

Harter, S. (2002). Authenticity. In *Handbook of positive psychology.* (pp. 382–394). Oxford University Press.

Harvey, D. (2005). *A brief history of neoliberalism.* Oxford University Press.

Hashim, R., Ahmad, H., Mazuki, M. A., Bahrin, N. L. Z., & Ahmad, A. (2017). Sibling rivalry and offspring conflict: A review. *Advanced Science Letters, 23*(1), 3–6. https://doi.org/10.1166/ASL.2017.7167

Henrich, J., Boyd, R., Bowles, S., Camerer, C., Fehr, E., Gintis, H., & McElreath, R. (2001). In search of homo economicus: Behavioral experiments in 15 small-scale societies. *The American Economic Review, 91*(2), 73–78. http://www.jstor.org/stable/2677736

Higuchi, A. (2014). The mechanisms of social exclusion in modern society: The dilemma of active labor market policy. *International Journal of Japanese Sociology, 23*(1), 110–124.

Hochschild, A. R. (2012). *The managed heart: Commercialization of human feeling.* University of California Press.

Hochschild, A. R. (2013). *The outsourced self: What happens when we pay others to live our lives for us.* Picador.

Hoffman, M. L. (2001). *Empathy and moral development: Implications for caring and justice.* Cambridge University Press.

Hogg, M. (2007). Uncertainty-identity theory. *Advances in Experimental Social Psychology, 39*, 69–126. https://doi.org/10.1016/S0065-2601(06)39002-8

Horkheimer, M., Adorno, T. W., & Noeri, G. (2002). *Dialectic of enlightenment.* Stanford University Press.

Javaid, O, Shamsi, A., & Hyder, I. (2018). *Building a theoretical model of socially sustainable entrepreneurship through comparative case analysis of ethnic entrepreneurial communities.* Institute of Business Management. http://prr.hec.gov.pk/jspui/handle/123456789/11058

Javaid, O. (2024). The significance of moral agency for socioeconomic justice and its absence in islamic economics and finance. *Journal of King Abdulaziz University: Islamic Economics, 37*(1 SE-English Language), 3–20.

Javaid, O., Shamsi, A. F., & Hyder, I. (2020). Religious entrepreneurial communities as a solution for socioeconomic injustice. *Journal of Enterprising Communities: People and Places in the Global Economy, 14*(3), 415–446.

Joseph, E. (2000). *A welcome engagement: SMEs and social inclusion.* London: Institute for Public Policy Research (IPPR).

Karra, N., Tracey, P., & Phillips, N. (2006). Altruism and agency in the family firm: Exploring the role of family, kinship, and ethnicity. *Entrepreneurship: Theory and Practice, 30*(6), 861–877.

Kernis, M. H., & Goldman, B. M. B. T.-A. in E. S. P. (2006). *A multicomponent conceptualization of authenticity: Theory and research* (Vol. 38, pp. 283–357). Academic Press. https://doi.org/10.1016/S0065-2601(06)38006-9

Kowal, A. K., Krull, J. L., & Kramer, L. (2004). How the differential treatment of siblings is linked with parent–child relationship quality. *Journal of Family Psychology, 18*(4), 658–665. https://doi.org/10.1037/0893-3200.18.4.658

Krier, D., & Worrell, M. (2016). *Capitalism's future: Alienation, emancipation and critique.* London: Brill.

Labonte, R. (2004). Social inclusion/exclusion: Dancing the dialectic. *Health Promotion International, 19*(1), 115–121.

Landes, D. S., Mokyr, J., & Baumol, W. J. (2010). *The invention of enterprise: Entrepreneurship from ancient Mesopotamia to modern times.* Princeton University Press.

Lawson, C. A. (2002). *Understanding the borderline mother: Helping her children transcend the intense, unpredictable, and volatile relationship.* Jason Aronson.

Le Breton-Miller, I., & Miller, D. (2006). Why do some family businesses out-compete? Governance, long-term orientations, and sustainable capability. *Entrepreneurship Theory and Practice, 30*(6), 731–746. https://doi.org/10.1111/j.1540-6520.2006.00147.x

Ledoux, J. (2015). *The emotional brain: The mysterious underpinnings of emotional life.* Simon & Schuster.

Levi-Strauss, C. (2016). *The elementary structures of kinship.* Beacon Press.

Levitte, Y. M. (2004). Bonding social capital in entrepreneurial developing communities-survival networks or barriers? *Journal of Community Development Society, 35*(1), 44–64.

Lockwood, D. (1999). Civic integration and social cohesion. In I. Gough & G. Olofsson (Eds.), *Capitalism and social cohesion essays on exclusion and integration* (pp. 63–84). Macmillan Press Ltd.

Magis, K. (2010). Community resilience: An indicator of social sustainability. *Society and Natural Resources, 23*(5), 401–416. https://doi.org/10.1080/08941920903305674

Marcuse, H. (2013). *One-dimensional man: Studies in the ideology of advanced industrial society.* Taylor & Fancies.

Masarik, A. S., & Conger, R. D. (2017). Stress and child development: A review of the family stress model. *Current Opinion in Psychology, 13*, 85–90. https://doi.org/10.1016/j.copsyc.2016.05.008

Maté, G., & Maté, D. (2024). *The myth of normal: Trauma, illness, and healing in a toxic culture.* Ebury Publishing.

Mauss, M. (2015). *The gift: Forms and functions of exchange in archaic societies (classic reprint).* London: 1 kg Limited.

Moon, J. (2001). Business social responsibility: A source of social capital? *Philosophy of Management, 1*(3), 35–45.

Morris, A. S., & Williamson, A. C. (2019). *Building early social and emotional relationships with infants and toddlers* (1st ed.). London: Springer. https://doi.org/10.1007/978-3-030-03110-7

Neumann, E. (2015). *The origins and history of consciousness.* Taylor & Francis.

Norris, F. H., Stevens, S. P., Pfefferbaum, B., Wyche, K. F., & Pfefferbaum, R. L. (2008). Community resilience as a metaphor, theory, set of capacities, and strategy for disaster readiness. *American Journal of Community Psychology, 41*(1), 127–150. https://doi.org/10.1007/s10464-007-9156-6

Olofsson, G. (1999). Embeddedness and integration. In I. Gough & G. Olofsson (Eds.), *Capitalism and social cohesion: Essays on exclusion and integration* (pp. 38–60). Macmillan Press Ltd.

Oxoby, R. (2009). Understanding social inclusion, social cohesion and social capital. *International Journal of Social Economics, 36*(12), 1133–1152.

Papanek, H. (1972). Pakistan's big businessmen: Muslim separatism, entrepreneurship, and partial modernization. *Economic Development and Cultural Change, 21*(1), 1–32.

Parcel, T. L., & Menaghan, E. G. (1994). Early parental work, family social capital, and early childhood outcomes. *American Journal of Sociolog, 99*(4), 972–1009.

Pearson, A. W., Carr, J. C., & Shaw, J. C. (2008). Toward a theory of familiness: A social capital perspective. *Entrepreneurship: Theory and Practice, 32*(6 Spec. Iss.), 949–969.

Peattie, K. (2007). Business and social inclusion. In D. Abrams, J. Christian, & D. Gordon (Eds.), *Multidisciplinary handbook of social exclusion research* (pp. 169–192). Wiley.

Peredo, A. M., & Chrisman, J. J. (2006). Toward a theory of community-based enterprise. *The Academy of Management Review, 31*(2), 309–328.

Perry, B. D., & Szalavitz, M. (2006). *The boy who was raised as a dog and other stories from a child psychiatrist's notebook: What traumatized children can teach us about loss, love, and healing.* Basic Books.

Peterson, J. B. (2002). *Maps of meaning: The architecture of belief*. Taylor & Francis.

Polanyi, K. (2001). *The great transformation: The political and economic origins of our time.* Beacon Press.

Portes, A. (1998). Social capital: Its origins and applications in modern sociology. *Annual Review of Sociology, 24*(1), 1–24.

Portes, A., & Sensenbrenner, J. (1993). Embeddedness and immigration: Notes on the social determinants of economic action. *American Journal of Sociology, 98*(6), 1320–1350.

Poutziouris, P. Z., Steier, L., & Smyrnios, K. X. (2004). Guest editorial: A commentary on family business entrepreneurial. *International Journal of Entrepreneurial Behavior and Research, 10*(1/2), 7–11.

Prime, H., Wade, M., & Browne, D. T. (2020). Risk and resilience in family well-being during the COVID-19 pandemic. *The American Psychologist, 75*(5), 631–643.

Putnam, R. D. (1993a). *Making democracy work: Civil traditions in modern Italy.* Princeton University Press.

Putnam, R. D. (1993b). *The prosperous community: Social capital and public life.* The American Prospect.

Putnam, R. D. (2020). *Bowling alone: Revised and updated: The collapse and revival of American community.* Simon & Schuster.

Ritzer, G. (2016). The mcdonaldization of society. In E. Mofield & T. Stambaugh (Eds.), *In the mind's eye* (1st ed.). London: Routledge.

Robbins, P. (2019). *Political ecology: A critical introduction.* Wiley.

Robinson, R., Hocking, C., & Payne, D. (2016). Toilet training practices and subjectivities in 1980s Aotearoa New Zealand. *New Zealand Sociology, 31*(1), 49–71.

Rogers, C., & Webb, D. (2013). *Significant aspects of client-centered therapy.* CreateSpace Independent Publishing Platform.

Rohner, R. P., & Britner, P. A. (2002). Worldwide mental health correlates of parental acceptance–rejection: Review of cross-cultural and intracultural evidence. *Cross-Cultural Research, 36*(1), 16–47. https://doi.org/10.1177/106939710203600102

Rothausen, T. J. (2009). Management work–family research and work–family fit: Implications for building family capital in family business. *Family Business Review, 22*(3), 220–234.

Sandel, M. J. (2012). *What money can't buy: The moral limits of markets.* Allen Lane.

Sarasvathy, S. D., Ali, I., Block, J., & Lutz, E. (2016). Partitioning socioemotional wealth to stitch together the effectual family enterprise. In K. Randerson, C. Bettinelli, G. Dossena, & A. Fayolle (Eds.), *Family entrepreneurship: Rethinking the research Agenda* (pp. 14–46). Routledge.

Sbert, J. M. (2010). Progress. In W. Sachs (Ed.), *The development dictionary: A guide to knowledge as power* (pp. 212–227). Zed Books.

Scott, J. C. (2020). *Seeing like a state: How certain schemes to improve the human condition have failed*. Yale University Press.

Shiva, V. (2016). *Staying alive: Women, ecology, and development*. North Atlantic Books.

Simmel, G. (2004). *The philosophy of money*. Routledge.

Stolle, D. (2003). The sources of social capital. In M. Hooghe & D. Stolle (Eds.), *Generating social capital civil society and institutions in comparative perspective* (pp. 19–42). Palgrave Macmillan.

Swartz, T. T. (2009). Intergenerational family relations in adulthood: Patterns, variations, and implications in the contemporary United States. *Annual Review of Sociology, 35*, 191–212. https://doi.org/10.1146/annurev.soc.34.040507.134615

Swyngedouw, E. (2010). Impossible sustainability and the post-political Condition. In M. Cerreta, G. Concilio, & V. Monno (Eds.), *Making strategies in spatial planning: Knowledge and values* (pp. 185–205). London: Springer. https://doi.org/10.1007/978-90-481-3106-8_11

Tata, J., & Prasad, S. (2015). Immigrant family businesses: Social capital, network benefits and business performance. *International Journal of Entrepreneurial Behavior and Research, 21*(6), 842–866.

Tomasello, M. (2015). *The cultural origins of human cognition.* Harvard University Press.

Waldinger, R., & Schulz, M. (2023). *The good life: Lessons from the world's longest scientific study of happiness*. Simon & Schuster.

Wang, K., & Ke, Y. (2024). Social sustainability of communities: A systematic literature review. *Sustainable Production and Consumption, 47*, 585–597. https://doi.org/10.1016/j.spc.2024.04.031

Wellman, B., & Wortley, S. (1990). Different strokes from different folks: Community ties and social support. *American Journal of Sociology, 96*(3), 558–588. https://doi.org/10.1086/229572

Woolcock, M. (1998). Social capital and economic development: Toward a theoretical synthesis and policy framework. *Theory and Society, 27*(2), 151–208.

Zeanah, C. H. (2018). *Handbook of infant mental health.* Guilford Publications.

Zhuravlova, L., Chebykin, A. I. A., & Chebykin, O. (2021). *The development of empathy: Phenomenology, structure and human nature.* London: Routledge.

Chapter 4
The Moral Basis of the Social and the Teleological Basis of the Moral

The moral can be described as a prerequisite for the social, as without it, the idea of sustaining a social reality is unlikely. In the previous chapter, social capital was also referred to as a moral resource, as social capital requires trust, which necessitates individuals to honor their commitments and show empathy and compassion toward each other. However, it can get complicated as a person has to juggle their commitments and compassion with multiple stakeholders and withhold their compassion against the antisocial elements if necessary. However, if compassion is purely based on emotions, then it may or may not flow where it is due, while the rational may not even engage the compassion in the first place. Would you help a person you badly despise if the person is in desperate need, like stuck in a car on fire? Or would you allow violation of some terms in a contract (a rational construct) when the other party is stricken with a financial emergency, a provision of which is not part of the contract? The limitation in the emotional and rational approaches, therefore, necessitates invoking a third faculty that is referred to here as moral, which will be described here in contrast to the emotional and the rational (Haidt & Graham, 2007; MacIntyre, 2013; Sandel, 2012).

The aim here is not to come up with a universalizable theory of morality, because this perhaps cannot be achieved in the first place. Attempts have been going on since the beginning of human history to accomplish this task. No consensus has been achieved yet. The problem, perhaps, lies in certain perennial questions, answers to which can only be speculated with our rational faculties. Like who are we, where did we come from, were we created? Or how it all came to exist, is there a purpose to all this that we call the universe or life? Based on these answers, cultures have been setting criteria to describe what's good and what's bad, what's harmful despite it may be pleasurable, and what's beneficial even when painful, but help us advance toward our ultimate purpose, whatever it may be (MacIntyre, 2013; Sen, 2017). Despite the ambiguity, we have an instinct that pushes us to consider the rightness or wrongness of an act, despite the act being endorsed by our emotions or logic. This instinct is typically referred to as our conscience, which Kant referred to as the

O. Javaid, *Socioeconomic Sustainability Through Moral and Social Capital*, Entrepreneurship and Development in South Asia: Longitudinal Narratives, https://doi.org/10.1007/978-981-96-8134-1_4

'Moral law' within him (Guyer, 2006), which the relevant research shows is very much biologically ingrained as well (Bloom, 2011; Hamlin et al., 2007).

4.1 The Mediator

Every human interaction, by definition, is moral as it may leave the parties better or worse off as per the agreed-upon criteria to judge the better from the worse (Hallaq, 2013). We typically prefer not to cause harm, as we perceive it, as our conscience may make us feel guilty. However, while facilitating others, when we can, especially in situations where there is no material benefit, can make our conscience feel content. Research on happiness often suggests that happiness is a function of how a person can benefit others (Stillman et al., 2009; R Waldinger & Schulz, 2023) while receiving something from others rather induces pleasure (Lembke, 2021). But when we are in survival mode, threatened with uncertainties, our focus can potentially shift to what we can receive for ourselves or for the people we deeply care about (Brewer, 1999). In high-stress scenarios, our self-interest can triumph over our altruistic spirit for strangers, shrinking its focus to people whom we value most, making us susceptible to committing injustice against those who are outside our 'moral circle' (Graham et al., 2017; Loewenstein, 2005). Those who do not intend to cause harm to others or attempt to facilitate others as much as they can and compensate for the harm incurred unintentionally are seen in a positive light in any society. Such individuals are acknowledged as heroic even if they prioritize others' interests during times of crisis (assuming there is no ambiguity in what is referred to as harmful or beneficial).

However, what if the understanding of the benefit or harm of this well-intentioned person is not correct? There are often hidden side effects that may become obvious in the long run, which outweigh the benefits eventually, and the receiver, often a child, may also not even understand what brought this harm to them (like some medical treatment). Would the purity of intentions be sufficient to consider someone moral, or would their understanding of the potential harm also count? What about the capacity of the individual, which may be constrained due to intrinsic or extrinsic reasons beyond one's control, like the policies at an organization where one is employed? Should we call the person moral if they prioritize their self-interest due to a sense of insecurity, despite they do not intend to cause any harm to others? How do we even know if positive intentions are there in the first place in such circumstances? What if the capacity to act in a particular way is constrained by culturally assigned roles, which may limit one's capacity, and even shape the perception of the harm in a specific situation, like often witnessed in a parent–child relationship in a modern individualistic culture (Maté & Maté, 2024)? Fromm (1994) described that a society can normalize harmful behavior, the culture may begin to endorse it, and even create institutions to regulate and perform certain harmful behaviors under legal cover. Would an individual, who cannot escape such a culture, despite being aware of the consequences, be considered moral or otherwise? Likewise, if one is employed in a particular institution that expects the employees to perform certain roles that may end up causing harm to society in certain ways that are not declared illegal as yet, but also considered normal within the dominant 'social imaginary', will one be referred to as moral in such a context? (Trueman & Dreher, 2020). In short, the question is, how do we judge if the act of the individual, under institutional, cultural, or instinctual constraints, is immoral, even though it may be considered legal and normal within a society?

Calling the situation complex appears like an understatement, which is why perhaps many resort to religion for that matter; however, we also have various options, some have more depth and breadth than others. Nevertheless, there are certain generally agreed-upon standards of morality, like truthfulness, being respectful, not causing unnecessary harm or pain, avoiding injustice (but defining it first), giving what's due, honoring commitments, avoiding arrogance, wastage and excess (beyond the needs), or the infamous golden principle of choosing for others that which is chosen for oneself. Haidt has recently suggested moral choices related to six categories: care/harm, fairness/cheating, loyalty/betrayal, authority/subversion, sanctity/degradation, and liberty/oppression (Haidt, 2013). And then we also have a list of seven deadly sins, which are (1) pride, (2) greed, (3) lust, (4) envy, (5) gluttony, (6) wrath, and (7) sloth. And a corresponding set of virtues, which are (1) humility, (2) charity, (3) chastity, (4) gratitude, (5) temperance, (6) patience, and (7) diligence (Petruzzello, 2024). The list goes on, the complete set would depend on one's beliefs; however, that is not the end of the story, perhaps. Whatever moral standard one believes in, it is still possible to fall short of complying with it, due to a variety of intrinsic and extrinsic reasons, so one needs to be aware and capable of managing these obstacles if one ought to be moral. These obstacles include our self-interest, cultural constraints, or the conflicting commitments that we make in family, community, or marketplace. The diverse nature of engagements, therefore, creates a conflict between our instincts, emotions, and rational faculty, which we then attempt to resolve using an inner guiding compass referred to as 'Moral Intuition' by Haidt (2013). McGilchrist (2019) writes that moral "values are linked to the capacity for empathy, not reasoning; and moral judgments are not deliberative, but unconscious and intuitive" (p. 135). It is often backed by our tribal instinct (Greene, 2014), but not always necessarily, as some individuals can go against the unjust social customs or norms despite huge risks (Neumann, 2015; Peterson, 2002).

For example, if my family member commits an injustice against a stranger, my conscience needs to support the stranger, even when doing so is economically or emotionally damaging for me. In organizational settings, a nepotistic attitude or bias toward one's family members may have an emotional cause; however, one may avoid it to ensure justice in a context where people outside of the family, particularly strangers, are also involved. This typically happens in a context where engagement between a group of people, including the family members, is more of a rational nature, regulated by a structure of rules, like in a large family-owned firm (Kubíček & Machek, 2020). Here, a person in charge may favor his or her family members when there is a conflict between them and the rest (Barnett & Kellermanns, 2006; Brewer, 1999). In state institutions, nepotism and cronyism are seen as problematic for the same reason, as state institutions are not meant to favor a particular ethnic group, for example (Fukuyama, 2011). The same can happen within the context of the family, a parent may be more emotionally attached to one of their children; however, doing justice among all would require the parent to treat them without discrimination (Hashim et al., 2017; Kowal et al., 2004). On the flip side, too much insistence on equal treatment may also create harm when the needs of each child are different due to some sickness or natural incapability (Jeannin & Van Leeuwen, 2015; Padilla et al., 2019). Like a child hitting puberty, it cannot be treated like an infant. The same may apply to a group of people working together; they may form certain rules to regulate their engagement, but strict adherence to the rules may sometimes leave behind a struggling member (Edmondson, 2004). An entrepreneur I interviewed suggested that when he finds one of his authorized retailers with a good record struggling to pay back, he offers them more supplies on credit to help them recover from the financial challenge, instead of charging a penalty as per agreed-upon rules that may include the use of legal force to recover the dues. This altruistic exception to the rules also has a good rational reason, that is, it improves the possibility of recovery of old debts as well. Likewise, at the time of inheritance distribution as per a pre-agreed criterion, a rational activity, financially stable siblings may sacrifice their share and give it to a sibling in financial trouble, although doing so may not be appreciated by their spouse or children.

The preceding discussion implies that our moral intuition, our conscience, is not always at odds but can also be endorsed by our emotional or rational judgments. A rational understanding of a moral principle, however, doesn't imply that we also arrive at it rationally. In fact, in high-pressure, emotionally charged emergencies, one may not be capable of rational analysis at all, and in the absence of our intuitive voice, our rational brains may get overloaded with cognitive dissonance. The intuitive voice of conscience may thus provide a third option when the emotional and the rational are in a state of conflict. From acts of compassion toward a particular person, or a group of people not associated with you, to following standards of justice within groups to avoid discriminating or unfair treatment, or commitment to truthfulness, or integrity, as and when needed, therefore, require a conscience operating independently of our instinctual, emotional needs and the rational criteria. One must be truthful and respectful, or compassionate when needed, for the sake of being truthful and respectful, not because there are some emotional or rational outcomes, which may also eventually follow, of course. Our conscience may, therefore, guide us to delicately navigate between the needs of the individual, or the collective (micro, meso, macro) as and when needed. However, if following the voice of the conscience can invite resistance from others, then one has to proceed with caution, finding the right moment to express or act, to avoid possible resistance from those who may be adversely affected, like the members of your family or tribe. The conscience, therefore, also often needs a criterion to justify its choices to others around, a facility often provided by cultural values, religion in particular, due to its transcendental significance. Nevertheless, the intuitive voice of the conscience is to be followed tactfully, particularly when it is at odds with the requirements of our emotional bonds or rational commitments.

4.2 The Moral and the Rational

Honoring commitments and truthfulness, for example, can be socially challenging, emotionally difficult, and economically damaging, sometimes, to an individual or a group of individuals, like partners in a family firm, at least in the short run. For example, a struggling business may need to sell its fixed assets to pay back suppliers or creditors. In my doctoral research, I came across an example of an individual who even sold his house to pay back, despite his family had nowhere to go. Often socioemotional and economic cost that comes with the commitment to a standard of morality opens the possibility of deceitfulness; however, one's conscience may opt for the moral standard even at a personal loss. The rational understanding—that honoring one's commitment or being honest would preserve one's goodwill in the long run—may not always be powerful enough to counter the survival instinct that may be triggered due to the anticipation of immediate loss (Kahneman & Tversky, 2012) that may be incurred as a result of upholding the moral principle. The emotion of guilt generated by the conscience, therefore, comes in handy to back up the rational understanding (Damasio, 2009; Tangney & Dearing, 2002). Things are not so ideal all the time, as we see frequent examples where individuals with weaker consciences, may opt for dishonesty and preserve their self-interest in the short term (Gneezy et al., 2013; Mazar et al., 2008; Wang et al., 2021). However, if they are eventually exposed, it may cost them everything gained via deceitfulness (Ellemers et al., 2013; Javaid et al., 2019). Such individuals, either driven by pure self-interest or concern only for their family or dependents (Ariely, 2013), may cause disturbance in the lives of victims, which eventually would create ripple effects, as people who get hurt often unintentionally hurt others as well (Gino et al., 2009). The part of society that is affected because of dishonest behavior is unlikely to be in balance anymore. If dishonest, unethical, or exploitative behavior is coming from the elite of a society, who even have the means to get away or manipulate the law for their advantage, the society is unlikely to sustain itself (Ferguson, 2014; Fukuyama, 2014; Putnam, 2020).

Certain personalities, unfortunately, are prone to deceitful, manipulative, and exploitative behavior, for which they also yearn to be in a position of power. Psychopaths, sociopaths, or those with narcissistic personalities, whose brain regions responsible for empathy and compassion remain undeveloped or damaged (Hambrick et al., 2019; McGilchrist, 2019), may end up doing quite a lot of harm, more so if society has been organized in a way that it gets easier for them to get to the position of power. Unfortunately, capitalism is said to have created such a society. In capitalism, it is argued by some that a range of institutions have emerged where it is not just easier for such individuals to get in power, rather such individuals are often required by these institutions (Brooks & Fritzon, 2016; Fuchs & Lingnau, 2024). These include corporations, financial firms on Wall Street, or the stock market, where individuals are required to act as rationally as possible (Babiak & Hare, 2006; Croom, 2021). There are frequent examples where corporations have resorted to manipulation, exploitation, and single-minded pursuit of quantitative (financial) results irrespective of the effects on the lives of the general population or the natural environment (Bakan, 2020; Béchervaise & Benjamin, 2013; Hickel, 2020; Marcuse, 2013; Zimbardo, 2007). In this realm of capitalism, therefore, morality appears to exist as a marketing tool for many in the corporate world (Béchervaise & Benjamin, 2013; Metcalf et al., 2019). So, those market institutions, which are structurally designed to prioritize profits, often get inclined to use the idea of morality as a resource in the process of capital accumulation, even defining it in the context of the ultimate aim of accumulation. The idea of morality is thus often instrumentalized for cosmetic appeal, a marketing tactic, where numerous corporate entities twist and distort it for the sake of rational goals (Adewale, 2017; Albert Bandura, 2002; Dari-Mattiacci & Fabbri, 2023; Jackall, 1983). So, the process of deterritorialization and reterritorialization (Deleuze et al., 2013), it may be argued, also prevails in the domain of morality, complemented by the phenomenon of 'repressive desublimation' as described by Marcuse (2013).

Modern market institutions, corporations in particular, have also been referred to as having psychopathic traits (Babiak & Hare, 2006; Bakan, 2019; Stibbe, 2013). Bakan (2019, 2020) has extensively documented numerous examples of corporate entities caught in various forms of criminal activity. The law does come into action sometimes, explains Bakan, penalizing corporate criminals with huge fines for their crimes. The penalty is often seen as a cost of doing business in the corporate world. However, the law often does not catch up to regulate (Brownsword & Somsen, 2009; Marchant, 2011) many of the potentially harmful substances or activities. From sugar (DiNicolantonio et al., 2018) to social media (Haidt, 2023) to fossil fuels (Klein, 2015) to plastics (Williams et al., 2019) to military-industrial complex (Loewenstein, 2023), and now the emerging use of artificial intelligence (Crawford, 2021), are just a few examples. The damage to the biosphere and the rest of the living world is also unprecedented (Hickel, 2020; Klein, 2015). It also takes the law too long to respond. In the case of cigarettes, despite persistent efforts by the concerned scientific community and doctors, the product is not banned, even when it kills around 8 million people, including around 1.3 million non-smokers who were unlucky to be around someone smoking for long enough (WHO, 2023). When the law catches up, it may sometimes allow the sale of a harmful product like cigarettes, despite it being known that the product is harmful. A rational measure of putting extra taxes is applied often to disincentivize demands or make it mandatory for the company to inform the customer about the harmfulness of the product, letting the customer decide, who if addicted to the product, still knowingly choose the product.

The PR firms, instead, are reportedly hired by many corporations to make sure that the corporate image is maintained in the eyes of the general public (Bakan, 2020). Even scientists are sometimes funded by some corporations to produce fabricated research, which is then used by PR agencies to claim that a certain product is safe for the people and(or) environment. This phenomenon of producing fake science is so widespread that it is formally studied under the academic domain of agnotology (Galison & Proctor, 2020; Kourany & Carrier, 2020; Proctor & Schiebinger, 2008). This is a glimpse into a reign where the rational is devoid of the moral, where the rational or the economic rather holds too much power. Historians and political analysts have noted that in a society where morals are used to appear good and feel good, then actually doing good, and the law is seen as a cost of doing business by the rich, the society is on its path to collapse. Such a society cannot be deemed sustainable by any meaning of the word (Diamond, 2013; Fukuyama, 2014; Polanyi, 2001; Sachs, 2010; Tainter, 1988).

It can be, therefore, argued that in the world of global capitalism, the primary cause of such unsustainability is recognized to be too much economic and political power held by market institutions, where law and morals are seen as exploitable resources or an obstacle to manage in pursuit of capital accumulation. The economic institutions of the modern world, where economic aims are prime, are essentially referred to as amoral (Bakan, 2019; Friedman, 2007). A key reason for its amorality is the very rational nature of institutional structures that operate more like a machine, which cannot possess a conscience. Friedman (2020) would suggest that humans who work in market institutions rather have a conscience, but the institutions themselves do not; they are mere structures of rules. However, what Friedman does not mention is that the humans within modern institutions can typically survive only if they submit to the aims of the institutions and keep their moral sense at bay (Adewale, 2017; Dari-Mattiacci & Fabbri, 2023). Human-to-human interaction becomes moral when two individuals interact in ways where their capacity to exercise moral judgment is available to them (Javaid, 2024), which often gets constrained or even diminished when the two individuals interact as agents of the institutional structure (Jackall, 1983; Kakavelakis & Edwards, 2022). Institutions set the rules and responsibilities that the employees are supposed to perform in exchange for a paycheck. Most employees aim to perform their job, without asking many questions, in exchange for a salary, as they are expected to behave like a homo-economicus (Bandura, 2002).

So, the more human-to-human interaction happens through the roles assigned to them by their employers in a society, the more amoral a society can potentially become (Podvoyskiy, 2022; Fevre, 2000; Ritzer, 2016; Weber & Tribe, 2019). Bowles (2016) and Sandel (2012) also suggest that moral action loses its spirit in an environment where everything is bought and sold. So, even morality can become McDonaldized when subjected to the market logic, that is, when people are encouraged to do good in exchange for an incentive. Moral, therefore, may only maintain its essence when it is pursued for its own sake, not for some emotional or rational ends. The modern market environment, or the environment created by modern market institutions, or the environment of modern market society, therefore, is typically devoid of morality; the environment can be referred to as amoral, precisely because it is predominantly rational. The degree of a society being moral would, therefore, be inversely proportional to the degree of institutionalization and McDonaldization. The social, which is also fundamentally dependent on the moral would logically suffocate in such a society, raising a question about its social sustainability as well. The social and economic relationships can be considered as moral when individuals can use their conscience or moral sense at will, where they act as free agents, and not as agents of an institutional entity. Therefore, it can be suggested that the possibility of turning social and economic activity into a means for a moral end can likely happen in contexts where individuals can freely exercise their moral agency.

4.3 Moral Agents and Homo-economicus

Individuals may exercise their moral agency in a society that would not constrain their moral agency, implying that the reign of rational institutions would be within healthy limits, while the culture and social imaginary would also value individuals operating at will. That would also imply that individuals have been raised to operate not based on their self-interest alone, but on their moral intuition, while also keeping in view the well-being of the larger community or society they are a part of (Gintis, 2000; Hallaq, 2013; Javaid, 2024). Is it possible to create such a society, or have such societies even existed in human history? If so, then it would be intriguing to explore what it would take to raise individuals to become moral agents rather than be driven by their self-interest or the interest of their immediate social group. After the seventeenth century, the transformation of European society, however, took the opposite route, gradually turning individuals to act more in their self-interest. The invention of modern institutional design, bureaucratic that is, that attempted to constrain human agency, also implies a decline in communal spirit, cohesion, and trust (Fukuyama, 2011; Weber & Tribe, 2019). The shift in individual behavior created an atmosphere that Herbert Spencer described as 'Social Darwinism' (Spencer, 2017), where only the fittest would survive.[1] Thomas Hobbes had already preceded Spencer's idea:

> ... like man, we find three principal causes of quarrel. First, competition; secondly, diffidence; thirdly, glory. The first maketh men invade for gain; the second, for safety; and the third, for reputation. The first use violence, to make themselves masters of other men's persons, wives, children, and cattle; the second, to defend them; the third, for trifles, as a word, a smile, a different opinion, and any other sign of undervalue, either direct in their persons or by reflection in their kindred, their friends, their nation, their profession, or their name. (Hobbes & Missner, 2016, p. 82)

The indigenous population in the Americas, after having a nightmarish experience with such a European man, concluded that they had a sickness in their minds, they are only concerned about their self-interest, and are willing to destroy others for their benefit. This sickness was referred to as 'Wetiko' disease by the indigenous community in the American region (Forbes, 2008). Today, we call such individuals sociopathic or psychopathic. How such an individual was produced in European society is a question for anthropological investigation. A glance may attribute the cause to a variety of factors such as plagues (Cantor, 2015), famines and wars (Armstrong, 2014; O'Boyle, 2014), and the declining significance of religion and subsequent undermining of the very foundation of moral conduct toward others (Horkheimer et al., 2002). Further, the rise of scientific worldview as inspired by Cartesian dualism (Dika, 2020; Goldsmith et al., 1995), ideological shift toward materialism (Hickel, 2020), rise of capitalist values inspired by Protestant (Weber & Kalberg, 2013), Puritans and Calvinists beliefs (Munro, 2010), and subsequent spread of ideas like Social Darwinism that inspired the individualistic ethos (Hofstadter, 2017), can be cited as potential explanations. The idea of original sin within the Christian worldview (Augustine & Chadwick, 2008) may also have its influence. The enclosure

[1] Charles Darwin, however, originally suggested the survival of the most adaptable (Bowler, 2009).

movement, also leading to wars (Hickel, 2020; Polanyi, 2001), likely shaped how a typical peasant would view the aristocratic or capitalist class, who was directly responsible for destroying their traditional way of life, in Europe and the Colonies. Many wars were also fought over control of land in the same context. In this chaotic environment, intellectuals like Hobbes, Bacon, and later Spenser declared that human nature was greed-driven, selfish, and revenge-seeking, thus establishing the need for methods that could manipulate and control individuals for the aims sought by the capitalist elite of the society.

The presence of such individuals in noticeable quantity along with the continuous wars were two key contributing factors that led to the creation of rational institutions, also known as the bureaucratic system, that would constrain and exploit the agency of the (sic) selfish individuals (Abdelnour et al., 2017; Curtis, 2007; Weber & Tribe, 2019). The rational institutional design would manipulate individuals toward specific goals, isolating them into separate departments and sub-departments, so they remain divided, are easier to manipulate and control, and are less likely to gang up against the top management (Foucault, 2012; Fukuyama, 2011; Mcdonald, 2017; Weber & Tribe, 2019). The presence of such a system, its procedures, its structure of processes, rules, and policies, presumes that the individuals who will be employed operate like homo-economicus. They will be selfish, therefore, untrustworthy; thus must be constrained for the aims of the institutional structure, through a system of performance measurement tied with quantitative rewards and punishment, in exchange for the job performed within a very narrow compartment inside the institution.

The creation of bureaucratic machinery also sparked the need for human resource that would work in institutions of a public or private nature employing the bureaucratic system (Fukuyama, 2011). The destruction of the commons also created a supply of labor, but they were not conditioned to work within bureaucratic institutions. The British education system was thus created for the peasants, not just in Europe, but also for the disgruntled population of the colonies, so that the next generation would be tamed and conditioned to get employed in industry and state institutions (Mitra, 2015). The education system in Europe and its colonies also attempted to disconnect students from their past so that the students would not see their inclinations and orientations in the context of their history, but as a part of their nature (Freire, 2000). For example, it can be inferred from the work of concerned experts that the resentment that the student felt—a feeling that was inherited from their parents or grandparents, whose livelihood was destroyed by the people in power, either in Europe or in colonies—lost its context. When such students got disconnected from their history, the feeling was projected by the system on fellow students who were defined as adversaries in a race for grades (Bourdieu & Passeron, 1990; Giddens, 2013).

The education system would attempt to put every student in a competitive race against the rest, systemically inculcating an individualistic spirit and a sense of obedience to a seemingly meaningless set of instructions, while filtering out those who resist such transformation. The subsequent pedagogy treated every student under the Hobbesian assumptions about human nature, eventually producing individuals in the same image (Orr, 2004). A deliberate application of what Giddens (2013) later referred to as Double Hermeneutics, more commonly known as self-fulfilling prophecy, a phenomenon that happens subtly in modern institutions, happens directly within schools while producing the human resources for modern institutions. That is, the view of a man that emerged during the development of the capitalist machine in Europe, eventually, reproduced the same kind of man directly or indirectly, that is, selfish, competitive, but obedient if tamed using carrot and stick, and yet untrustworthy to be left unsupervised unless proven otherwise (Apple, 2004; Bowles & Gintis, 2011).

The colonies where these institutions did not grow through a historical process but rather were forcefully imposed, like in the Indian subcontinent, also produced the same kind of individuality among the population they engaged (Chande, 2023). The culture in the southern and eastern parts of the world typically had a collectivist and religious orientation before colonization, where people saw each other as generally trustworthy unless proven otherwise (Fuchs & Lingnau, 2024; Maffi, 2018; Yi, 2004). The onslaught of colonial institutions did not completely disintegrate the collectivist culture or their religious orientation, which rather prevailed and continues even today in many parts of the world (Gilmartin, 2014; Lieven, 2012). These regions are not free from social ills; however, they may not be exactly like the ones that created the rationale for modern rational institutions, like in Europe. However, the contemporary onslaught of globalization is blurring the lines and often creating new forms of challenges in the global south, which include inequality, social disintegration, and class division (Norberg, 2016; Sachs, 2010). Still, a significant number of the population in such regions consider religion to hold the final verdict on morality and human nature, despite often personally falling short in conduct (Turner, 2011).

Religions other than Christianity also offer their unique concept of human nature. Islam, for example, which was the official religion in a lot of colonies, does not consider humans to be immoral or selfish by default, but to have the potential to act both morally and immorally (al-Ghazzali et al., 2015). Further, Islamic discourse recommends ways to nurture and train people to become moral and thus trustworthy. It is interesting to note that nowhere in the Muslim world do we see the rise of complex bureaucracies to constrain human agency like they did in Europe (Hallaq, 2013). However, the Ottoman military, to some extent, copied the institutional format of the Church by not allowing its officers to get married to prevent nepotism, but it is perhaps a far cry to call it a modern bureaucracy (Fukuyama, 2011). The Muslim society in general kept the human agency intact and was generally administered by those who demonstrated their strength of character (Hallaq, 2013). Islam's view of human nature provided a distinct basis for the Muslim world to organize complex societies, once after the spread of Islam from Arabia, and then again for the Ottoman (Mikhail, 2021) and Mughal Empires (Alam, 2021; Dale, 2009). Safavids in Iran (Dale, 2009), and cultures in the Far East, including Indonesia and Malaysia regions, also thrived with the same view of human nature and world view for hundreds of years (Weintraub, 2011). Things were not perfect, nor they are today; however, despite the damage done during colonization, the subsequent establishment of a modern state, and the economies turning capitalist, the social fabric of the Muslim world still takes inspiration from the same set of beliefs, and remains socially cohesive to a significant extent (Javaid, 2024; Pew, 2012). Forces of globalization, an inflow of technology, and consumer culture, however, could be creating a social shift unprecedented in Muslim history (Raquib et al., 2020). Hinduism, another dominant religious system, also does not consider humans to be sinners by default, but in the context of their belief about reincarnation, the nature of the person or their fate depends on how the previous life was led (Frazier, 2017). Likewise, many indigenous cultures consider humans to be more cooperative by default than competitive (Dunbar-Ortiz, 2023; Forbes, 2008; Graeber & Wengrow, 2023). More examples can be cited here. However, the intent of this very rough and often overgeneralizing sketch above is to point toward the fact that the European view of a human as a brutish, competitive, self-centered, untrustworthy by default, which is even declared as morally superior in the modern economic paradigm, is a product of unique European history. A significant majority globally do not share such a view. Also, many cultures have thrived and have sustained themselves socially and economically for much longer, while balancing the social and economic, even maintaining harmony with the biosphere, with a more optimistic view of human nature (Graeber & Wengrow, 2023; Norberg, 2016; Pullanikkatil & Hughes, 2023).

In the context of the non-Western historical experience, it is critical to acknowledge that we have an innate capacity to do well, and our conscience is a natural part of our existence. It has also been scientifically documented that as infants, we have an innate capacity for making moral judgments that is deeply embedded in our biology, implying that our moral instinct is not merely a social construct (Bloom, 2011; Hamlin et al., 2007). Having said so, it must also be acknowledged that we do indeed have a dark side, or the potential to act in ways that are immoral, harmful, and evil. We often demonstrate a set of behaviors identified as terrible father and terrible mother, the examples of which are found throughout ancient history, not just in European culture (Campbell et al., 1991; Neumann, 2015; Peterson, 2002). That is why perhaps complex societies eventually had to invent a legal system and define a penal code, violation of which would invite action from law enforcers. Fukuyama (2011) has argued that for a society to sustain, everyone from the very bottom to the very top must be answerable to the same set of laws. This idea, Fukuyama identifies, was first introduced and practiced by Hinduism many millennia ago. He further asserts that if the elite consider themselves above the law, even use the law to manipulate the public, society unsurprisingly falls into chaos. The question eventually emerges: how to ensure that the elite or any person abides by the law, let alone acts morally, when they can escape easily, either because of the incapacity of the law enforcer or because of the power one holds against the law-enforcing apparatus.

The ancient cultures, belief systems, and religions, therefore, would put ample emphasis on nurturing the moral agency that would remain active even in the absence of any external incentive or cost. The ancient mythologies had the concept of a hero, who would act righteously despite temptations to act otherwise. The hero would even sacrifice and fight against the intrinsic forces of human nature that may rather push the hero toward adhering to the unjust tyranny of the cultural norms. A hero, in short, would confront the terrible father (Campbell et al., 1991; Neumann, 2015; Peterson, 2002). Ancient belief systems, like Buddhism, Abrahamic religions, or Hinduism, explain elaborate 'mystical' ways where one would recognize and tame the tempting forces, rather than utilize them for the greater good (Krüger, 2018). In contrast, the mystical is seen as comical in the material world of capitalism (Horkheimer et al., 2002), which rather engages our temptation, one after the other, and creates a world that does not understand the idea of balance (Han & Butler, 2017; Harvey, 2005). The dominance of the rational and undermining of the emotional has rather paved the way for the base temptations to be the driving force, a phenomenon that is referred to as Enantiodromia by psychologist Carl Jung (Jung, 2016). Therefore, it can be argued that the unbalance within the psyche of the modern man, with no moral compass to calibrate, has created a world prone to imbalance, both socially and environmentally.

4.4 The Moral and the Emotional

The concept of enantiodromia refers to the tendency for one extreme to provoke a counter-reaction that shifts an individual or society to the opposite extreme (Jung, 2016). Similarly, nature has a way of restoring homeostasis, an equilibrium state, through a counter-movement in the opposite direction, like a pendulum swinging back after reaching one extreme. Over time, with each oscillation, the amplitude diminishes, potentially stabilizing at an equilibrium state (Lembke, 2021). However, conscious efforts can reduce both the number and amplitude of these swings. In a societal context, ancient mythologies also suggest that excessive tyranny can eventually lead to conditions ripe for anarchy or chaos, as described in Chapter 2. Chapter 2 also discussed examples from European history suggesting that tyranny in various forms—religious, political, and more recently, institutional—eventually created a counter-reaction every time, the most recent of which is broadly referred to as post-modernism (Foucault & Rabinow, 2020). The post-modernists critically saw modern society for its tendency to impose rigid standards on its citizens, compelling them to be rational, objective, and productive members of society (Bauman, 2013a, 2013b). Educational institutions that emerged in the modern world, and subsequent employment environments in public or private institutions, perpetuated this conditioning, straightjacketing individuals at the expense of their authenticity (Foucault, 2012; Weber & Tribe, 2019). This excessive focus on external standards triggered a counter-reaction that prioritizes being authentic (whatever that means to an individual) over becoming what the 'biopolitical' modern world demands, paving the way for 'psychopolitical' (Han & Butler, 2017). This reaction rejects established standards of morality, religious, traditional, cultural, or historical norms, and any prescriptive notions of what one ought to become. It replaces objectivity with subjectivity, external focus with internal focus, rationality with emotion, and becoming with being. In this context, morality is often framed in terms of feelings or desires, where the moral action is what makes a person feel good. Concerned scholars refer to this as Emotivism. Macintyre (2013) suggests:

> Emotivism is the doctrine that all evaluative judgments and more specifically all moral judgments are nothing but expressions of preference, expressions of attitude or feeling (pp. 11–12)

Trueman (2020) traces back the origin of Emotivism to Rousseau, who established the idea that our inner sentiments are the source of moral judgments. Many subsequent thinkers gradually pushed the idea a little further, Nietzsche being the most notable one. Post-modernism took it further and turned it into a mass movement in recent decades, eventually making it a worldwide phenomenon. The idea that 'my way or the highway' is now becoming a common ethos of the day, often fervently advocated by the entertainment industry. In a society adhering to emotivism, each individual, whom we may call a homo-emoticus, driven by their emotions and using them to guide their conscience, may potentially turn a social group into a crowd of people often going in different directions, and finding others obstructing their way. In such a society, how would an agreement on right and wrong be reached? It would perhaps be a matter of chance, as emotions and feelings are not constants, so the idea of right and wrong would also not be constant; they would be in a continuous state of flux, and agreements that happen would be temporary. Agree to disagree could become the order of the day. How would two individuals in a state of conflict find a mutual ground in such a society? The lack of order, the anarchic nature of it, and too much chaos may ensue (Bauman, 2013a).

Emotions are described as essentially the energy to achieve something on a social level; they make us bond with others or can cause conflict as well (as discussed in Chapter 3). They become meaningless when not shared (Barrett, 2020). Being emotional for the sake of it would go against the very purpose the emotional energy is meant to serve. The discourse in positive psychology suggests that an aim is necessary for our emotions, which comes from a sense of a purpose, that gives a direction toward which the emotional energy can be channelized, a purpose that is beyond the self, preferentially benefiting others around as well (Doris & Group, 2010; Seligman, 2017). Moral, therefore, needs to guide the emotional, as the act of becoming has a positive intent, that something is being improved from what is. The act of becoming is moral, in its essence. Being and becoming thus are two sides of the same equation. Our state of being is also the starting point, so genuine becoming may stem from being. A new reality of the self is created only after accepting the present reality as suggested by Rogers (2013), earlier by Jung (1993), and even earlier by Heidegger (1962). The act of becoming that is beneficial may emerge from the state of being. Two or more individuals may also facilitate each other in the process of becoming while offering a genuinely accepting (motherly) space to each other (Hayes et al., 2003). Becoming, when grounded in our state of being, aiming at improvements for the self and others, therefore, can be considered a moral act.

However, if the idea of becoming is externally imposed, which does not acknowledge our state of being, it creates a disconnect, as it is often said to have happened in the project of modernism. It has been argued that a questionable understanding of human nature in the modernist worldview (Cartesian Dualism), inspired a set of aims in the modernism project, that undermined our state of being (emotional, intuitive), eventually creating a split that imposed a set of standards (individualistic, materialistic, economic) that suffocated our core nature (Jung et al., 2013). Traditional cultures and religions (not when demagogues are using them to manipulate people) often attempt to avoid this disconnect. They have aimed to structure a society where the instinctual, emotional, and rational forces harmoniously interplay with each other (Campbell et al., 1991; Jung et al., 2013; Peterson, 2002). Traditional cultures typically define individual identity in the context of their historicity, which gives them a perspective to understand their state of being. Understanding history and how it shaped the collective would also provide a direction to orient their becoming with time. Their understanding of the history and future is often not individualistic, but rather seen as a collective project, as in their worldview individuals do not exist in isolation from others, but are related to those with whom they are born and raised, including members of the extended family and community (Diamond, 2012; Graeber & Wengrow, 2023). So, their project of becoming eventually is expected to be aligned with the historical trajectory that gave birth to the state of being in traditional cultures and communities.[2] The rejection of the historical, traditional, or the sacred, in the paradigm of emotivism, is, therefore, also a denial of becoming. However, keeping in view the denial of the state of being in the collective path set by modernism, the emotivism's urge to 'be' has rejected any possibility of becoming that is often collectively and historically constructed.

There appears to be a possibility that the homo-emoticus, in their insistence on being emotive and constantly in flux, may find it difficult to sustain long-term relationships due to their hyper-individualistic pursuits. However, a healthy human society is fundamentally interdependent. In our formative years, we are dependent on our mothers, then our fathers, and subsequently on the extended family, growing up in an interdependent environment. Gradually, during adolescence, we achieve some degree of independence. Adolescence is typically a period - free of significant responsibility - in a healthy family, where the individual is not yet mature enough to have a family of their own but is old enough not to be dependent on elders. This stage, assuming the family is financially stable, represents a period of maximal freedom for the individual (Erikson, 1994). Adolescence is then followed by an age of responsibility, as individuals enter into a state of interdependence once again, this time having children as dependents. A young man, before becoming a father, often views his father negatively due to the latter's restrictive, albeit healthy, role. Consequently, adolescence can be seen as an age of being, if allowed by the circumstances. Neumann (2015) suggests the possibility of getting stuck in a specific developmental stage. If the environment imposes harsh and unrealistic expectations during growth, individuals may reject the idea of becoming in harmony with family or community. Neumann argues that this phenomenon can affect entire segments or societies, which may cling excessively to the past to justify maintaining the status quo, thereby acting tyrannically against efforts to improve circumstances. Some members of such social groups may reject

[2] This historical experience of ancestors is also genetically passed on to the next generations, so without understanding ancestral experiences, it is difficult to make sense of our natural dispositions. (Wailoo et al., 2012).

the concept of fatherhood entirely, even in its healthier form. This state is referred to as Peter Pan Syndrome in psychology, where individuals refuse to accept responsibility and remain stuck in an adolescent state even as they age (Kalkan et al., 2019). The homo-emoticus may be similarly stuck, reacting against the rationalistic tyranny of modernism by aggressively rejecting any social construct and considering their instincts or emotions as the sole criteria for defining their axiological or teleological positions (MacIntyre, 2013).

The rejection of emotional expression, along with the rejection of religion and culture that traditionally provided a teleological medium for emotional energy, has created a shadow in the psyche of the modern individual, according to Jungian psychology. Jung defined the shadow as a part of one's nature that one has learned to reject through social experiences, typically during the upbringing phase, often feeling disgust and hatred toward it (Jung, 2014). For example, the Peter Pan syndrome leads one to reject their fatherly nature. The rejected side is then projected externally, and any stimuli that remind one of the shadow's contents trigger the same emotions felt against those personal shadow contents (Neumann, 2015). It is possible to walk toward shadow integration, which depends on one's teleological position. If the goal, however, is to continue in the Peter Pan mode, shadow integration is unlikely. Instead, Peter Pan would see shadow projection and subsequent reactions to any stimuli as morally justified. The cancel culture that has spread in recent years may point toward a similar dynamic. Individuals prone to canceling, because something offends them, may be driven by their shadow contents. Such individuals may not see reality objectively, so their subjective becomes their objective (Twenge & Campbell, 2010). This does not mean that canceling is inherently unhealthy; there can be valid reasons to cancel something harmful. However, if canceling is based purely on subjective criteria and excludes any objective measure or transcendental concept of morality, it has the potential to cause injustice (Lukianoff & Haidt, 2019). Shadow content, if not integrated, may distort one's view of reality, causing one to see certain incidents as threatening even if they are not. If one does not understand the source of their view of reality and how their psyche may be distorting it, their response can potentially lead to injustice (Haidt, 2013). Recognizing the difference between the objective and the subjective is, therefore, critical. The doctrine of emotivism, however, overrides the objective with the subjective. What is perhaps needed is the recognition of the subjective from the objective and ensuring their co-existence without rejecting either, while keeping their difference in mind as well (McGilchrist, 2019). Without such recognition, the balance between the objective and the subjective is not possible, and the rational would not be balanced with the emotional, nor being would be balanced with becoming. Often to bring balance between the two, the presence of a moral standard, which may come with a teleological premise that transcends the realm of both emotional and rational, objective and the subjective, that gives meaning to our state of being and a corresponding aim for becoming, therefore, becomes necessary (MacIntyre, 2013; Taylor, 1992).

4.5 The Question of Balance

The possibility of conflict between the rational and the emotional, being and becoming, would perhaps require nurturing a moral agency within individuals that would operate independently of rational and emotional considerations. This would happen when individuals are also aware of the influence of their base temptations, socioemotional activity, and rational faculty, on moral judgments. More specifically, each individual ideally needs to have sufficient inner understanding and self-awareness, to notice the influence of instincts and emotions, and differentiate it with moral intuition (Joshua Greene & Haidt, 2002), and have sufficient agency, unconstrained by external cultural or institutional obstacles, to follow the voice of their conscience whenever needed. Many of the ancient belief systems prescribed the path of mysticism to nurture such a level of self-awareness and capacity, where becoming aware of temptations, emotions, or rational brain activity can help to identify moral intuition distinctly from the rest (Underhill, 2017). However, that would often require cutting from society for long periods, often turning into a monk, for example. If most people follow this path and resort to some monasteries, the human world may not be sustained like that either. Human needs such as procreation, shelter, protection, to be seen and loved, and exchanging stuff in the market as per needs, would require a healthy social and economic life. The real challenge is to remain moral in the storm of temptations, amidst emotional and rational engagements with other humans in a complex society. Monasticism in this context is perhaps anti-life; however, to some extent humans need a space to reflect on what is going on in their inner worlds of emotions and temptations, which is now also extensively recommended as a prerequisite of psychological health by many psychologists (Hayes et al., 2003; Jung, 2006).

Although humans can nurture each other's moral faculty through the process of upbringing, mentorship, and self-reflection, protocols of which are also often prescribed in many belief systems (Krüger, 2018; Underhill, 2017). However, on the flip side, it is also entirely possible for humans to act in pure self-interest, often causing harm to others to protect oneself and one's immediate family (Gino et al., 2009; Mazar et al., 2008; Zimbardo, 2007). Acting in self-defense is not immoral, but while doing so, we can get overwhelmed by temptations or cause injustice by an overreaction. Therefore, on one side, a mechanism of self-regulation by increasing self-awareness and strengthening human conscience is indeed needed. On the other hand, another mechanism of external regulation is perhaps pertinent. Therefore, the idea of reward and punishment keeps the potential offenders from preferring the immoral, or scares them from going toward the wrongful, particularly during tempting times, when the survival instincts or lust can potentially hijack the moral agency. Moreover, many individuals are in the process of developing their conscience, or perhaps many may not get the chance, but it is necessary that they also do not get carried over by their temptations or survival instincts. For example, the religious idea that they will eventually be punished for any wrongdoing on the Day of Judgement may come in handy to create some resistance. Neurological studies also have shown that when driven by pure self-interest, the brain region responsible for empathy and compassion is often bypassed (Joshua Greene & Haidt, 2002; McGilchrist, 2019; Singer et al., 2004). A comprehensive framework to regulate, motivate, and nurture resistance to the immoral (Krüger, 2018) is, therefore, needed to address the entire range of our potentialities.

In this context, it also becomes necessary that any individual is not pushed by others to the point of desperation, where acting in self-interest, even at the risk of crossing the moral limits, becomes unavoidable. Injustice has the potential to breed more injustice, while kindness also breeds more kindness, hence the term social and moral capital, as when they are invested, they multiply (Bubolz, 2001; Putnam, 1993; Wang, 2015). Therefore, a morally healthy society must try its best to ensure that all individuals' physical and socioemotional needs are met with respect so that the point of desperation may not arrive. Every individual in a society must try to facilitate others to fulfill their needs to the extent of their capacity, which would require a healthy conscience. Today, this task of fulfilling the needs of every person around has been outsourced to the modern state, or the non-profit sector in the modern capitalist world, as most individuals are forced to spend almost all of their available time in the market, and much of their income on survival. They barely get any time to spend even with their children, spouse, or the elderly in their immediate family. Further, the capacity of the state in a market society or the civil society, including the non-profits, remains limited in terms of the number of individuals or the extent of their socioemotional needs they can address. Humans, particularly when vulnerable rather require a healthy organic social environment, the sustainability of which has been increasingly threatened in the individualistic world of neoliberal capitalism. As discussed earlier, this focus has also been constricted by a limited view of who we are (homo-economicus?), a view shaped by a unique historical experience in Europe.

4.5.1 Tyranny of the Church to the Tyranny of Liberalism

The European historical march toward enlightenment removed the external and internal regulatory mechanisms that were used to control human temptations. External controls were earlier imposed by the Church and were embedded in a culture shaped under religious influence (Kee, 1998). The religious worldview, particularly the concept of accountability on the Day of Judgement, also served as an internal regulatory mechanism for individuals to keep their temptations in check (McNeill, 1951). However, these controls reportedly became overly oppressive and exploitative (Cohn, 2000), which motivated the emerging enlightenment movement to advocate for a set of ideas that were later described as liberalism. Liberalism rejected these external and internal controls, viewing them as limiting human potential. The rebellion against the church's exploitative influence did not originate with the (sic) enlightened or the liberal class, but rather with Martin Luther in the sixteenth century. Luther, a priest, openly opposed the Church's abuse of power in the name of religion. His actions resonated with many who shared his concerns about the Church's exploitation of power. Luther advocated for individuals to directly read the Bible and connect with the Divine without the Church as an intermediary, thus suggesting to limit the role of the Church in the life of a devoted individual. He also proposed that God would reward honest and hardworking individuals with worldly riches, which resonated with the aristocratic class in Europe (Lindberg, 2011). Weber's (2013) thesis in "The Protestant Ethic and the Spirit of Capitalism" suggests that Protestant ethics, particularly Calvinist principles, contributed to the development of capitalism by promoting values of hard work and frugality (Brouwer, 2002). Tawney (2016), another notable historian, has suggested a similar relationship between religious transformation in Europe and the rise of capitalism. The scientific view of the world, promoted by the Enlightenment project, eventually removed religion from its position of power, making the ideological environment ripe for an alternative telos and ethos (Horkheimer et al., 2002). For those who bought into the new telos and ethos, human reason was now the ultimate arbitrator of the truth, and material outcomes were no more a reward from God but an outcome of human effort and ingenuity. In short, the Church's constraining and exploitative influence on individual potential paved the way for the rise of individualism and capitalism, which has evolved into what we now refer to as neoliberalism (Harvey, 2005).

Nietzsche, for example, has been one of the fiercest proponents of individualism, who also referred to religion as an excuse to justify the herd mentality, where being moral was a means to remain part of the social group who were manipulated by the religious demagogues of the Dark Ages. The idea of morality was instrumentalized, in Nietzsche's view, for socioemotional and even political ends. Nietzsche's observation about the general tendency of the public to avoid taking a stand against the injustice perpetuated by those who held social and religious power in society contributed to his view against religion (Nietzsche, 2020). He eventually proclaimed the death of god, highlighting the erosion of religion's authority over the moral, which was rather used as a tool for mass manipulation by the authorities of the Church. Nietzsche argued for the concept of the Übermensch, or "overman", a so-called ideal chased by individuals who transcend societal constraints and forge their path based on personal values and convictions. Nietzsche's overman was supposed to follow their conception of morality, or at least some moral principle that transcends the need to be part of a collective for a sense of security or emotional attachment (Nietzsche, 2021). Later philosophers like Ayn Rand further advocated for selfishness by considering one's rational self-interest as the defining principle of morality (Rand & Branden, 2016). The segments of society that took inspiration from such ideals, however, lacked any sense of a grand narrative, a higher sense of purpose that would transcend one's self (Chande, 2023). The likely result is the creation of a hedonistic culture where the ultimate aim is to get a dopamine hit from the next act of consumption, a culture driven by base temptations, instead of a higher purpose (Courtwright, 2021; Lembke, 2021).

The developments in modern times initially ignored the moral capacity of the individual while also rejecting religious authority as it lost its credibility, therefore, losing the traditional regulatory apparatus. The modern individual was then encouraged to turn hedonistic, to be driven by base temptations, self-interest, and the chaos of emotivism. This individual, despite serving capitalism as a good consumer, presented a challenge for the capitalist state, whose aim has been to maintain discipline and order. This task was at first handed over to rational institutions, predominantly public at the beginning, but these were gradually superseded by private corporations, now increasingly digital and employing AI, similar to the social credit system in China. Neoliberalism, which spread throughout the world particularly during and after the Cold War, in the name of increasing individual freedom, ironically appears to be taking the path toward establishing a digital tyranny led by tech unicorns, while keeping the general public busy in an ever-speeding cycle of production and consumption (Han & Butler, 2017; Zuboff, 2019). This leaves little time for the individual for reflection or introspection. Neoliberalism fails to provide a transcendental sense of purpose for the individual or the collective, yet encourages the pursuit of self-interest in ways dictated by the corporate world. This cycle represents a new form of socioemotional manipulation for rational ends. The consequences are not difficult to imagine. Given such imbalances at archetypal levels, it is questionable whether it is possible to generate a socially and environmentally sustainable world in the world of neoliberalism.

From monasticism, to the tyrannical control exerted by religious authorities, and eventually to the advocacy of a completely free society devoid of any form of moral authority, to the creation of a digital tyranny, the Western experimentations when evaluated through the lens of socio-environmental sustainability do not lead to an appraisable picture. Throughout Western history, we can find examples where the unconscious forces of temptation, particularly the desire for power, have wreaked havoc by manipulating the sacred, moral, and socioemotional domains. This manipulation was evident first during the reign of the church and later during the dominance of the capitalist class. The logic of exchange, based on cause and effect, such as "do this and you will receive that" or "avoid this to prevent loss", has been a key characteristic of religious orders (Weber & Parsons, 1999) and has persisted into the secular era of capitalism. Moreover, the concept of repressive desublimation (Marcuse, 2013), where moral and socioemotional aspects are exploited as resources to gain and maintain power for rational goals, demonstrates a similar archetypal character during both the church's dominance and the capitalist reign. However, the latter has reduced the processes of exchange, reward, and punishment to a purely material and quantifiable realm (Podvoyskiy, 2022; Han & Butler, 2017; Klein & Smith, 2008).

4.6 Towards Balance

The material and quantifiable is the realm of the rational, where becoming happens, and where the aim is to adapt for survival and triumph in the objective material world. Exclusive focus on the objective undermines the subjective. The realm of the rational is the realm of the fatherly, which then triumphs over the motherly. The motherly rather dwells in the subjective realm, the socioemotional, where being is put before becoming. Exclusive focus on the becoming has also compromised the state of being. The vengeful mother, the post-modern goddess of chaos, is again in the grips of the terrible father, which now manifests as a digital tyranny, using the whip of psychopolitics to maintain control. To rescue humanity from chaos and tyranny, a hero is, therefore, needed, one who attempts to rebalance the overdominance of the rational or the emotional, while making the two exist for the sake of a transcendental goal, not for their own sake. The forces that form the emotional, the rational, and the moral dwell in our inner world, so to align the two under the guidance of the moral, one has to turn attention to the world that exists inside, while not losing the focus of the external.

An alternative societal model is needed that recognizes and nurtures people's natural inclination to do good, where individuals have enough time, guidance, and support to reflect on and develop their moral agency and capacity for self-regulation. The socioeconomic and political environment may also be regulated based on criteria that transcend personal or group biases, without excessive control or manipulation seen in modern market institutions that prioritize capital accumulation at the expense of human moral agency. However, critiquing the design philosophy of modern institutions requires an alternative perspective on human nature, which may necessitate moving away from a Eurocentric view of human history. What's needed is a more inclusive understanding of human history and who we are as humans, an alternative 'master narrative' in terms of Taylor (2018). The significance of having a master narrative to keep the society cohesive and resilient during crisis has been acknowledged by scholars from varying schools of thought (Habermas, 2015; Harari, 2015; Lyotard & Van den Abbeele, 1999; MacIntyre, 2013; Peterson, 2002; Ricoeur et al., 1990). Drawing from a master narrative, a unique approach to organizing and structuring society on socioeconomic and political levels is required to allow for the natural expression of human conscience in pursuit of moral and just aims to help ensure sustainability across all dimensions of human existence. World religions had been providing such a master narrative until their message was forgotten by those tempted by hunger for power, who subsequently used religion as a tool to manipulate and control the masses, a tendency that did not cease in the contemporary secular order. Many consider religion to be a thing of the past; however, even today, a significant number of the world's population still find solace in the worldview offered by religion, which helps them make sense of their existence, their life circumstances, and maintain peace among their communities.

4.6.1 *Nurturing Moral Sense*

Human beings, at the very start of our lives, lack moral agency as our primary instincts dominate. For example, as babies, we cannot effectively respond to our mothers who may be unable to take care of our needs during moments of exhaustion or sickness. We cannot exercise patience when mother takes some rest. It has been suggested that although the infants may show limited forms of empathy, complex moral reasoning develops much later (Bloom, 2011). It has been demonstrated that social evaluation by infants is limited and evolves significantly with age (Hamlin et al., 2007).

So, as we grow up, as we begin to interact with others, we eventually are struck with this dilemma between what we require and what others require. We realize that often prioritizing our self-interest over that of others can potentially hurt them, and vice versa. We may grow up in an environment where we see others prioritizing their self-interest. So, eventually, we may also copy their behavior. However, if others show us compassion and care without making us feel ashamed for it, we may also nurture our innate capacity to be moral and compassionate. Bruce D. Perry, the pioneer of the neuro-sequential model of brain development, suggests that the parts of our brain involved in empathy and compassion are developed when others act toward us with genuine empathy and compassion during our upbringing phase (Perry & Szalavitz, 2006). Empathy and compassion would produce more empathy and compassion, intergenerationally, hence the term moral capital. Likewise, if caretakers are either absent, or perhaps shame too much, or remain negligent due to their life stresses, the child may get the message that 'I am on my own, I need to take care of myself'. Unsurprisingly, this may likely happen more in poorer households (Evans et al., 2013; Maté & Maté, 2024). Thomas Harris also linked too much physical or emotional abuse by caretakers as a primary cause behind this belief that "I am okay but they are not", while everyone else is a threat to manage (Harris, 1969). Both Bruce D. Perry and Harris, in their separate works, explain the likelihood of a person turning into a sociopath if the early parenting environment leaves a child devoid of experiencing empathy and compassion.

Fromm (2017) also suggests that a very negative self-image that is likely shaped during early childhood, as a result of too much shaming, may lead to narcissistic personality disorder as compensation for the self-hate inculcated, for example, in a highly shaming and emotionally abusive environment. The development of psychopaths, sociopaths, or narcissists is not entirely because of early childhood experiences; however, it is believed that they likely contribute. A person who has been raised in unhealthy environments may change, as our brain and biology are not fixed; we do change often through self-realization or with the help of a caring company (Cozolino, 2014). Nevertheless, children must be given due care, through their development stages, so that the chances of turning them into an antisocial personality remain minimal. Children, therefore, who grow up experiencing that others are not a threat by default may be more capable of sacrificing their self-interest to ensure fairness and justice in their relationships when necessary (Laible & Thompson, 2007). Likewise, children who are raised with self-respect and a sense of worth would also not allow others to treat them unfairly as well (Baumeister et al., 2003).

However, there is more to it, as both bittersweet moments are part of life, tragedies can happen, and everyone can make mistakes, so a system of beliefs that helps give meaning to the painful moments in life that are experienced individually or collectively, eventually becomes a necessity. Nietzsche (1997) suggests that if we have a purpose to live, we can bear any life circumstances, no matter how painful they might be. Camus (2015), Frankl (1997), and Jung (2006) are among others who have also pointed out the significance of having meaning in life that helps us make sense of otherwise unbearable circumstances. Meaning is often derived from our beliefs about, for example, who we are, why the world exists, and what our role is in this world. A set of beliefs provides meaning and purpose to the life of believers, facilitates them to constructively channel emotional energy such as anger, frustration, fear, and hatred, tackle hopelessness, or counter the forces of temptations like greed, lust, or jealousy. This, as per Carl Jung, has been the primary aim of religion, that is, to provide a mechanism to contain or channel such psychic energies by providing them a context. A key aim is also to ensure justice and fairness for all stakeholders, particularly in circumstances when the emotional energy becomes too powerful for our rational minds to contain; a conceptual framework offered by religion, therefore, comes in handy. Jung notes:

> The individual who is not anchored in God can offer no resistance on his resources to the physical and moral blandishments of the world. For this he needs the evidence of inner, transcendent experience which alone can protect him from the otherwise inevitable submersion in the mass … [Religion's] evident purpose is to maintain the psychic balance, for the natural man has an equally natural "knowledge" of the fact that his conscious functions may at any time be thwarted by uncontrollable happenings coming from inside as well as from outside. (Jung, 2006, p. 15)

The family or the early upbringing environment eventually becomes the prime medium through which these beliefs or their absence are first experienced by a child, particularly when the child sees the adults go through and cope with difficult experiences beyond their control. The presence of a healthy social environment, therefore, becomes critical so that any healthy beliefs, values, norms, and understanding about who we are, are transmitted to the next generation (Jungert et al., 2015; Wiese & Freund, 2011). This understanding may also include the emotional challenges that particularly emerge from within (Maté & Maté, 2024). In a family environment where the relationship between children and adults remains strained, children do not take inspiration from adults, or learn much from them, let alone become self-aware (Laible & Thompson, 2007; Maté & Maté, 2024; Neece et al., 2012). Lack of such self-awareness increases the susceptibility of being driven by their temptations, insecurities, and lusts, which may often culminate in the form of lust for power (Finzi-Dottan & Karu, 2006; Perry & Szalavitz, 2006). In the absence of awareness about such potentialities, our rational faculty may become their instrument, which may even use religious beliefs or moral values for its advantage (Jung et al., 2013).

A healthy upbringing environment, therefore, must also nurture the necessary self-awareness, something that has been considered mandatory by the mystical side of almost all religions.

A healthy family and community environment where everyone mutually facilitates each other in all kinds of difficulties becomes mandatory for the appropriate upbringing of the children (Hoffman, 2001). Social capital on a community scale also reproduces moral capital, which in turn would produce more social capital, in a positive virtuous cycle of co-creation (Emery & Flora, 2006; Putnam, 2020). The moral, however, has to take the lead, which can happen when the idea of morality is emphasized by a source that is seen as sacred by the collective. Religion, along with the idea of an all-seeing God, often serves this end (Candland, 2001; Dana et al., 2007; Putnam & Campbell, 2012). The communities that I studied in my doctoral thesis adhere to Islam for that purpose, that is, a religion claimed to be followed by around two billion people in the world. Other entrepreneurial communities also adhere to other religions like Christianity and Hinduism, which often guide their members to ensure a healthy family environment and cohesion within the community, which can be expected to contribute to their socioeconomic sustainability as well. Therefore, it can be argued, social is morally embedded, while moral is embedded in a religious worldview in many communities around the world. In other words, religion sets the criteria for the moral, which guides the social, which then creates the stage for economic activity that is referred to as socially embedded. Such an economic activity, then, is said to work for the socioeconomic needs of all stakeholders within a community, often including extra-community members as well in the process. In the coming chapters, the book explores how members of some specific communities engage with each other socially, how they do business, form economic ties, support each other in difficulty, raise their children, and eventually ensure their socioeconomic survival within a particular ideological and moral framework. Since in my primary research, I focused on the entrepreneurial communities in Pakistan, therefore, the flow of discussion will be guided by the findings from these communities; however, the discussion will also incorporate the experience of entrepreneurial communities from other parts of the world to find common patterns for greater generalizability of the findings. The discussion done so far will also guide in assessing any prevailing or shifting patterns within the communities explored for this research.

References

Abdelnour, S., Hasselbladh, H., & Kallinikos, J. (2017). Agency and institutions in organization studies. *Organization Studies, 38*(12), 1775–1792.

Adewale, A. (2017). Does bureaucracy stifle moral agency? *International Journal of Public Administration in the Digital Age, 4*(2), 1–13.

Alam, M. (2021). *The Mughals and the Sufis: Islam and political imagination in India, 1500–1750*. State University of New York Press.

Al-Ghazzali, A. H. M., Daniel, E. D., & Field, C. (2015). *The alchemy of happiness*. London: Taylor & Francis.

Apple, M. W. (2004). *Ideology and curriculum*. RoutledgeFalmer.
Ariely, D. (2013). *The (honest) truth about dishonesty: How we lie to everyone—Especially ourselves*. HarperCollins.
Armstrong, K. (2014). *Fields of blood: Religion and the history of violence*. Random House LLC.
Augustine, & Chadwick, H. (2008). *The confessions*. London: OUP Oxford.
Babiak, P., & Hare, R. D. (2006). Snakes in suits: When psychopaths go to work. *Applied Psychology, 44*(2006), 171–188.
Bakan, J. (2019). *The corporation: The pathological pursuit of profit and power*. Free Press.
Bakan, J. (2020). *The new corporation: How "good" corporations are bad for democracy*. Penguin Canada.
Bandura, A. (2002). Selective moral disengagement in the exercise of moral agency. *Journal of Moral Education, 31*(2), 101–119. https://doi.org/10.1080/0305724022014322
Barnett, T., & Kellermanns, F. W. (2006). Are we family and are we treated as family? Nonfamily employees' perceptions of justice in the family firm. *Entrepreneurship Theory and Practice, 30*(6), 837–854. https://doi.org/10.1111/j.1540-6520.2006.00155.x
Barrett, L. F. (2020). *How emotions are made: The secret life of the brain*. Pan Macmillan.
Bauman, Z. (2013a). *Postmodernity and its discontents*. Polity Press.
Bauman, Z. (2013b). *The individualized society*. Polity Press.
Baumeister, R. F., Campbell, J. D., Krueger, J. I., & Vohs, K. D. (2003). Does high self-esteem cause better performance, interpersonal success, happiness, or healthier lifestyles? *Psychological Science in the Public Interest, 4*(1), 1–44. https://doi.org/10.1111/1529-1006.01431
Béchervaise, N. E., & Benjamin, C. G. (2013). Visionary or criminal: From profit through morality to socially sustainable entrepreneurship. *Procedia—Social and Behavioral Sciences, 99*, 339–350. https://doi.org/10.1016/j.sbspro.2013.10.502
Bloom, P. (2011). *Descartes' baby: How child development explains what makes us human*. Random House.
Bourdieu, P., & Passeron, J. C. (1990). *Reproduction in education*. Society and Culture.
Bowler, P. J. (2009). Darwin's originality. *Science, 323*, 223–226.
Bowles, S. (2016). *The moral economy: Why good incentives are no substitute for good citizens*. Yale University Press.
Bowles, S., & Gintis, H. (2011). *Schooling in capitalist America: Educational reform and the contradictions of economic life*. Haymarket Books.
Brewer, M. B. (1999). The psychology of prejudice: Ingroup love and outgroup hate? *Journal of Social Issues, 55*(3), 429–444. https://doi.org/10.1111/0022-4537.00126
Brooks, N., & Fritzon, K. (2016). Psychopathic personality characteristics amongst high functioning populations. *Crime Psychology Review, 2*(1), 22–44.
Brouwer, M. T. (2002). Weber, Schumpeter and Knight on entrepreneurship and economic development. *Journal of Evolutionary Economics, 12*(1–2), 83–105.
Brownsword, R., & Somsen, H. (2009). Law, innovation and technology: Before we fast forward—A forum for debate. *Law, Innovation and Technology, 1*(1), 1–73. https://doi.org/10.1080/17579961.2009.11428364
Bubolz, M. M. (2001). Family as source, user, and builder of social capital. *The Journal of Socio-Economics, 30*, 129–131.
Campbell, J., Moyers, B., & Flowers, B. S. (1991). *The power of myth*. Knopf Doubleday Publishing Group.
Camus, A., Brien, J. O., & Martinez, J. (2015). *The myth of sisyphus*. London: CreateSpace Independent Publishing Platform.
Candland, C. (2001). Faith as social capital: Religion and community development in Southern Asia. In J. D. Montgomery & A. Inkeles (Eds.), *Social capital as a policy resource* (pp. 355–374). Springer.
Cantor, N. F. (2015). *In the wake of the plague: The black death and the world it made*. Simon & Schuster.

Chande, A. (2023). Global politics of knowledge production: The challenges of islamization of knowledge in the light of tradition vs secular modernity debate. *Nazhruna: Jurnal Pendidikan Islam*. https://doi.org/10.31538/nzh.v6i2.3502
Cohn, N. (2000). *Europes inner demons: The demonization of Christians in medieval Christendom*. University of Chicago Press.
Courtwright, D. T. (2021). *The age of addiction: How bad habits became big business*. Harvard University Press.
Cozolino, L. (2014). The neuroscience of human relationships: Attachment and the developing social brain. In *The neuroscience of human relationships: Attachment and the developing social brain*, 2nd ed. W W Norton & Co.
Crawford, K. (2021). *The atlas of AI: Power, politics, and the planetary costs of artificial intelligence*. Yale University Press.
Croom, S. (2021, June 6). *12% of corporate leaders are psychopaths. It's time to take this problem seriously*. The Fortune.
Curtis, A. (2007). The trap: What happened to our dream of freedom? *BBC Newsnight, 2007*, 1.
Dale, S. F. (2009). *The Muslim empires of the Ottomans, Safavids, and Mughals*. Cambridge University Press.
Damasio, A. (2009). *Descartes' error*. Random House.
Dana, L. P., Paul Dana, L., & Dana, L. P. (2007). A humility-based enterprising community: The Amish people in Lancaster County. *Journal of Enterprising Communities: People and Places in the Global Economy, 1*(2), 142–154.
Dari-Mattiacci, G., & Fabbri, M. (2023). How institutions shape morality. *The Journal of Law, Economics, and Organization, 39*(1), 160–198. https://doi.org/10.1093/jleo/ewab016
Deleuze, G., Guattari, F., Hurley, R., Seem, M., & Lane, H. R. (2013). *Anti-Oedipus: Capitalism and Schizophrenia*. Bloomsbury Publishing.
Diamond, J. (2012). *The world until yesterday: What can we learn from traditional societies?* Viking.
Diamond, J. (2013). *Collapse: How societies choose to fail or survive*. Penguin Books Limited.
Dika, T. R. (2020). The origins of Cartesian dualism. *Journal of the American Philosophical Association, 6*(3), 335–352.
DiNicolantonio, J. J., O'Keefe, J. H., & Wilson, W. L. (2018). Sugar addiction: Is it real? A narrative review. *British Journal of Sports Medicine, 52*(14), 910–913.
Doris, J. M., & Group, T. M. P. R. (2010). *The moral psychology handbook*. London: OUP Oxford.
Dunbar-Ortiz, R. (2023). *An indigenous peoples' history of the United States*. Beacon Press.
Edmondson, A. C. (2004). Psychological safety, trust, and learning in organizations: A group-level lens. In *Trust and distrust in organizations: Dilemmas and approaches* (pp. 239–272). Russell Sage Foundation.
Ellemers, N., Pagliaro, S., & Barreto, M. (2013). Morality and behavioral regulation in groups: A social identity approach. *European Review of Social Psychology, 24*(1), 160–193. https://doi.org/10.1080/10463283.2013.841490
Emery, M., & Flora, C. (2006). Spiraling-up: Mapping community transformation with community capital framework. *Community Development, 37*(1), 19–35.
Erikson, E. H. (1994). *Identity and the life cycle*. W. W Norton.
Evans, G. W., Li, D., & Whipple, S. S. (2013). Cumulative risk and child development. *Psychological Bulletin, 139*(6), 1342–1396. https://doi.org/10.1037/a0031808
Ferguson, N. (2014). *The great degeneration: How institutions decay and economies die*. Penguin Publishing Group.
Fevre, R. (2000). *The demoralization of western culture: Social theory and the dilemmas of modern living*. Continuum.
Finzi-Dottan, R., & Karu, T. (2006). From emotional abuse in childhood to psychopathology in adulthood. *Journal of Nervous & Mental Disease, 194*(8), 616–621.

Forbes, J. D. (2008). *Columbus and other cannibals*. Seven Stories Press.
Foucault, M. (2012). *Discipline & punish: Birth of a prison*. Knopf Doubleday Publishing Group.
Foucault, M., & Rabinow, P. (2020). *The Foucault reader*. Penguin Canada.
Frankl, V. (1997). *The man's search for ultimate meaning*. Insight Books.
Frazier, J. (2017). *Hindu worldviews: Theories of self*. Bloomsbury Publishing, London.
Freire, P. (2000). *Pedagogy of the oppressed: 30th anniversary edition*. Bloomsbury Academic.
Friedman, M. (2007). The social responsibility of business is to increase its profits. In W. C. Zimmerli, M. Holzinger, & K. Richter (Eds.), *Corporate ethics and corporate governance* (Vol. 32, pp. 173–178). London: Springer.
Friedman, M., & Appelbaum, B. (2020). *Capitalism and freedom*. University of Chicago Press.
Fromm, E. (2017). *The sane society* (L. A. Anderson (Ed.)). Taylor & Francis.
Fromm, E. (1994). *Escape from freedom*. Henry Holt and Company.
Fuchs, F., & Lingnau, V. (2024). The homo economicus as a prototype of a psychopath? A conceptual analysis and implications for business research and teaching. *Journal of Business Ethics*. https://doi.org/10.1007/s10551-024-05638-7
Fukuyama, F. (2011). *The origins of political order: From Prehuman times to the French revolution*. Profile Books Ltd.
Fukuyama, F. (2014). *Political order and political decay: From the industrial revolution to the globalisation of democracy*. Profile.
Galison, P., & Proctor, R. (2020). Agnotology in action: A dialogue. In J. A. Kourany & M. Carrier (Eds.), *Science and the production of ignorance: When the quest for knowledge is thwarted*. The MIT Press. https://doi.org/10.7551/mitpress/12146.003.0004
Giddens, A. (2013). *The constitution of society: Outline of the theory of structuration*. Polity Press.
Gilmartin, D. (2014). *Civilization and modernity: Narrating the creation of Pakistan*. 312.
Gino, F., Ayal, S., & Ariely, D. (2009). Contagion and differentiation in unethical behavior: The effect of one bad apple on the barrel. *Psychological Science, 20*(3), 393–398. https://doi.org/10.1111/j.1467-9280.2009.02306.x
Gintis, H. (2000). Beyond Homo economicus: Evidence from experimental economics. *Ecological Economics, 35*(3), 311–322. https://doi.org/10.1016/S0921-8009(00)00216-0
Gneezy, U., Rockenbach, B., & Serra-Garcia, M. (2013). Measuring lying aversion. *Journal of Economic Behavior & Organization, 93*, 293–300. https://doi.org/10.1016/j.jebo.2013.03.025
Goldsmith, E., Khor, M., Norberg-Hodge, H., & Shiva, V. (1995). *The future of progress: Reflections on environment and development*. Green Books Ltd.
Graeber, D., & Wengrow, D. (2023). *The dawn of everything: A new history of humanity*. Picador.
Graham, J., Waytz, A., Meindl, P., Iyer, R., & Young, L. (2017). Centripetal and centrifugal forces in the moral circle: Competing constraints on moral learning. *Cognition, 167*, 58–65. https://doi.org/10.1016/j.cognition.2016.12.001
Greene, J. (2014). *Moral tribes: Emotion, reason and the gap between us and them*. London: Atlantic.
Greene, J., & Haidt, J. (2002). How (and where) does moral judgment work? *Trends in Cognitive Sciences, 6*(12), 517–523. https://doi.org/10.1016/S1364-6613(02)02011-9
Guyer, P. (2006). Introduction: The starry heavens and the moral law. In P. Guyer (Ed.), *The Cambridge companion to kant and modern philosophy* (pp. 1–27). London: Cambridge University Press. https://doi.org/10.1017/CCOL052182303X.001
Habermas, J. (2015). *The theory of communicative action: Reason and the rationalization of society* (Vol. 1). London: Polity Press.
Haidt, J. (2013). *The righteous mind: Why good people are divided by politics and religion*. Knopf Doubleday Publishing Group.
Haidt, J. (2023). Devices and desires: Social media is the major cause of the mental illness epidemic among young women. *New Statesman, 152*(5710–5711), 29.

Haidt, J., & Graham, J. (2007). When morality opposes justice: Conservatives have moral intuitions that liberals may not recognize. *Social Justice Research, 20*(1), 98–116. https://doi.org/10.1007/s11211-007-0034-z

Hallaq, W. B. (2013). *The impossible state: Islam, politics, and modernity's moral predicament (Reprint).* Columbia University Press.

Hambrick, E. P., Brawner, T. W., & Perry, B. D. (2019). Timing of early-life stress and the development of brain-related capacities. In *Frontiers in behavioral neuroscience* (Vol. 13). Frontiers Media S.A. https://doi.org/10.3389/fnbeh.2019.00183

Hamlin, J. K., Wynn, K., & Bloom, P. (2007). Social evaluation by preverbal infants. *Nature, 450*(7169), 557–559. https://doi.org/10.1038/nature06288

Han, B. C., & Butler, E. (2017). *Psychopolitics: Neoliberalism and new technologies of power.* Verso.

Harari, Y. N. (2015). *Sapiens: A brief history of humankind.* Harper.

Harris, T. A. (1969). I'm OK You're OK: A practical guide to transactional analysis. In *I'm ok you're ok: A practical guide to transactional analysis.* Harper & Row, London.

Harvey, D. (2005). *A brief history of neoliberalism.* Oxford University Press.

Hashim, R., Ahmad, H., Mazuki, M. A., Bahrin, N. L. Z., & Ahmad, A. (2017). Sibling rivalry and offspring conflict: A review. *Advanced Science Letters, 23*(1), 3–6. https://doi.org/10.1166/ASL.2017.7167

Hayes, S. C., Strosahl, K. D., & Wilson, K. G. (2003). *Acceptance and commitment therapy: An experimental approach to behavior change.* Guilford Press.

Heidegger, M., & Newcomb, T. (1962). *Being and time.* Basil Blackwell.

Hickel, J. (2020). *Less is more: How Degrowth will save the world.* Penguin Random House.

Hobbes, T., & Missner, M. (2016). *Thomas Hobbes: Leviathan (Longman library of primary sources in philosophy).* Taylor & Francis.

Hoffman, M. L. (2001). *Empathy and moral development: Implications for caring and justice.* Cambridge University Press.

Hofstadter, R. (2017). *Social Darwinism in American thought, 1860–1915.* University of Pennsylvania Press.

Horkheimer, M., Adorno, T. W., & Noeri, G. (2002). *Dialectic of enlightenment.* Stanford University Press.

Jackall, R. (1983). *Moral Mazes: Bureaucracy and managerial work.* Harvard Business Review. https://hbr.org/1983/09/moral-mazes-bureaucracy-and-managerial-work

Javaid, O. (2024). The significance of moral agency for socioeconomic justice and its absence in islamic economics and finance. *Journal of King Abdulaziz University: Islamic Economics, 37*, 3–20. https://journals.kau.edu.sa/index.php/JKAUIE/article/view/761

Javaid, O., Shamsi, A., & Hyder, I. (2019). How Memon, Delhi Saudagaran and Chinioti entrepreneurs create new ventures? *Pakistan Business Review, 21*(1), 63–73.

Jeannin, R., & Van Leeuwen, K. (2015). Associations between direct and indirect perceptions of parental differential treatment and child socio-emotional adaptation. *Journal of Child and Family Studies, 24*(6), 1838–1855.

Jung, C., & Hull, R. F. C. (1993). *The practice of psychotherapy: Essays on the psychology of the transference and other subjects* (R. F. C. Hull (Ed.)). Routledge.

Jung, C. (2006). *The undiscovered self (reprint).* New American Liberary.

Jung, C. (2014). *Aion: Researches into the phenomenology of the self.* Taylor & Francis.

Jung, C. (2016). *Psychological types.* Taylor & Francis.

Jung, C., Henderson, J. L., von Franz, M. L., Jaffé, A., & Jacobi, J. (2013). *Man and his symbols.* Stellar Classics.

Jungert, T., Landry, R., Joussemet, M., Mageau, G., Gingras, I., & Koestner, R. (2015). Autonomous and controlled motivation for parenting: Associations with parent and child outcomes. *Journal of Child and Family Studies, 24*(7), 1932–1942.

Kahneman, D., & Tversky, A. (2012). Prospect theory: An analysis of decision under risk. In *Handbook of the fundamentals of financial decision making* (Vol. 4, pp. 99–127). World Scientific. https://doi.org/10.1142/9789814417358_0006

Kakavelakis, K., & Edwards, T. J. (2022). The impact of structure and corporate ideology on leader-follower relations in the bureaucratic organization: A reflection on moral mazes. *Journal of Business Ethics, 181*(1), 69–82.

Kalkan, M., Batık, M. V., Kaya, L., & Turan, M. (2019). Peter pan syndrome "men who don't grow": Developing a scale. *Men and Masculinities, 24*(2), 245–257. https://doi.org/10.1177/1097184X19874854

Kee, H. C. (1998). *Christianity: A Social and Cultural History*. Prentice Hall.

Klein, N. (2015). *This changes everything: Capitalism vs. the climate*. Alfred A. Knopf Canada.

Klein, N., & Smith, N. (2008). The shock doctrine: A discussion. *Environment and Planning D: Society and Space, 26*(4), 582–595.

Kourany, J., & Carrier, M. (2020). *Science and the production of ignorance: When the quest for knowledge is thwarted*. MIT Press.

Kowal, A. K., Krull, J. L., & Kramer, L. (2004). How the differential treatment of siblings is linked with parent–child relationship quality. *Journal of Family Psychology, 18*(4), 658–665.

Krüger, J. S. (2018). *Signposts to silence: Metaphysical mysticism: Theoretical map and historical pilgrimages*. AOSIS.

Kubíček, A., & Machek, O. (2020). Intrafamily conflicts in family businesses: A systematic review of the literature and agenda for future research. *Family Business Review, 33*(2), 1.

Laible, D., & Thompson, R. A. (2007). Early socialization: A relationship perspective. In *Handbook of socialization: Theory and research.* (pp. 181–207). The Guilford Press.

Lembke, A. (2021). *Dopamine nation: Finding balance in the age of indulgence*. Penguin Publishing Group.

Lieven, A. (2012). *Pakistan: A hard country*. Penguin UK.

Lindberg, C. (2011). *The European reformations*. Wiley.

Loewenstein, A. (2023). *The Palestine laboratory: How Israel exports the technology of occupation around the world*. Verso.

Loewenstein, G. (2005). Hot-cold empathy gaps and medical decision making. *Health Psychology, 24*(4S), S49-56. https://doi.org/10.1037/0278-6133.24.4.S49

Lukianoff, G., & Haidt, J. (2019). *The coddling of the American mind: How good intentions and bad ideas are setting up a generation for failure*. Penguin Publishing Group.

Lyotard, J. F., & Van den Abbeele, G. (1999). *Postmodern fables*. University of Minnesota Press.

MacIntyre, A. (2013). *After virtue: A study in moral theory* (3rd ed.). Bloomsbury Publishing.

Maffi, L. (2018). Biocultural diversity. In *The international encyclopedia of anthropology* (pp. 1–14). https://doi.org/10.1002/9781118924396.wbiea1797

Marchant, G. E. (2011). The growing gap between emerging technologies and the law. In G. E. Marchant, B. R. Allenby, & J. R. Herkert (Eds.), *The growing gap between emerging technologies and legal-ethical oversight: The pacing problem* (pp. 19–33). London: Springer. https://doi.org/10.1007/978-94-007-1356-7_2

Marcuse, H. (2013). *One-dimensional man: Studies in the ideology of advanced industrial society*. Taylor & Fancis.

Maté, G., & Maté, D. (2024). *The myth of normal: Trauma, illness, and healing in a toxic culture*. Ebury Publishing.

Mazar, N., Amir, O., & Ariely, D. (2008). The dishonesty of honest people: A theory of self-concept maintenance. *Journal of Marketing Research, 45*(6), 633–644. https://doi.org/10.1509/jmkr.45.6.633

Mcdonald, D. (2017). *The golden passport: Harvard business school, the limits of capitalism, and the moral failure of the MBA elite*. HarperCollins.

McGilchrist, I. (2019). *The master and his emissary: The divided brain and the making of the western world* (2nd ed.). Yale University Press.

McNeill, J. T. (1951). *A history of the cure of souls*. Harper.

Metcalf, J., Moss, E., & Boyd, D. (2019). Owning ethics: Corporate logics, silicon valley, and the institutionalization of ethics. *Social Research: An International Quarterly, 82*(2), 449–476. https://muse.jhu.edu/article/732185

Mikhail, A. (2021). *God's shadow: Sultan Selim, his Ottoman empire, and the making of the modern world*. Liveright Publishing Corporation.

Mitra, S. (2015). From Hole in the Wall to school in the cloud. In P. Dixon, S. Humble, & C. Counihan (Eds.), *Handbook of international development and education* (pp. 368–376). Edward Elgar Publishing Ltd.

Munro, J. (2010). Tawney's century, 1540–1640: The roots of modern capitalist entrepreneurship. In D. S. Landes, J. Mokyr, & W. J. Baumol (Eds.), *The invention of enterprise: Entrepreneurship from ancient Mesopotamia to modern times* (pp. 107–155). Princeton University Press.

Neece, C. L., Green, S. A., & Baker, B. L. (2012). Parenting stress and child behavior problems: A transactional relationship across time. *American Journal on Intellectual and Developmental Disabilities, 117*(1), 48–66.

Neumann, E. (2015). *The origins and history of consciousness*. Taylor & Francis.

Nietzsche, F. (1997). *Twilight of the idols* (R. Polt & T. B. Strong (Eds.)). Hackett Publishing Company, Incorporated, London.

Nietzsche, F. (2020). *The gay science*. Dover Publications.

Nietzsche, F. (2021). *Thus spoke Zarathustra: (Illustarted)*. Independently Published.

Norberg, H. (2016). *Ancient futures*. Local Futures.

O'Boyle, C. G. (2014). *History of psychology: A cultural perspective*. Taylor & Francis.

Orr, D. W. (2004). *Earth in mind: On education, environment and the human prospect*. Island Press.

Padilla, J., Sang, S. A., Updegraff, K. A., McHale, S. M., Umaña-Taylor, A. J., & De Jesús, S. A. R. (2019). Siblings' appraisals of fairness and jealousy in response to parental differential treatment: Longitudinal links to Mexican-origin emerging adults' adjustment. *Emerging Adulthood, 9*(4), 267–280. https://doi.org/10.1177/2167696819851435

Perry, B. D., & Szalavitz, M. (2006). *The boy who was raised as a dog and other stories from a child psychiatrist's notebook: What traumatized children can teach us about loss, love, and healing*. Basic Books.

Peterson, J. B. (2002). *Maps of meaning: The architecture of belief*. Taylor & Francis.

Petruzzello, M. (2024). Seven deadly sins. In *Encyclopædia britannica*. https://www.britannica.com/topic/seven-deadly-sins

Pew. (2012). *The world's muslims: Unity and diversity*. https://www.pewresearch.org/religion/2012/08/09/the-worlds-muslims-unity-and-diversity-executive-summary/

Podvoyskiy, D. G. (2022). "Dangerous modernity!", or the shadow play of modernity and its characters: Instrumental rationality-money-technology (Part 2). *RUDN Journal of Sociology, 22*(1), 40–57.

Polanyi, K. (2001). *The great transformation: The political and economic origins of our time*. Beacon Press.

Proctor, R., & Schiebinger, L. L. (2008). *Agnotology: The making and unmaking of ignorance*. Stanford University Press.

Pullanikkatil, D., & Hughes, K. (2023). *Socio-ecological systems and decoloniality: Convergence of indigenous and western knowledge*. Springer.

Putnam, R. D. (1993). *Making democracy work: Civil traditions in modern Italy*. Princeton University Press.

Putnam, R. D. (2020). *Bowling alone: Revised and updated: The collapse and revival of American community*. Simon & Schuster.

Putnam, R. D., & Campbell, D. E. (2012). *American grace: How religion divides and unites us*. Simon & Schuster.

Rand, A., & Branden, N. (2016). *Virtue of selfishness: A new concept of egoism*. Paw Prints.

Raquib, A., Javaid, O., & Anjum, G. (2020). Creation of the Islamic self for sustainability: Can Muslim entrepreneurship positively contribute to the SDGs through Tazkiya and Tarbiya of the Muslim youth. *Journal of Islamic Business and Management (JIBM), 10*(02), 323–342.

Ricoeur, P., McLaughlin, K., & Pellauer, D. (1990). *Time and narrative* (Vol. 1). London: University of Chicago Press.
Ritzer, G. (2016). The mcdonaldization of society. In E. Mofield & T. Stambaugh (Eds.), *In the mind's eye* (1st ed.). London: Routledge.
Rogers, C., & Webb, D. (2013). *Significant aspects of client-centered therapy*. CreateSpace Independent Publishing Platform.
Sachs, W. (2010). *The development dictionary: A guide to knowledge as power* (W. Sachs (Ed.); 2nd ed.). Zed Books.
Sandel, M. J. (2012). *What money can't buy: The moral limits of markets*. Allen Lane.
Seligman, M. E. P. (2017). *Authentic happiness: Using the new positive psychology to realize your potential for lasting Fulfillment*. Nicholas Brealey Publishing.
Sen, A. (2017). *Development as freedom*. Macat Library.
Singer, T., Seymour, B., O'Doherty, J., Kaube, H., Dolan, R. J., & Frith, C. D. (2004). Empathy for pain involves the affective but not sensory components of pain. *Science, 303*(5661), 1157–1162. https://doi.org/10.1126/science.1093535
Spencer, H. (2017). *The principles of biology* (Vol. 1). London: Hansebooks GmbH.
Stibbe, A. (2013). The corporation as person and psychopath: Multimodal metaphor, rhetoric and resistance. *CADADD Journal, 6*(2). http://www.lancaster.ac.uk/fass/journals/cadaad/volume-6-2/
Stillman, T. F., Baumeister, R. F., Lambert, N. M., Crescioni, A. W., DeWall, C. N., & Fincham, F. D. (2009). Alone and without purpose: Life loses meaning following social exclusion. *Journal of Experimental Social Psychology, 45*(4), 686–694.
Tainter, J. A. (1988). *The collapse of complex societies*. Cambridge University Press.
Tangney, J. P., & Dearing, R. L. (2002). *Shame and guilt*. Guilford Press. https://doi.org/10.4135/9781412950664.n388
Tawney, R. H. (2016). *Religion and the rise of capitalism*. Verso Books.
Taylor, C. (1992). *Sources of the self: The making of the modern identity*. Cambridge University Press.
Taylor, C. (2018). *A secular age*. Harvard University Press.
Trueman, C. R., & Dreher, R. (2020). *The rise and triumph of the modern self: Cultural Amnesia, expressive individualism, and the road to sexual revolution*. Crossway.
Turner, B. S. (2011). *Religion and modern society: Citizenship*. Cambridge University Press.
Twenge, J. M., & Campbell, W. K. (2010). *The narcissism epidemic: Living in the age of entitlement*. Atria Books.
Underhill, E. (2017). *Mysticism: A study in nature and development of spiritual consciousness*. Devoted Publishing.
Wailoo, K., Nelson, A., & Lee, C. (2012). *Genetics and the unsettled past: The collision of DNA, race, and history*. Rutgers University Press.
Waldinger, R., & Schulz, M. (2023). *The good life: Lessons from the world's longest scientific study of happiness*. Simon & Schuster.
Wang, L., Song, F., & Zhong, C.-B. (2021). High compensation and unethical reciprocity. *Journal of Management, 48*(8), 2223–2254. https://doi.org/10.1177/01492063211040557
Wang, X. (2015). *On moral capital*. Yilin Press Ltd.
Weber, M., & Kalberg, S. (2013). *The protestant ethic and the spirit of capitalism*. Taylor & Francis.
Weber, M., & Parsons, T. (1999). *The sociology of religion*. Beacon Press.
Weber, M., & Tribe, K. (2019). *Economy and society: A new translation*. Harvard University Press.
Weintraub, A. N. (2011). *Islam and popular culture in Indonesia and Malaysia*. Taylor & Francis.
WHO. (2023). *Tobacco*. https://www.who.int/news-room/fact-sheets/detail/tobacco
Wiese, B. S., & Freund, A. M. (2011). Parents as role models: Parental behavior affects adolescents' plans for work involvement. *International Journal of Behavioral Development, 35*(3), 218–224.
Williams, M., Gower, R., Green, J., Whitebread, E., Lenkiewicz, Z., & Schröder, P. (2019). *No time to waste: Tackling the plastic pollution crisis before it's too late*.

Yi, E. (2004). Guild dynamics in seventeenth-century Istanbul: Fluidity and leverage. In *The ottoman empire and its heritage* (Vol. 27). Brill Publishers.

Zimbardo, P. (2007). The Lucifer effect: Understanding how good people turn evil. In *The Lucifer effect: Understanding how good people turn evil.* Random House, London.

Zuboff, S. (2019). *The age of surveillance capitalism: The fight for a human future at the new frontier of power: Barack Obama's books of 2019.* Profile.

Chapter 5
Socioeconomic and Ideological Particularities of Enterprising Communities

The previous two chapters discussed the moral and the (organic) social, how they reproduce each other, and their possible influence on the organization of economic activity. In this chapter, an attempt is made to outline what the economic would look like when it works for the social under a moral framework. Many 'enterprising communities' in the world offer examples that align their economic activity with social and moral goals. The moral aims themselves are often embedded in a transcendental myth, or a religion, that offers a worldview, a *Weltanschauung*, a master narrative, an idea about life, the world, the universe, and a purposive role of individuals in it, that gives a teleological context to the moral (MacIntyre, 2013; Taylor, 2018). This set of worldviews, beliefs, and purposes is referred to as meta-norms by Hollingsworth (2000). The meta-norms shape the social, that is, the organic family and community, and also the relationship of the social with the economic. So, before the economic becomes embedded in the social, the social is already embedded in the moral, while the moral is embedded in the meta-norms. The meta-norms, therefore, provide a space for the individual, the family, the community, the market, the firm, along with other stakeholders like the state, other communities, travelers, even the biosphere, to mutually co-exist in a specific order. The meta-norms thus also provide a criterion to evaluate the outcomes of any activity, including economic ones, but while corresponding to the social needs (even political ones). They also provide the basis for the feedback to adjust any activity, including the social or economic, based on the shifting needs of the collective that are also prioritized as per the meta-norms. In this context, it is needless

---

Sections 5.2.1, 5.2.2, 5.2.3 and 5.3 of this chapter draws from the author's doctoral thesis 'Building a Theoretical Model of Socially Sustainable Entrepreneurship through Comparative Case Analysis of Ethnic Entrepreneurial Communities' submitted to Dept. of Management Sciences, Institute of Business Management (IoBM), Karachi, Pakistan.

O. Javaid, *Socioeconomic Sustainability Through Moral and Social Capital*,
Entrepreneurship and Development in South Asia: Longitudinal Narratives,
https://doi.org/10.1007/978-981-96-8134-1_5

to mention, that the act of entrepreneurship, or the process of initiating, organizing, and carrying out an act of production for the sake of selling in the market, is also inseparable from the meta-norms of the collective where the entrepreneurial activity takes place (Weiskopf & Steyaert, 2009). The meta-norms will thus establish the meaning, significance, and normative criterion to evaluate the outcome of entrepreneurial activity as well. Religions like Islam, Christianity, Judaism, and Hinduism, for example, offer a set of meta-norms, some more comprehensive and detailed than others. To perform a cross-examination of the religious beliefs or cultural mythologies, like Buddhism, is not the aim of this book.[1] The coming discussion will rather see how different communities adhering to different religions, organize themselves in ways that help them sustain in all dimensions.

It is pertinent to mention that the nature of economic activity, either organized on the gift model, or trading, typically work for the betterment of the whole collective when it is grown bottom up and evolve as per the dynamic needs of the collective (Greif, 1994; Javaid, 2022a, 2022b; Schumacher, 2010). In this context, the trend of imposing foreign institutional designs or methods of production or consumption of European or Western origin in traditionally organized communities all around the world (Escobar, 2012; Hong, 1995; Sachs, 2010) should be seen critically. This was unfortunately the norm during colonial times, while today the development discourse also attempts to take the free market design or its compatible institutions everywhere in the world, which often results in social tensions that eventually rupture the social fabric of the traditional communities. The social unsustainability that ensues from such a capitalistic way of organizing society has already been discussed in previous chapters. Often, an external intervention is necessary in emergencies that the community members are unable to address; however, this does not undermine the fact that any model that may help any community sustain itself in the long run typically emerges from within, not outside. Adoption from the external may happen, but again, the adoption is done in a bottom-up fashion, where a community culture integrates an externally evolved method into their own and keeps it if it works for them (Schumacher, 2010). Often, the cost of doing so is not visible, and it may take a long time for the results to emerge, the realization of which may also require a community to adjust if it is causing any substantial harm. I found many such examples in my doctoral thesis, the consequences of which are gradually being realized, but it appears that the corrective measures are yet to be taken in the communities I studied. More details are discussed in Chapters 6 and 7.

Such experiences, and the experience documented in the literature, suggest that the evolution of methods and techniques needs to happen in a bottom-up manner. It should be restated here that resisting necessary evolution in the name of following the tradition degenerates a community. The pressing needs of the individual or the collective are not frozen in time due to many endogenous and exogenous

[1] For a comparison between how the meta-norms of Buddhism and Islam affects the organization of the production and the consumption cycle in a society see Javaid (2019).

factors, so the response to the changing needs or the corresponding challenges needs to be dynamic, yet should ideally emerge from within the community. The meta-norms must therefore provide such provision of cultural dynamism, or change in socioeconomic institutions or methods, to prevent any degeneration at the hands of the tyrannical rule of the terrible father, that is, the cultural traditions that do not allow any change. The moral framework thus emerging from such meta-norms would also need to be flexible enough to accommodate the needs. In Islam, for example, lying is a great sin; however, there are three occasions where lying is considered acceptable, that is to save one's life, to deceive one's enemy in war, and to mend the relationship among people in a state of conflict, especially a husband and a wife.[2] Such a set of meta-norms and the corresponding set of moral principles that offer adaptability as and when needed may eventually form a healthy basis for the social and the corresponding economic institutions, or the activity of entrepreneurs in the socioeconomic context set by the meta-norms. The moral framework outlined by many religions, like Islam, which is followed by the communities I studied, typically prioritizes the social over the economic and describes the economic as a means toward the social, which may organize the economic activity around the social needs if the respective moral standards are adhered to by its agents. Other religions may also produce a similar socioeconomic arrangement.

Since the social cannot be sustained without the economic, healthy economic activity is therefore critical. However, to keep the two in a healthy relationship, it was proposed in the previous chapter that the two must become a means for a common aim. Solving the problem related to the fulfillment of the material needs of the members of the community and beyond is, therefore, seen here as a moral problem. This also requires a response from the market to ensure social stability, which can be threatened because of the scarcity of anything fundamental to sustain human life. What is produced, how it is produced, and how it is distributed in a community, therefore, could be deeply influenced by the sociocultural, moral, and religious environment that prevails within a community, understanding of which also entails looking at the historical circumstances, which is briefly done in this chapter. Since, in my doctoral thesis, I specifically studied Memon, Chinioti, and Delhiwala communities that reside in Pakistan, therefore, the flow of discussion will be guided by my findings of the three communities; however, for generalizability, a quick review of some historical and contemporary examples will precede the discussion on the three Pakistani communities. This chapter broadly reviews the community characteristics, while Chapters 6 and 7 look at specific

[2] "Umm Kulthum bint 'Uqbah (May Allah be pleased with her) reported: Messenger of Allah (ﷺ) said, 'The person who (lies) in order to conciliate between people is not a liar, when he conveys good or says (something) good". [Al-Bukhari and Muslim]. The narration in Muslim added: She said, "I never heard him [she meant the Prophet (ﷺ)] giving permission of lying in anything except in three (things): war, conciliating between people and the conversation of man with his wife and the conversation of a woman with her husband". Source: Riyad as-Salihin 249, https://sunnah.com/riyadussalihin:249 (retrieved: 1st July 2024).

family norms, business practices, startup methods, conflict prevention and resolution tactics, to understand how the social and the economic weave together in the communities in focus. A lot of work has already been done and is being done to understand how these communities also can guide us to live in harmony with the natural environment (Maffi, 2018; Pullanikkatil & Hughes, 2023). However, the focus in this book is on what we can learn about the practices that help in socioeconomic sustainability.[3]

5.1 A Look into History

A key feature of the pre-modern markets noted by Marx (2012) was that the trading was done to satisfy human needs, while money was used as a medium of exchange. The idea of money as capital as an ever-increasing quantity through the cycle of production and consumption was not born. More broadly, the aims and methods employed for production and consumption were determined by sociocultural or even religious beliefs adhered to by the traditional communities. Numerous examples from various cultures suggest that the aim of economic activity was typically to provide sustenance to the family but also to have the capacity to contribute to various community-related causes, as one's reputation within the community was (is) often based on how much one can contribute. Mortensen suggests that the primary motive of producers within the household was not to maximize their gain; rather, community meta-norms sanctioned individuals to remain committed to the well-being of their collective as a whole (Mortensen, 1999) while discouraging them from "accumulation of personal wealth" (Hudson, 2010, p. 10). The institution of voluntary trade has been in existing since the Paleolithic era; however, in Hudson's view, more recent "tribal experience" (p. 10) suggests that such a trade was in the form of "reciprocal gift exchange" (p. 10). Hudson further argues that the primary objectives of such an exchange have been to reinforce "cohesion among the community's members and peaceful relations among chiefs of neighboring tribes" (p. 10).

Hudson (2010) notes that leading and well-placed families during earlier times had been given control over "land, mineral rights, and other enterprises [by their respective political authority who even had given these affluent families the right to lease the land] … for a stipulated rent to be paid to the civic authority" (p. 26). According to Wunch (2010), productivity enhancement techniques were encouraged by the political authority in the neo-Babylonian era. The economic environment typically encouraged entrepreneurs (as voluntary risk-takers, and initiators of economic activity in its simple form) to bridge between the basic consumer and production on one hand, and between the individual landholder and "all levels of

[3] This is also critical for environmental sustainability as per literature (Dillard et al., 2008; Javaid, 2022a, 2022b; Sachs, 2010), but not a main focus of the exploration here.

royal or temple administration on the other" (Wunsch, 2010, p. 56). These entrepreneurs perhaps facilitated the production of agricultural products and other raw materials. They also typically acted as financial intermediaries, generating liquidity to facilitate transactions in various sectors of production. The level of innovation pursued by neo-Babylonian entrepreneurs was not seemingly technological but rather social and financial. Those entrepreneurs often focused on improving their relations with key stakeholders by providing them financial leverage, sometimes on a profit-sharing basis, and improving product distribution techniques to reduce wastage (Wunsch, 2010).

The form of exploitation that existed during the capitalist or colonial era was non-existent during earlier times because of its "own form of cheap labor", notes Hudson (2010, p. 26). Nevertheless, there has been evidence that some family-oriented businesses in early Mesopotamia and Babylonia were able to amass a fortune and grow their material standards of living (Hudson, 2010) for multiple generations in some cases (Wunsch, 2010) under a conducive political and economic atmosphere. Typical occupations in the neo-Babylonian period are said to be related to farming, husbandry, transportation, tax farming, money lending, food processing and distribution, and textile production (Wunsch, 2010). In Hudson's (2010) view, these entrepreneurs, instead of specializing in a commodity or service, usually preferred to have a diverse portfolio of income generation opportunities, including "organizing and managing voyages, fields, workshops, or other productive units" (p. 19). Their approach, it appears, was collective rather than individualistic, as they typically operated through guilds like the ones organized by "Assyrian traders early in the second millennium, Syrian and 'Phoenician' traders with Aegean and Mediterranean lands by the eighth century BC" (Hudson, 2010, p. 19). Various family-based entrepreneurs such as "Balmunamhe in Old Babylonian times, Assyrian traders in Asia Minor, the Egibi in Neo-Babylonia, Cato and other Romans" (Hudson, 2010, p. 19) were found to have invested in diverse income generation mechanisms such as long-distance and domestic trading. Such trading practices, according to Hudson (2010), enabled entrepreneurs to serve the monarchic authorities or religious temples with "food and raw material" (p. 19) (in exchange for some form of benefit), providing financial services, leasing fertile land, workshops, and real estate management.

It appears that economic exchange occurred between families or between families and the political or religious authority. The process of redistribution within the family and the extended family was typically done on the principle of voluntary reciprocity. In Polanyi's (2001) view, "all economic systems known to us up to the end of feudalism in Western Europe were organized either on the principle of reciprocity or redistribution, or householding, or some combination of the three" (p. 57). Mortensen (1999) notes:

> In tribal societies, the kinship system plays the role of securing simultaneously social integration, i.e., an institutional order of normativity, and system integration, i.e., the steering system of the existence and survival of the material subsistence of the members of society. The kinship system secures norms, world-views, and does not allow types of socialization that go beyond the kinship system. At the same time, it lays boundaries on the development of the productive forces, since it does not include a systematic motive to produce over and above an inherited and customary level of subsistence. (p. 22)

Such principles were embedded in the social fabric of the community, which also utilized "the patterns of symmetry, centricity, and autarchy" (Mortensen, 1999, p. 22). Curl (2009) describes the socioeconomic order of the natives living in the North American region while discussing the history of cooperatives. Before the establishment of Puritan capitalists arriving from Britain, the native's organization of production was typically structured along the lines of communal harmony, reciprocity, cooperation, and sharing. Curl (2009) notes:

> Tools were commonly shared within the communal group. It was unthinkable, for example, for one unit in a band to have two harpoons while another had none." (p. 15) … "The Shoshone traditionally divided the catch equally among the families until common survival needs were met … Cooperation and collectivity also formed the backbone of the way of life of agriculture-oriented peoples. Since ancient times, the Southwest Pueblos have practiced collective and cooperative farming (and later herding). The Rio Grande Valley Pueblos used cooperative irrigation and, in the high desert further west, the Hopi practiced cooperative dry farming. (p. 16)

The lack of a modern entrepreneurial ethic kept these earlier entrepreneurs from achieving "technological progress and economic growth" (p. 19). The use of money was considered restricted as a measure of the value of a transaction rather than an instrument for capital accumulation. Often, money as a unit of exchange was missing altogether in some places as well; however, the basic social order of such places was not much different than those where some form of a unit of exchange was present. The economic activity as a whole remained primarily as a medium to serve various social objectives (Polanyi, 2001).

Polanyi (2001) further explains that such a socioeconomic order, built around the needs of the extended household, continued throughout the "Greco-Roman [period] … up to the end of the Middle Ages" (p. 57), despite ever-increasing complexity of trade. The market did not grow in its scope and significance to dominate other "sociocultural institutional patterns" until the sixteenth century in Europe. Murray (2010) suggests that the primary driver of economic activity in Europe "was not individual profit maximization, but dedication to a variety of communal goals … Individuals from the leading commercial cities of Europe could become immensely rich from their entrepreneurial endeavors, but wealth was rarely the ultimate goal of their ambition … This was true all over Europe and well into modern times" (p. 103). A Laissez-faire self-regulating economic order perhaps came much later in Europe, as until the seventeenth century, the markets operated under the strict control of the political authority. It is suggested that the modern entrepreneur, as envisioned by Jeremy Bentham, Adam Smith, and later by Schumpeter, had not been born yet. Murray (2010) argues that "In many (if not most) times and places, the creative destruction in the name of economic progress that Joseph Schumpeter posited was neither present nor desirable" (p. 105). Murray's argument may be considered valid for entrepreneurial activity happening during the Ottoman era, parallel to the Middle Ages in Europe, and much earlier in Islamic Civilization also (Javaid, 2015). During the Ottoman era, business was typically done via various family-driven guilds, which, in Yi's (2004) view, were "egalitarian, communalistic organizations that suppressed internal competition and the profit motive" (p.

57). Throughout the history of Islamic civilization, Muslim communities in general emphasized the "spiritual aspects of life rather than materialistic ideas" (Javaid, 2015, p. 377). The economic activity in general obeyed the social norms or can be said to be embedded in the social, and the social was rather inspired by spiritual values, or the meta-norms of the religion that dominated the region. A pattern that continues even today in many communities around the world.

5.2 Some Recent Examples

Today, across the globe, numerous entrepreneurial communities arguably exist where the economic is embedded in social, and the social has been shaped by the meta-norms of a particular belief system that weave the social and economic together into a meaningful whole. Despite the odds not always being in their favor, the members of these communities have sustained and thrived economically, not because of some individualistic spirit, but because of a religiously inspired spirit of mutual support. There are many such communities around the world, such as Marwaris, Chettiars, Sikhs, Jews, Parsis, Druze, Mennonites, Amish, Armenians, Mormons, Quakers, Lebanese Christians, Syrian Christians, Baha'is, Bohra, Ismailis, Jains, Overseas Chinese, Nigerian Igbo, Yazidis, Maronites, and Chaldeans, just to name a few. There are also several indigenous communities around the world, such as Yoruba from Nigeria, Maori in New Zealand, Quechua in Peru and Bolivia, Sami in Norway, Navajo now living in the United States, and Inuit in Canada and Greenland. Further, the details about the Mapuche in Chile and Argentina, Zulu in South Africa, Ashanti in Ghana, Hmong in Vietnam, Laos, Thailand, and China can also be mentioned here. To explore their economic, social, and ideological dynamics would require volumes; here is a quick summary with some examples from the list.

Marwaris are one such community that is typically based in India. They are known for their acumen in trade and commerce. They have been thriving in finance, manufacturing, and retail, and use family networks and community associations to operate in their domains of expertise (Timberg & Das, 2015). Jews are another global community, with very ancient origins, known for their success in the domains of finance, investment banking, technology, law, and medicine (Baron, 1993; Sarna, 2019). Parsis are yet another example, whose history goes back more than a thousand years. They have also been historically successful in a variety of trades and industries. Many of the richest people in India today belong to this faith. They are generally praised for their ethical business conduct and community welfare (Desai & Bharat, 2017; Luhrmann, 1996). Another example is the Druze in the Middle East, who adhere to the faith of Islam. They engage in diverse entrepreneurial activities, such as agriculture, commerce, and now increasingly in the domains of medicine and engineering. They are also known for maintaining a strong internal support system (Firro, 2021). Mennonites and Amish, based in North America, adhere to a sect of Christianity known as Anabaptist Christianity.

They are particularly renowned for their simplistic traditional lifestyle and non-reliance on modern facilities. They focus on agriculture, crafts, and small-scale manufacturing, with the help of cooperative business models (Hostetler, 1993; Thiessen, 2013). Armenians, who reside in West Asia, likewise have worked in trade, crafts, and more recently, in technology and education, through mutual support and tight-knit community networks (Suny, 1993). Sikhs who originated in the Punjab region of India, and now reside in many countries, are also prominent in agriculture and transport. Many of them now own global business ventures. Sikhs in general value hard work and emphasize community service (Elsberg, 2019). Mormons, who are mostly based in the US, also engage their internal social networks to operate in various industries like finance, real estate, and retail. They have achieved success in many fields while helping each other (Benedict, 2007). Indigenous communities like the Maori in New Zealand and the Yoruba in Nigeria are active in sectors like tourism, agriculture, and cultural industries. Unlike Mennonites and Amish, they are more inclined to blend modern methods while keeping their traditional cultural integrity intact. They are particularly inclined to maintain their kinship networks and preserve their cultural heritage (Falola & Adebayo, 2000; Kawharu & Tapsell, 2019). These are just a few examples where entrepreneurial success can be said to be an outcome of cultural and religious values that emphasize mutual support and cooperation.

The moral values followed by the members of these communities often appear to be inspired by their respective religions or belief systems, which can also be noticed to shape their economic behavior and social dynamics. Marwaris are often found to practice *karma* and *dharma* (duty), which are fundamental tenets of Hinduism. The values, it has been noted, motivate them to remain ethical in their business practices and contribute to their community. Doing so, they believe, would lead to their spiritual salvation (Dhanania & Gopakumaran, 2005). The Jewish community believes in a similar concept referred to as *tikkun olam* (repairing the world) in Judaism. This inculcates the spirit of philanthropy among Jews toward their fellow community members. Religious Jews would often see their wealth as a means to fulfill their religious obligations by contributing to the betterment of their community, and often the society as well (Krasner, 2013). Likewise, Zoroastrianism, the religion followed by Parsis, also motivates them toward righteous living. It strongly emphasizes maintaining a strong work ethic and social responsibility among Parsis. Parsis, therefore, are often found to use their wealth to benefit the community (Luhrmann, 1996). In Sikhism, likewise, the concept of *Vand Chhako* (sharing with others) has been encouraging Sikhs to use their resources to support the less fortunate, as it would generate communal harmony (Kaur, 2013). Similarly, Mormonism emphasizes self-reliance and service to the community. It inculcates a view that one's wealth is a means to achieve spiritual and communal goals. Mormonism is also said to encourage a frugal lifestyle and generosity (Cranney, 2011).

The economic resources, therefore, are generally seen in these communities as a means to an end, not an end in itself. Wealth is often a means to the well-being of the collective, for which a part of the surplus is frequently used by well-off members. The Druze, for example, are noted for their culture of self-sufficiency and prioritize communal well-being. They reportedly view wealth as ordained by God, which is then to be used to help others in the community, particularly in lesser privileged segments. Druze, therefore, prefer to socially organize for the collective good over wealth accumulation as the religion they follow encourages them toward social justice and to support the needy (Firro, 2021). Mennonites have a culture of simple living and self-sufficiency, as their religious belief positions wealth as a source of evil. Their religion thus emphasizes humility and detachment from worldly possessions. They do engage in economic activity, but spend a small portion of their earnings on basic needs only and prioritize contributing to the community instead of wealth accumulation (Naka, 2011). The Chettiars, a community in southern India that adheres to the Hindu faith, are generally known for their entrepreneurial orientation and money-lending practices. They traditionally practiced a form of delayed gratification. For them, wealth has been a means to secure their family's future and fulfill their religious obligations inspired by the Hindu beliefs of karma and reincarnation. They believe that living a life of service in the current life would lead to a better future in the next reincarnation (Rudner, 2023). The Amish, on the other side of the world, engage in economic activity for self-sufficiency while prioritizing community well-being over individual accumulation. Their religious teachings expect them to live a life of simplicity while avoiding worldly temptations. However, they acknowledge the need for financial resources to maintain their community and way of life (Kraybill, 2003). Armenians also generally view wealth as a tool for survival and community advancement. Their Christian beliefs tell them to prioritize stewardship and charity, and to use their resources to support their families, the church, and those who are less fortunate (Saroyan, 2022; Suny, 1993).

In the examples being highlighted here, economic activity is generally embedded within social structures and informed by religiously inspired moral frameworks. The reputation of the entrepreneur in these communities is often found to be based on their contributions to the community. This dynamic is observed across the communities being discussed, where a balance between personal success and communal responsibility is frequently noticed. For example, among the Marwaris, reputation is based not just on business acumen but also on philanthropy and social contributions. Wealthy Marwaris have historically funded educational institutions, hospitals, and religious sites (Nakatani, 2014). Prominent Marwari families like the Birlas and the Goenkas are known for their extensive philanthropic work (Taknet, 2016). Also, in Jewish communities, the concept of tzedakah (charitable giving) is central to social reputation. Wealthy individuals are expected to support communal institutions, such as synagogues, schools, and welfare organizations (Sarna, 2019). This practice is believed to not only fulfill religious obligations but also elevate one's social standing within the community (Baron, 1993). For the Parsis, their faith emphasizes 'good thoughts, good words, and good deeds', encouraging them to invest in community welfare. Notable Parsi philanthropists have established numerous educational and healthcare institutions wherever they thrive economically (Vevaina, 2023). Within the Druze community, individual reputation is generally tied to one's role in maintaining community cohesion and providing support to fellow members. In their practice of providing mutual guarantees referred to as kafala, the community members vouch for each other's debts, which is unlikely in the absence of strong trust and a sense of communal responsibility (Firro, 2021; Van Eijk, 2014). The Anabaptist Christian beliefs of Mennonite and Amish communities emphasize humility, mutual aid, and communal living. Individual reputation in Mennonite and Amish is thus built on contributions to communal projects, such as barn raisings and disaster relief efforts (Reid, 2015; Rogers et al., 2013). Armenians, who are also Christian, hold those in high regard who contribute to maintaining the cultural and religious institutions (Cora, 2018; Suny, 1993). For Sikhs, those who show adherence principle of seva (selfless service) would be regarded higher than those who fall short in doing so. Sikhs, therefore, often run communal kitchens (langars), educational initiatives, and organize disaster relief efforts. Prominent Sikh figures engage in significant acts of charity and community service (Nippoldt, 2022). Mormons, another Christian community, also value members who exemplify self-reliance and support the community (Benedict, 2007). Among Indigenous communities such as the Maori and Yoruba, traditional values and communal living are again significant in shaping individual reputation. For the Maori, the concept of mana (spiritual authority and prestige) is often linked to one's contributions to the community and the preservation of cultural heritage (McCarthy et al., 2013). Similarly, the Yoruba value those who maintain communal ties and support family and clan networks. The reputation of individuals is said to be enhanced by acts of generosity and leadership within the community (Adekson, 2004). In each of these communities, individual reputation does not appear to be a measure of accumulated wealth rather is linked with one's contributions to the collective as prescribed in the meta-norms of the community. The meta-norms or religious beliefs of each community appear to nurture an environment in general where economic activities are often conducted with a focus on social responsibility and mutual support, which then makes individual and communal prosperity two sides of the same coin.

It is interesting to note that many of these communities emerged from a historical experience of persecution or marginalization. The Marwaris, a mercantile caste in India, faced exclusion at the hands of the Brahmin and Kshatriya castes, and later during the British dominance. The exclusion forced them to rely on each other and contributed to the development of a culture of self-reliance (Timberg & Das, 2015). Similarly, the Jewish diaspora has suffered centuries of displacement in Europe, which perhaps contributed as well to their strong sense of community and self-reliance. This may also explain their high emphasis on education and the use of commerce as a means of collective well-being (Baron, 1993). The Parsis, likewise, had to flee religious persecution in Persia and then established themselves in India in the eighth century onwards. Further, their belief in honesty, hard work, and ethical conduct in business dealings likely contributed to their economic success as well (Luhrmann, 1996; Palsetia, 2001). The Sikhs, another example from the list, also suffered from religious persecution during the Mughal era, which perhaps contributed to the development of a strong communal identity

(Mandair et al., 2013). Mormons, who also faced persecution and displacement in the United States, had to develop a cooperative economic setup on a communal scale to survive. A religiously inspired sense of mutual support also helped them survive when the odds were not in their favor (Bushman & Bushman, 2001). The persecution of indigenous communities around the world during the colonial era is no secret as well.

Socially these communities can be said to exemplify a strong sense of solidarity grounded in their distinct cultural and religious identity, which has likely been intensified due to the difficulties they experienced in the past. The community members formally and often informally facilitate each other in a variety of different ways. The Marwaris, for example, operate a network of Marwari Associations across India that provides financial and social support to fellow community members venturing into business. These associations not only offer mentorship and access to capital but also reportedly serve as a platform for information sharing and building trust with potential business partners (Timberg & Das, 2015). Likewise, Jewish communities have a long history of Tzedakah (charity) by for example, creating loan societies that provide access to capital for fellow Jews (Tenenbaum, 1993). Sikh entrepreneurs are also known for providing mentorship, capital, and market access to new ventures within their community (Takhar & Jakobsh, 2023). On the other side of the planet, the Mormon Church in America operates welfare programs that aim at providing employment opportunities, also offering financial assistance and job training to its members (Bushman & Bushman, 2001).

The entrepreneurial success of these communities, cannot be attributed solely to individual contributions; there can be exceptions in every community; however, the inferences drawn here are based on general trends. So, as per the reported description of respective communities, it can be argued that the religious beliefs of the aforementioned communities often provide a moral framework that shapes social organization, which in turn shapes the dynamics of economic activities. The strong sense of community and religious values, coupled with a shared history, can be said to create a fertile ground for trust, cooperation, and mutual support. Social networks offer not just financial resources but also a safety net during challenging times, often helping the struggling members or supporting new entrepreneurs establish themselves. The moral frameworks derived from their respective religions shape these communities' relationship with wealth, leading them to view it as a means toward collective well-being, which seems to have helped the members of these communities to sail through hard times. Table 5.1 provides a summary of the community characteristics described in Sect. 5.2.

It also appears from preceding examples that the market has been used as a social tool, at the service of various morally inspired goals often sanctified by a particular religious worldview. Not primarily aiming at wealth accumulation would not necessarily imply that the enterprise would resist any opportunity to grow. A respondent told me that 'a stagnant firm is destined to fail, growth keeps the momentum going'; however, the ultimate aim for the existence of the firm was often to help the next generation sustain themselves. Growth of the firm can be

Table 5.1 Socioeconomic characteristics of religious enterprising communities described in Sect. 5.2

Community	Entrepreneurial activities	Sociocultural characteristics	Religious characteristics	Concept of wealth	Concept of individual success	References
Marwaris	Trade and commerce, finance, manufacturing, retail, extensive family networks, and community associations	Strong family networks, community associations, philanthropic contributions	Hinduism: Karma and Dharma, emphasis on ethical business practices and fulfilling community obligations	A means to fulfill dharma and karma, ensure community welfare	Based on business acumen, philanthropy, and social contributions	Timberg and Das (2015), Nakatani (2014) and Taknet (2016)
Jews	Finance, technology, law, medicine, education, and charitable organizations	Emphasis on education, philanthropy, and social justice	Judaism: Tzedakah (charitable giving), Tikkun Olam (repairing the world)	Means to fulfill religious obligations, promote social justice	Based on charitable giving, support for communal institutions	Baron (1993), Sarna (2019) and Tenenbaum (1993)
Parsis	Trade, industry, textiles, shipbuilding, ethical business conduct, and community welfare	Strong community welfare, ethical business practices	Zoroastrianism: Good thoughts, good words, good deeds, using wealth for community benefit	Tool for righteous living, community welfare	Based on contributions to community welfare, ethical business conduct	Desai and Bharat (2017), Luhrmann (1996) and Palsetia (2001)
Druze	Agriculture, commerce, medicine, engineering, and the internal support system	Closed social system, communal cohesion, mutual guarantee (kafalah)	Islamic principles of social justice and supporting those in need	Means to ensure the community's security and prosperity	Based on maintaining community cohesion and mutual support	Firro (2021) and Van Eijk (2014)

(continued)

Table 5.1 (continued)

Community	Entrepreneurial activities	Sociocultural characteristics	Religious characteristics	Concept of wealth	Concept of individual success	References
Mennonites	Agriculture, crafts, small-scale manufacturing, and cooperative business models	Simple living, mutual aid, communal projects	Anabaptist Christianity: Humility, detachment from worldly possessions, focus on meeting basic needs, and community	Means to meet basic needs, contribute to the community	Based on contributions to communal projects, mutual aid	Hostetler (1993), Thiessen (2013), Reid (2015) and Rogers et al. (2013)
Amish	Agriculture, crafts, small-scale manufacturing, and cooperative business models	Simple living, mutual aid, communal projects	Anabaptist Christianity: Humility, detachment from worldly possessions, focus on meeting basic needs, and community	Means to meet basic needs, avoid worldly temptations	Based on contributions to communal projects, mutual aid	Hostetler (1993), Thiessen (2013), Reid (2015) and Rogers et al. (2013)
Armenians	Trade, crafts, technology, education, and tight-knit community networks	Formation of guilds and benevolent societies, supporting cultural and religious institutions	Christian values: Stewardship, charity, supporting families, the church, and the less fortunate	Tool for survival, community advancement	Based on support for cultural and religious institutions, benevolent societies	Suny (1993), Cora (2018) and Saroyan (2022)
Sikhs	Agriculture, transport, global business ventures, and community service	Strong sense of community, focus on hard work, and communal harmony	Sikhism: Vand Chhako (sharing with others), Seva (selfless service)	Means to support the less fortunate, ensure communal harmony	Based on acts of charity, community service	Elsberg (2019), Kaur (2013) and Takhar and Jakobsh (2023)

(continued)

Table 5.1 (continued)

Community	Entrepreneurial activities	Sociocultural characteristics	Religious characteristics	Concept of wealth	Concept of individual success	References
Mormons	Finance, real estate, retail, self-reliance, internal social networks	Cooperative economic setup, mutual support	Mormonism: Self-reliance, service, viewing wealth as a means to achieve spiritual and communal goals	Means to achieve spiritual and communal goals	Based on self-reliance, support for the community	Benedict (2007) and Bushman and Bushman (2001)
Maori	Tourism, agriculture, and cultural industries	Communal living, preservation of cultural heritage, and blending traditional practices with modern techniques	Māori spirituality: Concept of mana (spiritual authority and prestige), contributions to community and cultural preservation	Means to preserve cultural heritage, support the community	Based on contributions to the community, preservation of cultural heritage	McCarthy et al. (2013)
Yoruba	Agriculture, trade, crafts, and cultural industries	Strong family and clan networks, communal ties	Yoruba religion: Emphasis on communal ties and family support	Means to support family and clan networks	Based on acts of generosity, leadership within the community	Falola and Adebayo (2000) and Adekson (2004)

sought to expand one's capacity to contribute more, or ensure the financial future of the coming generations of the family. A firm may exploit new opportunities to grow without compromising its primary aims to facilitate the community members directly or indirectly. There are many examples of enterprises initiated by the members of a particular enterprising community, including the ones I studied, which rose to prominence on a national scale, if not internationally. Still, the pride of the founding family typically remained with the idea of how well they can contribute to the community or society at large. In the three communities I studied, the image of a family owning large enterprises is typically built around what they give back, not how much they accumulate (Javaid et al., 2020; Papanek, 1972). Many firms eventually get listed in stock exchanges also, and are among the largest in Pakistan (Sikandar & Mahmood, 2018).

However, the affluence comes with its own, as the family owners, at some point, may turn their interests toward profits and support the community more as a show-off. This points to the possibility that the charitable legacy of the family after gaining riches may be broken as the third or fourth generation takes over, where the focus may shift toward financial interests, and less toward how the firm benefits the community. The subsequent generation of affluent families can likely forget how their elders rose to prominence, that is, not by striving for their self-interest, but with the help of their community, through mutual support. Such mutual support becomes critical for the long-term survival of the community, as each individual and family needs community support at some point in their lives. The communities I studied could not have been able to sustain themselves economically in the absence of such an environment. This becomes evident when a review of each community's history reveals the various crises they have experienced. In this context, I will now provide a brief background of the three communities I explored in my doctoral research.

5.2.1 Memon

In 1424-1425AD Thatta, the capital of the Sindh province at that time, some 700 Hindu families belonging to the Lohana tribe changed their religion to Islam. The Muslim saint who inspired them to change their religion called them *Momin* (Pious Muslim), which later changed to Memon. The locals were furious and became hostile to the group, pushing the new Muslims to migrate to Kathiawar in the district of Gujarat. Later, due to some socioeconomic reasons, the community got dispersed into several geographical regions, "all over Kutch and Gujrat" (Memon, July 2011, p. 8).[4] Those who settled in the Hala region were later known

[4] Reference to the periodicals from the Memon community is made as '(Memon, Mon 20XX, p. ##)' from now onwards. Memon magazine until November 2014 can be downloaded from http://www.wmopc.com/indexma.php, while magazines after April 2015 can be downloaded from http://wmoworld.com/the-Memon/.

as Halai or Halari Memon. The ones who settled in Kutch were called Kutchi; likewise, those who settled in Okha Bundar were later called Okhai Memon. Similarly, Memon settled in Sindh and was referred to as Sindhi Memon. The division continued in later centuries, and the Memon community was further subdivided into smaller fragments over time. Some of these sub-groups were open to other sub-groups for "assistance or information they required" (Memon, July 2011, p. 9) while some were not. For example, "Kutchi Memon jamaats had this policy of mutual trust without any discrimination. However, in sharp contrast, the Memon castes of Kathiawar and Gujarat excluded members of other castes for the benefit of the local membership. Their exclusionary nature, likely a result of a self-centric tendency, did not work for them either, eventually breaking them down into smaller fragments of sub-groups (Memon, July 2011). Despite migration, the Memon community kept on facing tough times due to the dominance of other communities, Marhattas and Marwaris specifically, on the economic landscape of the region.

Browsing through the newsletters and magazines published by the Memon community, one may note that the community members would migrate to regions in the subcontinent and around the world when their survival would become difficult due to either famine or worsening law and order situation. Outside the subcontinent, Memons migrated to East Africa, South Africa, Burma, Sri Lanka, further down the Far East, etc. After 1947, some community members belonging to sub-groups like Bantva, Okhai, Halari, Jaipur, Agra, kathiawari, and Kutiyana, even came to Karachi and established themselves permanently in the port city of Pakistan, which later became the economic hub of the country. Nowadays, they reside in many parts of the world connected through the World Memon Organization. The community's monthly periodical reported that Memons "organized themselves and continued to face the odds with courage, patience, endurance, fortitude and hard work ... discipline, decorum, and unity" (Memon, July 2011, p. 9). Memons, it is said, started from small and local trades, traveled to far-off places with caravans, and gradually raised their economic status. During the British era, the Hindus lost their dominance in the power structures and trade, and the Memon rose as one of the affluent communities in the subcontinent. Their trade relations with the British government during the First World War also reportedly contributed greatly to their rise toward economic affluence in the region. Later, affluent Memons financially supported Muhammad Ali Jinnah (also known as Quaid-e-Azam), whose efforts led to the creation of Pakistan. Memon also contributed to the Pakistan Movement (Memon, July 2011). Memon's resilience as a community, it appears, helped them thrive after every crisis that often destroyed much of what they had. Despite the odds, they are still believed to be one of the most affluent and thriving business communities in Pakistan.[5]

[5]For more details: see https://www.wmona.com/the-origin-of-memons-as-community-and-their-history/

5.2.2 Delhiwala

According to a tradition, the ancestors of Delhi Saudagaran (traders), commonly known as Delhiwala, were the descendants of the Aryan race (Saudagar, May 2015, p. 62)[6] who converted to Islam in 1324 AD in the subcontinent, some 700 years ago, in the Indian region. According to the community periodical, their spiritual mentor, who inspired them to change their religion, advised them to 'live as a community, establish matrimonial ties among one another, do trade as it has more *barakah*,[7] preach Islam so that missionaries are raised among the community, and establish religious seminaries to produce more Hafiz'.[8] He prophesied that if they followed this advice, then wherever they go, 'they will shine like a sun', and that 'they will be religiously minded and would be involved in worldly life only on a need basis'. In 1656 AD, around half of the population of Delhi died in a famine. Several families left the city. By that time, the groups who were unfriendly to the Mughals began to dominate the trade, while the local Muslims did not have an entrepreneurial appetite. So Khurram, the third son of the Mughal Emperor Shahjahan, from 1628 to 1658 AD, reportedly established a colony in Delhi by the name of Shahjahanabad. The emperor's son dedicated a large area to Delhi Saudagaran in that colony. The land was allotted in 1657 AD to 64 Khoja Sheikh and Chinioti families at the request of Allama Saadullah Chinioti, who was Shahjahan's top vizier. With the permission of the Emperor, the land was sanctioned, and the families were invited to settle in the dedicated location in the colony. Allama Saadullah Chinioti himself traveled to Bahira, Khoshab, and Sargodha to invite the families. On the promise of the Emperor to provide subsidies, the 64 families mutually decided to send a few of their members to Delhi and evaluate the situation. Some 350 men, women, and children traveled to Delhi, Shajahanabad, under the protection of the security provided by the Emperor. Hakeem Shamsuddin Chawala led this caravan. After arrival, those families not only established their homes but also set up markets and factories (Saudagar, Apr 2010, p. 48–50). The community remained there and later fought against the British army in the War of Independence of 1857. After the British won, the land that was gifted by Shahjahan's son to the members of the community was taken away; however, later, after receiving amnesty from the Victorian Queen, the community reportedly returned to Delhi. After the partition, a significant majority of them migrated to Pakistan and settled there, and eventually had to start yet again (Saudagar, May 2014, p. 89).[9]

---

[6] Reference to the magazine Saudagar, a periodical of Delhiwala community, is made as '(Saudagar, Mon 20XX, p. ##)' from now onwards. These periodicals can be downloaded from https://saudagar.pk/?page_id=38

[7] Barakah: Extra ordinary but unexplained and unplanned efficiency in some outcome, that is believed to be a gift by God for following the moral code.

[8] Hafiz: A person who has memorized the entire book of The Holy Quran, from cover to cover.

[9] More details: https://web.archive.org/web/20040324015425/http:/www.hinduonnet.com/thehindu/mp/2003/03/06/stories/2003030600560300.htm.

5.2.3 Chinioti

Chinioti Sheikh, another dominant entrepreneurial community in Pakistan, originated from a small city called Chiniot, some 158 km northwest of Lahore, the capital of Punjab province, in Pakistan. This city gained its significance as a trade center during the era of the Mughals in the subcontinent. According to tradition, some Hindu business families, namely Talawar, Puri, Khanna, and Kapur, who became Muslim during the reign of Mughal emperor Akbar some five centuries earlier, came to be known as Chinioti Sheikhs. After accepting Islam, they continued their trading profession. Later, they identified themselves as *Sheikh*, *Khuwaja*, or *Khoja* (Saqib, 2016).[10] At the beginning of the nineteenth century, some families from the Maggun tribe situated in the Pani Pat area also migrated to a village called Wara near Chiniot. Some of them settled in Mohalla Bhoran in Chiniot district. These migrants gradually established matrimonial ties with local Muslims in Chiniot. Additionally, some families belonging to the tribes situated in other regions migrated to Chiniot. Vohra families who migrated from Gujrat (India) are now in the majority in the Chiniot community. These were a few trade-oriented families who further established social and economic ties with the locals in Chiniot. The present generation of these families still mentions the sub-caste with their names. (Saqib, 2016).

Historically, the city was dominated by Hindu landlords and moneylenders, who are said to have restricted the economic opportunities for Muslims. At the end of the nineteenth century, poverty made some locals migrate with their families to other cities in the subcontinent for the sake of economic opportunities. Several of them led the foundation of firms, which later became business empires of Pakistan despite beginning from small-scale roadside shops with negligible resources. Some of them landed on the list of the richest families in the country (Saqib, 2016). At the time of the partition of the subcontinent and the creation of Pakistan, several of these families, who established businesses in various parts of India, had to return. Despite the incident of partition destroying their business and disconnecting several of them from their family members, their entrepreneurial spirit reportedly remained intact. They again migrated to cities in West and East Pakistan to set up their businesses. These cities include Karachi, Lahore, Faisalabad, Hyderabad, and Sukkur in West Pakistan; whereas in East Pakistan (now Bangladesh), they selected Dhaka, Khulna, Chittagong, Narayn Gung, Sandar Band, etc. The selection of these cities was made keeping in view the nature of the information they received regarding the opportunities available in each city. They started again with negligible resources and regained their status as another affluent community in Pakistan by the end of the twentieth century. The prominent success stories in the community, reports Saqib, motivated others to escape poverty through perseverance, improvising with minimal resources, and

[10] Saqib (2016) was the only credible and the most detailed source found on Chinioti history, therefore, the particulars about community's history is based on his work.

personal sacrifice to achieve economic prosperity for their family and community (Saqib, 2016).

The success story of several Chinioti entrepreneurs started with a modest trade of hides. All other kinds of trade until the late nineteenth century were dominated by other communities adhering to Hinduism, who would avoid working with hides because of religious reasons. This niche was the only venue that early entrepreneurs of the community identified as an opportunity to excel. They, it is said, started frugally, worked like laborers, sold their products through street shops while transporting them on bicycles and donkey carts, and maintained a frugal lifestyle to reinvest profits in business. However, through hard work, intelligence, determination, and strength of character, family and community support their trade of raw leather and related products is believed to have expanded to multiple continents in a few decades. The handful of early success stories likely inspired the whole community. The next generation of these entrepreneurs expanded into textile, manufacturing, and other industries. Saqib (2016) suggests that the total number of Chinioti families across Pakistan and worldwide would be around 40,000, while the total population of the community is around 300,000. The majority of top entrepreneurs from the community do not live in Chiniot City but have maintained their connections and participated in several social welfare projects in the city. The Chinioti story is also an example of how a community can strive to raise itself from poverty to one of the affluent classes in the country through hard work and determination, despite being completely derailed multiple times in the last 100 years.

This rise of these three communities in Pakistan has not been a walk in a park for their members, as the partition event in 1947 brought many families to bare subsistence level as they had to migrate to Pakistan, where again in 1973, the nationalization movement, they lost what they had built in the meantime (Akhter & Rafiq, 2022). The political conditions inside Pakistan, and in the region due to the Russian Invasion of Afghanistan, then the American invasion, and the subsequent involvement of Pakistan in the (sic) war on terror, adversely affected the economy as well (Jamshed et al., 2022; Lieven, 2012). Despite all these ups and downs, the communities persisted and were able to regain their economic affluence after every phase of a downward spiral. Many among them also left for other places, where they replicated the same communal environment through trust, cooperation, and reciprocity. Peredo (2014) enlists various natures of crises that spark a communal effort for economic survival, some of which were faced by the aforementioned communities multiple times. Peredo's list includes "(1) economic crisis and a lack of individual opportunity in the community, (2) processes of social and cultural disintegration, (3) social and political alienation of the community from mainstream society, (4) environmental degradation, and (5) post-war reconstruction" (p. 266). From this list, the aforementioned communities have at least faced the first, third, and fifth during their history, often several times, yet they managed to sustain themselves.

The persistence of communities during times of crisis several times in their history hints toward the presence of a high degree of social cohesion and a motivation to support each other, which likely increases during difficult times. An increase in resilience under pressure is a property referred to as 'antifragility' by Taleb (2012). The time of crisis tests how much individuals or families within a community are willing to support each other. Helping each other restart businesses, even providing refuge or taking responsibility for other community members during extreme circumstances. It implies that a crisis that pushes a community toward its limits can either effectively disintegrate it or become a source of increased cohesion as well during and after the crisis, depending on the capacity of each individual to sacrifice and support others voluntarily. Disintegration is likely to happen if individuals prioritize or individual families consider their self-interest over the interest of other families. A community is perhaps not a community to begin with if the individuals are more concerned about themselves, and a crisis would immediately expose the superficial nature of their engagement. A certain degree of we-ness is required at the heart of individuals capable of exercising their moral agency fully. If someone in the community gets hurt, others need to voluntarily offer support, thus increasing cohesion during the time of crisis. As per Taleb (2018), this is possible when there is a commonly held worldview that also sets a teleological purpose for the community, but is also voluntarily followed by each member of the community; however, the 'I-ness' is exercised with a sense of 'we-ness' (Falzon, 2004). A strong degree of social cohesion, embedded in a moral framework, is perhaps a prerequisite that provides the impetus for action directed toward the well-being of the collective. The crisis thus provides an excuse for social cohesion to demonstrate its effectiveness by bringing the community even closer, eventually increasing the social capital of the community.

During a time of crisis when personal survival is at stake, it appears counterintuitive that individuals become more sacrificing. It is perhaps natural for our survival instincts to get triggered in such circumstances. Paternal instincts, where parent sacrifice for their children, are also understandable. However, if the contrary, that is, altruistic behavior for a wider audience, is happening, then one may wonder what drives such behavior. Religious beliefs may explain this. A study finds that religious people are motivated by a sense of obligation rather than emotion, leading them to help others beyond their close circle, driven by their religious beliefs rather than personal attachment (Saslow et al., 2012). Multiple cross-national studies suggest that nonbelievers are less likely to "endorse moral values that serve group cohesion" and are more likely to have a more "consequentialist view of morality" (Ståhl, 2021). These studies were not conducted in a crisis-like situation; however, one can only speculate how, during the uncertainty of a long-term crisis, in particular, like forced migration due to a threat of a more powerful dominant community, nonbelievers with a consequentialist view would react.

Irrespective of the potential reaction of a nonbeliever, these studies show that a believer may have a strong rationale to remain moral and altruistic during the uncertainty and chaos of a crisis. A crisis can be micro, like related to the survival of a family firm, or it could be more macro, as mentioned above in the preceding examples. It could be natural or manmade, either social or economic. Whatever its cause, scale, or form, a crisis has the potential to evoke tension within the affected individuals, details of which were discussed in previous chapters. The meta-norms set by Islam were found to be facilitative during moments of crisis, as per the respondents of the three communities I studied, which motivate individuals or families to balance the social and the economic while appropriately choosing a response, keeping in view the nature of the crisis. Respondent's religious beliefs emphasized nurturing and empowering an individual's moral agency and instilling the concern of the collective, even making it mandatory to facilitate others as per one's capacity. Islam's tendency to decentralize collective responsibility to the individual level perhaps makes the religion antifragile. As soon as believers of Islam become aware of a need, individuals are expected to respond to it, often more proactively, without waiting for permission from a centralized institutional authority (Hallaq, 2013; Javaid, 2024). Such spontaneity can increase trust and cohesion among the collective, particularly during moments of crisis. Even during ordinary times, mutual care and reciprocity have been demonstrated by community members. The following is a brief description of the social and socioeconomic landscape, along with how the community members support each other formally and informally. This description is based on a review of limited literature and the research I conducted in my doctoral thesis.

5.3 Characteristics of Pakistani Enterprising Communities

Some of the prominent communities in Pakistan are Memon, Delhiwala, Chinioti, Dawoodi Bohra, and Ismaili. I studied the first three for my doctoral research, while the particularities of the last two are described here in light of the limited literature available on them. The subsequent discussion focuses on the social character, socioeconomic landscape, and mutual support mechanisms within the communities, encompassing both formal and informal dimensions. Relevant literature is cited accordingly. When presenting verbatim quotes from respondent interviews, citations will follow the format (AS23), where "AS" denotes the respondent's initials and "23" refers to the specific code assigned to the quote extracted from the interview transcripts available with the author. Apart from interview data, Newsletters from the Memon community and community periodicals of the Delhiwala community titled Saudagar were also used. There are many overlapping themes between the communities and fewer differences, therefore, it is possible to discuss their characteristics simultaneously, which now follows:

5.3.1 The Community Character

Memon often live close to one another, tied to each other via social and economic lines. There are specific areas in the city that are famous for housing the majority of the Memon, such as Kharadar (MF 17, 18). Memon are believed to be one of the peaceful and affluent communities in Pakistan. A respondent affirmed, 'if a Memon's son becomes a gangster, then it would be the day of judgment' (MA 47). A prominent Memon entrepreneur paints the following picture of community life and how he feels about it in the community newsletter:

> I yearned to go home, to the camaraderie, warmth, and brotherhood of the Memon Community. I sensed that our people were different. We were a united, helpful, and benevolent tribe that was compassionate towards our fellow human beings. Philanthropy was in our blood, and although we had very little of our own, we were keen to share with our brothers and sisters … [it was] a close-knit community, where everybody knew each other, had time for one another, and help was always at hand. (Memon, Feb 2016, p. 2)

The Memons are known—even mocked often—for their frugal lifestyle. However, their frugality, simplicity, and humility were originally a religious-spiritual practice that eventually became part of their culture. The Bohra community appears to come closer, while members of other communities, especially the elders, maintain a humble lifestyle; however, the Memon community's character is renowned in this context. The respondents who were selected through purposive sampling without having 'humility' as a selection criterion in mind were still found to be very humble. Dressing very modestly, naturally presenting themselves as down to earth, attributing all their financial success to God's grace, for example. The frugal lifestyle also has some economic and social advantages. Frugality enables them to keep the cost of business to its minimum. A Chinioti respondent even praised and said, 'We cannot out-compete the Memon today as we have increased our expenses, as our children want to go on vacations to Singapore and Switzerland and eat KFC all the time' (SJ 24). Many memons still live in their ancestors' homes, maintaining a very simple lifestyle, despite being billionaires. The money saved reportedly helps them in business, particularly during market recessions, and contributes greatly toward welfare activities. However, the new generation is described by respondents as being influenced by consumerist trends, often spending more on luxuries. The consumerist trend is also apparent in the new generation of Chinioti and Delhiwala. In the Chinioti community, a show-off culture has penetrated to an alarming extent. According to multiple members of the Chinioti community, some members, including Chinioti women, even show off their affluence through the choice of their wardrobe, for example, in social gatherings, including funerals, where a silent competition of sorts appears to be happening. This is a recent phenomenon with potential adverse consequences for social integration that is discussed in Chapter 6.

Social gathering is an integral part of the Chinioti community culture. A Chinioti respondent suggested 'we love to flock together' (SJ 26). Community members often socialize with each other at events like wedding ceremonies, funerals, religious festivals like Eid, and specially planned events like Eid Millan parties. Product exhibitions are often arranged by women entrepreneurs at community events (SJ 37). Face-to-face interaction, which was deeply embedded in Chinioti culture, however, is said to have reduced due to digital interactions (SJ 33, 34). Chinioti respondents referred to their community as *baradari*, that is, an extended kinship network, where members are connected through social and matrimonial ties (SJ 1). The literature highlights that strong family linkages can play a key role in business development and subsequently sustain family and community life in enterprising communities. For example, Memon often shares key management positions in companies owned by their relatives, subsequently overlapping their social and business interests. The owners of "Adamjee's and Bawany's [Memon entrepreneurial families]... have long been related to each other through family ties" (Levin, 1974, p. 239). Many decades ago Papanek also made a similar observation about Memon and other communities that still holds true:

> Additional features of the business communities include the prevailing traditional custom of arranged marriages within the group, which often affects the ownership and inheritance of assets, and a frequently highly conservative tendency about the status of women and the role of formal education. (Papanek, 1972, p. 30)

Marriages typically happen within the Memon community, and the examples of a Memon marrying a non-Memon are rare (MT 81). According to a respondent, marriages only happened within the sub-groups or casts within the community; however, he also suggested that now different casts are getting connected through matrimonial ties (IO 71). Delhiwala also prefers to establish matrimonial ties within the community (KS 44). They claim to be related to each other through ancestral ties, as rhetorically, 'everyone's grandmother in the community is the same' (Saudagar Magazine, March 2014, p.100, 103; TP 6). The social and family ties are valued to such an extent that after the demise of any elder in the Delhiwala community, their immediate and extended family members, friends, and community associates write memoirs to express their grief, containing accounts of memorable interactions with the deceased. These memoirs are published in the community's monthly magazine, Saudagar. Some of the issues of Saudagar are filled with these memoirs, particularly when the deceased is a famous community figure with an active record of participation in community development activities (see, for example, Saudagar, Jan 2011, Feb 2011, Mar 2011, Sep 2011, Feb 2012 issues). In the editions of the Saudagar reviewed, it was observed that any personality with a track record of community service was praised. The details about economic life and entrepreneurial achievements of personalities were also found on several occasions; however, their mention was overshadowed by the details related to community service, praises of their character, and the nature of relationships they had with other community members. They resemble the Memon in this context as, according to Levin (1974), "reputation for being pious Muslims, which has been attached to the Memons, contributes greatly to their commercial success" (p. 232). However, things are rapidly changing in the newer generations.

The kinship network remained inclusive of every related member, irrespective of their capability to make an economic contribution toward the family or community. In case a person is handicapped temporarily or permanently, the community would unconditionally come forward to take care of such a person. Adherence to a religious code further reinforces such behavior. However, such support may not be available to individuals who are not part of the community, at least directly (indirectly, maybe via the welfare organizations managed by the communities). Egbert (1998), while analyzing the Bohra community of Tanzania, argued that it is only by birth or marriage that a person can become a member. Only a small minority in a country can enjoy the economic advantage offered by the Bohra community. The Ismaili community, being similar to Bohras, perhaps follows a similar exclusivity. At the time of establishing matrimonial relationships, one may assume that there is a significant bias toward their community members; an alternative scenario hasn't been reported either by Papanek (1972) or Levin (1974). Such exclusivity is perhaps a general trend among kinship-based ethnically oriented community networks. To establish matrimonial and subsequently business relationships, elders need to be aware of the whereabouts of the other party. Since most marriages are decided by the elders, it's easier to decide choose a bride for their sons or a husband for their daughters who have grown up in front of their eyes. The same would perhaps be true for business relationships, as building trust with a stranger is relatively difficult in the sociocultural context of the subcontinent, which includes Pakistan and India (Afghan & Wiqar, 2007; Menning, 1997). One can safely assume that this exclusivity, at least in the context of building matrimonial relations, which are often done by affluent families with an economic interest in mind, is perhaps a cultural phenomenon, as the Islamic teachings do not encourage such exclusivity. However, this observation may not be generalized in the context of the employment opportunities created by other communities like the Memon in Pakistan. For example, factory labor in their firms need not belong to the same community (Papanek, 1972). A similar observation can be conveniently made for other businesses owned by Delhiwala and Chinioti in Pakistan.

5.3.2 Socioeconomic Character

Until the previous generation, the economic environment was more egalitarian and less competitive. Competition was typically avoided with fellow community members (Levin, 1974), a norm that now seems to be changing. Excessive risk-taking was also not the norm. Yet their entrepreneurial success was not much affected. This implies that pro-cooperative behavior leads to a win–win for all stakeholders and is believed to add barakah. Islamic values also encourage altruistic behavior, sharing instead of accumulating, and avoiding conflicts (Al-Ghazali, 2007). According to Akhtar et al. (2015), demonstration of such a behavior is an extension of the aura of the family, beyond the family, as competitors in the market are not seen as competitors, but as members of an extended kinship network. Even if you do not know them, the likelihood that they could be a distant relative cannot be ruled out. Even if they are not, they may become a family member after forming matrimonial ties with one's son or daughter with a potential match on the other side. The urge to remain part of the collective, reinforced by religious meta-norms, eventually strengthens the spirit of cooperation over material competition, or at least suppresses the ugly forms of competitive behavior. The sense of competition at a personal and professional level is said to be rising among younger Memon; however, the community elders seem to be more concerned about maintaining communal ties even today. Delhiwala maintains a soft corner for their *baradari* as long as the person is genuinely in need; however, this may not be the case with potential competitors in the market, despite the competitor being from the community. However, it is unlikely that this competition takes ugly forms where attempts to destroy or take over the business of one's competitor are actively sought. The Chinioti also compete with each other as rivals in the marketplace. It is believed by Chinioti that healthy competition benefits all (Saqib, 2016). 'Incidents of unhealthy competitions are seldom', suggests a respondent (SS 36). The elders of the community have been particular about not harming others for the sake of their own benefit (Saqib, 2016). 'The culture of hard work, honoring commitment and mutual support was common in the community and is considered the key to success' (WK 20; SS 2). Such cooperative behavior induces a level of trust between members of the community as well, which also reinforces the culture of solidarity among the baradari members (Afghan & Wiqar, 2007). Menning (2010) emphasized the significance of this 'personalized trust' when entrepreneurs of Surat City (India) face uncertain market conditions, which applies to the environment within Pakistani enterprising communities as well. Menning notes:

> "This general-purpose aspect of personalized trust is especially important under conditions of highly imperfect information, such as are present in the widely fluctuating markets in Surat. In these situations, trust in person functions as a sort of bounded rationality in the face of uncertainties about external events and system … "Reliance on moral bonds and reputation may prove more rational in some circumstances than adherence to formal rules and routines as a means of improving efficiency, reducing transaction costs and insuring compliance in business deals." (Menning, 1997, p. 83)

A much broader system of support exists in different communities where well-off individuals or families are assumed responsible for providing support to the underprivileged class of their community. The ease of entry through community support, easily available financial support, social capital, information access, and connections with suppliers and potential customers make self-employment a preferred career choice for community members. Such support can potentially produce a continuous stream of opportunity creation within an enterprising community (Dana et al., 2019; Danes et al., 2008; Javaid et al., 2020). In this context, cultural and religious values play their part in providing a discourse to reinforce the shared experience (Farooq et al., 2019; Kumar et al., 2022). The *baradari*, the kinship network, also becomes a source of labor, expertise, market intelligence, and connections with potential suppliers, vendors, and investors. When a Chinioti starts a business, often the customer is already known, making it convenient to make the first sale (JV 7; WK 2). A customer who facilitates a new entrepreneur does not mean that there is any unusual compromise on the delivery and quality of the product, and new entrepreneurs are also not supposed to expect a buyer in the community to compromise on product quality for the sake of maintaining relationships. Suppliers can be located likewise in the community, and new suppliers from the community may be preferred over those outside the community if there is no considerable difference in price, product quality, and delivery (WK 59). The community-organized events often facilitate the maintenance of social ties and also serve as a means to share business opportunities and market experiences. The flow of information related to market opportunities is said to enable Chinioti entrepreneurs to make investment and business decisions (SS 18; WK 24; KL, p. 245). Such interactions can also allow Chinioti people to learn about the new ventures their fellow *baradari* members have started (JV 1). Likewise, the new venture can find customers within the community from such socializing activities, while their potential customers can also expect products or services at a lower price. New entrepreneurs can sometimes also find sympathetic buyers within the community (SJ 13, 37; WK 59).

According to the respondents from the Delhiwala community, the opportunities were also exposed to them by some of their 'friends or relatives' (TP 36; IO 9), or during their experience within the family business at the early stages of their entrepreneurial career (SAR 29, 30, 31). They were also introduced to them via 'the potential partners in their friend's circle' (KS 2, 5) or by 'a past employer' (FA 3). There are examples where the Delhiwala started something with considerable corporate experience (FA 1, 18; KS 1, 51). In all cases, business opportunities emerged from the family, personal, or professional networks of the respondents. There is no data on how many Delhiwala do business; however, according to Mr. Irfan Asli Pari, Honorary General Secretary of the social welfare wing JPSD (Jamiyat Punjabi Saudagaran Delhi), around 70% of the 200,000 families could have an entrepreneurial orientation (IAP 62). The community elders have continued their family business or have extended it; however, the millennials and the Gen-Z in the community appear to be experimenting with new business ideas (SAR 13; NS 59; Saudagar, Feb 2016, p.42). The rationale for the respondents to have their own business has been to follow the family legacy (NS 1; TP 1, 35; SAR 1; RS 1), also because they were brought up at home (KS 16; NS 43). A Delhiwala respondent suggested that money earned through a business done honestly has 'barakah' (TP 73), and business is expanded to accommodate the coming generation, not primarily to expand personal riches (TP 63; NS 48). 'It is in our genes,' (FA 9).

After the partition Delhiwala restarted their businesses with negligible resources (RS 4; TP 18; JBS 4; 1212, p. 69; SAR 22, 24; Saudagar, June 2016, p. 90, 92), some also carry forward their family businesses (RS 1; TP 1, 35; NS 1). A significant number of the respondents were in the business their fathers had established after immigration. Some also diversify into new markets, perhaps right after migrating to Pakistan or after several years of operating in the same market. It was also mentioned by a Delhiwala respondent that there is a negligible unemployment rate in the community because community members actively facilitate those in need (TP 92; SAR, 54). It was exclusively mentioned by one respondent that Delhiwala does not share opportunities and resources with other community members (NS 35, 36). However, there are other examples to counter this claim. Stories regarding business failures were shared within the close circle (SAR, 14), and respondents received business ideas from friends (TP 36; IO 6). Several Delhiwala have been reported to help others in starting their own business (SAR 55; IAP 60; Saudagar, Jan 2011, p.79; Apr 2014, p.21). Some community elders are also famous for mentoring the young ones (TP 5). Papanek (1972) has also endorsed this trend in the entrepreneurial communities he studied, suggesting that these communities allow a 'considerable amount of social mobility' within their boundaries. There is no class barrier for any member having entrepreneurial intentions. Delhiwala often sends their children to businesses owned by other community members, as fathers may have a soft corner and a lenient attitude toward their children (TP 3).

The guidance available in the immediate network is also a critical factor that enables Chinioti entrepreneurs to select which business proposition to pursue (UL 2, 4, 6; KL, p. 116). Informal partnerships (within and outside the family) where multiple partners pool in their capital to start a business are reported as common (SS 53), implying a general level of trust already among the partnering members. It is recommended that, to start or expand a business, profits can be reinvested or capital borrowed from the family (father in the majority of cases, father-in-law in some cases) on an interest-free basis, or a partner can be sought who already has enough capital (SJ 3; AsB 45). Banks are exclusively avoided because they charge interest, which is strictly prohibited by the religion they follow (Usmani, 2002). Technical guidance to start a business is also typically available from anyone within the Chinioti community, or necessary knowledge can be acquired by working in a business owned by an immediate or distant relative (UL 2). If an idea is novel and there is a lack of necessary guidance in the community, then the elders may discourage the young ones because of a greater likelihood of failure (WK 23; UL 56).

Chinioti people are rather 'generally seen as street smart' according to one respondent (WK 69); those who do not typically look for jobs can find communal sympathies which appear to be more prevalent in the previous generation. 'Hard-working nature often encourages established businesses to accept them as working partners, if needed, in businesses owned by their relatives' (WK 17, 18, 21). Sometimes, involving an immediate or a distant relative is seen as cost-effective and a fix for trust issues. If so, then nepotism may also become a favorable phenomenon, creating a win–win-win (3 times) scenario for the employee, the employer, and the community (UL 13; JV 6). According to the respondents, such qualities enable a Chinioti to become employed and then self-employed (AB 2; KL, p. 114). 'Unemployment is rare', according to the respondents (UL 53; WK 60); however, there is no secondary data to back this claim. A Memon respondent also suggested that it is rare to find anyone unemployed in the community; again, the claim cannot be statistically substantiated. Resourceful ones often are reported to help the needy find employment within the community or facilitate them in setting up their business on a small scale (MA 28). There are several examples of Memons in the data who started their business with negligible resources. It is believed by the community members that their rise to affluence and economic dominance in the country has been a result of their character, hard work, and perseverance. The bonding within the community thus has facilitated community-based entrepreneurs to find investors, customers, and suppliers (who can also be from outside the community) through referrals and recommendations provided by community contacts. Facilitation during difficult times from stakeholders within the community, which often comes unconditionally, is also encouraged by religiously inspired cultural values. The support sustains economic activity during uncertain times and facilitates recovery after collapse.

5.3.3 *Formal and Informal Support for the Needy*

The financially struggling members of the communities in question are facilitated in a variety of formal and informal ways. This facilitation ranges from providing interest-free loans to starting their ventures, which is often done formally and informally. Loans have to be interest-free as interest is strictly prohibited in Islamic law. Apart from loans, other support in setting up a business is also provided. Memon and Delhiwala have also formally organized institutions that facilitate struggling members of the community with their health and education. For example, the All Pakistan Memon Federation is responsible for providing a platform for Memon sub-groups to interact with each other, whereas the World Memon Organization connects all Memons globally. The well-being of a respective caste or a sub-group is typically managed by a locally managed organization referred to as a *jamaat*, which is operated by volunteering elders. It is financed by the wealthy elite of the community. A jamaat collects the demographic information of the poor, which enables them to better plan for the development and welfare activities. Other key responsibilities may include setting up educational and health care institutions, providing financial support to those in need, providing residential support, helping to set up businesses, arranging marriages, issuing marriage licenses, resolving matrimonial and business disputes, running community centers and managing low-cost transport services for the community members, etc. (Memon, July 2011). It was noted that the young ones are also encouraged to participate in welfare activities, such as several young volunteers who went to the northern areas of Pakistan when it was struck by an earthquake in 2005. It was reported that such volunteerism has been part of the community's legacy. For example, before the partition of the subcontinent, a prominent member of the community was "awarded the medal of Qaiser-e-Hind" (Memon, July 2011, p. 12) for his contribution at the time of an earthquake in Quetta during the 1930s. In earlier times, some religious seminaries were also run through the donations of Memon elites. Even after the creation of Pakistan, several schools, colleges, and universities were established by the community. Memon Alam magazine reports:

> For promoting education, the large groups of Memon businessmen set up foundations & Trusts. Prominent among them are the Dawood Foundation, Suleman Dawood Dialysis Centre, Adamjee Foundation, Aziz Tabba Foundation, Aisha Bawany Waqf, and many others. These foundations and trusts donated generously toward the establishment of educational institutions throughout the country and gave generous scholarships to students of all communities for higher education. There are many vocational institutions, including Rangoonwala Centre, World Foundation Community Centre, and many ladies' tailoring schools. During the last 3 years, the World Memon Foundation Community Centre has alone trained 11,000 girls in different vocational subjects. (Suriya, 2011, p. 12)

Table 5.2 A list of facilities managed by the Memon community as described in community newsletters

Educational	Healthcare
Dawood Engineering College	Kutiyana Memon Hospital
Adamjee Science College	Bantva Khidmat Committee Hospital
Rounaq-e-Islam Girls College	Memon Medical Hospital
Usman Institute of Technology	Usman Memorial Hospital
Aisha Bawany Academy	Kathiawar Hospital
Suriya Parekh College of Liberal Arts	Hussaini Hospital
Hussain Ebrahim Jamal Institute of Chemistry-Karachi University	Bantva Anis Hospital
	Patel Hospital
Ahmed Bawany Academy	Memon Medical Complex
Dawood Public School	Bagh-e-Halar Hospital
Hashmani Post Graduate Eye Institute	Suleman Dawood Dialysis
Memon Institute of Data Processing	Memon Charitable Hospital, Hyderabad
Adamjee Institute of Information Technology	
Bagh-e-Halar School & College	

The above-mentioned welfare initiatives are generally known to facilitate people irrespective of their ethnic and religious affiliations. Likewise, in the domain of health, several hospitals have also been established by the community, which typically provide healthcare services at a subsidized price to the community members and the general population, as shown in Table 5.2.

Likewise, Jamiyat Punjabi Saudagran-e-Delhi (JPSD), the welfare wing of the Delhiwala community, claims to provide monthly financial support to widows, orphans, poor of the community. Some of the elders in the community also play an active role in mediating family, domestic, and business disputes through the platform of JPSD. Improving social bonding is another reported aim of such community-led organizations. Several affluent community members are involved in the management of the organization and actively contribute their time and charity as well. The organization runs several welfare hospitals and educational institutions in Karachi, listed in Table 5.3. The community monthly magazine Saudagar publishes a summary of welfare activities organized in these institutes.

Papanek (1972), who made his observations almost half a century ago, suggested that such initiatives are considered mandatory for wealthy individuals. Prominent businessmen within the community preside over various

Table 5.3 A list of facilities managed by JPSD as described in the community literature

Healthcare	Education and community service
Haji Fazal Ilahi General Hospital	Ismail Allahwala Boys Campus
Baigum Haji Hospital	Najam Girls School
Bilqees Memorial Hospital	Riaz Masjid
Marrium Batla Hospital	Saudagaran Cooperative Housing Society
Yahya Sootwalay Hospital	Jamiyat Taalim Al Quran
Abdul Khaliq Abdul Razzaq Hospital	Ameeniya Muslim Girls School, etc.
B.H.Y. Hospital	
Jamiyat Sabira Clinic and Diabetic Centre	
M.Y. Chandiwala Clinic	

community-managed organizations. The wealthy further supported the community in different ways, such as by giving donations, mediating conflicting parties, and providing business acumen and personal connections for solving financial problems. In this context, Papanek also gave an example from the Khoja Ismaili community:

> The most dramatic illustration of such a combination of activities and the use of leadership prestige to advance economic goals is provided by the Khoja Ismailis. One of the major functions of the well-known Jubilee 'weighings' of the Aga Khan has been the collection of funds from his followers as a religious obligation. In the last such weighing, conducted in Pakistan in the early 1950s, these funds were collected in terms of shares in a finance corporation (Platinum Jubilee Finance Corporation), and capital was subsequently lent out to members of the community through credit cooperatives and other community institutions. (Papanek, 1972, p. 28)

Dobbin (1996) has also noted the role of wealthy Ismaili families in the development of their communities on similar lines. The Bohra community's organized support is also noteworthy in this context. Egbert (1998) notes that in Tanzania Bohra community has organized an "extensive financial security system [to facilitate] ... the local community members in private and business affairs" (p. 131). The Bohra community all over the world claims to organize support for their needy members similarly. The fund is organized through the collection of "deposits, tax payments, and voluntary contributions" (p. 131), particularly from the established Bohra entrepreneurs for those in situations of individual hardships (p. 131) or those who intend to start their business for the first time. In adherence to the Islamic code, the Bohra entrepreneurs avoid investment in banks or other interest-bearing financial products. For the same reason, the fund organized by the community provides interest-free loans, which are particularly useful during economic recessions, preventing businesses from going bankrupt. On the contrary, the high interest rate on loans from the banks during economic recessions reportedly created cash flow problems for small businesses in addition to the spiritual discomfort caused to the borrower. The community fund would therefore help the members during a crisis, but also can be used to set up businesses, thus enabling the community members to achieve economic independence and become contributing members of the community. In exchange for such support, the community members have to adhere to the communal code established by the Bohra religious authority. To provide loans, the Bohra community has one of the most organized setups to provide interest-free loans to its members. There are examples also in the Chinioti community of struggling entrepreneurs who received interest-free loans from the affluent class within the community (Saqib, 2016); however, nowadays, startup capital is typically provided by an immediate family member, particularly by the entrepreneur's father (SS 17; UL 5). Collapsing Entrepreneurs can receive support to bounce back on their feet from immediate relatives and community members, depending on their level of relationship with others (WK 41, 61). This happens informally in the Chinioti community.

The significance of informal support has been observed by Basu (1998), who studied Pakistani entrepreneurs in the UK. He noted that the long-run success of

Pakistani entrepreneurs depended on "access to and use of informal (personal and family) sources of capital at the time of business start-up … access to informal sources of information through other family or community members being in the same line of business" (p. 317) is another advantage community-based entrepreneurs have. Similarly, in Surat city (India), various entrepreneurial communities do business on informal lines, according to Menning (1997). The financial and information support that exists within the "extended kin ties and the putative or mythical kinship uniting members of the same caste or religious community … [is preferred over] "formal and impersonal types of outside support and organization (p. 73) by the community members. Menning notes:

> "When an individual has access to zero-interest loans from his family firm or his ethnic community, he has little need to approach lenders such as banks or moneylenders for capital. In the same way, entrepreneurs often prefer to get advice and training from family and caste members rather than relying on external sources like state agencies, vocational schools, and so on." (p. 73)

Papanek (1972) describes that the younger members belonging to the underprivileged class within the communities in Pakistan were facilitated first through employment and later in acquiring "entrepreneurial positions" (Papanek, 1972, p. 30) by the wealthier businessmen of the same community. Papanek further notes that the junior "members of business communities have had extensive training [from seniors in their community] in business skills and established connections with a network of information and credit facilities within the community itself. In addition, membership in a business community serves to identify a person in terms of a significant network when his creditworthiness is evaluated by outside agencies or when he seeks employment … [This tendency] to include a range of socioeconomic classes is are extremely significant aspect of the operation of these traditional social groupings" (p. 30). A Chinioti entrepreneur in Karachi, who owned a family-managed business of manufacturing and exporting tents, even housed an entire ancestral village within the premises of the factory. A hostel of sorts was maintained for the villagers who were expected to work as laborers. The son of the owner whom I interviewed was not happy with the arrangement, as these villagers barely contributed to the productivity of the firm; however, they were still tolerated as his father wished to support them. Whether the new generation of the respective communities will continue the legacy of their elders to support each other formally and informally or not has become a point of concern for the community elders I interviewed. The new generation was claimed to be more materialistic and concerned more about improving their lifestyle. In the Delhiwala community, there is a rising concern about class consciousness, which is increasing the distance among community members. There are examples where community members have refused to help each other and yet have spent lavishly on their children's weddings. If such trends spread, then the consequences on the social sustainability of the communities are not hard to anticipate.

The above sketch is based on the primary data I collected through interviews and some previous studies. It shows how certain social and economic activities in the community are shaped by religious beliefs, where economic resources are essentially seen as a means for the well-being of the community. By putting the economic at the service of the social—that is not built around the tribal (emotional) instincts, but rather on a moral framework, sanctioned by a set of transcendental meta-norms—the conflict between the devouring nature of the economic (as seen in capitalism) and the exclusionary nature of the socioemotional (as seen in tribalistic cultures) can perhaps be avoided. The meta-normative framework of Islam, for example, does not encourage accumulation for the sake of the family and tribe, but rather expects the affluent ones to keep expanding their contribution beyond the circle of their family, and tribe. This is done both by paying charity, and also by forming economic relationships, like giving employment to outsiders as long as they qualify, and by engaging with vendors and suppliers irrespective of their community background. The communities discussed above, perhaps, have been doing the same, except until recently; examples are emerging that indicate a rise in material competition for personal gains that should alert the elders concerned about the social sustainability of their community. More details on a micro level, that is, a sketch of what happens inside the family and the family enterprise, are discussed in the coming chapters.

References

Adekson, M. (2004). Indigenous family work in Nigeria: The Yoruba experience. In *Global perspectives in family therapy* (pp. 146–160). Routledge.

Afghan, N., & Wiqar, T. (2007). Succession in family businesses of Pakistan: Kinship culture and Islamic inheritance law. In *CMER working paper no. 07-54*.

Akhter, N., & Rafiq, S. (2022). An analytical study of the socio-economic condition of Pakistan from Nationalization to Islamization. *Peshawar Islamicus, 13*(01 SE-Articles), 49–57. http://ojs.uopisl.pk/index.php/peshawarislamicus/article/view/60

Al-Ghazali, A. H. (2007). *Ihya Uloom ul-Din: Volume 2 (Reprint)*. Darul-Ishaat.

Baron, S. W. (1993). *A social and religious history of the jews: Index to volumes IX-XVIII* (Issue v. 9–18). Columbia University Press.

Basu, A. (1998). An exploration of entrepreneurial activity among Asian small businesses in Britain. *Small Business Economics, 10*(4), 313–326.

Benedict, J. (2007). *The Mormon way of doing business: Leadership and success through faith and family*. Warner Business Books.

Bushman, C. L., & Bushman, R. L. (2001). *Building the Kingdom: A history of Mormons in America*. Oxford University Press.

Cora, Y. T. (2018). Female labor, merchant capital, and resilient manufacturing: Rethinking Ottoman Armenian communities through labor and business. *Journal of the Economic and Social History of the Orient, 61*(3), 361–395.

Cranney, R. D. (2011). *The good life: Mormons and money*. Brigham Young University.

Curl, J. (2009). *For all the people: The hidden history of cooperation, cooperative movements, and communalism in America*. PM Press.

Dana, L., Gurau, C., Light, I., & Muhammad, N. (2019). Family, community, and ethnic capital as entrepreneurial resources: Toward an integrated model. *Journal of Small Business Management, 58*(5), 1003–1029.

Danes, S. M., Lee, J., Stafford, K., & Heck, R. K. Z. (2008). The effects of ethnicity, families and culture on entrepreneurial experience: An extension of sustainable family business theory. *Journal of Developmental Entrepreneurship, 13*(03), 229–268.

Desai, A. S., & Bharat, S. (2017). *The Parsis of India: Continuing at the crossroads*. SAGE Publications.

Dhanania, K., & Gopakumaran, S. (2005). Marwari business discourse: An analysis. *Journal of Asian Pacific Communication, 15*(2), 287–312.

Dillard, J., Dujon, V., & King, M. C. (2008). Understanding the social dimension of sustainability. In *Routledge studies in development and society*. Routledge. https://doi.org/10.4324/9780203892978

Dobbin, C. (1996). *Asian entrepreneurial minorities: Conjoint communities in the making of the world-economy, 1570–1940*. RoutledgeCurzon Ltd.

Egbert, H. (1998). Entrepreneurial advantages and disadvantages of belonging. *GeoJournal: Identities in Sub-Saharan Africa, 46*(2), 129–134.

Elsberg, C. (2019). Bootstraps and Turbans: Sustenance, belief and entrepreneurship in 3HO/Sikh Dharma. *Nova Religio, 23*(1), 89–111. https://doi.org/10.1525/nr.2019.23.1.89

Escobar, A. (2012). *Encountering development: The making and unmaking of the third world*. Princeton University Press.

Falola, T., & Adebayo, A. G. (2000). *Culture*. Transaction Publishers, London.

Falzon, M. A. (2004). *Cosmopolitan connections: The Sindhi Diaspora, 1860–2000*. Brill.

Farooq, R., Joern, B., & Christian, F. (2019). Entrepreneurship in Islamic communities: How do Islamic values and Islamic practices influence entrepreneurship intentions? *Journal of Enterprising Communities: People and Places in the Global Economy, 13*(5), 557–583.

Firro, K. M. (2021). *The Druzes in the Jewish State: A brief history*. Brill.

Greif, A. (1994). Cultural beliefs and the organization of society: A historical and theoretical reflection on collectivist and individualist societies. *Journal of Political Economy, 102*(5), 912–950.

Hallaq, W. B. (2013). *The impossible state: Islam, politics, and modernity's moral predicament (Reprint)*. Columbia University Press.

Hollingsworth, J. R. (2000). Doing institutional analysis: Implications for the study of innovations. *Review of International Political Economy, 7*(4), 595–644.

Hong, E. (1995). The impact of modernization on indigenous people: The case of Sarawak. In H. N. Hodge, P. Goering, & S. Gorelick (Eds.), *The future of progress: Reflections on environment and development* (pp. 129–140). Green Books Ltd.

Hostetler, J. A. (1993). *Amish society*. Johns Hopkins University Press.

Hudson, M. (2010). Entrepreneurs: From the near eastern takeoff to the Roman collapse. In D. S. Landes, J. Mokyr, & W. J. Baumol (Eds.), *The invention of enterprise: Entrepreneurship from ancient Mesopotamia to modern times* (pp. 8–39). Princeton University Press.

Jamshed, U., Jahangir, A., & Fazil, N. (2022). War on terror: Socio-economic ramifications for Pakistan. *Global International Relations Review, V*(I), 1–10. https://doi.org/10.31703/girr.2022(v-i).01

Javaid, O. (2015). The original socio-cultural and economic context for practicing shirkat-ul-aqd. *International Journal of Pluralism and Economics Education, 6*(4), 371.

Javaid, O. (2019). Islamic system of production and consumption: A guide for Muslim entrepreneurs. *Journal of Business Innovation, 4*(1), 1–12.

Javaid, O. (2022a). An Islamic vision and approach for entrepreneurship: Developing through a multi-stage comparative analysis of systems, ideologies and code of ethics. *International Journal of Ethics and Systems, 38*(1), 125–146.

Javaid, O. (2022b). The principles of a circular economy in the light of Islamic values and beliefs. *Journal of Islamic Thought and Civilization, 12*(1), 214–230.

Javaid, O. (2024). The significance of moral agency for socioeconomic justice and its absence in Islamic economics and finance. *Journal of King Abdulaziz University: Islamic Economics, 37*(1), 3–20.

Javaid, O., Shamsi, A. F., & Hyder, I. (2020). Religious entrepreneurial communities as a solution for socioeconomic injustice. *Journal of Enterprising Communities: People and Places in the Global Economy, 14*(3), 415–446.

Kaur, I. N. (2013). Addressing economic inequality—An expanded interpretation of the 3-Pillars Sikh Theory in Sri Guru Granth Sahib. *Second Annual Conference Celebrating Prakash Utsava of Sri Guru Granth Sahib, Sponsored by Sikh Gurdwara San Jose and Chardi Kalaa Foundation, San Jose, CA, September, 14.*

Kawharu, M., & Tapsell, P. (2019). *Whāriki: The Growth of Māori Community Entrepreneurshi.* Oratia Media.

Krasner, J. (2013). The place of tikkun olam in American Jewish life. *Jewish Political Studies Review, 25*(3/4), 59–98.

Kraybill, D. B. (2003). *The riddle of Amish culture.* Johns Hopkins University Press.

Kumar, S., Sahoo, S., Lim, W. M., & Dana, L. P. (2022). Religion as a social shaping force in entrepreneurship and business: Insights from a technology-empowered systematic literature review. *Technological Forecasting and Social Change.* https://doi.org/10.1016/j.techfore.2021.121393

Levin, S. (1974). The upper bourgeoisie from the Muslim commercial community of Memons in Pakistan, 1947 to 1971. *Asian Survey, 14*(3), 231–243.

Lieven, A. (2012). *Pakistan: A hard country.* Penguin UK.

Luhrmann, T. M. (1996). *The Good Parsi: The fate of a colonial elite in a postcolonial society.* Harvard University Press.

MacIntyre, A. (2013). *After virtue: A study in moral theory* (3rd ed.). Bloomsbury Publishing.

Maffi, L. (2018). Biocultural diversity. In *The international encyclopedia of anthropology* (pp. 1–14). https://doi.org/10.1002/9781118924396.wbiea1797

Mandair, A. P. S., Shackle, C., & Singh, G. (2013). *Sikh religion.* Culture and Ethnicity. Taylor & Francis.

Marx, K. (2012). *Economic and philosophic manuscripts of 1844.* Dover Publications.

McCarthy, C., Dorfman, E., Hakiwai, A., & Twomey, Ā. (2013). Mana Taonga: Connecting communities with New Zealand museums through ancestral Maori culture. *Museum International, 65*(1–4), 5–15.

Menning, G. (1997). Trust, entrepreneurship and development in Surat city, India. *Ethnos, 62*(1–2), 59–90.

Mortensen, N. (1999). Mapping system integration and social integration. In I. Gough & G. Olofsson (Eds.), *Capitalism and social cohesion: Essays on exclusion and integration* (pp. 13–37). Macmillan Press Ltd.

Murray, J. M. (2010). Entrepreneurs and entrepreneurship in medieval Europe. In D. S. Landes, J. Mokyr, & W. J. Baumol (Eds.), *The invention of enterprise: Entrepreneurship from ancient mesopotamia to modern times* (pp. 88–106). London: Princeton University Press.

Naka, T. (2011). The spirit of giving: Mennonite narratives about charitable contributions. *Culture and Religion, 12*(3), 317–338.

Nakatani, S. (2014). Hometowns of the marwaris, diasporic traders in India. In *Regional routes, regional roots? Cross-border. Patterns of human mobility in Eurasia* (pp. 63–76). Hokkaido Slavic-Eurasian Reserarch Center.

Nippoldt, L. J. (2022). *Serving others: Individual and societal transformation through Seva in a Sikh community.* University of California.

Palsetia, J. S. (2001). *The Parsis of India: Preservation of identity in Bombay City.* Brill.

Papanek, H. (1972). Pakistan's big businessmen: Muslim separatism, entrepreneurship, and partial modernization. *Economic Development and Cultural Change, 21*(1), 1–32.

Peredo, A. M. (2014). Poverty, reciprocity and community-based entrepreneurship. In T. Baker & F. Welter (Eds.), *The Routledge companion to entrepreneurship* (pp. 263–280). Routledge.

Polanyi, K. (2001). *The great transformation: The political and economic origins of our time.* Beacon Press.

Pullanikkatil, D., & Hughes, K. (2023). *Socio-ecological systems and decoloniality: Convergence of indigenous and western knowledge.* Springer International Publishing.

Reid, J. (2015). Old order Mennonites in New York: Cultural and agricultural growth. *Journal of Amish and Plain Anabaptist Studies, 3*(2), 212–221.

Rogers, A., Horst, M., Rogers, F., Lee, J., & Reihart, M. (2013). From the barn to the operating room and back: The Amish way of life leads to improved throughput and outcomes following trauma. *Journal of Trauma and Acute Care Surgery, 75*(5), 916–918.

Rudner, D. W. (2023). *Caste and capitalism in colonial India: The Nattukottai Chettiars*. University of California Press.

Sachs, W. (2010). *The development dictionary: A guide to knowledge as power* (W. Sachs (Ed.); 2nd ed.). Zed Books.

Saqib, A. (2016). *Kamyab log*. Sang-e-Meel Publications.

Sarna, J. D. (2019). *American Judaism*. Yale University Press.

Saroyan, A. (2022). *The origins of Armenian Philanthropy: Nersēs The great and the question of the Greek influence (critical examination)*. Durham University.

Saslow, L. R., Willer, R., Feinberg, M., Piff, P. K., Clark, K., Keltner, D., & Saturn, S. R. (2012). My brother's keeper? Compassion predicts generosity more among less religious individuals. *Social Psychological and Personality Science, 4*(1), 31–38.

Schumacher, E. F. (2010). *Small is beautiful: Economics as if people mattered*. HarperCollins.

Sikandar, S., & Mahmood, W. (2018). Corporate governance and value of family-owned business: A case of emerging country. *Corporate Governance and Sustainability Review, 2*(2), 6–12.

Ståhl, T. (2021). The amoral atheist? A cross-national examination of cultural, motivational, and cognitive antecedents of disbelief, and their implications for morality. *PLoS ONE, 16*(2), Article e0246593. https://doi.org/10.1371/journal.pone.0246593

Suny, R. G. (1993). *Looking toward Ararat: Armenia in modern history*. Indiana University.

Suriya, A. H. T. (2011). The spread of generations. *Memon Alam, 2011*, 15–16.

Takhar, O. K., & Jakobsh, D. R. (2023). *Global sikhs: Histories*. Practices and Identities. Taylor & Francis.

Taknet, D. K. (2016). *The Marwari heritage*. IntegralDMS.

Taleb, N. N. (2012). *Antifragile: Things that gain from disorder*. Random House.

Taleb, N. N. (2018). *Skin in the game: Hidden asymmetries in daily life*. Random House Publishing Group.

Taylor, C. (2018). *A secular age*. Harvard University Press.

Tenenbaum, S. (1993). *A credit to their community: Jewish Loan societies in the United States, 1880–1945*. Wayne State University Press.

Thiessen, J. T. A.-T. T. (2013). *Manufacturing mennonites: Work and religion in post-war manitoba (Canadian social history series)* (NV-1 onl). University of Toronto Press.

Timberg, T. A., & Das, G. (2015). *The Marwaris: From Jagat Seth to the Birlas*. Penguin Books Limited.

Usmani, M. T. (2002). *An introduction to Islamic finance*. Kluwer Law International.

Van Eijk, E. (2014). Pluralistic family law in Syria: Bane or blessing? *Electronic Journal of Islamic and Middle Eastern Law, 2*, 73.

Vevaina, L. (2023). Trusts on the monsoon winds: Parsi transnational religious philanthropy. *Ethnography, 24*(3), 316–333.

Weiskopf, R., & Steyaert, C. (2009). Metamorphoses in entrepreneurship studies: Towards an affirmative politics of entrepreneuring. In H. Daniel & S. Chris (Eds.), *The politics and aesthetics of entrepreneurship: A fourth movements in entrepreneurship book* (pp. 183–201). Edward Elgar Publishing Limited.

Wunsch, C. (2010). Neo-Babylonian entrepreneurs. In D. S. Landes, J. Mokyr, & W. J. Baumol (Eds.), *The invention of enterprise: Entrepreneurship from ancient mesopotamia to modern times* (pp. 50–61). London: Princeton University Press.

Chapter 6
Family as a Producer of Moral and Social Capital

The tendency to see material wealth as a means for morally embedded social ends is generally preserved and transferred from generation to generation from the very institution of the family (Bubolz, 2001). The new generation eventually continues the same values on the community level. The respondents in my study also believed that when the new generation is born, they see how the family elders set the priorities as they grow up, that the economic has a secondary significance over the social or moral, or otherwise, also, if the meta-norms of the community sanction such a prioritization of social over economic. The family, therefore, can be seen as an incubator where the new generation learns the values and beliefs upheld by the elders (Swartz, 2009). The younger ones are also influenced by other external factors like the environment in the community, formal education process, religious authority figures, and today also by TV and digital media (Anderson & Cavallaro, 2002). Although modern mediums offer tough competition today (Postman, 2006); however, their penetration would perhaps depend on who provides a growing child more company, if it is the safe, fulfilling, and nurturing presence of family members then it may be assumed that their values will be mirrored by the child (Cozolino, 2014), and if it's the TV and gadgets, then one can anticipate (Haidt, 2023). The community culture can thus be described as the net aggregate set of values and norms transferred to the next generation in each family within a community (Pierre Bourdieu, 2011; Coleman, 1994).

A family (in an extended sense) that sustains and maintains bonding social capital may also have some economic implications for the community as a whole. A family, when it breaks down, can also potentially break down the business owned by the

Sections 6.1, 6.2 and 6.3 of this chapter draw from the author's doctoral thesis 'Building a Theoretical Model of Socially Sustainable Entrepreneurship through Comparative Case Analysis of Ethnic Entrepreneurial Communities' submitted to Dept. of Management Sciences, Institute of Business Management (IoBM), Karachi, Pakistan.

O. Javaid, *Socioeconomic Sustainability Through Moral and Social Capital*,
Entrepreneurship and Development in South Asia: Longitudinal Narratives,
https://doi.org/10.1007/978-981-96-8134-1_6

family, which could have been facilitating the community both directly and indirectly. This is critical when a key factor that keeps the community together is the capacity of the families to support each other or support various community-related causes, as discussed in the previous chapter. This significantly depends on how much a family earns through their entrepreneurial activity, and how much they can contribute from what they can save (Coleman, 1988). It was observed in the data I collected that the conflict arising from relational issues inside the family may even convince some family members to change their careers altogether and seek employment elsewhere, like in the corporate sector, potentially risking the survival of the business owned by their family. In this chapter, the focus will therefore be on the family culture more, and how the norms of the family culture affect the bonding between family members. Also, the chapter sheds some light on what changes are emerging in the family culture for good or for worse, as highlighted in the primary data I collected, which also offers insight into a way to keep the family sustainable in its extended sense.

6.1 The Family Norms

To ensure transmission of family values, customs, and norms to the next generation, the members of the communities I studied were highly selective in choosing the brides or grooms for their children. They typically avoided establishing matrimonial ties outside the community for the same reason (MT 81). Marriage was not (and often is) not a merger of two individuals into a family unit, but rather a merger of two extended families into a bigger extended family (Islam, the religion followed by the communities; however, gives autonomy to two individuals to form or break the relationship of marriage, the family members are expected to comply). The trend is reported to be easing out, as in the case of Memon. Earlier, they would not even consider finding a match outside their sub-caste, but now they are reportedly doing so; however, still not outside the Memon community (IO 71). The trend to marry outside the community is believed to be on the rise in Delhiwala, but it was seen critically as a source of community disintegration (RS 36, 37). If the marriage happens outside the community, and the family of the bride or the groom is from a dissimilar culture, then eventually the possibility of transmission of community and family culture may be dependent on the extent of influence of either family on the children. The likelihood of children coming into the family business or adopting an entrepreneurial career path, for example, may be higher if both the father's and mother's family members have an entrepreneurial orientation. The quantum of support for the budding entrepreneurs from their maternal and paternal sides may also be high only when the relatives on both sides are also business oriented.

It is believed, even by some community members, that the social order in their respective communities follows a more patriarchal orientation. This looks apparent as in any typical family in the respective communities, the breadwinning role is assumed by the males while the females take care of the home, the upbringing of the children (Afghan & Wiqar, 2007; Seaman et al., 2016), and maintaining social ties. Amongst Bohra (Egbert, 1998) and Ismaili community (Dobbin, 1996), the religious authority, males, also have a significant influence on the way family and community life are organized, and how community resources are distributed. In the available literature, such dominance of religious authority in the Memon, Delhiwala, and Chinioti communities is not discussed, nor it is generally heard of. Afghan and Wiqar (2007) note about the typical family structure in the country:

> Pakistani culture is characterized by high power distance because the structure of organizations is hierarchical and power is typically centralized. Families, too, support a structure of hierarchy with the father being the head of the family and the eldest son having more say in decision-making than the younger ones. Children are expected to respect and obey their parents and generally refrain from questioning their authority. The elders of the families, or buzurg, such as paternal or maternal grandparents or great-grandparents, are also considered wise and experienced and are to be treated with respect and reverence. Sibling rivalry is discouraged, and siblings are instructed to respect each other from an early age. (p. 8)

The same can be easily said about the family norms in the communities I studied. In such a form of family order, referred to as a corporate family, the authority flows from top to bottom. The role of parents and elders is not typically tyrannical toward the younger ones, but rather supportive, as the elders assume the responsibility to take care of the young ones until they are old enough. What is expected in return is respect for parents and other elders, and adherence to the moral standards of the family and community. But there is a possibility that compliance with standards may become too suffocating, for women in particular, where the social or family orientation is enforced on women more through fear of disrespect or 'what people would think about it' and less through positive encouragement or inspiration, particularly to keep women from earning opportunities. On the contrary, women in the Ismaili community, however, often work in the education and health facilities managed by the community. Some Chinioti women are also now coming forward to participate in family businesses (Saqib, 2016), likely because of various sociocultural reasons (like rising divorce rates) and the influence of global trends. Memon vocational training centers in the city also teach women various skills that can be used to start a home-based venture. It is often portrayed in the Western media that the women in Pakistani households are trapped inside their homes, where they are also often mistreated. Mistreatment of women is not absent; stories of which are often described in community periodicals as well, with an intent to make corrections in community character. A Delhiwala disclosed that many newly married girls ask for a 'divorce after being treated like a maid by their in-laws' (SI 21). Typically, this mistreatment is said to happen at the hands of the mother-in-law. However, such examples cannot be said to be a representative description of women's character or the treatment they receive in the community. A community simply would not sustain for long in a toxic environment in most homes. The key role that the women in the respective communities appear to be performing is to keep the social alive, bonding social capital to be specific, in the short run and the long run by nurturing the next generation with the right set of values; would this continue in future or not, is a question however.

6.1.1 The Women and the Social

Chinioti women, for example, are active socially. In well-off families where the home chores are often performed by the maids, keeping contact with the extended family, and taking care of the needy by distributing charity in the community are often done by the women. Men typically focus more on the economic, as their nature of relationship with other members is more rational (as opposed to emotional), while women tend to focus more on the social in general. Due to the culturally sanctioned division of responsibility, a greater focus of women on the social may be evaluated in the context of the worldview held sacred by the community, where the social is more important than the economic. A mother's role is therefore considered pivotal to strengthening the family bonding among the immediate and extended family. Chinioti women in general reportedly act as a binding force and a role model for the rest to emulate in this context (Saqib, 2016, pp. 257–270). The quantity of social connections maintained by the women may be less than the quantity of economic relations formed by the men in the marketplace. However, in terms of the quality or strength of relationships, specifically in the respective communities, it would be plausible to argue that it comes more naturally to women, with some exceptions, of course. This claim also goes in line with the studies endorsing that women, in general, are more interested in people, and have more agreeable and compassionate personalities as compared to men, who are rather more interested in material stuff (Su et al., 2009; Weisberg et al., 2011). Such studies do not claim that women or men cannot do the opposite, but rather highlight what comes more naturally to them. Social and cultural conditioning may reinforce such roles, the evaluation of which needs to be done as per the meta-norms adhered to by the respective cultures. Meta-norms of the communities in question here encourage men to take up financial responsibility, while also encouraging women to focus more on the social, while not prohibiting the opposite, which often becomes necessary as well.

Further, in Islam's cosmological view of the family, fathers are to be respected; however, mothers should be respected three times more than fathers. The paradise is believed to be 'under the feet of the mother' in Islam (Boudreaux, 2022), a view deeply held throughout Muslim cultures, including the communities being discussed. If that's the general norm, then the entire notion of the communities being patriarchal comes into question. Mothers can be assumed to be ruling by proxy through their sons, but with a motherly character. A top Memon entrepreneur was asked in an interview published in their monthly newsletter about the patriarchal nature of the community and his views about women empowerment, he claimed to be a staunch believer of women empowerment but described it under the pretext of the motherly archetype that he believed also manifest in meso and macro contexts. He said:

> We cannot disregard the importance of the role of women in WMO [World Memon Organization]. One of the main areas where I intend to focus ... is women's empowerment. I firmly believe that knowledge comes not from the father but the mother, because it is the mother with whom the child spends most of his time. Whenever we praise a person, we always say that his/her mother must be good. No one says his father must be good. Even if you look globally, all the countries are known as motherlands; no country is known as a fatherland! This is the power of women, and this is the power which we have to unleash and develop in this organization. (The Memon, Feb 2021, Issue 32, p. 19)[1]

The archetypal significance of the motherly is hard to miss from the quote. Women's empowerment is also been described as an extension of the motherly character beyond the family and into the platform of WMO, which attempts to connect the globally dispersed community and channel their resources to take care of the needy. The notion of communities being patriarchal becomes questionable when we see the dominating role of women at the time of forming matrimonial relationships, where the permission of the grandmothers and mothers is considered essential, who often have more say than the male members of the family in such matters. The groom also typically complies with the choice of their mothers. Matriarchy likely supersedes patriarchy in many families in social contexts.

Mothers are highly regarded in community periodicals[2] also, often highlighted as a source of inspiration, someone who builds character and harmony between siblings, which then is believed to contribute to *barakah* in the financial outcomes of the family business later in life. This character is tested in difficult times. When someone in the immediate or extended family collapses economically, socially, or becomes physically ill, other family members may come forward to help them until recovery (WK 41, 61; SS 46). Such a motherly character among siblings or family members, where members are willing to sacrifice the little they have for other members, is said to be unlikely without the proper role modeling by parents, mothers in particular (WK 4). The motivation for mutual support and the strength of character needed for it ought to be inculcated through role modeling by mothers which may eventually contribute not just to the socioeconomic sustainability of the family in its extended sense, but also enable individuals to contribute to maintaining a supportive community environment. The monthly periodical Saudagar along with the respondents identified various qualities to be inculcated among children such as 'spirit to sacrifice' (Saudagar, Feb 2011, p. 24), 'strong character, high morals' (Saudagar, May 2012, p. 59), 'spirit to serve', 'frugal life', 'earning a legitimate income' (Saudagar, May 2013, p. 84), 'humility' (RS 14), 'socializing nature', 'being empathetic', 'professional integrity' (Saudagar, Apr 2014, p. 74) 'frugality' (JBS 65). In community literature, mothers and grandmothers are

[1] The Issue can be download using the following URL: https://wmoworld.org/wp-content/uploads/2021/02/32-WMO_Newsletter_February-2021-FINAL-COMPRESSED.pdf (Last accessed: 9th July 2024).

[2] Saudagar, Mar 2012, p. 55, 67; Apr 2014, p. 138; May 2014, p. 49. The issues can be accessed on their website: https://saudagar.pk/; The Memon, Nov 2015, p. 4; Feb 2016, p. 6; July 15 (Eid Edition), p. 7.

therefore described as heroes of the nurturing process, as fathers are often at work for long hours. Appreciation of their motherly role in the community literature, however, remains confined within the context of the immediate family. The motherly side of women, it may be argued, due to their greater capacity for compassion and connectedness, has the potential to perform a key strategic function in the context of socioeconomic sustainability of the community environment generation after generation, which also deserves to be highlighted and appreciated. The role of the mother is generally underappreciated by other family members, particularly by the mother-in-law, who sees the new bride as someone sharing his son's attention, which is often a source of the mother's sense of importance. Mistreatment of the new bride can ensue, creating a trickle-down effect on how the new mother eventually treats her children as they grow up. This can have adverse consequences on the upbringing process and subsequent bonding among the next generation of family members.

6.2 The Family Bonding

A healthy upbringing environment is recognized for its potential for creating a strong relationship between siblings, a bonding social capital, which is believed to be a potent resource to sustain the family business where brothers may eventually work together. The role of emotionally available mothers cannot be overstated in this context (see Sect. 3.1). Bonding becomes critical also during prolonged uncertain recessionary times, as family members are more likely to stay with the family business instead of searching for jobs elsewhere. As mentioned earlier, the family business is an entity that creates the financial capital for the community. Sustenance of the family business is thus critical for keeping the community together, as in the absence of support coming from inside, the community members in need will look elsewhere. To sustain the family business, the family's internal social capital is recognized as a critical component in the literature (Lu et al., 2013; Pearson et al., 2008). Other than that, the family value system, wisdom of the ancestors also known as folk wisdom, technical expertise of all family members, experience and expertise of the elders, network of the family within the community and the market, the credibility of the family name, financial resources, are some of the key resources offered by the family. These resources facilitate the family business, or any extension that emerges out of it (more about it in Chapter 7). The entire pool of tangible and intangible resources is termed family capital in the literature (Bubolz, 2001; Danes et al., 2009; J. Hoffman et al., 2006; Rodriguez et al., 2009), which is developed across multiple generations. Access to the family capital depends on the bonding between the family members. If bonding weakens due to some unresolvable conflict, then it becomes difficult for the estranged family member to access the family capital. The access to family capital, therefore, keeps the family members motivated to remain on good terms with each other (Danes et al., 2008).

Literature has highlighted the significance of fair treatment by parents in preventing conflicts in the family business at the time of success planning (Avloniti et al., 2014). It is suggested that fair treatment during upbringing plays a significant role, as otherwise, siblings may develop grudges against each other, while those who have received preferential treatment may develop a sense of superiority. The cause of preferential treatment may be genuine, like a sibling having some permanent or temporary disability. However, if favoritism is purely due to emotional reasons, then a sense of injustice and inferiority can be developed among those who were treated less, while a sense of arrogance may develop among those who are given preferential treatment (Buist et al., 2013; Jenkins et al., 2003; Kowal et al., 2004). In some families, boys are treated better as compared to girls, or a younger sibling may receive a higher parental focus than an older sibling (Padilla et al., 2019). The imbalance can have detrimental effects on the bonding of the siblings, eventually causing trouble when the siblings have to work together in a family business. The friction may push siblings to part ways, splitting the business resources in the process. At the time of inheritance distribution as well, some siblings may feel entitled to receive more than the others and eventually end up taking a greater share, or even all assets, especially that belongs to the sisters (SAR 43, IAP 56, NS 31, IAP 10). These issues were known to the respondents, as they emphasized the significance of fair treatment and justice repeatedly in their assertion over the significance of the bonding between siblings. For inheritance distribution, adhering to the Islamic law of inheritance was specifically prescribed as a just criterion to distribute inheritance, as it transcends the personal bias of any individual in the family or community (UL 47, MN 15, MT 88).

The religiously inspired meta-norms adhered to by the respondent appeared to influence their realization of the significance of fair treatment. The engagement of elders with their siblings was often inspired by their religious orientation, which emphasizes sacrifice, altruism, and kindness. This provided a role model for the new generation to emulate while maintaining relationships with their siblings. It was unanimously believed by the respondents that their income was ordained by God, and they had no contribution in the 'quantity' of money or wealth they own (NS 51, SS 56, TP 86, JBS 14, IS 48, SAP 56, MT 74, ARJ 90, IO 31). They nevertheless worked hard also as one has to put in their side of the effort. However, the outcome is believed to be determined by so many other factors that are beyond one's control, like the opportunities arriving from the network, the inflow of customers, competitor's behavior, overall market, and economic conditions, all of which were seen to be influenced by forces beyond one's control. Often, they would experience serendipity, like a customer finding them at the right moment when the businesses needed the most, which was seen as God's intervention. They said their planning barely led to any meaningful outcome, perhaps because of unpredictable macroeconomic conditions, and yet their business thrived as their customers would approach them often at the right moment. The worldview offered by Islam also provided them with a narrative to explain the cause of such incidents, which they would call 'God's grace' (Saqib, 2016). The holy book they follow, The Qur'an, frequently mentions that the 'rizq' is determined by God, that is, anything that one needs to sustain.[3] The Qur'an further states that God would provide more to some, while less to others; some will be tested with riches, while others will be tested with poverty.[4] Some degree of inequality is divinely ordained as per the Quran; however, the believers who have been bestowed with more are required to remain humble, remain in a state of gratitude, express their gratitude by helping the lesser off, and spend on their family members. Wealth needs to be distributed, never hoarded, which becomes easier when one maintains a very frugal and modest lifestyle (Al-Ghazali, 2007). Such views and practices are said to instill humility, encourage an altruistic attitude, and incentivize sharing. All respondents kept referring to God's grace while describing the cause of their financial success. Those who were more well off acted with even greater humility.

I interviewed owners of leading pharma companies, large textile units, and a distribution company. These people were billionaires, but very down to earth, never boasting about their success. I even mistook the owner of a pharma company as a house help when he first entered the guest room where I was waiting, and then I was introduced by a mutual contact that he was the owner of a leading pharma company in the country. The old fellow came in a very simple traditional dress (shalwar kameez) and also spoke as if he were just an ordinary guy. There are even examples from their past when fewer people owned cars. The children would walk to the school, even when the parents owned a car and could have used it to drop off the kids at the school. Chinioti entrepreneur interviewed by Saqib (2016) shared that when he and his siblings were of school-going age, their father would park the car at a distance and then let the respondent and his siblings walk to the school so that their classmates would not feel a sense of inferiority; it is rare to see such an example today. The humbleness, modesty, frugality, and humility, therefore, were key traits practiced by the elders, which likely prevented any material competition among the siblings. Thus, it may be argued that the voluntary self-enforcement of equality can potentially have a positive effect on social cohesion (Stolle et al., 2008). There were examples where one particular sibling could not contribute enough to the business sufficiently due to a natural limitation or disability, but was still respected by other siblings, even by his nephews. This was so because their father instructed 'not to disrespect your uncle and support him financially' even when he is unable to contribute and focuses more towards his 'missionary activity to spread the message of Islam' (IO 75).

In the data, Islam's meta-norms were frequently referred to emphasize mutual support, avoiding conflict over worldly matters, forgiveness, patience, kindness, and that sustenance is determined by Allah (of course, not everyone strictly demonstrates such traits as conflicts do happen eventually). Those who claimed to follow also claimed to live in harmony while avoiding conflicts and resolving disagreements without damaging social bonding. Islam's worldview is also said to provide a rationale for abiding by the meta-norms. It is believed that avoidance

---

[3] For example, see Surah 11, verse 6; or Surah 2, verse 212 in The Qur'an.

[4] For example, see Surah 2, verse 155; or Surah 16, verse 71 in The Qur'an.

of conflicts will increase *barakah*, prevent accidental harm, and ensure immense reward on the Day of Judgement, while indulging in conflict for selfish gains will have adverse consequences in the world and the hereafter. Exercising patience on smaller losses was seen as a means to prevent bigger losses. The focus is to be on sacrifice, but that is believed to become easier when it is known that material wealth has been given precisely to facilitate others, and not to show off (AsB 19, TP 73, KS 14, JBS 14, ARJ 92, MA 13, MF 52, 60). However, it is perhaps unrealistic to expect sacrifice from a person who has experienced unfair treatment frequently during their upbringing experience, or someone who believes himself to be more entitled than others due to the preferential treatment received by a parent. A fair environment where one typically receives what is due by adults who demonstrate modesty and sacrifice themselves may potentially inspire the next generation to follow suit.

6.3 The Disintegration

A noticeable number among the younger generation, however, does not seem to be following suit in the three communities I studied. The conflicts are said to be rising, divorce rates are reportedly increasing, and class consciousness is said to be emerging between the richer ones and those who are relatively less well off. Divorce between a married couple is seen as a potentially irreversible rupture between not just two individuals, but two families. There is no statistical data; however, it may be assumed that their frequency is sufficient to spark concern and motivate community members to frequently highlight these issues in community literature and suggest antidotes. Respondents also showed concerns, shared their understanding of the root causes, and recommended solutions as per their understanding. For example, in the Delhiwala community economic disparity and class consciousness were referred to as a major cause of social disintegration in the community magazine (Saudagar, Aug 2012, p. 71, 73; Mar 2015, p. 125; Dec 2014, p. 114; 1305, p. 83; Feb 2014, p. 55). It was asserted by a respondent, 'class division now does exist among Delhi Saudagaran', while 'material affluence and its show off by the elite in the community are increasing the divide among the community' (TP 70, 71, 72). The Saudagar has frequently published articles emphasizing the maintenance of a simple lifestyle for the same reason (Saudagar, Mar 2012, p. 73; Oct 2010, p. 75; May 2015, p. 54, 55). The community members are advised in the monthly periodicals, for example, to organize the wedding ceremonies of their children frugally (Saudagar, Feb 2014, p. 59; Mar 2014, p. 59). The periodical asserts that the show-off of affluence on such occasions can reinforce class consciousness among everyone participating in the ceremony, unlike any other public event (Saudagar, Aug, 2014, p. 63). The new generation of the Chinioti community also appears to be more inclined toward showing off their affluence. The social gatherings used to be a medium to share experiences, market opportunities, and business initiatives, are now said to be becoming a platform for women to show off their riches. Such trends are also increasing the financial pressures on earning members of the family (KL, p. 132; SJ 41, 52).[5] If the business is not doing well, then such family pressures can become a source of conflict among siblings working together in a family business. It was also mentioned by a respondent that such pressures from his wife encourage him to work harder as well (AB 8); however, in case the market is going through a recession, or competition is giving him a tough time, the consequential stress may also hurt social relationships. The parents, for example, may spend more time in the market and have less time for children during recessionary periods.

Overspending on luxuries, wedding ceremonies, and subsequent show-offs is believed to be causing a rise in class consciousness also among the members of the Chinioti community, and therefore a sense of disconnect among community members. Chinioti now have a sense that they belong to different classes. Such trends are also said to increase the self-serving mindset, as increased personal expenses on luxuries can reduce the likelihood of financially supporting immediate or distant relatives (AB 47). Fathers spending lavishly on their daughter's upbringing and on her wedding ceremony, for example, also shape the lifestyle expectations their daughter has with her husband and in-laws. If the husband is not as well off as the father of the bride, then the bride's unfulfilled expectations can create resentments, which may even lead to divorce. Such trends are causing a rise in divorce rates in the community, suggests one respondent (SJ 50). The affluence of the previous generation, as per another respondent, has encouraged the current generation to significantly increase their living standards, causing a rise in the cost of living as well. The shift from frugality to extravagance is believed to make many in the new generation less diligent and passionate about reaching new heights (KL, p. 206), due to which job orientation appears to be on the rise as it offers a more stable routine. Such a shift goes in line with the work of Ibn Khaldûn (2015), a Muslim historian from the fourteenth century, famous for his thesis on the rise and fall of societies.

Memon respondents also shared their concerns about the rising levels of education, which they believe correlates with a decline in the respect for elders, and subsequent lowering of moral, religious, and family values (MA 43; MF 28; IO 97; MA 47; MN 41; IS 37; MN 42). The generation gap between the traditional 'simple-minded' elders and 'modern millennials' is said to be increasing (SAP 29; IO 88, 89). The impact of media, modern education (IO 47), and technology is seen as negative (Memon, Sep 2012, p. 1; ARJ 59) and 'a cause of disconnection across generations, families and community members' (MT 79). It was mentioned by a respondent that 'community members have less time now for each other and are becoming more materialistic' (MA 32). 'Self-centeredness', 'show-off culture', and 'lavish lifestyle' are blamed on the media and technology (IS 34, 41; MN 34; MA 42, ARJ 88; MT 79). The pressure to raise consumption, shift toward a lavish

[5] KL refers to Kamiyab Log (Successful people) a book by Saqib (2016). The purpose of mentioning it like this is to blend it with the references pointing to respondent's statements.

lifestyle (MA 42; ARJ 88), and 'the race to increasing living standards have forced the Memon people to swell their expenses' (IS 29), 'pushing some entrepreneurs to even cut corners to increase their earnings' (MN 33). Another respondent suggested that the 'herd mentality makes people follow such trends blindly, leading to class consciousness' (IS 34). 'Such short-sightedness has also led people away from religion' (IO 99), or perhaps a lack of religiosity is responsible for it. Due to such trends, the community is disintegrating, the respondents asserted that 'the defaults in the market are increasing', and the level of trust among community members seems to be on a decline (ARJ 58, MN 28; MT 80; SAP 35; IO 83; MF 21).

A significant number among the new generation of Memons is reported to be inclined toward acquiring higher education for several reasons (SAP 45; IO 41; ARJ 18; MF 6; MF 5; IO 49; IS 57, 61). For some, it is a requirement of professionally managing a firm (MN 40), while others consider it detrimental to the traditional ways of managing a business, as it can contribute to creating a rift between family elders and newcomers (IO 35). 'The modern education also does not talk much about ethics,' suggested one respondent (IO 21). Despite all these limitations, formal tertiary education was considered important (IO 39, 40; MN 40; IO 58; Memon, Aug 2013, p. 3). Another respondent suggested that professionalization is the requirement of an expanding business, so newcomers need to have the necessary knowledge to develop a more professional approach to managing the family business.

In the Chinioti community also there are examples among the new generation who emphasize educating the young with modern education, even sending them abroad for that matter (KL, p. 26, 160). One of the reasons mentioned is the increasing demands of business as the operations are professionalized and the market has become global (AB 39, 40). However, to work locally, practical experience is considered to have more significance than formal education (KL, p. 116). To interact with professionals and international stakeholders, the elders felt the need for modern education. Some respondents, however, believe that an unintended consequence of increasing levels of education is a rise in job orientation in the coming generation (UL 32, 33, 57; AB 38; WK 29). Further, modern education is believed to be nurturing a self-serving mindset, and an increasingly felt generation gap, as the educated ones with modern education often find it difficult to accept the traditional family values. Modern education, therefore, is believed to be creating a divide between the old and new generations. The new generation increasingly embraces a different set of values and uses a different language. Previously, elders were seen as the guardians of traditional values, guiding the younger generation to engage with the extended family. However, the generation gap caused by modern education may be leading the new generation to become disconnected from elders and their resources.

Education is not just seen as the only source of the modern individualistic ethos; media is another, both TV and digital, according to the Saudagar magazine of the Delhiwala community, which stands in contrast with the traditional family values (Saudagar, Jun 2014, pp. 63–64). The influx of technology in daily lives is also seen as a primary culprit behind moral degradation; for example, cell phones are believed to be making children less social (JBS 51; KS 47; Saudagar, Mar 2013, p. 53, 56), and 'exposing them to profanity and vulgarity' (Saudagar, Apr 2011, p. 55, 56). Modern education however, is additionally blamed for the decline in religious orientation and promoting secular and materialistic values (Saudagar, Jan 2011, p. 64; Aug 2012, p. 81). The religious, social, and family values that kept people connected and humble are now believed to be disappearing because of the influence of digital mediums (Saudagar, Jul 2012, p. 135). Religious orientation is said to be on a decline (SAR 46, 47; IAP 30, 81) while the family-oriented role of women is said to be under threat due to the exposure to modern liberal values (Saudagar, Mar 2012, pp. 66–67). Marriages are increasingly happening outside the community, which is seen as a sign of disintegration (RS 36, 37). Despite the stated risks, the magazine still highlights the importance of acquiring education on several occasions (Saudagar, Apr 2014, p. 131, 133; FA 22, NS 18, KS 27).

However, job orientation is also seen as a result of the rise in education in the Delhiwala community (IAP 64; NS 44). 'The new generation is believed by respondents to be 'less hard-working, not interested in getting their hands dirty to gain experience and struggling their way to the top' (TP 89, 90; JBS 45), a concern shared by Chinioti respondents as well. Their previous generation, on the contrary, 'started with negligible resources and gained affluence through hard work and determination' (RS 4; TP 18; JBS 4; SAR 22, 24; Saudagar, Dec 2012, p. 69; Jun 2016, p. 90, 92). However, it was reported in Saudagar that the millennials in the community are 'more prone to lavish lifestyle, perhaps depending on the level of affluence in their family' (Saudagar, Aug 2012, p. 71, 73). In addition to 'modern education' (IO 34), 'lack of interest in father's business' (TAP 14), or 'decline in business expansion' (NS 65) can be another contributor toward job orientation. 'Employment can encourage people to relocate themselves closer to the employer and away from the family, sometimes traveling abroad, causing disconnect, loneliness, and depression' (Saudagar, Jul 2012, p. 151). Chinioti sources also asserted that an employed person may get less time to interact with their family members and experience less interaction with family. When all family members collaborate in a thriving family business, it can serve as a unifying force for the family. This is especially true if parents try to foster an environment of mutual respect and cooperation among siblings (KL, p. 201; WK 4), or otherwise, when the business suffers losses, it may become a likely source of blame game among the family members, and bring out unresolved resentments.

It can be inferred from the data that parents' influence is perhaps one of the reasons why the new generation tends to connect with their extended family. When the parents are gone, children may minimize the ties with their relatives (JBS 50; Saudagar, May 2015, pp. 50–51). Saudagar reports that there is a disconnection between parents and children, and an increasing trend of sending parents into old age homes (Saudagar, Aug 2014, p. 59). The nuclear family structure is rising, while the joint family system is going away, according to a respondent (KS 46). It was also suggested that a self-serving mindset is also on the rise in the community

(NS 55; Saudagar, Jan 2011, p. 63). Saudagar raised concerns that previously everyone was geographically connected, living nearby, but now the community is geographically dispersed (Saudagar, Jan 2011, p. 63). The number of conflicts appears to be rising; unjust property and inheritance distribution is considered key cause (SAR 43, IAP 56). Disputes were resolved previously at the family level, but not the case anymore, according to one respondent (KS 45). Rising levels of greed, materialism, and reduced moral values are considered the primary culprits (IO 31). Saudagar suggests that decreasing morals and higher levels of education (Saudagar, Mar 2015, p. 77) are also contributing to an increase in divorce rate (Saudagar, Jul 2014, p. 58; Aug 2012, p. 61; Jul 2013, p. 46; Mar 2013, p. 63; Mar 2015, p. 77; Sep 2016). Another reason is perhaps the ill-treatment of daughters-in-law by in-laws (IAP 24; IO 31), which likely creates a rift between the families of the bride and the groom. The articles in the magazine Saudagar have been stressing to mend the social ties. The contributors have recommended several solutions. These solutions also hint toward a diverse set of presumptions held at the community level about the causes behind the disintegration and what can likely reverse the process in the community:

- Need to change self-serving mindset to a family and community-oriented mindset (Saudagar, Jan 2011, p. 63)
- Curing self-centeredness through increasing religious orientation (Saudagar, Apr 2014, p. 49, 59; IAP 36)
- Elimination of dowry from marriage (Saudagar, Mar 2014, p. 129)
- Improving moral values, strength of character, and kindness toward others (Saudagar, May 2014, p. 58; Feb 2015, p. 63)
- Adopting a simple lifestyle (Saudagar, Jun 2012, p. 43; May 2015, p. 54, 55; Mar 2012, p. 73)
- Emphasis on increasing socializing activities (Saudagar, Mar 2012, p. 82)
- Strengthening family relations and bonding through increased tolerance, patience, and morals (Saudagar, Aug 2012, p. 71, 73; Mar 2015, p. 125; Apr 2014, p. 126; Apr 2012, p. 112, 116; Mar 2013, p. 61, 62)
- Respect for parents (Saudagar, Feb 2014, p. 57, 123), particularly mothers (Saudagar, May 2014, p. 49), heirs, daughters (Saudagar, Jul 2014, p. 126, 127), husband (Saudagar, Jan 2014, p. 45), wives (Saudagar, Jan 2015, p. 123) and family as a whole (Saudagar, Feb 2014, p. 63) to increase social bonding across immediate and extended families, particularly the in-laws.

These suggestions go in line with the values and beliefs of other communities also. If we assume respondents and observations documented in community periodicals to be correct regarding the rising levels of conflicts, divorces, class consciousness, increasing moral degradation, self-serving mindset, decline of religious orientation, and geographical dislocation, the families afflicted with these ills within the respective communities may be heading toward potential disintegration. The quantity of such families is not known but can be assumed to be noticeable, keeping in view the extent of the discussion. Despite the warnings by the community members—published frequently in the monthly magazine or newsletters—a reversal of the disintegrating trends or any fruitful measures taken by the community elders for that purpose has not been reported anywhere in the data sources. If we concur with these views, the disintegrating factors can also have unfavorable consequences for socially embedded entrepreneurial activity within the community; therefore, countermeasures compatible with the community's values and beliefs are perhaps necessary. Nevertheless, the not-so-counterintuitive suggestions hint toward the factors that may keep the families within the communities bonded together.

6.4 A Deeper Look

These suggestions boil down to a single proposition: In this clash of modern 'isms' like individualism and materialism with religious guidance and traditional values, the latter must be adhered to. Within an individual family, some are more inclined already toward the latter, mostly the elders, while others, mostly the younger generation, are becoming more inclined toward the former. The elders emphasize on frugal lifestyle and prioritize relationships over individual material success as a means of keeping the kinship networks together. The penetration of an alternative value framework through education, TV, and digital media, and engagement with the rest of the (rapidly transforming) society are some factors that are accused of creating a split and having adverse consequences on the bonding between family members directly and indirectly. Directly, the split manifests as a generation gap, and indirectly as a result of material competition between family members, which can potentially cultivate jealousy and envy among siblings, cousins, or other members of the extended family. A reluctance to help those in need may also have emerged as a result of maintaining a lavish lifestyle, particularly during recessionary times when the request for help may also increase. The problem likely emerges not with more wealth but with the intent of maintaining a lavish and exceptional lifestyle.

The religion followed by the community discourages such material competition, as a believer is discouraged from comparing themselves with those who are richer, but rather with those who are better in piety and strength of character.[6] A jealousy-inducing material competition through exuberant spending and the subsequent rise of class consciousness could be because a religious worldview has been superseded by something else. It is hard to ascertain what exactly triggered this shift, or if there is a deeper underlying cause to it. Is it unfair treatment of children

[6] Abu Huraira quotes Prophet Muhammad (ﷺ): When one of you looks at one who stands at a higher level than you in regard to wealth and physical structure he should also see one who stands at a lower level than you in regard to these things (in which he stands) at a higher level (as compared to him). Ref: Sahih Muslim 2963a; Book 55: The Book of Zuhd and Softening of Hearts; Source: https://sunnah.com/muslim:2963a (last accessed: 10th July 2024).

in the upbringing process, and if such treatments eventually manifest as material competition later in life? A feeling of insignificance cultivated in the psyche of a person during the upbringing process may lead to the development of a coping mechanism of seeking external validation involving show-off. But is this the case? Questions like these can be answered through some longitudinal ethnographic studies where the observer somehow gains access to the very private space where the mother and children spend most of their time, just to see if that is the cause or not. The observation also needs to be taken without the mothers or their children noticing the observer. Accessing this private sphere discreetly for a long enough time is a challenge due to cultural limitations. If mothers are asked directly, or if those showing off are asked about their motives (assuming they give permission to be interviewed), it is unlikely that the researcher will get an honest answer. Mothers are nevertheless assumed to be the most compassionate, fully capable of loving the child, while unhealthy cultural norms may likely be described as normal as well. Therefore, keeping in view the challenge, perhaps the best that can be done is some intelligent, research-backed speculation, based on the existing body of evidence regarding what gives rise to a compulsive obsession toward consumerism for external validation.

6.5 The Insecure Mother and Consumerism

There is ample evidence to back the claim that financially and emotionally secure mothers raise emotionally secure children with a high sense of self-worth. So when they grow up, they do not have an irresistible urge to prove their worth, and thus will not be typically inclined to show off or to seek external validation, and vice versa (Bowlby, 2012; Grossmann et al., 2008; Morris et al., 2007; Sroufe et al., 2009; Waters et al., 2000). However, in the subcontinent region as well, newlywed brides often do not feel secure in many households due to the infamous antagonism between the mother-in-law and the bride (Gangoli & Rew, 2011; Gopalakrishnan et al., 2023; Ijaz et al., 2021; Khan, 2021). This antagonism also exists in the communities I studied and was highlighted in Sect. 6.3 while discussing the causes behind rising divorce rates. These causes were:

(a) Mistreatment by in-laws, particularly the mother-in-law, while the son also sides with the mother, as required by religion,[7] sternly sometimes;
(b) Modern education and exposure among women are increasing their general awareness about their significance and rights; thus, they no longer tolerate any mistreatment, which can be referred to as a positive development.

[7] The religion followed by the communities also prohibits mistreatment of brides, rather recommends the bride be treated with respect and not burdened with responsibilities without her consent, a directive which is often ignored.

(c) Brides who are raised in affluent families often expect their husbands to provide the same level of affluence, who are often at the start of their career and not financially capable enough, which creates rifts that may often end up in divorce.
(d) Ego issues on either or both sides, over-expectations of all sorts, or lack of understanding, while not making enough effort to resolve the communication gap, is another likely cause.

The first cause, if present, could be due to the insecurity mothers may be experiencing due to their husband's family environment. The insecurity may make mothers more dependent on their sons as compared to daughters, as daughters are typically wedded off into another family and no longer available to provide support, financial support in particular (a trend which may be reversing in the communities). The children are also required by Islam's meta-norms to value their mother three times more,[8] which may give the mother a sense of significance that she may not have experienced earlier in life, or at least in the context of her post-marriage experience. So, when her daughter-in-law arrives, she becomes a natural rival who shares her son's attention. The bride of her son would not experience a welcoming reception unless the mother-in-law did not possess any insecurities. If the treatment of the bride is too hostile, then separation is likely sought; however, often the treatment is subtle, passive-aggressive, and pleasant on the surface or in the social sphere, blurring the signs of passive hostility. This does not give enough material to the bride and the bride's family to seek a divorce.[9] Then, there is social stigma attached to seeking divorce as well, which, if present, may further reduce the chances of separation.

So, if the marriage is sustained, but if the son sides more with the mother in a combined family environment, and if the environment is dominated by the insecure mother-in-law, it may eventually turn the new bride insecure. If the bride continues to live in this environment,[10] may also repeat the same pattern when she becomes a mother-in-law herself in the future (not necessarily, of course). Insecure mothers may live in a survival mode, where their compromised intuition and compassion for their children may not fully create a healthy upbringing environment for the children. Such mothers may often become biased in favor of or against a particular child depending on whether the child reminds them of the character of

[8] Ibn Salamah As-Sulami quotes Prophet Muhammad (ﷺ): "I enjoin each one to honor his mother, I enjoin each one to honor his mother, I enjoin each one to honor his mother (three times), I enjoin each one to honor his guardian who is taking care of him, even if he is causing him some annoyance". In Sunan Ibn Majah 3657, Chapter 1: Honoring One's Parents, Book 33: Etiquette, source: https://sunnah.com/ibnmajah:3657 (last accessed on: 11th July 2024).

[9] The bride's family is also involved in the separation process as marriage is not a relationship between individuals, but two families, as mentioned earlier.

[10] Sometimes the son realizes the issue and decide to live separately. A friend of mine, who is not a member of any of the communities being discussed here, even left the country to protect his wife from her mother's wrath, which, according to him, caused a miscarriage during her first pregnancy.

their own family or that of their in-laws. She may also become emotionally distant, if not fully unavailable, or overly attached to a particular child, and may also overreact more often. The children may grow up in such upbringing environments with a sense of inadequacy, as also suggested in the literature (Bowlby, 2012; Grossmann et al., 2008; Morris et al., 2007; Sroufe et al., 2009; Waters et al., 2000). They may end up seeking external validation or approval from their social circle to feel significant, which may manifest as a tendency to live lavishly, even when it is beyond one's means. They would show off their material success, even pretending to be more successful than they are. A tendency amplified by social media these days (Freitas, 2017; Schroeder & Cavanaugh, 2018; Storr, 2018).

The insecurity of parents can also lead to helicopter parenting or over-pampering of children during the upbringing process, which could be a sign of compensatory behavior by parents, likely caused by their deep-rooted sense of insecurities (Srivastav & Mathur, 2020; van Ingen et al., 2015). Mothers in particular, who may themselves have suffered during their upbringing experience, perhaps due to the emotional unavailability of their parents, can turn this into an intergenerational phenomenon (Bowlby, 2012). Helicopter parenting can nurture a sense of entitlement among children as well (Gao et al., 2024; Segrin et al., 2012), which can eventually affect their marriage in the future, as mentioned in 3rd and 4th causes of divorce above. Further, based on anecdotal evidence and previous studies, it can be argued that parents' or mothers' sense of insecurity likely compromises the developmental needs of children, which is then compensated through indulgence in consumer culture as they grow up. The consumer culture, as per concerned scholars, may cultivate an individualistic-materialist spirit as well (Baudrillard, 2016; Bauer et al., 2012; Curtis, 2002). If it becomes widespread, then class consciousness on the community scale can also be a subsequent outcome (Baudrillard, 2016; Bauman, 2013; Veblen, 2012).

The spread of these modern-'isms', it may be inferred from my primary exploration, could have been much more rapid and widespread among the communities if it were not for the religious beliefs and values that shun individualism and materialism. The problem in discussion here, however, cannot be solved with more materialism and individualism either, let alone consumerism, which rather uses insecurities as a means to keep the consumers hooked on consumption. In the long run, at least the problem may be addressed by ensuring the sense of security of the new bride, assuming that is the only hindrance for them in their role of nurturing the new generation. If so, then the mother-in-law has a very critical role to play in this context, as their experience and internalized sense of security often turn them into unjust tyrants who even turn their sons against their brides. The intergenerational cycle has to be broken in families where the problem persists. The victims of the past, the mother-in-law, must choose the path of the hero and not of the villain, by not choosing to repeat the cycle. If not, then the husbands need to step in to create the necessary distance, which is not too much that the children feel isolated from the extended family, or too little that the bride feels the heat of a hostile environment.

6.6 The Model Family

In the light of the discussion in this chapter and available literature, a sketch of a model family can be created. A model family would provide a healthy, nurturing environment for the children that does not just cater to the child's physical and psychological needs, but would also enable children to follow the healthy patterns and norms of the family that keep the family, in its extended sense, together. The environment that is conducive to the healthy upbringing of the next generation, which requires, for example, a secure mother and a healthy relationship with the mother-in-law (if the two are living under the same roof), is also replicated in each consecutive generation. The availability of the extended family is also critical for the upbringing process, as the famous saying goes, 'it takes a village to raise a child'. The parents in their upbringing experience need support from others, especially when a new child arrives, mothers especially need all kinds of emotional, physical, and financial support so that they are not distracted from catering to the physical and psychological needs of the infant, and do justice with the older children also to the extent possible. Of course, the father needs to be there; however, the children need more than just two adults to depend on, as the two parents are often not available for a variety of reasons. Older siblings and cousins, who are not married as yet, or the elderly may provide this support.

The elderly also need care, which is provided by the young. Studies also suggest that the time spent by the elderly with their grandchildren also significantly improves their health and life expectancy (Arpino & Bordone, 2014). Increased life expectancy would allow them to keep spreading their wisdom, provide moral support to their children and grandchildren, and continue to be a center of gravity for the extended family to remain bonded together. The elderly often embody the motherly, where arms are always open for anyone, especially when one is broken, burned out, vulnerable, defeated, wounded, and let down by the outside world. The elderly are the people who can give refuge, who may help one heal and get back on their feet (elderly with toxic personalities may do the opposite; however, their toxicity hints toward some serious flaws in the upbringing they received, as discussed earlier). The elderly help in conflict mediation as well, if a conflict arises among family members. The elderly may also role model altruism and inspire others to follow the same. This inspiration would imply the elderly are seen as a moral authority, which can happen when their children and grandchildren have a healthy relationship with them, which involves open communication. Everyone must speak the same language for such communication to happen. The formal education that the children receive must also facilitate this process of connection with the elderly (something that is yet to happen). The consumer culture which rather tempts youngsters to look for short-term gratification comes in direct contradiction to the environment the elderly intend to create, therefore, access to digital technology which exposes the developing minds to consumerism, must also be restricted until a certain age at least (Charmaraman et al., 2022; O'Keeffe et al., 2011).

The altruistic spirit is reinforced by the meta-norms, which could be religiously inspired and can prevent material competition from surfacing in the first place.

The elderly also role model for practicing their belief system, which provides a rationale to act in an altruistic manner. Altruism may also require everyone to walk at the pace of the slowest member of the family unless the slowest member is supported by others to move at a pace with others. The aim is not to go fast, but far, (borrowing from an African proverb) a perspective which is reinforced by religion as it instructs its followers to look for the long-term over immediate gratification, and even be concerned about what will happen in life after death. The ultimate prize is the union with the most secure and permanent source of nourishment, God, as every other resource, either social or economic, is not permanent and, therefore, does not offer the same sense of security and peace. The detachment from the material, which is achieved by maintaining a frugal lifestyle removes the distractions from connecting with God and also makes it painless, rather bountiful for family members to support and help each other out emotionally, socially, and economically when needed. The selflessness that is achieved may also cultivate patience even when treated unfairly, preventing escalation, and may allow the use of wisdom to address the offense to make the offender realize their mistake, apologize, and make corrections.

The new generation would learn to follow suit when they take inspiration from the elderly; however, this may not happen when they see the ways of the elderly as outdated and incompatible with the demands of the modern age, where the individualistic pursuit of material success is glorified. The inspiration cannot be enforced; a tyrannical environment created by elders, therefore, would naturally tempt the new generation to rebel. The reaction of the elderly during the moments when the young ones are swayed by their temptations would set the tone of the relationship. If the elderly overreacts harshly, they eventually create an environment where fear triumphs over love. Patience, tolerance, and compassion are the key virtues elders should demonstrate. However, they should remind the young ones at the right moment that there are worldly and otherworldly consequences for their actions, especially when these actions harm others. Such harm can occur when one's empathy fails during moments when self-serving temptations override concern for others. One must therefore become cautious and fear the consequences of being swayed by temptations. Such exemplary behavior can only be motivated and sustained when the relationship between elders and the young is based on inspiration, not fear. Taking inspiration from the elderly does not imply becoming stuck in traditional patterns; instead, it involves recognizing the need for change and improvement, especially in the context of the family business in an ever-changing market landscape. Risk-taking, experimentation, and acknowledging gaps or unmet needs in both family and business keep the family firm alive and relevant.

A critical role of the elderly is to distribute property as per the laws of inheritance before they die. At least they would write a will and involve a family lawyer. Preferably, the distribution would be done beforehand to avoid any disputes later on. Daughters are to be given their due share as per the law of inheritance, which has been clearly described in Islamic jurisprudence. Daughters, when denied their share of inheritance, add to their level of insecurity, particularly after their marriage. The sense of security of women in the family is of critical importance in its role, but also due to its implication for the upbringing process of the next generation. As mentioned earlier, insecure mothers likely raise insecure children, and vice versa. Daughters, therefore, also need to be valued for the strategic role they ought to play eventually after becoming mothers, which has implications not just for the social and economic future of the family, but also for the community as a whole. Further, when they acquire the role of being a mother-in-law, they also need to provide a secure environment for the bride, which is only possible when they feel secure themselves. Women in their different roles create a nurturing space, which is critical to raising secure individuals who also possess a strong character or morals. Women also reinforce the bond between old and new generations, and maintain healthy ties between extended family members, as women (when they feel secure) in general are naturally more capable as compared to men for such a task.

The nurturing space with its motherly character, therefore, is a place where social capital is created, a resource that not just comes in handy for the family's internal cohesion, but also for the social sustainability of the community as well. Ideally, every individual who emerges from the nurturing atmosphere should possess a strong character, a sense of security and worth, a hardworking attitude, wisdom to balance between social and economic roles, and empathy to understand the social and economic needs of family and community members. Such an individual should possess an altruistic spirit that remains alive, particularly when it gets difficult to give, but rational enough also to consider the economic sustainability of the family and the family business. When a community can produce such individuals, who interact with each other for social and economic ends, and help each other out whenever needed, the community is expected to sustain itself socially as well. Of course, not everyone embodies such a personality in the community, nor is every family capable of providing the environment described above. An increasing number of individuals and families are perhaps departing from such ideals. However, there is an understanding, quite clear in the community literature, also in the responses of the respondents, which hints toward the ideals that the individuals must set in front of them as a benchmark to emulate, and thus remain altruistic in all levels of their engagement to the extent possible.

To help each other, the giving spirit also requires something to give. This is where the mention of the economic resources and how to generate them becomes significant. Realistically speaking, economic resources are also needed to some extent for a sense of security among individuals. So far, the discussion has been on the social aspect of engagement of family members in this chapter, while Chapter 5 reviewed the socioeconomic character of the community culture. It is pertinent now to look at how the economic activity is organized, how the family is engaged in the process, particularly when it comes to creating a family business, and what enables the businesses to sustain and grow, and become a perpetual source to help the struggling members in the community as well. The data gathered for this study and the previous literature offer valuable insights into this context, which is the topic of Chapters 7 and 8.

References

Afghan, N., & Wiqar, T. (2007). Succession in family businesses of Pakistan: Kinship culture and Islamic inheritance law. In *CMER working paper no. 07-54*.

Al-Ghazali, A. H. (2007). *Ihya Uloom ul-Din: Volume 2 (Reprint)*. Darul-Ishaat.

Anderson, K. J., & Cavallaro, D. (2002). Parents or pop culture? Children's heroes and role models. *Childhood Education, 78*(3), 161–168.

Arpino, B., & Bordone, V. (2014). Does grandparenting pay off? The effect of child care on grandparents' cognitive functioning. *Journal of Marriage and Family, 76*(2), 337–351.

Avloniti, A., Iatridou, A., Kaloupsis, I., & Vozikis, G. S. (2014). Sibling rivalry: Implications for the family business succession process. *International Entrepreneurship and Management Journal, 10*(4), 661–678. https://doi.org/10.1007/s11365-013-0271-6

Baudrillard, J. (2016). *The consumer society: Myths and structures*. SAGE Publications.

Bauer, M. A., Wilkie, J. E. B., Kim, J. K., & Bodenhausen, G. V. (2012). Cuing consumerism: Situational materialism undermines personal and social well-being. *Psychological Science, 23*(5), 517–523.

Bauman, Z. (2013). *Liquid modernity*. Polity Press.

Boudreaux, J. (2022). *"Under Her Feet": A case study on motherhood discourse in an American Muslim community*. The University of Memphis.

Bourdieu, P. (2011). The forms of capital (1986). *Cultural Theory: An Anthology, 1*(81–93), 949.

Bowlby, J. (2012). *A secure base*. Taylor & Francis.

Bubolz, M. M. (2001). Family as source, user, and builder of social capital. *The Journal of Socio-Economics, 30*, 129–131.

Buist, K. L., Deković, M., & Prinzie, P. (2013). Sibling relationship quality and psychopathology of children and adolescents: A meta-analysis. *Clinical Psychology Review, 33*(1), 97–106. https://doi.org/10.1016/j.cpr.2012.10.007

Charmaraman, L., Lynch, A. D., Richer, A. M., & Grossman, J. M. (2022). Associations of early social media initiation on digital behaviors and the moderating role of limiting use. *Computers in Human Behavior, 127*, 107053. https://doi.org/10.1016/j.chb.2021.107053

Coleman, J. S. (1988). Social capital in the creation of human capital. *American Journal of Sociology, 94*, S95–S120. http://www.jstor.org/stable/2780243

Coleman, J. S. (1994). *Foundations of social theory*. Belknap Press of Harvard University.

Cozolino, L. (2014). The neuroscience of human relationships: Attachment and the developing social brain. In *The neuroscience of human relationships: Attachment and the developing social brain, 2nd ed.* W W Norton & Co.

Curtis, A. (2002). *The century of self (documentary)*. BBC Two.

Danes, S. M., Lee, J., Stafford, K., & Heck, R. K. Z. (2008). The effects of ethnicity, families and culture on entrepreneurial experience: An extension of sustainable family business theory. *Journal of Developmental Entrepreneurship, 13*(03), 229–268.

Danes, S. M., Stafford, K., Haynes, G., & Amarapurkar, S. S. (2009). Family capital of family firms: Bridging human, social, and financial capital. *Family Business Review, 22*(3), 199–215.

Dobbin, C. (1996). *Asian entrepreneurial minorities: Conjoint communities in the making of the world-economy, 1570–1940*. RoutledgeCurzon Ltd.

Egbert, H. (1998). Entrepreneurial advantages and disadvantages of belonging. *GeoJournal: Identities in Sub-Saharan Africa, 46*(2), 129–134.

Freitas, D. (2017). *The happiness effect: How social media is driving a generation to appear perfect at any cost*. Oxford University Press.

Gangoli, G., & Rew, M. (2011). Mothers-in-law against daughters-in-law: Domestic violence and legal discourses around mother-in-law violence against daughters-in-law in India. *Women's Studies International Forum, 34*(5), 420–429. https://doi.org/10.1016/j.wsif.2011.06.006

Gao, W., Hou, Y., Nelson, L. J., Xu, Y., & Meng, L. (2024). Helicopter parenting and Chinese university students' adjustment: The mediation of autonomy and moderation of the sense of entitlement. *Journal of Adult Development*. https://doi.org/10.1007/s10804-024-09483-w

Gopalakrishnan, L., Acharya, B., Puri, M., & Diamond-Smith, N. (2023). A longitudinal study of the role of spousal relationship quality and mother-in-law relationship quality on women's depression in rural Nepal. *SSM-Mental Health, 3*, Article 100193.

Grossmann, K., Grossmann, K. E., Kindler, H., & Zimmermann, P. (2008). *A wider view of attachment and exploration: The influence of mothers and fathers on the development of psychological security from infancy to young adulthood.*

Haidt, J. (2023). Devices and desires: Social media is the major cause of the mental illness epidemic among young women. *New Statesman, 152*(5710–5711), 29.

Hoffman, J., Hoelscher, M., & Sorenson, R. (2006). Achieving sustained competitive advantage: A family capital theory. *Family Business Review, 19*(2), 135–145.

Ijaz, S., Ajmal, A., Asad, S., & Kanwal, S. (2021). Perception about mother-in-law. *Pakistan Journal of Social and Clinical Psychology, 19*(2), 22–30.

Jenkins, J. M., Rasbash, J., & O'Connor, T. G. (2003). The role of the shared family context in differential parenting. *Developmental Psychology, 39*(1), 99–113. https://doi.org/10.1037/0012-1649.39.1.99

Khaldûn, I. (2015). *The Muqaddimah: An introduction to history-Abridged edition* (F. Rosenthal, N. J. Dawood, & B. Lawrence (Eds.)). Princeton University Press.

Khan, T. (2021). *Husbands and mothers-in-law as perpetrators of domestic aggression against married women in Pakistan.* Åbo Akademi University. https://www.doria.fi/handle/10024/182724

Kowal, A. K., Krull, J. L., & Kramer, L. (2004). How the differential treatment of siblings is linked with parent–child relationship quality. *Journal of Family Psychology, 18*(4), 658–665. https://doi.org/10.1037/0893-3200.18.4.658

Lu, J., Xie, X., & Wu, M. (2013). Research on social capital and conflict management mechanism of family business's top management team. *Asian Social Science, 9*(11), 70–74.

Morris, A. S., Silk, J. S., Steinberg, L., Myers, S. S., & Robinson, L. R. (2007). The role of the family context in the development of emotion regulation. *Social Development, 16*(2), 361–388.

O'Keeffe, G. S., Clarke-Pearson, K., Media, C. on C. (2011). The impact of social media on children, adolescents, and families. *Pediatrics, 127*(4), 800–804.

Padilla, J., Sang, S. A., Updegraff, K. A., McHale, S. M., Umaña-Taylor, A. J., & De Jesús, S. A. R. (2019). Siblings' appraisals of fairness and jealousy in response to parental differential treatment: Longitudinal links to Mexican-origin emerging adults' adjustment. *Emerging Adulthood, 9*(4), 267–280.

Pearson, A. W., Carr, J. C., & Shaw, J. C. (2008). Toward a theory of familiness: A social capital perspective. *Entrepreneurship: Theory and Practice, 32*(6 Spec. Iss.), 949–969.

Postman, N. (2006). *Amusing ourselves to death: Public discourse in the age of show business.* Penguin Books.

Rodriguez, P., Tuggle, C. S., & Hackett, S. M. (2009). An exploratory study of how potential "family and household capital" impacts new venture start-up rates. *Family Business Review, 22*(3), 259–272.

Saqib, A. (2016). *Kamyab log*. Sang-e-Meel Publications.

Schroeder, A. N., & Cavanaugh, J. M. (2018). Fake it 'til you make it: Examining faking ability on social media pages. *Computers in Human Behavior, 84*, 29–35.

Seaman, C., Bent, R., & Unis, A. (2016). Family entrepreneurship culture, entrepreneurial intent, futures and foresight in Scottish Pakistani communities. *Futures, 75*, 83–91.

Segrin, C., Woszidlo, A., Givertz, M., Bauer, A., & Taylor Murphy, M. (2012). The association between overparenting, parent–child communication, and entitlement and adaptive traits in adult children. *Family Relations, 61*(2), 237–252.

Srivastav, D., & Mathur, M. L. (2020). Helicopter parenting and adolescent development: From the perspective of mental health. *Parenting-Studies by an Ecocultural and Transactional Perspective, 2020*, 1.

Sroufe, L. A., Egeland, B., Carlson, E. A., & Collins, W. A. (2009). *The development of the person: The Minnesota study of risk and adaptation from birth to adulthood*. London: Guilford Press.

Stolle, D., Soroka, S., & Johnston, R. (2008). When does diversity erode trust? Neighborhood diversity, interpersonal trust and the mediating effect of social interactions. *Political Studies, 56*(1), 57–75.

Storr, W. (2018). *Selfie: How the west become self-obsessed*. Pan Macmillan.

Su, R., Rounds, J., & Armstrong, P. I. (2009). Men and things, women and people: A meta-analysis of sex differences in interests. *Psychological Bulletin, 135*(6), 859–884. https://doi.org/10.1037/a0017364

Swartz, T. T. (2009). Intergenerational family relations in adulthood: Patterns, variations, and implications in the contemporary United States. *Annual Review of Sociology, 35*, 191–212. https://doi.org/10.1146/annurev.soc.34.040507.134615

van Ingen, D. J., Freiheit, S. R., Steinfeldt, J. A., Moore, L. L., Wimer, D. J., Knutt, A. D., Scapinello, S., & Roberts, A. (2015). Helicopter parenting: The effect of an overbearing caregiving style on peer attachment and self-efficacy. *Journal of College Counseling, 18*(1), 7–20.

Veblen, T. (2012). *The theory of the leisure class*. Dover Publications.

Waters, E., Merrick, S., Treboux, D., Crowell, J., & Albersheim, L. (2000). Attachment security in infancy and early adulthood: A twenty-year longitudinal study. *Child Development, 71*(3), 684–689.

Weisberg, Y. J., DeYoung, C. G., & Hirsh, J. B. (2011). Gender differences in personality across the ten aspects of the big five. *Frontiers in Psychology*. https://doi.org/10.3389/fpsyg.2011.00178

Chapter 7
Family Firm as a User and Producer of the Moral and Social Capital

The family is a microcosm of the community itself; Chapter 6 discussed the prevailing and required dynamics for it to sustain and produce individuals with a character necessary for social and economic sustainability in the context of the three Pakistani communities. To sustain the social dimension, it is needless to mention that a healthy economic activity is also critical. This chapter describes how the families in the three communities organize themselves economically with the help of moral and social capital and reproduce them with the help of the economic activity. The key instrument used for this purpose is the family firm, which is started, owned, and managed by the family members, or if it is already started or established by the previous generation, then it is carried forward by the new torchbearers. In the process of initiating new ventures or managing the old ones, the involvement of social relationships is profound. The social thus facilitates the economic, the economic then in turn sustains the social.

7.1 Early Training

The impact of the family on cultivating personality needed for the economic sustainability of the family and community was explicitly expressed in data gathered from the three communities. The traits and motivation required to start a venture, if referred to as an entrepreneurial character, were said to be transferred from generation to generation, as newcomers see their elders in the family and extended family starting and running their businesses from an early age. By the time the new generation

This chapter draw from the author's doctoral thesis 'Building a Theoretical Model of Socially Sustainable Entrepreneurship through Comparative Case Analysis of Ethnic Entrepreneurial Communities' submitted to Dept. of Management Sciences, Institute of Business Management (IoBM), Karachi, Pakistan.

O. Javaid, *Socioeconomic Sustainability Through Moral and Social Capital*, Entrepreneurship and Development in South Asia: Longitudinal Narratives,
https://doi.org/10.1007/978-981-96-8134-1_7

reaches the adolescent age, they have already observed several entrepreneurial examples. Often, three generations are found to be living under the same roof. Nurturing of a child is typically done not just by the parents but also by the entire extended family, which acts as a natural incubator to cultivate not just the necessary character, as explored in Chapter 6, but also the entrepreneurial spirit. From an early age, children may start observing the economic activities performed by the adults in the family (IO 22; 23).

In the Memon community, when children pass puberty, their direct training in the family business begins (IS 1; MA 20; IO 1; MF 1; MN 4; MT 1). The family business, therefore, becomes the first training facility for the newcomers. They are typically expected to spend their free time, like summer vacations, in the father's business so that they gain firsthand experience of it (IO 54; MN 38; MT 14; ARJ 37; IS 14). Gaining practical experience is often seen as more important than formal education when it comes to starting and managing a business (IO 56; MA 45; MN 39; IS 55). New comers start working as laborers and work their way to the top only by proving themselves worthy through hard work. In this whole process, the father is seen as a role model and a source of inspiration, as his offspring typically understand that their father also worked his way to the top, so they also have to follow suit (SAP 46; Memon, Jun 2015, p. 5; Aug 2015 p. 6; Aug 2016, pp. 7–8). The family businesses, started by the previous generation of the respondents, typically had a humble start through negligible resources (ARJ 5, 6; Memon Eid Edition, Jul 2015, p. 7; MF 42; MN 11). Multiple decades of hard work and demonstration of perseverance with integrity by elders are considered to be the cause of the affluence enjoyed by the third generation. Having one's grandparents and parents as role models thus inspires the next generation (Memon, Aug 2015; Nov 2015, p. 4; Aug 2016, p. 10, 11; IS 72; ARJ 1; SAP 2; MT 66).

Respondents belonging to the Delhiwala community also suggested that when their children reach the age of adolescence, they receive training in the family business owned by the father (RS 22; SAR 5; JBS 64) or any close relative. Like Memon, their training would start right after school hours, as they were required to spend their spare time in business. In some cases, newcomers were asked to do odd jobs which included 'mopping the floor and serving tea to the guests'. The odd jobs were meant to dissolve any sense of pride they had (TP 7; JBS 7, 66; RS 14). There are no shortcuts, as offspring of the owner of a business, children are not seen as having the natural right to replace their fathers overnight, 'One [rather] has to prove himself worthy by working their way from the lowest to the top through hard work and earning respect' (JBS 7; RS 16, 17). The training of newcomers in Delhiwala happened in the businesses owned by their father typically; however, there are examples where the business is owned by the grandfather (Saudagar, May 2013, p. 84), by a relative (KS 28), or a family friend (TP 3), who played a part in providing experiential learning to the newcomers. As a young apprentice, one respondent described how he learned 'to deal with customers' (FA 21), 'to take a risk' (NS 62), or 'to control operations'. The choice of formal education for newcomers in Delhiwala is likely based on the requirements of the family business (NS 45). Despite formal education, the value of practical experience was considered greater than formal education by some respondents (RS 29, 34; JBS 36, 61; FA 28).

In the Chinioti community, the newcomers are also typically trained in their father's business at an early age. The process often begins as the son enters high school, and continues in parallel with studies (KL, p. 114; AsB 41; UL 12; WK 32). It is believed by respondents that a special protocol for the owner's son would unnecessarily boost his ego. There are examples where the son is expected to start working like a laborer and find his way to the top by only proving he is capable through hard work and persistence (KL, p. 57, 158). Sometimes, young ones are encouraged to work in other businesses also for the same reason (SJ 15). The Chinioti elders may judge the capability of their offspring before assigning responsibilities to them in the business. In the case of multiple siblings, the father typically evaluates the strengths, nature, skill set, and mindset of each son before assigning him responsibilities in the business. For example, those who are strong in calculations may be assigned responsibilities related to accounting and finance. Keeping in view the nature of the father's business and a child's potential, it may be decided to include them in a family business or perhaps help them start a new one (AsB 26, 28, 30; KL, p. 186). The training process is expected to inculcate various character and personality traits summarized in Table 7.1.

Table 7.1 Personality characteristics for entrepreneurial success

Memon	*Delhiwala*	*Chinioti*
'appetite for expansion' (MF 51), 'being bold and vigilant' (MF 37), 'courageous' (MF 65) 'quick learner (IS 13) 'good at calculations' (IO 87; MT 63) 'hard-working' (ARJ 108) 'perseverance' (SAP 74) 'drive for continuous improvement' (MF 54) 'risk-taking' (Memon, Sep 2015, p. 6; MF 55) 'passionate' (Memon, Apr 2016, p. 12) 'self-control' (MT 23) 'having a long-term perspective in mind' (MT 26) 'belief in the Creator' (IO 31) 'patience' (MN 52, 51) 'stress regulation' (MT 21) 'frugal lifestyle' (MT 25) 'avoid being greedy' (MT 27) 'avoid hastiness' (MT 24), and 'keep one's faith in the Creator is the sole provider' (MN 37)	'appetite to learn' (SAR 8) 'strong communication with employees and customers' (FA 41) 'Courage' (FA 40) 'emotional maturity' (RS 33) 'hard-working' (IAP 20; TP 22; JBS 25) 'perseverance' (TP 16; SAR 35), 'humility' (FA 32) 'intuition' (FA 27, 45) 'judgment of character' (KS 6) 'ability to take the risk' (NS 63) 'financial management' (TP 67), 'having skin in the game' (JBS 59) 'visionary' (Saudagar, Feb 2015, p. 13) 'self-reliance' (Saudagar, Sep 2011, p. 29; May 2012, p. 59) 'belief in Creator to provide sustenance' (NS 51; SAR 56; TP 86; JBS 14)	'strong character' (AB 52) 'Courage' (UL 58) 'emotional intelligence', and 'self-control during difficult times' (KL, p. 101, 86, 223, 93) 'self-confidence' 'street-smartness' (WK 69) 'time management' (KL, p. 177, 147) long-term thinking' (KL, p. 253) 'passion' (KL, p. 112) 'hard work and perseverance' (KL, p. 156, 116, 70, 100, 191; SJ 22; AB 13)

7.2 Early Support

It was mentioned by multiple Memon respondents that many among the new generation now want to do a separate business (ARJ 46; MT 1). When they do, the first investment is made by their fathers in a majority of cases (MA 3; IO 4; SAP 20; MT 18). The goodwill of the family typically facilitates budding entrepreneurs to receive credit from the suppliers and orders from the customers (MA 17; MN 22; SAP 59). In the process of setting up a new business, which may take around 3 years (ARJ 25; SAP 9; MT 35), moral support, motivation, guidance, and connections of family elders are often available to help the young ones move forward. The support from elders typically continues well beyond the inception period of a business; rather, it is available for life lifetime (Memon, Aug 2016, p. 6; MT 2; IO 101). Similar support may also be available for the son-in-law (MA 22). Family connections are considered pivotal in finding reliable suppliers and customers, and providing access or knowledge about new opportunities in the market (SAP 58, 10; MT 6, 10). The support from the family and the extended family is believed to reduce the risk of failure so much so that the respondents claimed that the failure rate of new businesses in the community is less than 20% (IS 51; IS 53; ARJ 89; MN 48).

In the Delhiwala community, family elders are generally available for advice and support as well (NS 4; SAR 41; Saudagar, Jan 2011, p. 33; KS 7). The elders also advise on what type of key strengths an entrepreneur should develop (FA 20) or offer moral support in case the business is suffering from a loss (Saudagar, Jan 2011, p. 34). The father's office is often available free of cost when his children are starting a new venture (SAR, 35). The family elders, the father in several cases, are regarded as the first financiers for budding entrepreneurs (IO 26; NS 10; RS 5). Children, once trained, are also trusted to take the father's business forward or expand it horizontally or vertically (Saudagar Dec 2012, p. 69; 1606, p. 64). In one case, the father even left for missionary activities with the *Tablighi Jamat* while leaving the business to his sons (Saudagar, Sep 2010, p. 30). A respondent suggested, 'If the next generation is not ready or is not available for any reason, the business might face a collapse' (FA 39). Elder siblings' role in setting up a business has also been acknowledged on multiple occasions (Saudagar, Jan 2011, 33; Oct 2011, p. 45; KS 39). There are also numerous examples where siblings have been working as partners in the family business (Saudagar, Dec 2012, p. 68; Feb 2015, p. 55; June 2016, p. 64, 92; NS 3).

The Chinioti community also presents a similar picture. In the case of affluent families, when someone intends to start a new business, family elders can provide the necessary guidance, technical knowledge, and connections with suppliers and potential customers to kick-start the business (UL 3). However, before that, the upcoming entrepreneur in the family might have already spent considerable time in his father's or some of his relatives' businesses to gain experience and knowledge about the processes. Customers within the community may be contacted before starting the business to understand their requirements; the potential customer may purchase the product or service once launched if the offering fulfills the requirements (JV 7). Entrepreneurs in the Chinioti community also 'start from what they have' (AB 17;

KL 95), 'what they know' (KL, p. 93), and what resources are available in their network. It is advisable to 'gain some experience in a small business and learn how to manage the whole supply chain' (WK 67, 71, 70, 68; SJ 58, 60). 'Knowing the customer in advance' is also considered important (JV 7; WK 2). Business opportunities can be identified from the information received from the community network (as mentioned earlier). Personal and family credibility is considered important to gain the trust of all stakeholders. Maintaining and growing that credibility through honesty and honoring commitments is, therefore, crucial. The Chiniotis seek investment from the entrepreneur's father (in the majority of cases), father-in-law, or a partnership with some relative or friend (SJ 16; UL 11, 17). It was suggested that if capital is not available within the immediate network, then the person either makes and saves money through a brokerage or by working as an employee for some years (SS 20; SJ 32; JV 12, 13). It is considered important to work firsthand to learn the basics of the business (KL, p. 199, 97, 155; WK 28), which typically happens in a business owned by someone in a family network.

For Memon young entrepreneurs, family goodwill is a key asset when starting a business, which is a product of hard work and integrity sustained for multiple generations (SAP 11, 59; ARJ 14; MT 4). The budding Memon entrepreneurs also need to prove through their conduct with stakeholders that they can uphold the goodwill of the family by honoring their commitments to the customers and suppliers (MT 11). It was mentioned by respondents that suppliers would also give credit if they already know the entrepreneur's father or their family background (MN 22; SAP 19; MT 9). Further establishing the trust with the supplier can be done through timely payments (SAP 16; SAP 12; MT 7; MT 8). In case the business is a B2B, the first customer can also be found within the family's network. Sometimes the customer is already known to the entrepreneur before starting a business. It was noted that established entrepreneurs develop newcomers in their family network by becoming customers. This customer would also bear with the teething problems of the newcomers when they struggle to produce the desired quantity and quality of product at the right time while they go through their early learning curve (IO 3; SAP 58, 3). The assurance of the first customer can give confidence to the newcomers, minimizing their risk, and subsequently reducing their chances of failure as well. It was emphasized that 'one should begin with improvising on the resources already available' (ARJ 10, 8; IO 102, 108) with the family and that 'one should gain the knowledge of the supply chain before entering into a new line of business' (IS 70; IO 105) by engaging with the experts available within the family network; like asking a friend or a family member who is already experienced in the domain (IS 69; MA 2). Further, initial experience can also be gained by working as an employee for someone in the same line of business in the family's network (MT 13; Memon, Nov 2015, p. 4).

Likewise, in Delhiwala, at the time of starting a business, the family's or father's credibility is seen as a bridge to connect with potential suppliers. A win–win mindset and honesty of intentions are a prerequisite (JBS 58). Partners can be from the entrepreneur's immediate network, friends, and relatives (KS 10, 11, 18, 32; FA 6). In several cases, the opportunity to start a business was discovered from within the immediate family network (TP 34; IO 4, 6; NS 5). In several examples, the initial customers are approached using one's personal and family connections (FA 30, 3, 25; KS 2, 5, 8; SAR 31, 27, 30, 29). An entrepreneur's network beyond the family and community can also help find customers or partners (KS 21, SAR 20). Chinioti entrepreneurs evolve in their entrepreneurial endeavors likewise. Chinioti considers mentorship by family or community elders important during the entire process (UL 2, 3, 4, 6, 55; SJ 9, AB 12). The persistent moral and financial support and guidance from the immediate network, coupled with social bonding with the stakeholders, facilitate the budding entrepreneurs. Entrepreneurs also have to do the necessary hard work, with dedication, honesty, strength of character, and other entrepreneurial traits mentioned above, to increase their chances of success. The entrepreneurial failures, as per Chinioti respondents, are less than 15–20% of all businesses started by community members (SS 54), a claim also made by Memon and Delhiwala respondents. However, this claim needs to be verified through statistical data.

7.3 Family Goodwill

Parents' relations with their siblings and other relatives can become a benchmark for the next generation to emulate, as the way parents treat their siblings becomes a template for the children to treat others outside the family. This experience, which is a part of the nurturing process, is considered crucial to developing the strength of character and strong morals, which can help sustain the family's goodwill or credibility in the market. Stakeholders often trust anyone in the market who has a track record of honoring their commitments. The goodwill is thus seen as one of the important assets of the family business in the Memon community (ARJ 14; MT 4; MT 3; SAP 11). In Pakistan, there is a lack of legal enforcement of contracts in the market; it is only the credibility of a person that allows a transaction to happen, particularly when credit is involved. Since such transactions often happen on verbal commitments, they are considered to increase the speed of doing business, while reducing the transaction cost (IS 60; IO 46). The volume of credit from the suppliers is often dependent on the amount of credibility a person has been able to establish over the years. It can take a lifetime to develop goodwill, which even the children can benefit from (SAP 14; MA 16; Jun-16, p. 6). According to one Memon respondent, goodwill used to be the hallmark of the Memon community as they were known to be trustworthy among all (MN 30). A Memon mentioned that the suppliers themselves approach entrepreneurs with strong goodwill and willingly facilitate them by offering raw materials on credit (SAP 17). Partnerships to expand a business can also be possible (IS 27). Honoring commitments to either deliver the service or supplies or make payments as promised is critical to develop and maintain goodwill, and vice versa. Persistent business failures, however, can damage the credibility of an entrepreneur in the market (IS 52; MT 76; ARJ 64, 65; MF 13; MN 26; SAP 16, 12; MT 7, 8). Children emulating the moral standards of family elders can allow the continuation of the family's goodwill across generations (IS 44; Memon, Aug 2016, p. 10).

The data from Delhiwala also emphasize that apart from honoring commitments, being principle-oriented, caring about other's benefit, and being honest, establishes goodwill (Saudagar, May 2014 p. 58; Feb 2015, p. 55, 62; June 2016, p. 64, 63, p. 95; Aug 2016, p. 63, 64). The goodwill ensures long-lasting relationships with suppliers and customers. The idea of putting the customer first was also mentioned repeatedly by Chinioti respondents. If the benefit of the customer is considered supreme and demonstrated through product delivery at the right time, of the right quality, and at the right price, then the loyalty of the customer can be ensured. Going beyond customers' expectations is also practiced in some cases (KL, p. 152, 153, 158; WK 57, 58). Consistency in quality standards can be a source of customer loyalty (SS 27). Delhiwala respondents believed 'giving benefit to the customer even at a loss' (SAR 32), 'remaining honest about the product quality' (TP 30), while remaining 'consistent in delivery' (TP 28) is believed to contribute toward developing customer loyalty and generate a positive word of mouth (TP 29). It was unsurprisingly mentioned by a Delhiwala that 'it takes years to develop such credibility' (IO 41; FA 29). The next generation of Delhiwala also naturally benefits from the goodwill of the previous generations or parents (Saudagar, Oct 2013, p. 71; Feb 2014, p. 28). Access to credit in the market and support from suppliers or vendors are naturally dependent on an entrepreneur's goodwill (IO 41; KS 33).

Every Delhiwala respondent acknowledged the significance of goodwill in achieving business goals to the extent that it was recommended that one's goodwill must not be compromised even if the business suffers a financial loss; as a single negative example can ruin years of hard work of goodwill (RS 41; KS 20; JBS 15; IAP 4; FA 23; IO 41; KS 34; FA 29). Some of the frequently highlighted qualities of prominent personalities in the memoirs in Saudagar Magazine tell us about the dominant values and virtues in the community. Some frequently mentioned qualities include: 'balanced approach toward life', 'collective approach', 'empathy', 'forgiveness', 'hard work', 'humility', 'integrity', 'kindhearted', 'patience', 'perseverance', 'politeness', 'sacrifice', 'self-reliance', 'silah-e-rehmi' (mutual care for immediate family), 'simplicity', 'socializing nature', 'straight forward in communication', 'willpower', 'piety' (God-fearing). It can be deduced that practicing such virtues establishes the reputation or goodwill of an entrepreneur in the community (see Saudagar, Sep 2009, p. 35; Jan 2011, p. 75; Feb 2015, p. 56, 63; Feb 2016, p. 41; Jun 2016, p. 89).

Data from Chinioti sources also endorse that the character of an entrepreneur contributes toward building goodwill, which can help establish strong business relationships with other stakeholders (SS 11; AB 56; KL, p. 116). A track record of honoring commitments with suppliers and customers, along with the demonstration of a win–win approach, is also considered pivotal by Chinioti for developing long-term business relationships (KL, p. 116). The goodwill established by family elders is to be carried forward by the next generation by following the footsteps of their elders, which is an important stepping stone for the new ones to establish themselves as well (SS 23, 37). As seen in the other two communities, easy access to credit from suppliers and establishing customer loyalty are typically linked with the credibility of the owning family (AB 18; UL 15). Financial loss, even the collapse of a business, is seen as a temporary loss, as with the support within community networks, entrepreneurs can reestablish themselves if their goodwill is not damaged; however, the loss of goodwill is considered fatal for the future of the owning family. It is recommended that, in case one has to opt between financial loss and the loss of credibility, then one should opt for the financial loss and maintain credibility (KL, p. 101, 164). The data from the Memon community also contains examples where a person sold his property, even his house, and took his family to a relative's house to make sure he did not default on his payments after one of his major customers refused to pay the owed amount. The data from the Chinioti community also had similar examples.

7.4 Influence of Religion: Taqdeer, Barakah, and Avoiding Haraam

The respondents from all communities would agree that the character and the efforts to develop and sustain goodwill are not meant to impress others, or even for the sake of financial success, but because it is mandated by religious beliefs. The financial success that follows is also typically seen as a blessing of the Creator or God, irrespective of how much one follows religious guidelines in every aspect of their business and personal life. Business outcomes, in other words, are perceived as a result of fate or *taqdeer*, which suggests that the amount of income is determined by the will of the Creator that is ordained when an entrepreneur works hard with purity of intention. The quantum of output (profit) is not believed to be a result of effort, let alone piety. Respondents considered new business opportunities a function of the will of the Creator. Delhiwala likewise believes the same (JBS 3, 5, 14) but the Divine blessing comes only when one works hard (TP 87; SAR 56; NS 51, 52) with honesty (Saudagar, Feb 2012, p. 94) and pure intentions (JBS 46, 55). In other words, it will require hard work to achieve whatever quantity of output is ordained by the Creator. Abidance to the teachings of Islam, while avoiding *haraam*[1] (KS 9, RS 39), is believed to be the key to pleasing the Creator, who would provide sustenance and *barakah*[2] in income. There are examples where the choice of business and product advertisement (Saudagar, Jan 2011; p. 34; IAP 66) was influenced by the religious mindset of the entrepreneur. 'One needs to work hard, keep intentions pure' (JBS 46, 55), and 'leave the results to Allah' (NS 52). 'When people think

[1] Haraam is anything prohibited in the teaching of Islam, like interest-based transactions are strictly prohibited, selling alcohol or anything intoxicating substance is prohibited, earning through cheating is prohibited, or by causing undue harm or injustice to any living being etc.

[2] Barakah is an Islamic concept which implies that more is less, as one is able to achieve more with fewer resources. It also implies that the work is done with ease, and barriers in a path toward a legitimate goal are removed through Divine intervention.

that they are in control, they invite trouble' (TP 86). 'The wealth is considered as a trial; the Creator would test his subjects with less and more of material prosperity to check the level of their piety' (TP 42). *Taqdeer*, the Islamic concept that *rizq*[3] is determined by the Creator, is a dominant belief, as per a Chinioti respondent (SS 40). 'God is the primary owner of everything' (KL, p. 142). 'An entrepreneur's job is to work hard; however, the result is determined by the will of the Creator,' suggests another Chinioti respondent (SS 12). 'The result is not seen as a cause of the hard work'; rather, hard work is believed to only open the possibility of receiving what is willed by the Creator (KL, p. 152). The pleasure of the Creator is rather seen connected to charitable giving, instead of hard work, and the prayers of the parents and grandparents (AB 57) which adds *barakah* in rizq. The wealth is also seen as a test, given in excess for the sake of distribution, that is, to what extent the receiver can spend it as per the teachings of Islam. Success is also defined in non-material terms like respect in the community and salvation on the Day of Judgment (JV 11, AsB 81).

For Memon respondents, more important than income is the peace of mind that emerges from creating a positive impact on the lives of others and family members. Further, more important than the quantum of income is *barakah* which emerges when the Creator is pleased with a believer's actions (IS 48, 65; ARJ 90; MA 11, 40; MF 43, 49, 50, 48; MN 36, 49, 12, 37; SAP 56, 72; MT 74). Memon respondents believed that, along with the grace of the Creator, *barakah* in the income can be a desired outcome of avoiding any prohibited action, like missing commitments, dealing in prohibited items. Several respondents consulted religious scholars to make sure about the legitimacy of their transactions and business practices, for that matter (ARJ 63, MT 70; MT 89; MF 56). Delhiwala also concurs, 'One needs to remain steadfast while avoiding any business practice prohibited in Islam' (Saudagar, Jan 2014, p. 47; Apr 2014, p. 69) and 'give charity as required' (Saudagar, Apr 2014, p. 69, NS 42; JBS 42). Giving charity (JBS 42, NS 42, TP 88), taking care of the needs of the deserving and stakeholders (JBS 16), and abiding by the principles of Islam are considered to be a source of *barakah* in the business (TP 88; KS 15). Likewise, Chinioti also believes that doing any activity prohibited in Islam, like dealing in usurious loans or transactions, is believed to reduce *barakah* (AsB 19). Doing a form of business that is prohibited in Islam, like opening a cinema, may also reduce *barakah* from the income (KL, p. 180). Cheating and unfair dealing with customers and suppliers is also considered another way to remove *barakah* (AB 64). According to a Delhiwala respondent, community members generally believe that employment has less *barakah* than trade; for the same reason, ancestors of community members were encouraged to come into business (TP 73). Doing business may have more *barakah* than doing a job, 'which is another of the reasons why Memons do business', according to a Memon respondent (MF 52). *Barakah* has been defined in many ways by Memon, for example, being able to pay all employees and generate profit, despite the calculations showing that the business is in loss (MF 60); having

[3] Rizq is the amount of tangible and intangible things upon which a person's survival and well-being is dependent.

good health; having children with sound character; no conflict in the family (ARJ 93); money and opportunities coming in unexpectedly; and removal of barriers when one intends to accomplish any legitimate goal (MA 13; ARJ 97, 92). Mother's prayers are considered important in this context for Memon (MF 47). Memon respondents believed charity to be another important way of increasing barakah in business, particularly the amount made compulsory for well-off Muslims known as *zakat.* A part of *zakat*, charity contribution for philanthropic activities, appears to be a part of Memon's culture. The *jamaat* of every sub-group within the Memon community, it was noted, collects and disperses the zakat and other forms of donations to the needy 'in an organized and disciplined manner' (MN 59, 60; IO 76; MA 24; MF 24; ARJ 101; Memon, Oct 16 p. 1; Jul 15).

Religious orientation, such as their belief in *taqdeer*, was also identified as an inhibitor of conflict between family members. It was said that 'everyone eats from what has been provided by Allah ... 'We are given not to consume but rather to benefit others, particularly our family members and relatives', such a belief and moral code is said to strengthen the bonding between family members (ARJ 96; MN 47, 33, 68). So, any family member who may not contribute equally to the business because of a genuine reason is still supported by the rest (IO 33, 68). Chinioti also sees business as worship due to its ability to positively contribute to the lives of family members and employees (KL, p. 124, 233). Charity is also considered by Chinioti a prerequisite for business expansion (KL, p. 233). Community entrepreneurs often believe that giving to charity will expand their business and add *barakah* to their income (KL, p. 87, 219, 101). Data suggested that the women from the Chinioti community are dedicated to charity work and helping the needy. According to a Chinioti respondent, the philanthropic nature of their women is the reason behind the affluence of the Chinioti community (SS 13, 47, 48). Women can act as role models in this context and teach their children to give back to society (KL, p. 84, 257). There are examples of hospitals, schools, mosques, and community centers that are run by the donations of the Chinioti affluent class (UL 54; SJ 28). Zakat, the compulsory charity according to Islamic Shariah, is given with due diligence (KL, p. 87, 86). The charity work is typically done without show-off and kept confidential, as recommended in Islam (SJ 63, SS 47). A common trend is to support deserving community members to become entrepreneurs or help them find employment (WK 60). Business success is seen as a reward from the Creator (KL, p. 128, 152, 198, 233; AB 57; SS 12; UL 44) for doing all the good, following the principles of Islam in business and personal life, paying alms and charity. The tendency to respect elders and sacrifice self-interest for the immediate family, relatives, the community, and all stakeholders in the business is an outcome of religious orientation, which is also said to positively impact the relationship with stakeholders in the business (KL, p. 146).

Avoiding interest-bearing loans or borrowing from banks to run or expand a business is seen as another major contributor to the barakah of a business, as per Memon (MA 12). Hence, the Bank loans are avoided by all means possible by all Memon respondents (MT 33; MT 68; IS 24; IO 5; MF 26; ARJ 22; SAP 57; MN 16,

23). Expanding organically, by reinvesting profits, doing *Musharakah*[4] (ARJ 24, MF 44), or borrowing from a family elder (when in need), are possible ways to establish or grow a business. One respondent even suggested that his family business grew faster when banks were avoided altogether (IO 8). Delhiwala also avoids bank loans. None of the respondents suggested it as a legitimate option for business expansion. The profits are typically reinvested (Saudagar, Jan 2011, p. 34, JBS 9; TP 24, 69) or a partnership is sought with potential investors to expand the business (NS 39; RS 21; TP 41). One respondent even shared his experience of getting into financial trouble after getting a loan and recovering from the trouble after paying off the bank loan (IO 12, 13). Islamic banking is considered a legitimate option by a few respondents in case there is a requirement for financial leverage to expand the business or manage the running expenses in larger businesses (IAP 49, RS 42). Also, as per Chinioti respondents, small and medium entrepreneurs avoid taking a loan on interest from banks, as it is prohibited by the teachings of Islam (WK 39, AsB 17; SS 39; UL 39). The respondents often believe that bank loans are responsible for business failures due to increased vulnerability to unforeseen mishaps like unexpected disturbances in law and order in the city. The Chinioti people's aversion to bank loans leads them to seek capital from alternative sources, such as family members and relatives. They often partner with potential investors to expand the business. Alternatively, they can reinvest their profits to expand the business without incurring external liability. Reinvesting profits can sometimes slow down the business expansion; however, it may also improve the business's stability during difficult times, which is perceived as increased *barakah* in business.

7.5 Sociocultural Particularity of Business Strategies

7.5.1 Goals

The primary goal sought by the Memon to expand a business is to contribute toward the financial security of the new generation, particularly when siblings in the family are partners in a family business and their children are likely to take charge of the business in the coming future (IS 9; IO 29, 61; MN 9; MT 53). It is believed by respondents that diversification in product portfolio according to the developing market requirements is critical to sustaining the business, 'if willed by Allah', of course (MT 52, 16, 86; ARJ 13, 74, 83, 7). Despite these intentions, according to a Memon respondent, community entrepreneurs of small and medium sizes often do not plan in detail ahead for their expansion. Strategic goals do exist, however, strategic planning to achieve those goals is unheard of among the Memon community in general (IS 66, 67, 68). The reason could be the uncertain nature of the macroeconomic conditions of the country, and also that outcomes are seen more as a result of God's grace and less due

[4] A form of profit and loss sharing partnership as advocated by Islamic jurisprudence.

to personal efforts. In the Chinioti community, business diversification is seen as a requirement to survive and take the business forward. It is not advisable to put all eggs in one basket. Market saturation and expanding families can create pressures on the business to diversify (KL, p. 153, 156, 203, 71). To diversify, ideas and guidance can come from the family networks. The interactions in social events can allow Chinioti entrepreneurs to share and discuss experiences of investing and extending a business in a particular domain. The success of an entrepreneur can encourage others to follow suit (as highlighted earlier). In Delhiwala, future trends can be determined through customer engagements (KS 19, TP 31). The expansion is often motivated by the intention of creating space for the upcoming generation (NS 49; TP 63). New lines of business are often started to accommodate the children once they are ready (TP 65). Hence, horizontal integration into related markets and vertical integration across the supply chain are perhaps two convenient options (IAP 1; JBS 12; TP 27, 32) thanks to the resources available in personal and professional networks (JBS 43).

7.5.2 Financial Management

Experimentation has a cost; therefore, Delhiwala respondents claimed that knowledge about the entire supply chain before starting a business is fundamentally important. It was recommended to find a job in the SME (Small and Medium Enterprise) sector of interest (IAP 83, 84) to gain relevant experience (Saudagar, Feb 2016, p. 42). Knowledge about the competition and consumer behavior was also considered important; it was suggested that 'spending time as a salesman can help an aspiring entrepreneur to understand how the market works' (FA 10, 20). In two cases, there were multiple years of job experience before the respondent started their business (KS 1; FA 1). Keeping the cost low is naturally seen as critical; however, what is notable is the insistence on keeping personal expenses low while maintaining a frugal lifestyle, as the cost of living of an entrepreneur and his family also eventually becomes the cost of doing business (Saudagar, Jun 2016, p. 72). This was also endorsed by Chinioti respondents (AB 20, 34; SJ 59; SS 3). A respondent even emphasized that 'any unnecessary office expense also needs to be avoided to keep costs low' (JBS 58). All of this gets difficult when there is a need to show off. So, to override the temptation, apart from the religious reason, if there is one, there is also a strong economic reason, that is, 'minimization of the cost, to increase the net profits and reinvest in businesses. Reinvestments are preferred over taking investments, as the preference appears to be financial independence, instead of speed of expansion, which is preferred to be 'organic, slow and steady' (FA 17; KS 17; IAP 85), a tactic also used by Chinioti entrepreneurs. It was also suggested that at least 3 years should be given to a new business to achieve breakeven, 1 year in case of the service industry (FA 53, 53; SAR 33). Entrepreneurs start with the available resources (Saudagar, Dec 2012, p. 68; SAR 21). It was suggested that 'not more than 50% capital at hand should be invested' (NS 62), 'one must not go beyond his means' (JBS 58), and 'chosen domain must be according to a person's skill set' (SAR 18). Memon here would also agree with Delhiwala. It was further recommended by a Memon respondent that while starting a venture, it is better to avoid two things: (1) credit of the supplier, and (2) blocking cash by acquiring inventory without assurance from any customer (MA 5, 6). Another key tactic Memon uses to keep the cost low is to partner with someone in the family and friend circle who possesses the necessary experience instead of hiring a professional or a consultant. In the Chinioti community also, getting family members and relatives on board is a norm; they eventually share responsibilities, take a share in profits, and do not take salaries during the struggling phase of the business, in comparison to an employee who may leave during such times.

7.5.3 Raising Capital

Most Delhiwala respondents believed that organic expansion strategies are better than taking large jumps using bank borrowings. The profits need to be reinvested thus, while the cost of doing business has to be controlled and minimized (TP 68; 60; 31). Several respondents agreed that change is necessary for survival and expansion (IO 36; NS 2; TP 14, 15; RS 19, 24), and if the business is not expanding, then the possibility of decline may increase (RS 25; NS 47, 49). To expand a business, profits are typically reinvested and bank loans are avoided by Memon as mentioned above (IO 10; SAP 57; MT 71). Apart from religious reasons, several practical reasons were also described by Memon. The bank loans can make it difficult to see the incurred loss unless they become large enough to be damaging; the debt-to-equity ratio can be disturbed, and pressure to pay to a bank can reduce the efficiency of managing a business. Sometimes, with a bank's money, one may expand a business to an extent that it becomes difficult to manage, often leading to failure. The bank interest can increase the cost of production, reducing the profit of a business. One Memon respondent, after getting rid of bank loans, liquidated some of his property to generate cash for the business. 'Working with cash', suggested one respondent, 'makes an entrepreneur more careful and risk-averse' thus reducing failures (IO 12–18). To expand the business, a partnership is often done with potential investors in the entrepreneur's personal or professional network (ARJ 23; SAP 6, 61). Chinioti also typically arrange capital to expand their business from the family, in-laws, partners, and suppliers willing to offer credit, and reinvest business profits, as mentioned earlier. The trust and reputation that exist between the family, relatives, and friends are considered pivotal here. Banks are typically avoided, first and foremost, by Chinioti, due to religious reasons, and also because a business running on bank finance is considered more vulnerable to market shocks. Chinioti respondents described the market scenario to be generally unpredictable, and also due to the law and order situation, doing business became difficult. In such a scenario, liabilities owed to financial institutions may negatively influence business performance and lead to bankruptcy (AsB 16). The rise in the cost of business due to interest on bank loans is another reason for business failure mentioned by Chinioti respondents. Borrowings from family members may not create such threats, provided that financial resources are available. Nevertheless, the business can be expanded keeping in view the available resources, not beyond that, often restricting the expansion, but keeping the business stable and under the control of the owners. Some of the business giants in the community, however, do involve banks to run and expand their operations. However, medium or smaller firms prefer reinvesting profits or finding capital in their immediate network.

A religious belief can help to keep profit margins high. Religion advocates living a modest lifestyle. This reduces the personal expenses of the owners and thus allows them to keep the selling prices low, increase their profits, and reinvest more capital into the business (SS 3, 15, 16; UL 43; KL, p. 68, 76, 95, 157, 255, 257). 'Doing ordinary things by hand [that can be done easily by hand] was mentioned as one of the ways' (UL 36) to keep the costs down, particularly in small businesses or when businesses are in the startup phase, as buying machines would incur extra cost. A Memon respondent also suggested that small businesses are more cost-effective (MA 7) and easier to maintain by a family (MT 46). However, if the family is prone to lavish spending, it can negatively affect the balance sheet, ultimately risking the survival of the business (UL 50; SJ 40, 41). One respondent suggested that minimizing the cost of business is one of the key attributes of Chinioti entrepreneurs; 'we are very smart purchasers', said one respondent (SJ 14), as 'it is in how we purchase that determines the profit margins'. The trend of living a frugal life may not be carried forward by the coming generations in the Chinioti community, as they are more concerned with showing off their affluence, as discussed earlier. Elders, however, kept the cost low by avoiding unnecessary expenses, and also by avoiding banks that eliminate the financial cost, the savings were then reinvested in the business for expansion (KL, p. 84, 89, 90, 121, 126, 191; AsB 20, 21, 54; AB 51).

7.5.4 Professionalization and Hiring

Chiniot may prefer to hire family members due to emotional reasons; however, the tilt toward family members or relatives is to an extent that it does not damage the business, 'meritocracy' was not typically absent while engaging with the family members (AsB 36; WK 46, 51), the rational approach therefore keeps the emotional angle within limits. Relatives are also hired, but they are not typically preferred as they are expected to leave as soon as they gain experience and start their own business. However, relatives are accommodated if there is a prior understanding with them about their plans. Professionalism and meritocracy, however, would not be compromised when managing large enterprises. There are examples where family members and relatives can only be a part of the organization if they qualify. Their compensation can also be decided through a professional human resource management system (KL, p. 186, 193). As a business expands, professional systems are often incorporated by the Chinioti owners to control the operations. 'For businesses larger than SMEs, hiring of professionals to run a business may become indispensable', also suggests one Memon respondent (ARJ 47). 'Hiring of professionals and delegating their responsibilities is an initiative of the educated generation in Chinioti'

(KL, p. 159). The responsibilities can be delegated to hired professionals, making the decision-making process decentralized and independent of the owner's personality (KL, p. 159). 'Such a delegation is considered necessary for business expansion' (WK 55; SS 10). Professionalization may involve creating documented policies and procedures regarding business operations, particularly HR and production, defining working boundaries of departments and individuals, and setting up performance and quality standards (KL, p. 193, 127, 184; AsB 28; SS 32). Hiring professionals, departmentalization, defining roles and responsibilities, respecting merit, and rewarding performance are also considered by several respondents in the Memon community. It was mentioned by a Memon respondent that the employees are hired on merit, and community-based relations often help in finding the right employee who can perform the job as required (IS 31, 34; SAP 54; MT 37, 36). Relatives are often helped in finding a job in some other businesses instead (MT 38). Smaller businesses may, however, be maintained informally (IO 57; IS 59). Community members with strong references can be hired in smaller businesses only if they prove trustworthy and fulfill the performance expectations of the employer (IS 34). Delhiwalas, however, were more particular about the 'selection of employees and suppliers as per merit' (TP 25). However, 'through personal connections, employees would also be located' (KS 48). It appeared that there was little preference for community members at the time of hiring; rather, respondents hired employees from all backgrounds on merit as and when needed (TP 45, SAR 48). One Delhiwala respondent was particular about not hiring relatives as it can hurt the performance of the business (JBS 56, 57). Smaller and newer firms owned by Delhiwala find employees through referrals (FA 48; TP 52, 55); one respondent suggested that smaller businesses in the community usually also prefer to hire qualified professionals to the extent a business can afford (TP 49). The bigger firms can also use job-hunting websites or other formal mechanisms to find employees (IO 30, SAR 56).

If family members are directly involved in the business, then responsibilities need to be divided according to the skill of each family member, and induction of family members into the business can be done systematically to avoid any disruption in the business, as recommended by one Delhiwala respondent (NS 7). Systems and SOPs are believed to be important to develop when the business grows out of the startup phase (FA 44). According to a Memon respondent, 'documentation in a smaller business is done to an extent required for taxation purposes and to avoid any conflict between partners' (MT 90). One respondent even asked his son to work for a professionally run firm to learn how a corporate system works, for the sake of implementing it in his organization (ARJ 75). In Chinioti businesses, also, often the departments are maintained by siblings, who appear to respect each other's authority in their respective domains (AsB 30). The development of a hierarchy with a system to enforce performance is seen as important to curb nepotistic tendencies, as relatives and family members are then subjected to the rules of the business instead of their personal preferences (KL, p. 186, 193). It is well understood by Chinioti that nepotism will not be allowed to hinder product delivery and customer relationships, and if family members are employed, then they need to be trained appropriately to avoid any pitfalls in business performance.

If siblings prefer to work in a Chinioti family business, then they work as partners and share responsibilities with mutual consensus in the family-owned business (WK 6; AsB 24, 27; KL, p. 90, 105, 156, 201). However, when the cousins arrive in the next generation, the business division may become a preferred option if there is no proper system to share responsibilities and profits (KL, p. 101, 273, 131; UL 25, 18). However, in case there is a family constitution already devised by the elders that defines the process of inducting the new generation, then such a division can be averted. The family constitution can document the process of induction, define the responsibilities of the new entrants, and how much share they will receive from the profits, or if they will be appointed on salaries in the early years of their engagement (KL, p. 131, 186, 193). There are examples in the Chinioti community where family-owned business groups in Chinioti families accommodate their fourth or fifth generation. If the necessary systems are in place, then the next generation can start from where the previous ended, and take the business to new heights, like a relay race' (KL p. 204). However, such a transition may require a detailed family constitution, training, and character development of the new generation, which is deemed necessary for creating synergy and interdependence among all heirs (KL p. 204).

7.5.5 Working Environment

Managing employees was mentioned as a challenging aspect of doing business by a Chinioti respondent (AsB 32). An inclusive employment policy was in place, suggesting that people from outside the community were also employed (UL 22; SS 30; AsB; 58). However, for jobs related to inventory and cash handling, they can prefer someone from their community, a relative, or a family member who is naturally seen as more trustworthy (UL 13). Relationship with employees, however, was mentioned by respondents to be family-like and friendly (KL, p. 88, 149, 153). A lenient attitude over minor discrepancies in performance was expressed (AsB 36; WK 46, 51). Special attention was given to employee personal needs by Chinioti entrepreneurs as religion requires taking care of one's employees (KL, p. 77, 88, 206; SS 50). In this context, business has been regarded as a means to make a positive contribution to the lives of stakeholders, particularly employees (KL, p. 124, 233). The result is often a negligible turnover rate and better output by employees (AsB 38; SS 49). Respondents from Memon (MA 38) and the Delhiwala community (TP 58) also emphasized that good relationships with employees can lead to a negligible turnover rate, particularly in smaller or medium-sized businesses. The Memon respondents also highlighted that the relationship with employees is kept more personal and less bureaucratic (SAP 47). In Delhiwala also the relationship in the working environment was facilitative and friendly instead of impersonal or bureaucratic, in businesses owned by at least three respondents (FA 50; KS, 29; TP 12). However, in businesses bigger than SMEs, the relationship was noticed to be more impersonal in Delhiwala. In Memon, there are examples where employees are even treated and facilitated like family members (MA 37; SAP 48), and the owner also helps them in case of a crisis at home (IS 30). Firing an employee who has received years of training is considered more costly as compared to hiring a new one by a Memon (MA 18). The Memon monthly periodical reported that 'minor negligence by employees should be ignored' (SAP 49, 50), and 'employees should be cared for and trusted' (Memon, Aug 16, p. 10). According to one respondent, a 'friendly, even family-like relationship can improve productivity' (SAP 47). Likewise, senior employees are often seen as assets (MA 18; ARJ 50; SAP 51). In the Delhiwala community also the working atmosphere for the employees was mentioned as cordial on several occasions, as employees were allowed to express their concerns openly with the owner (JBS 28, 38; FA 33, 50, 38, 34; SAR 6). For a Delhiwala respondent, employees were like family members. Some of the respondents even helped their employees start their own business while partnering with them, and some helped them in difficult times (JBS 23; FA 57; KS 35, 36, 37). In some examples from Delhiwala, the new generation of owners was required to earn respect from senior and older employees before assuming authority over them (RS 16, 17; TP 17; SAR 6).

7.6 Conflict Prevention and Resolution

Involvement of family members in managing the same firm increases the possibility of conflict, as discussed earlier also as rational factors, which aim at the survival and growth of the business, can go against the emotional expectations of family members with each other. To prevent conflicts and resolve them when they arise, several tactics and measures were mentioned by respondents. Before the list of more proactive prevention strategies, below is a quick overview of all the causes behind conflicts found in the collected data; eliminating them would also help prevent conflicts:

1. **The absence or loosely written agreement:** As per a respondent, "the lack of documentation and subsequent collapse of trust leads to conflict and business failure" (KS 18). Partners who are also family members often assume that a written agreement is unnecessary. They might believe that a simple verbal agreement suffices, leading to misunderstandings and disagreements that could escalate into disputes needing mediation. Even when a written document outlining the terms and conditions exists, it may lack clear guidelines for managing unexpected financial issues. This ambiguity can lead to disputes among partners regarding the distribution of losses or decisions on reinvesting versus withdrawing funds for personal use in the event of substantial profits. A respondent explained, "The documents were in place, but we had agreed that there would be no profit taking for the first 6 months. However, a personal issue arose. [metaphorically] The chickens grew up quickly and started laying eggs. The egg sellers started arguing about who would eat the eggs" (WK 59).

2. **Unequal contributions:** In a family business, elders might allocate an equal share of profits or responsibilities to siblings or cousins, regardless of the actual contribution they are expected to make. For instance, a respondent explained, "One brother's children are interested in getting more education, they are going to college. The other brother's children are not interested in studying but rather working in the business instead. Now their wives complain about why we are getting the same share despite more members of our family working?" (SAR 44). If the elders have not correlated income shares with the level of contribution in the business, or if they have not established a mechanism to address future disparities that may arise for various reasons, it could lead to or exacerbate existing resentments among siblings or cousins who are also business partners.
3. **Personal expenses:** Divergent family needs can lead to varying spending preferences among partners. For instance, a partner's wife from a wealthy background might wish to preserve her accustomed lifestyle, unlike another partner's wife who comes from a modest background. These lifestyle disparities can result in different spending levels between partners. Such differences may breed resentment if one partner is perceived to have more than the others, potentially cultivating animosity. One respondent explained, "If the home expenses of one partner are high, then he keeps using his profit in that, but this thing has to be considered. Conflict emerges when expenses increase, and income does not increase that much" (IS 31).
4. **Consumer culture:** The spread of consumer culture has already been discussed in Chapter 6. One explained, "This new generation is much more influenced by things like branding and materialism. We want to travel all over Europe, wear those branded shirts, and have expensive watches ... older folks, our parents... were very simple, all focused on saving, and not materialistic at all. Hardworking and simple. A whole different world" (UL 23). Overspending, therefore, may create a sense of competition between partners or their families, subsequently creating financial pressure both on the business and family relations.
5. **Generation gap:** Several respondents noted that modern education and internet usage among the new generation of family business owners have led to changes in lifestyle choices and family dynamics. The greater exposure to modern values and trends has led to situations where younger members sometimes display disobedience and disrespect toward elders, undoing the elders' efforts to maintain family unity. One respondent explained, "I have also seen a business in our communities where the son was telling his father, 'What have you done? We could have made four times more money.' The old father stepped aside and said, 'Okay, you go ahead.' And today that factory is no more" (MF 24).
6. **Control over business:** A respondent shared, "The conflict that arises is due to a difference in authority. It is seldom on the pay scale. ... You think you will be able to run it better your way ... your partner also believes that he will be able to run it better his way [conflict happens]" (AB 14). This may stem from a partner's belief that their skills, expertise, and capabilities surpass those of the other members, making them more appropriate for the leadership role. Conversely, the partner

might perceive the contributions of other family members as less valuable to the venture than their own, thus deserving greater control.

7. **Coherence among cousins:** As per a respondent, "there is a natural love [that exists between siblings] that does not exist in cousins. This is natural because even if we meet at home or their house, my parents are different, your parents are different, their parents are different, we are all raised differently" (NS 25). The likelihood of disagreement among the third generation is higher due to their varied upbringings, distinct values, life goals, and priorities. These variances may result in the cousins desiring to steer the business in different directions. Additionally, the unequal contributions from the previous generation can create friction among the cousins, particularly if someone's parents, who invested more, claim more control over the business.
8. **Inheritance distribution:** The respondents indicate that inheritance distribution is usually formalized through a will written by the deceased's parents. In the absence of a will, family elders or the heirs themselves often decide the distribution. However, disputes among heirs can arise if the assets are distributed unfairly. Most "disputes occur because of the injustice done in inheritance distribution" (FA 18). Additionally, respondents feel that non-adherence to Islamic law in inheritance distribution can cause conflict within the family.
9. **Systemization of business:** The data indicates that in smaller firms without well-defined processes and proper record-keeping protocols, partners may grow suspicious of each other due to the sums withdrawn from the business accounts. According to a respondent, "the absence of documentation creates an obstacle in resolving conflicts, perpetuating suspicion and eroding trust" (MT 42). Such mistrust can ignite disputes among family members who are partners, especially on days when profits are low or losses occur.

7.6.1 Conflict Prevention

The following is a list of factors identified in the data that may prevent conflict from occurring in the first place. If these factors are absent along with the causes mentioned above, there is a greater likelihood of conflict. Their absence can also be seen as a cause. Some have already been discussed in Chapter 6, so details will not be discussed here, only a brief mention. These factors are listed below:

1. **Religious orientation:** Many respondents mentioned that their religious beliefs helped them view their life as a temporary experience and their wealth as a test from God. These beliefs make material possessions less important, so when a loss occurs, it is not felt as strongly. If someone else is responsible for the loss, such as a family member or business partner, forgiving is easier. On the other hand, becoming too attached to material possessions can lead to anger and cloud one's judgment when experiencing a loss. This can make it difficult to investigate the actual cause of the loss. However, if one's partner makes an honest mistake, forgiving and moving forward is easier. Additionally, religious orientations that

encourage modesty and giving can help limit material competition among partners. This can prevent rifts from forming, especially during a recessionary phase in the business. Ultimately, these religious beliefs can help individuals address difficult situations calmly and tactfully, even when malpractice is involved. Here are some examples from the statements made by respondents: "Where one does not fear Allah, there is mischief going on" (SA 21); "Avoiding conflicts adds Barakat" (CH4); "We avoid conflicts by saying that is Allah's will" (TP 13); "Being a Muslim we support each other, Everyone eats from his *naseeb* [what Allah ordains], not effort" (JV 47).

2. **Social cohesion.** In case of a conflict, mutual respect and understanding among the members can ease the situation. The parents must model the spirit of cooperation, sacrifice, mutual support, and tolerance during their children's upbringing. This spirit of cooperation can also help avoid or resolve conflicts among partners outside the family or community. However, all partners must possess these traits and reciprocate accordingly. It was suggested that "as your family grows, you have to invest in creating a bond between those family members. On the other hand, the bond between brothers is natural in a family, it does not have to be created. They are also living in the same house and celebrating Eid [a religious festival] together. However, in the growth of the family, you have to ensure that bonding happens" (IAP 28).
3. **Interdependence:** As reported by the respondents, the elders would often identify the natural abilities or potential of the new members of the family. They would then nurture an environment where every family member could contribute as per their potential, and receive a fair share of the profit accordingly. The parents instilled mutual respect and understanding, which was considered essential for sustaining this cooperative environment. Furthermore, having interdependent relations with family members adds another dimension to the logic of maintaining ties. According to the respondents, the cost of conflict is dependent on the extent to which two or more people rely on each other's skills, resources, and networks. A respondent from the Chinioti community suggested, "All of our brothers are involved in this business. The brother who is good at math looks after accounts, and the brother who has a cool temperament deals with labor. We have defined our boundaries; no brother interferes in the work of another" (SS 45). Apart from economic, interdependence is also socioemotional and spiritual. The details are discussed in Chapter 8.
4. **Emotional Maturity:** Rapid expansion or sudden loss may lead to emotionally challenging situations. Therefore, it is essential to remain modest, and humble, and avoid any arrogant behavior, one respondent suggested "They have to teach you … to be modest, you need to be humble. Or the air that is filled inside you in the beginning, you have to deflate it" (MF 19). A steadily expanding business, with dedicated, interdependent, emotionally mature partners, was referred to as an ideal state that may avert the possibility of disputes. Emotional maturity may, however, depend on the upbringing experience of partnering members as discussed earlier.

5. **Family constitution and documentation:** Some respondents mentioned the need to develop a family constitution to ensure the survival of the business across generations. It was reported, "… a family business professor … promised to prepare a strategy for us. Now we are working with him to create a family constitution so that the business can move forward under regular principles and its fruits can continue from generation to generation" (SJ 46). A family constitution is a document that outlines the roles, responsibilities, rights, induction processes, boundaries, exit protocols, shares in profits, ownership transfer or investment processes, and more. The process of revising the family constitution with mutual consent can also be a part of the document. The document serves as a defining criterion, providing a structure for the new generation to continue the family business, which helps in avoiding and resolving disputes. The process of developing consensus can also be described in the constitution during ambiguous situations.
6. **Professionalism:** Respondents recommended clearly defining, documenting, assigning, and agreeing upon all operational processes, rules, policies, roles, and responsibilities within the organization. "We have probably kept this in a very professional way. Everyone does one job, there is no mixed, no joint responsibility … we have a complete proper hierarchy, in which I have a role, others have theirs" (SI 35) shared one respondent. It was stressed that all transactions must be recorded diligently, and all contracts should be documented under legal supervision.
7. **Justice by elders:** Another possible way to avoid conflicts recommended by respondents during inheritance distribution is by following the prescribed standard of Islamic law. "Where the decisions in inheritance distribution are correct, as prescribed in Islamic law, then there will be no injustice, but where discrimination happens, there will be problems" (ARJ 65), it was suggested. If parents take certain steps during their lifetime, it can help maintain the quality of relationships among family members. For instance, the father may choose to assist each offspring in setting up their own separate business and ensure that each one receives their due share of the parental investment. This will prevent any potential conflicts among siblings after the father passes away. However, this approach may also divide the resources of the family business among heirs, thereby reducing the buying power of each new business and compromising their ability to achieve economies of scale. One Delhiwala suggested in his interview published in Saudagar that the reason for such separation is 'growing levels of intolerance within the members of the community' (Saudagar, Jan 2011, p. 62).
8. **Upbringing atmosphere:** The need for proper upbringing has already been discussed. A respondent in this context suggested that "The best thing that parents can give to their children is education or character, money is nothing. The character will help them to become responsible and strong individuals. While money is only a part of their development that is not the most important" (MT 81). Festivals such as Eid were celebrated together to preserve the bond between family members. The elders made sure that family members interacted frequently during

every occasion to maintain the connection between siblings and cousins, so that differences did not create any rifts between them.

Conflicts nevertheless happen, and when they do, the elders often volunteer to mediate so that conflicting parties come back to terms, or at least the dispute is resolved, even if the two sides decide to part ways. Often, there are misunderstandings, which lead to false accusations; sometimes, one or both of the parties have ill intentions, which necessitates the intervention of a third party. This mediation role is performed by elders either informally or formally. The elders do not have the legal authority to punish an offender, but to decide if the claim of either or both of the parties is legitimate, and advise a way forward for the two to end their feud. If compensation is due, they would recommend it. Once the decree has been passed, if the offenders do not agree to compensate as decided, the only consequence is bad word of mouth, which eventually affects the credibility of the entire family of the offender in the community, reducing their prospects to find support within the community. Also, while establishing matrimonial or business ties, there is a norm of checking the background of the prospective partner, which, if tainted due to conflict and its aftermath, would have consequences for the offenders. There were examples where religious jurists, a *mufti,* were also consulted in matters where the violation was also against the legal code of Islam, like inheritance distribution, violation of a formal written contract between partners, or matters about divorce. The disturbing part is that everyone I interviewed was concerned about the rise of conflicts, the rise in betrayals, violation of agreed-upon terms of contracts, and the increasing number of divorces, all creating cracks in the social fabric of the communities. The good news is the realization among community members and the willingness to take corrective measures. But will these corrective measures will hit the root cause of social disintegration is a question worth exploring.

In this chapter, we saw the extent to which family and community relationships facilitate the process of establishing and running an enterprise. The firm, once established, typically, through the support available in the community networks, supports the community eventually as well. The support for the community either happens formally when the firm or the owners financially contribute to various philanthropic activities as listed in Sect. 5.3.3, but also informally, by offering training to newcomers, offering advice, sharing connections, becoming a customer of a new business, and bearing with it during its early struggles. All of this support, often offered unconditionally, can be expected to strengthen the bonds between the community members. Betrayals or conflicts, naturally, do the opposite. Avoiding conflicts during social and economic engagements or resolving them significantly depends on the moral capacity of the individuals, which is also reinforced and contextualized by religious beliefs, as discussed.

The religion is said to advocate that the love of people around must supersede the attachment to material belongings, while the love of God must supersede the love of people around. Love of the people instills kindness, while love of God nurtures the courage to exercise justice even when doing so does not please everyone. The hierarchy emphasized in the belief system, therefore, emphasizes the moral over the social, and the social over the economic. The social and the economic are not ignored; rather, they have their significance, but as a means, not as an end. The end is moral, which itself is a means to remain connected to God. The nature of relationships with family and community members, therefore, can have at least three layers: social, economic, and moral. Cultural, contractual, and religious reasons to maintain connections may also exist. Each reinforces the other, especially when one of them weakens. More layers imply a greater degree of interdependence and bonding, and greater prospects of sustaining the socioeconomic landscape. This multidimensional interdependence is now the topic of the next Chapter.

Chapter 8
Multidimensional Interdependence for Socioeconomic Sustainability

In the previous chapter, it was shown how community members use family and community networks to start and maintain their ventures. The ability to maintain trust, avoid conflicts, or constructively resolve them was noted as a key factor in the process. The significance of the upbringing process, which produced the right character to create such an environment, was discussed in Chapter 5. Further, it has also been discussed how many community members nurture this character under a religion's belief and value system, which provides an incentive to sacrifice and a moral standard for all believers to agree on. From the viewpoint of the respective communities, religion inspires the necessary character, which is cultivated in a healthy family environment, creating a supportive environment within the family and then the community. The same also comes in handy to start and sustain a firm, as the key tangible or intangible resources are arranged through the network. If the owners possess the right character, the firm will contribute to the community by creating employment or helping new ventures grow by supporting new entrepreneurs from the beginning of their journey. Such owners can also help struggling suppliers or vendors through financial facilitation while not breaking business ties, also by giving them advance payment for orders, and providing them supplies in case the struggling firm is on the receiving end. People or families who were on the verge of becoming poor, if pre-emptively helped by their network were recovered in due time. Owners who generated a surplus also contributed financially to various community causes organized by the *jamaat* of each community, as described in Sect. 5.2. Modesty, it was mentioned, increased this capacity to give. The support was typically due to their altruism, which also reproduced the moral and social capital in the process, inspiring others and strengthening the bond between community members. A firm that performs well may also keep the owner's family financially secure, mothers in particular, who, along with the rest of the family, and mothers-in-law, can focus on the upbringing of the next generation. Affluence can fuel temptations, which then must be tamed by maintaining

O. Javaid, *Socioeconomic Sustainability Through Moral and Social Capital*,
Entrepreneurship and Development in South Asia: Longitudinal Narratives,
https://doi.org/10.1007/978-981-96-8134-1_8

focus on the worldview offered by religion, that is, life is temporary, and to ensure success on the Day of Judgement, one must practice modesty and give charity in all forms. This can potentially shift the tone of relationships between family and community members from competitive to cooperative, where sharing is preferred over accumulation, contributing to socioeconomic sustainability.

A similar picture can be painted of several communities around the world where the economic activity is not an end in itself, but a means to facilitate others, a concept that is sanctioned by the religious or ideological framework of the community, as we saw in Sect. 5.2. All of these communities can be mentioned as an example where both the social and the economic reproduce each other, as the social resources facilitate the economic, while the economic resources then facilitate the social. The social, however, takes precedence over the economic under the moral pretext. The social, therefore, is found to be embedded in the moral, where the moral is embedded within a belief system that provides a teleological context to the moral. Interestingly, almost all these communities have an apparent patriarchal structure where the gender roles are divided, men focusing on the breadwinning, while women, including mothers and grandmothers, generally take care of the children and home, nurturing the necessary social and moral character that helps sustain the community both socially and economically. However, if the social takes precedence over the economic, then the roles that nurture the right character for the social would also take precedence logically over the economic roles. The role of men, therefore, becomes more of an operational nature, while women tend to play a strategic yet underrated role in the context of long-term socioeconomic sustainability, which is not possible perhaps without the necessary moral character nurtured by women in the community. Women's role in this context needs to be highlighted for its extra-economic significance.

The moral agents once raised can only exercise their moral agency if the collective socioeconomic arrangements allow the exercise of such agency; in the absence of the freedom to exercise such agency, raising moral agents would not make much sense. The idea that 'this is not my job/concern' or 'someone else should take care of it', like some state institutions, is not there in the 'social imaginary' (Taylor, 1992). Constraints to moral agency could be informal or cultural, or formal or institutional, that shape how someone views themselves as compared to others. If my circle of concern ends where my role ends, then I am not likely to be bothered about what the other person is going through. Modern institutionalism is often cited to have encouraged such individualism (Fukuyama, 2011). Collective culture, however, has an environment of 'we-ness', instead of 'I-ness' (Falzon, 2004), where my role does not end at myself, but rather it keeps expanding even much beyond my circle of influence. When I do not have the resources to help someone, I would encourage others to do so. More formalism, the dominance of the rational, it may be argued, discourages such involuntary organization, which rather requires an informal arrangement among people.

Individuals, whose free will has not been compromised can make moral choices at will. Such individuals may go beyond the agreed-upon legal or contractual rights or responsibilities, and help those in need, even when not formally required, but because it is required by their moral intuition, and perhaps encouraged by the ideals set by their belief system. Paying charity, forgiving, and maintaining ties even when it costs materially requires autonomy to exercise agency. Employees, for example, who are constrained by their job responsibilities and organizational policies, can find it difficult to extend a favor to a stakeholder when needed, even when not doing so can cause harm to someone. An employee cannot simply decide to help a supplier by giving him extra credit or supplies to a customer; the business owners, however, can make this decision. In a social context, this agency is available, so when the social supersedes the economic, it can be assumed that the agency will be exercised in an economic context as well, even when contractually not mandated. However, when the contractual nature of a relationship supersedes the economic one, the parties play within agreed-upon rules. However, if their sense of morality supersedes, then concession or support also follows, even when not mandated by the contracts. Morality may also save the day when social bonding is compromised or when apparent economic prospects are unwarranted, as discussed in Chapter 4. Moral agency in this sense can be said to go along with or go against several types of relationships that may prevail simultaneously, forming multiple types of interdependencies. The data reviewed in the previous chapters offers various examples in this context. To see how the moral balance out these interdependencies as described in the data, their interplay warrants a discussion.

8.1 Multidimensional Interdependence

The examples in Chapter 7 suggest that the nature of a relationship between individuals can have multiple dimensions, where each dimension creates a unique form of interdependence if the benefit is mutual. The data suggests that a relationship can be contractual, economic, social, moral, or sometimes exclusively encouraged by cultural norms or the religious code. All of these layers may also exist in a particular relationship. For example, a marriage can have all of these dimensions. The same can be observed between family members managing a business along with other stakeholders from the community. Each dimension introduces a degree of interdependence. Therefore, a relationship containing all of the dimensions may be assumed to be the strongest, while a relationship that has fewer dominating dimensions would be at a greater risk of disintegrating. A contractual relationship, for example, is typically formed to assign a cost of violating the terms that are agreed upon in writing before forming the relationship. A marriage is also a contract in this sense. However, if there is no social or emotional bonding, no moral consideration, and no reinforcement by religious or cultural norms, then the contract may be dissolved as soon as either or both parties no longer see it as beneficial for their interests. If ending the contract before the agreed-upon maturity mandates a penalty, then the parties would proceed if it were more beneficial in a purely utilitarian sense. A contractual connection, therefore, may keep the relationship hanging if the relationship does not yield any economic or social benefit to avoid the penalty. For example, an employer may keep an employee from firing them before the agreed-upon timeframe, risking legal action. Similarly, a marriage may be sustained for the same reason.

However, relationships are also formed and sustained without a legal contract. These relationships can be economic, socioemotional, moral, cultural, or religious. A relationship, for example, can be non-contractual yet purely economic, devoid of social, moral, cultural, or religious dimensions. Such relationships can be easily found, where two individuals or groups barter something of value and continue to do so as long as they benefit each other. Customer-seller relationships, particularly in small businesses, are typically of this nature. Even relationships between employers and employees in informal markets can be purely economic in this sense. Non-contractual relationships can also be purely social, based on emotional benefits rather than economic benefits, like between two friends or siblings. Moral relationships likewise can also exist in the absence of contractual, economic, social, cultural, or religious reinforcement, where a person may help someone out of compassion exclusively without showing off or without an intention to please God. Cultural dimension in a relationship dominates when an individual starts or maintains a relationship to look good in the eyes of the community, as opposed to religion, which may encourage starting or maintaining a relationship to please God exclusively. In both cases (contractual and religious), there may not be any economic or emotional benefit derived from keeping the relationship, nor there may be a legal requirement mandated in a contract.

A relationship, therefore, can have numerous dimensions. When the benefits of a relationship are multiple and mutual, it can be referred to as multidimensional interdependence. In modern market and institutional contexts, relationships are usually contractual and economic (Dari-Mattiacci & Fabbri, 2023; Ritzer, 2016). However, in the communities discussed here, relationships formed for economic reasons can have other dimensions as well. This is particularly true between family members who do business together, so the relationship between family members is both emotional and economic, a characteristic also highlighted in the literature (Caputo et al., 2018; Davies, 2019; Fathallah et al., 2020). The creation of a family constitution, system, processes, hierarchy, and putting things in writing, or the professionalization of the business as mentioned in Chapter 7, points toward this contractual dimension. In the three communities studied, the relationship between family members working together in a business used to be more informal until the previous generation, as the use of tools like family constitutions, creating formal hierarchies, and documenting the roles is a more recent phenomenon. At the inception of the communities, the economic interdependence between members was perhaps also significantly less, as most members of the communities were not well off. However, as the community members thrived economically and supported each other in the process of starting or expanding their ventures, the economic dimension can be assumed to have gained significance. Today, many businesses that choose to formalize, a contractual dimension is now being added among family and community members, working together as partners or in an employee-employer or B2B relationship.

Each dimension of interdependence brings unique benefits to either or both sides of a relationship. Family goodwill, for example, is considered among the most valuable assets, suggesting the significance of the cultural dimension, which also encourages philanthropic endeavors originally mandated by religion, as discussed in previous chapters, bridging the gap between different classes of community members, or preventing betrayal in economic relationships. The cultural dimension also brings in a sense of belonging to a wider social group. The religious dimension discourages material competition by emphasizing on frugal lifestyle, advising against conflict for selfish interests, which helps to maintain the sanctity of emotional bonding. To ensure a healthy relationship with God, one must maintain healthy relationships with everyone around, except for those with ill intentions, who must also not be treated unjustly. The religious dimension also gives a believer a sense of purpose for sacrificing. The moral dimension makes one feel content or free from guilt, while the social dimension has an emotional appeal to it.

The moral, social, cultural, and religious dimensions help maintain a relationship when the economic or contractual dimensions are not there. A relationship, then, is maintained via other dimensions, like with the parents or relatives who are too old to contribute or reciprocate. They are nevertheless supported by their children and everyone in the extended family, for emotional, moral, cultural, and/or religious reasons. Likewise, anyone who is economically vulnerable may not be able to reciprocate either but is supported again for moral, cultural, and/or religious reasons, even when no emotional bonding is there with the person. These dimensions, therefore, can also be seen as threads, as when one is broken or not available, other threads maintain the connection. The significance of each dimension of bonding may depend on the belief system of each individual and the nature of the relationship the individual has with others in the family or community. Like among family members, socioemotional bonding may dominate. In an informal relationship with significant power differences, cultural or moral dimensions may play a significant role. Religious mindedness would prioritize pleasing God, even when there is no socioemotional, cultural, or economic benefit associated with helping someone, nor is there any contractual obligation. Often, one's moral intuition is not working; there again, the mental understanding of pleasing God or accountability on the Day of Judgement can come in handy to choose a pro-social altruistic behavior, or simply avoiding harm or injustice to others. All of these dimensions together can potentially keep the relationship with significant power differences free from exploitative behavior, reinforcing the right behavior when one or more dimensions go missing.

From a religious perspective, the religious dimension must triumph over the others, or one's moral dimension must lead over the cultural or socioemotional one; however, real life is more complex, as often in matters where one needs to prioritize the social, or cultural, or religious, economic looks more attractive, or vice versa. The problem of nepotism is an example where socioemotional factors may dominate, or in the case of prioritizing community members while hiring for employment, one may comprise the benefit that could be reaped from hiring better talent from outside the community. Someone may become obsessed with

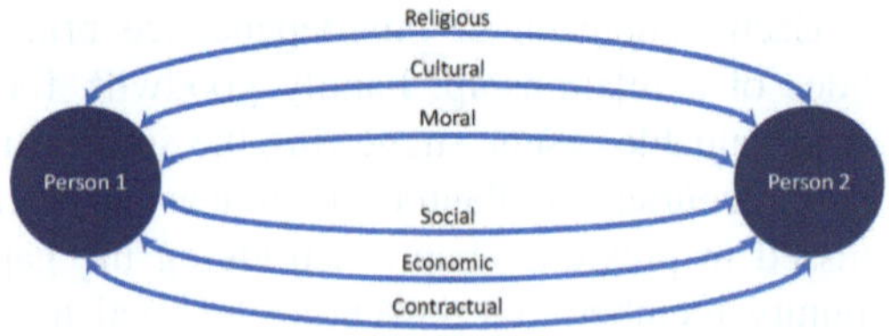

Fig. 8.1 Multidimensional nature of a relationship between two individuals

maintaining a positive outlook on a community scale while not paying attention to their social or familial responsibilities, like fathers not taking time to be fathers, or mothers interested in socializing more than mothering. Alternatively, some become overly cautious when it comes to adhering to religious code, often overstepping and stifling themselves under the fear of displeasing God, despite religious code being flexible in actuality. Overstepping in every dimension is perhaps a very human thing. However, the key is the extent to which a person has the humility to make corrections while using recommended anchors where necessary to prevent going off balance. Contracts are one example of such anchors. A culture of keeping an eye on each other and sharing feedback when necessary, while having the humility to listen to the feedback, is another critical trait, as emphasized by respondents in the previous chapters. Interestingly, signing contracts, having an environment of mutual accountability, and the necessary humility for the matter, are all mandated by the religion followed by the community. However, religion also notably empowered moral agency as well and cultivated the wisdom to know when the contractual terms are to be violated, but for the benefit of a struggling member. A customer who has not paid as promised may not be penalized even when the penalty is agreed in writing in the contract, because the circumstances that caused the customer to miss his payments were extraordinary. There can be many such examples in all kinds of social and economic relationships. An exercise of moral agency requires that one's moral intuition is nurtured enough to include the necessary composure and empathy to understand the situation, and the moral agent has the freedom to exercise the agency. A sense of inner security is critical here, which is also reinforced by the religious belief that it is God who sustains, who has promised to give more if a person facilitates those in need. The question is, how can such a capacity be made more common. Figure 8.1 graphically shows the dimensions of relationships possible between two individuals, while Table 8.1 enlists the benefits each dimension brings to either or both individuals.

Table 8.1 Benefits of each dimension of interdependence

Dimensions of interdependence	Benefit to either or both individuals
Religious	Pleasing god for salvation on the day of judgment
Cultural	Goodwill or reputation
Moral	Satisfaction of conscience
Social	Belongingness, sense of usefulness
Economic	Income, material needs, sustenance
Contractual	Sense of security due to certainty of outcome

The spread of materialism and consumerism in the communities perhaps create a motivation that may work against the moral, religious, and socioemotional dimensions. The criteria behind the cultural dimension, which valued enhancing the goodwill by doing good and not betraying trust, appear to be overtaken by the desire to look good only in terms of material affluence. Several respondents reported that there is a rise in betrayals among community members in business relationships, particularly by B2B customers who were supposed to make payments, or those who received investment money, were unable to honor their commitments because of alleged increase in the amount they spent on maintaining a luxurious lifestyle. The religion they follow, however, strongly advises against doing so, implying that love of temptations, which the religion requires its followers to strictly regulate, has triumphed over the moral and the idea of pleasing God. This was perhaps unprecedented among the community elders. Consumer trends are a product of materialist values that may effectively replace religious and cultural values, leaving emotional bonds as the only foundation for familial relationships. Morality may also be replaced by the common sense of the market and (or) the rationality of the institutions. The declining morality then can potentially disintegrate the social also, as discussed earlier, leaving market relationships to hang on to economic or contractual obligations. Such relationships are easier to break when either party cannot fulfill their obligations or when a more lucrative option is available. Relationships may only survive for the material benefit they provide, like hanging around someone for their material riches, as it also increases one's capacity to show off. It is not hard to understand how easily such a relationship would fall apart.

Globally, those who could not offer material or economic benefits, such as economically improvised, disabled individuals, the elderly, children, and expecting or lactating mothers, would rely on their families, communities, or social security programs provided by the state. However, thanks to neoliberalism, the subsequent disintegration of families and communities it caused, and the shrinking of the state's role in supporting the vulnerable, such segments of a society are often left stranded and alienated. However, due to their rational nature, the state institutions are not typically good at providing the emotional and moral support that exists naturally in healthy organic communities, which give a sense of purpose and belonging to their members. Therefore, the role of healthy organic families and communities cannot be overemphasized in addressing alienation, particularly in communities where culture and religion have been serving as a force to unify and bind the people together. If the three Pakistani communities go through the same process of disintegration at the hands of market forces due to increasing materialistic values, their future generation may also face the same problems already faced by the vulnerable and the poor in disintegrated communities in other regions. Therefore, it is pertinent to take measures that can prevent this process, a realization they seem to possess, but their understanding of the causes of such disintegration may need to go a little deeper. This is evident in their increasing willingness to send their children to an education system that prepares individuals for rational institutional environments. Nor is there any reluctance to expose their children to technology. The practice of encouraging children to live a modest life was also not found in the data. The three communities perhaps need to work in this context.

8.2 Building, Reproducing, and Preserving Interdependence

Previous chapters have already discussed the role of upbringing, involvement of extended family in the process, early exposure to business norms during family interactions, early training as an apprentice in the family business owned by one's family or a father's friend, in the process of nurturing the right character and personality. Other enterprising communities from around the world, as described in Sect. 5.2, also often raise their next generation for the necessary character and qualities as per available literature. The right character, grounded in an inner sense of security, was described as critical for nurturing moral agency. Further, the capacity and discipline to honor commitments make a person dependable. The existence of interdependence is, however, unlikely in the absence of the necessary character traits, personality, skillsets, and discipline. Such a character has often been noted to facilitate the struggling side in domains of interactions which are typically seen as purely rational by most mainstream economists. Some examples are discussed below:

8.2.1 Investments and Lending

A key area where the elders demonstrated their moral agency was honoring commitments regarding payments or being lenient when others failed to honor commitments for a genuine reason. Until the previous generation, it was assumed that a person would not miss a payment unless there was a legitimate crisis going on in their life. However, this perception may be changing, which will likely have far-reaching consequences on the culture of mutual support. In contrast, elders would even sell off their property to avoid defaulting on payments, while facilitating others. A young entrepreneur I interviewed also had done something similar after one of his major customers defaulted on his payments. However, he still managed to pay back his suppliers after selling his property. The experience and data suggested that business owners and investors would facilitate the other side if the trust had not been broken. It is critical to note in this context that family members or individuals who own a business typically have freedom over how to use their money or exercise their moral agency whenever needed. This may be referred to as a major factor that explains why, generally, there is a culture of avoiding financial institutions to finance business operations or expansions, as they do not offer the same degree of support, often leading to bankruptcies, particularly when market dynamics become turbulent. The city's law and order situation has been far from ideal for a few decades; it had fluctuated from worse to relatively better in the early 2000s, and then plunged again with the wave of terrorism and gang violence. Since 2018 or so situation has been relatively better, but the general dynamics of the market remain uncertain, because of macroeconomic situation, the pandemic and political turmoil in the country. There is also a general problem of a lack of work ethic in the market, which limits smaller firms from honoring their commitments in terms of the delivery of products or services. Keeping in view the kind of work environment within firms and the condition of the overall economy, it is difficult to work with an institutional lender who does not show much flexibility, but rather demands payments as per agreed terms, and compound interest payments when the debtor is not able to pay in due time. Respondents also identified that the cost of doing business goes up as well because of the markup on the borrowed amount from a bank. In contrast, the informal lending of money happens on an interest-free basis, as charging of interest over the principal amount, in any form, that is, some kind of a benefit made conditional at the time of lending, monetary or otherwise, is strictly prohibited by the religious code of the three communities. This religious restriction is also a major factor in avoiding banks. This allows community members who have enough surplus to facilitate others, which also strengthens the community bonds when both sides reciprocate their commitments, a trait which, unfortunately, is reported to be diminishing.

No banks means no bankruptcies, which are more likely due to uncertain market conditions. No banks also means a higher chance of multiplying moral and social capital, as the community members then support each other financially whenever needed. Socioeconomic interdependence is also reproduced. It is through their mutual support that the communities have been thriving despite the ups and downs of the last few centuries. During the 1970s, a socialist regime led by Zulfiqar Ali Bhutto nationalized many of the industries. After he was thrown away by a Military Dictator known as General Zia; the entrepreneurs had to start again from scratch, and they were able to do so with mutual support from the community. Going further back in the past, the partition event also created a lot of disruption, as many who were earlier settled in India had to migrate to Pakistan. Some were able to bring their valuables or savings; however, they had to start again in novel circumstances. A similar incident happened with Chinioti entrepreneurs who were doing business in Bangladesh in 1973 when the region, known as West Pakistan back then, plunged into chaos right before it claimed independence from Pakistan. One Chinioti respondent told me that his father had to escape overnight in a small boat; he was lucky to reach Pakistan alive. He then started again with the help of community members.

Unsurprisingly, during the startup phase of any business, the level of challenge rises to the extent of market instability. The financial institutions in the country do not even prefer to lend to small startups in general. In 2022, a Prime Minister Startup loan scheme was launched; however, few availed it as well, likely due to religious reasons. In this kind of situation, the help of an informal lender or investor, who is flexible with their terms, who offers support and guidance, and is patient while you work to establish a business, often for 3–5 years before achieving breakeven (as per respondents), is truly a blessing. It would especially be beneficial when the lender does not charge extra if the money is borrowed and does not demand repayment if the business fails for a valid reason (the borrower is, however, considered morally responsible to return the amount when feasible, as per the religious code). Investors who do a contract known as *Mudarabah* in Islamic law are required to bear the loss if the business collapses due to unforeseen circumstances, and it is this risk that gives them the right to claim a share in the profit, the percentage of which is agreed in advance. Those in the community who are aware and take the religious code seriously eventually opt for such contracts. It was possible to get such investments from the community circles, mostly from one's own family, that allowed the ventures to start and flourish, which is unlikely with the inflexible and costly intermediation from a financial institution. Such investors are generally known as angel investors. The data shows that their presence appears to be critical not just for the production of economic capital, but also reproduction of moral and social capital, as trust breeds more trust, which requires the right character to be reciprocated by both sides.

8.2.2 Benevolent Customers

As mentioned earlier, Investment is one kind of support that is received by individuals capable of exercising moral agency. In light of the data, there can be more ways to do that, like a B2B customer helping a new supplier start their business. The customers would keep buying and help the supplier streamline their operations until production runs smoothly. The new supplier could be a relative; in one case owner of a pharma company helped his nephew start a printing business, to print the packaging material, and supply it to him. The owner even provided investment to purchase a printing machine and some space in his factory. At the time I took the interview with this supplier, he had grown to a hundred employees and had several B2B customers in the pharma sector. A Chinioti who owns a textile exporting business also shared a similar story: an exporter, who was their first customer, helped them go through the teething phase, when they prepared their first consignment many decades ago. They had six hundred employees and were exporting to many countries when I interviewed them. Such support can come from an established B2B customer, but not when it grows too big.

The owners of large firms are often too busy or too distant to support small businesses in their local community or personal network. The structure of large firms is also relatively inflexible as compared to smaller firms, which may not tolerate the inconsistency from much smaller, struggling startups. An owner needs to remain approachable and flexible with the startup entrepreneurs while they struggle to streamline their processes. In large firms, which are often listed corporations, the owners may not be able to direct such interactions via the professionally managed company structure. A purchase manager in a large company, even if asked, may not be able to offer such support for obvious reasons to a nascent supplier (Freeman & Engel, 2007). In smaller firms, the managing entrepreneur is typically more accessible. Several entrepreneurs I interviewed showed a willingness to work with their employees as partners in a venture they wanted to initiate but could not because of time constraints. Therefore, they would identify an employee with the necessary talent and support them through finances, advice, and connections, while they become sleeping partners in the new venture. Therefore, the owners of small or Medium-sized firms may have a greater capacity to support new ventures, while larger firms may acquire smaller firms, often absorbing them unsuccessfully. The larger firms may even drive smaller firms out of the market if smaller firms are seen as competitors by the bigger players. Small is therefore beautiful, if I borrow from Schumacher (2010).

Similarly, news about emerging market opportunities is shared, without fearing that others may steal the idea, or turn into your competitor, preventing you from having the first mover's advantage. The spirit of sharing here dominates the spirit of competition. Those who venture forward before you, also come back and share their experience, and any challenges they may have faced, so that you do not have to face them if you are yet to start. Therefore, the moral, social, and economic capital can simultaneously multiply, creating a win–win scenario for all. Sharing advice, contacts, referrals, office space, space in your warehouse or factory, human resource, training the next generation in your friend circle, and even voluntarily helping partnering siblings to resolve their differences to prevent their venture from dissolving, are commonly observed. Through such acts, the moral and social capital facilitates the production of economic capital, which then strengthens the social ties and reinforces the moral behavior.

8.2.3 The Family Firm

Working together in a business can amplify the emotions existing among family members. If there is resentment, it can intensify, and if there is love, it can grow stronger as well. However, a firm growing too quickly or too slowly can also have its consequences. Generating too much profit or too little profit, as mentioned earlier, can put a strain on the relationship between family members. Excessive growth can spark greed and disagreement on how to use the extra profits. One sibling may want to reinvest extra profit for business growth, while the other sibling may want to take their family on a tour. Both the data I collected and the extant literature suggest that strong communication, cohesion, respect for differences, and a spirit of sacrifice would come in handy in addressing such situations (Arregle et al., 2007; Barbera et al., 2020; Pearson et al., 2008). The same traits can also be useful during times of market recession. Family members can continue to work together even if the income drops. While an employee, who only has contractual obligations and no socioemotional bonding with the family, may start looking for another job if the business is struggling, this is not the case when the working partners are family members, as noted earlier. This kind of family support is especially crucial during the startup phase of new ventures, as the business is not yet stable or credible enough to attract talent from the market. Family members working together may persist for longer periods, even if the business is struggling. This would strengthen the bond among family members, especially when their hard work and mutual support lead to the success of their venture. However, this support requires that the family's social capital already exists (Karra et al., 2006).

Socioemotional bonding among family members is therefore critical; however, it also raises the question of nepotism. Family firms with family-like environments can bring with them the possibility of free riding, shirking, consuming perks, excessive drawing of funds by a family member, and casual attitude toward business. These are some of the problems discussed in the literature that are associated with working with family members (Levitte, 2004; Poutziouris et al., 2004). This may be caused when a family member, a relative, or a community member is hired due to emotional reasons for a position, despite being unqualified, causing demoralization for the entire organization. Further, giving undue favor to an individual in the family can be a source of distress, thus causing conflict among family members (Alderson, 2015). Data indicate a strong understanding among the elders to train the new ones with the right skills and groom their personality as required. Once trained, the responsibilities assigned to the newcomers when they join the family business are also recommended to be in line with the individual's capacity. In this context, the respondents understood that emotional decision-making would harm the business. Nepotism, therefore, is consciously avoided in the communities. However, in case the business is successful, family or community members, who are not capable enough due to some disability, for example, are still accommodated to keep them from feeling useless. There have been examples where a person, with an obvious disability or negligible education, who would not have anything to put on their CV, would still be employed and assigned simple tasks as per their capacity, in a business owned by the family or extended family. Such inclusive tendencies also turn the working environment inside the firm more family-like, as the employees who often do not belong to the same community are treated with the same temperament. A respondent I interviewed invited me to lunch as it was lunchtime. In the dining hall, several employees were also present, along with the children and siblings of the business owner. All were given the same protocol, making the ambiance more like a family gathering.

Nevertheless, it was recommended that the newcomers be taught from an early age to keep the business and social relations separate, as not doing so would damage both. Giving undue advantage to family members over non-family employees was also considered equal to injustice from a religious point of view and thus was supposed to be avoided. The respondent's religious beliefs also did not allow discrimination based on ethnicity, race, or even religious differences; hence provided a rationale for an inclusive employment policy. Hiring employees purely on merit, without discrimination, was also seen as beneficial for the business. The data presented no evidence to substantiate the claim made by Portes (1998), DeFilippis (2001), and Woolcock (1998) about the possibility of the three ethnic communities becoming exclusionary to outsiders. Merit took precedence over ethnic affiliations. Many respondents suggested that they do not micromanage and rather ignore minor negligence of the employees. It is needless to mention that major offenders are not just caught but fired as well; however, one is not considered guilty unless proven otherwise. An inclusive and family-like environment is not present in all firms, as examples where the environment is the very opposite of that can also be easily found; some may find it hard to believe that such an environment even exists. However, smaller firms with around 50 employees, where family members have a healthy interpersonal relationship and are very much present to manage the operations, can be expected to have a more family-like environment. There is research in the international context that can support such a claim (Astrachan & Jaskiewicz, 2008; Barnett & Kellermanns, 2006). However, more evidence of the family businesses owned by the three communities is needed to further substantiate the findings in the local context.

8.2.4 Succession

The major test of the bonding comes at the time of transfer of ownership to the next generation, when the owners are too old or have passed away. Greed and resentment, if present, can work against the idea of keeping the family together. The religion has been very particular about distributing the inheritance and has described specific criteria about who will get what percentage.[1] Not following it, it is believed, would invite the displeasure of God.[2] Temptations, greed, and self-interest, multiplied by past resentments, or feelings of being treated unjustly, can generate strong motivation to take revenge at the time of inheritance distribution when the key decision makers also have more power than the rest. For example, when one of the two siblings who owned the business dies, the other one may take control of the firm and not let the offspring of the deceased brother take their share. Therefore, extra care during upbringing is critical to eliminate factors that can lead to resentment among descendants. Apart from socioemotional factors and religious reinforcements, the contractual dimension can also be added by putting things in writing in the form of a family constitution that documents how the next generation will receive the ownership of the family assets (Alderson, 2015).

The family constitution may also document the process of training, inducting, and raising the new family members to the position of authority in the company. The criteria regarding evaluation and assigning of responsibilities, and promotion through the ranks in the organization, also need to be documented and clearly articulated for all family members. The elders would use the document to gradually hand over the business to the newcomers, while relieving themselves of responsibilities. Alternatively, in case there are personality clashes among siblings or some resentment has developed due to unforeseen circumstances, then to avoid

[1] See the Qur'an, Surah 4, Verse 11.

[2] Anas bin Malik quotes Prophet Muhammad (ﷺ): "Whoever tries to avoid giving the inheritance to his heirs, Allah (SWT) will deprive him of his inheritance in Paradise on the Day of Resurrection". In Sunan Ibn Majah 2703, Chapter 3: Injustice In Wills, Book 22: The Chapters on Wills, Source: https://sunnah.com/ibnmajah:2703 (Last accessed: 21st July 2024).

any conflict, the elders may help each sibling set up a separate business. Starting separate firms, letting go of the family business, selling it off, or dissolving it into smaller units often do not go well in sustaining the family's goodwill across the community and the market. The existing literature also suggests that sustaining the family business is fundamental to sustaining the goodwill of the family name (Chaudhary et al., 2021; Zellweger et al., 2012). Therefore, measures must be taken, as early as possible, to eliminate the chances of brothers going sideways, to keep the goodwill of the family intact. When the newcomers start their professional journey and decide to have a side hustle for the sake of diversification (often essential for survival), they can use their family goodwill to establish relationships with suppliers, customers, and investors based on the market reputation established by the elders. If their side hustle turns out to be promising, it can act as a subsidiary of the family firm, or the firm may rebrand itself as a 'group of companies', so that the reputation of the family name is reinforced in the market. Understanding such benefits of streamlining the transition while ensuring the goodwill of the family may also make the succession free of conflict (Perricone et al., 2001).

8.2.5 The Bond Between Generations

For smooth succession planning, another key factor that was found to be contributing was the extent to which the newcomers adhere to the same values and beliefs as compared to their elders, a finding that also goes in line with extant literature (Le Breton-Miller et al., 2004; Sharma & Irving, 2005). In the data, these values and beliefs were noted to be about how elders and the next generations view themselves, how they relate to others in the immediate family, extended family, and the community, and how they see material wealth in comparison to their relation with others, and God. Further, what are their views about life's big questions like the purpose of their existence, or their role in the universe, and how to find answers to such questions? The three communities looked up to their religion for such answers. In cases where elders and newcomers have conflicting beliefs and values, tensions may escalate. Especially if there have been missteps in the upbringing process. For example, elders may have imposed their beliefs too harshly on the younger generation, or there may have been instances of injustice, leading to resentment and rebellion among the newcomers.

A key challenge emerging in this context is the communication gap between the elders and the new generation, which is often blamed on the Western-style education that the new generation is receiving. Further, there is an extraordinary level of content consumption from digital media. This has posed a challenge for those families, even where the upbringing environment has been conducive. However, where the environment is not so conducive, modern education and digital media have widened the gaps even further. Such gaps then block the transmission of the beliefs, values, and norms from one generation to the next, which may have kept the preceding generations together. The previous generation was also exposed to TV media that likely introduced the Western-style consumer culture in the communities. However, the flooding of foreign values through digital media is far more intense today. This creates a bigger challenge as there are studies that even suggest that addiction to digital media is changing the brain structure of children, where they are now becoming hardwired to short-term dopamine hits, significantly compromising their capacity for a long-term perspective (He et al., 2017; Montag & Diefenbach, 2018). Their capacity to regulate their emotions is also being significantly compromised. There is evidence about the rise in narcissistic values and self-esteem issues in a large number of teenage populations (Storr, 2018; Twenge & Campbell, 2010). There is also a rise in self-harm and suicidal behavior due to constant comparison on social media, which adversely affects the self-image of addicted consumers (Haidt, 2023).

The excessive use of social media was also reported to have been changing the culinary habits of youngsters. Popular trends in the market, the urge to post check-ins on social media, and posting food pictures to show off one's unique dining experience at a posh restaurant, were also reported to be a booming trend among the young generation, as per one Chinioti respondent. The shift toward processed foods can also have adverse behavioral effects, as reported in various studies (AlAmmar et al., 2020). Research shows that excess intake of sugary stuff is often followed by withdrawal effects that can increase one's irritability (Benton, 2002). It would be interesting to further explore the connection between the changing culinary habits of the communities, to what extent the change is influenced by social media consumption, and how it affects the bonding social capital of the members of the family, as irritable individuals may be more prone to conflicts.

Whether it is culinary habits, a race to upgrade one's luxury car, or a change in one's self-image, life goals, or social imagination, the influence of social media on the younger generation is a point of global concern. The data highlights that the younger generations of the community in question are also affected by the pathological spread of digital technologies. The effect ranges from departure from the traditional frugal lifestyle and individualistic values, and subsequent conflict with the previous generation on these lines. The possibility of such drastic, even pathological changes in the personalities of the new generation is expected to pose an even greater threat to the sustenance of the values and norms that have kept the communities sustaining and even thriving both socially and economically. Figure 8.2 describes how such changes can influence the social and economic sustainability of organic communities.

One way to preserve the traditional values could be perhaps to take inspiration from the upbringing strategy of top Silicon Valley icons like Bill Gates and Steve Jobs, who raised their children in tech-free environments.[3] Venture Capitalist Chamath Palihapitiya, founder of the firm Social Capital, and a former Facebook

[3] See https://www.businessinsider.com/screen-time-limits-bill-gates-steve-jobs-red-flag-2017-10 (Last accessed: 22nd July 2024).

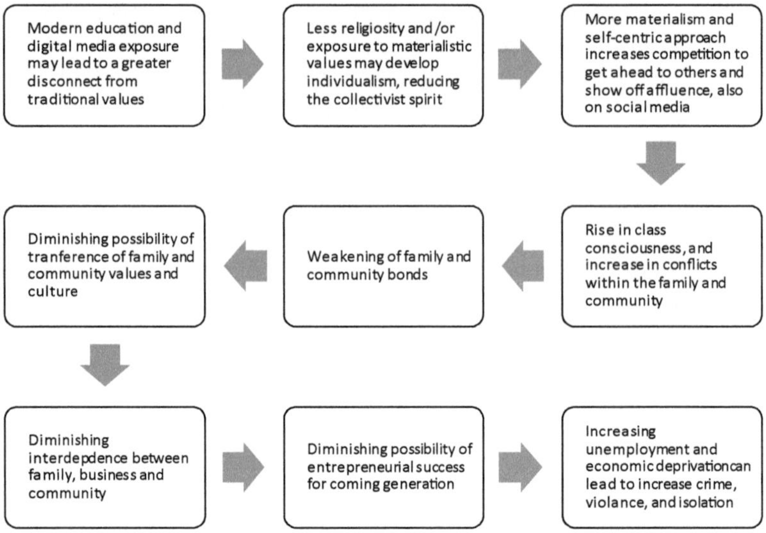

Fig. 8.2 Possible path toward social disintegration of religious enterprising communities

executive, having a net worth of more than a billion dollars (as of 2024), he is another example who proudly claims to have put a curfew in his home when it comes to the use of social media.[4] Tim Cook, Apple's CEO, also said in one of his interviews with CBS that Apple's phones are not designed to be used for long hours, only to make calls and send a few messages.[5] Peter Thiel recently said in an interview that he only allows his kids to have a screen time of 1.5 h per week.[6] Some individuals who are at the forefront of technological innovation perhaps know something about the technology they are producing. Or some inspiration can be taken from the Amish community in Ohio, USA, who try to remain as technology-free as possible for precisely the reason that technological adoption would disintegrate their culture and social cohesion (Kraybill, 2003). Therefore, perhaps it would be advisable that the children in the communities in focus here are raised tech-free in this context unless they are mature enough to understand what to absorb and what to filter out. However, this advice would be difficult to implement, as those children who are already addicted to their devices would find it hard to let go. Research on addiction also points toward the cause being alienation and not the substance or device itself. If children are addicted to phones, the question one should ask is to what extent they feel alienated, are their mothers

[4] See https://www.cnbc.com/2017/12/12/chamath-palihapitiya-my-kids-get-no-screen-time-whatsoever.html (Last accessed: 22nd July 2024).

[5] See https://www.youtube.com/watch?v=AwvLymAA2CM (Last accessed: 22nd July 2024).

[6] See https://www.businessinsider.com/peter-thiel-kids-screen-time-parenting-social-media-meta-tech-2024-6 (Last accessed: 22nd July 2024).

or the motherly presence of adults available, which offers them enough emotional presence and acceptance? If mothers in some families in the communities are in a state of survival among the in-laws or carry childhood trauma because of the emotional absence of their mother, then it is not hard to imagine how it would affect their emotional availability for children. Hence, the susceptibility among children to get addicted to something, including the readily and abundantly available digital devices.

It is not only the mother's job to keep their children safe from unwarranted digital exposure. The efforts of one parent may have limited impact when living in a combined family environment, where the children would eventually use the devices owned by grandparents, older cousins, uncles, or aunts if they were all living together. It can sometimes become nearly impossible for parents to even control screen time, due to the readily available devices owned by others. The entire family, and then the community, therefore, need to be involved and must invest in creating an environment where the children learn to use technology but healthily, that does not interfere with their developmental needs. A change would happen when perhaps there is a widespread realization on the scale of the community to do something about digital exposure and to maintain it within healthy limits. Keeping children occupied and busy in alternative engaging activities is also essential in this sense, which again requires necessary community-level realization followed by necessary arrangements, like infrastructure for outdoor and indoor sports, for example. Another aim, it is recommended here, should also be to create space for children to express their ingenuity while learning how to collaborate with others. An aim that can be achieved through formal education, details of which now follow.

8.2.6 Role of Formal Education

Unfortunately, the education system used by the communities today is the same as the one installed by the British Empire, which typically nurtures a spirit of individualism and competition, and prioritizes being efficient and productive instead of being moral and compassionate (Freire, 2000; Mitra, 2015; Orr, 2004). These qualities are inculcated pedagogically, while the content taught in the schools also focuses on details that have little relevance to the practical problems of the community. It can be argued that the educated individual who comes out of the system often internalizes various values and traits that are not helpful in the social sustainability of the family and the community. Many members of the three communities opted to send their children to such schools and then to universities, as education was reportedly seen as necessary for the professional needs of the business. However, what was perhaps overlooked was the incompatibility of the personality produced by the pedagogical and structural components of the prevailing education system with the values and belief system of the community. This incompatibility is contributing to the weakening of the bond between generations, and thus obstructing the transmittance of values and beliefs that have sustained the bonding social capital of the families, extended families, and the community as a whole. However, the gap between generations may be seen as an opportunity also to prevent the transmission of unhealthy family patterns, but only if there is a healthy alternative mechanism to restore the necessary values and character. This mechanism can be a new form of education system with the necessary pedagogical and structural characteristics, and the relevant content that allows the production of an individual who contributes to the socioeconomic sustenance of the family and community, and not the other way around. What traits such individuals must possess has been described above, but how they will be inculcated in an artificial incubation environment of a school or a college is an important question to explore.

The modern education system is often described as a replica of the modern factory environment, which was reportedly designed to ensure mindless obedience to a rational authority or filter out those who fail to obey (Freire, 2000; Orr, 2004). Therefore, the environment of formal education needs to mirror the external environment that graduates eventually participate in. The content taught and the methods of teaching also need to be in line with what is required. The desired environment, for example, needs to be more cooperative than competitive, where individuals share instead of hoarding, where they exercise agency for the benefit of others whenever needed, and where the pain of others is felt and addressed. For economic sustenance, a community member must also learn the necessary skills needed to start and manage a business, while accommodating the family members if necessary. Often, existing ventures serve as a school for newcomers, experientially teaching them the necessary skills and character. Before this time, a newcomer is exposed to an environment at home or school. If the environment at the family is not conducive, then the school must compensate; however, schools that are capable of doing so likely do not exist at the moment. In case if the community elders realize the need to create such an environment, several international examples may be looked upon for inspiration.

Lumiar School in Brazil can be mentioned here as a model to follow. This school is the brainchild of Brazilian entrepreneur Ricardo Semler. The school uses projects instead of subjects to teach students, who themselves decide which project they want to be a part of, irrespective of their age. Students of different ages join a particular group to collaboratively work on a specific project and experientially learn the concepts of different subjects. For example, a bicycle-making project introduces them to concepts of mathematics, physics, and geometry. The Indian educationist Sugata Mitra, winner of the TED annual prize for 2013, has invented a unique approach where the teacher only asks triggering questions from the students, who then use the internet or other sources to find answers. Mitra even found students capable of learning complex concepts on their own only if they are triggered with sufficient curiosity. The three communities, Memon and Delhiwala, in particular, run many schools and educational platforms for vocational training, often providing education at subsidized cost to all, showing their interest in this direction. However, they need to look at the structural and pedagogical elements, while also creating content that helps students internalize the values and ideals that are meant to create the desired personality, with sufficient moral agency required for maintaining socioeconomic sustainability

8.3 Interdependence and Balance

The significance of moral agents and their ability to exercise their agency was mentioned earlier in the context of interdependence in Sect. 8.1. The discussion on the multidimensional nature of interdependence, and how it is built, reproduced, and preserved by moral agents operating in an enabling environment (more informal than formal) hints toward the cyclic nature of the process of maintaining socioeconomic sustainability. The social relations were noted to facilitate the economic relations, while the economic relations sustained the social as well through interpersonal support and organized philanthropic activity. The moral agency, it may be argued, that is required for such a dance between the social and the economic is nurtured, expressed, and exercised within a cultural framework, a framework that is shaped by a concept of morality that transcends the culture itself. The culture must be grounded in a framework of morals, as otherwise, morality would become an instrument of propagating the culture itself. To prevent such circularity, the moral needs to be based on meta-norms that transcend culture itself. Religion, in its original form, has been serving this purpose in the communities in focus here and other similar communities around the world. The culture must therefore submit to a set of meta-norms, like that of religion, instead of using it, as often happens, otherwise, meta-norms become an instrument of imposing the culture's informal tyranny.

The culture of a community is supposed to set protocols of interactions, like how the individual families form relationships with each other and establish matrimonial ties in line with the teleological aims set by the meta-norms. The families in the community ought to raise the next generation with the necessary character, who then continue to socially and economically engage with the rest of the community members while maintaining interdependence. The economic activity emerges out of socializing, which then creates a rational reason for keeping the social ties as well, as noted. The material benefit that is derived from the socially embedded economic relationships can be reused to support the community members, either through informal support as discussed earlier, or more formally by giving charity to run various welfare organizations aimed at providing services like education and healthcare. Religion, followed by the communities, often sets the motivation to pay attention to the needs of others by reassuring the adherents that God will ultimately take care of their needs. The shunning of materialism in the religious worldview, and prioritizing of one's relationship with God, nurtures a moral consciousness as well, that aims to benefit others, even sometimes at a personal loss, to ensure one's connection with God.

Any institutional arrangements that compromise the moral agency of individuals become unattractive in this context, therefore, the economic organization is recommended to be more informal than formal, where the social remains alive, and is not superseded by the contractual. Formal is thus not shunned away totally, but is to be used carefully, with its limitations in mind. Like, contractual arrangements are nevertheless utilized often as a precaution to contain socioemotional energy, partnership contracts, use of organizational structure in family business, and family constitutions being good examples. The marriage contract is another example, but it falls in the social domain. However, the contractual arrangements must not constrain the moral from intervening where necessary. In the absence of the moral, the contractual can become too mechanical. In contrast, in the absence of the contractual, the socioemotional energy can create turbulence in case the moral agency is not there for the rescue. In the absence of socioemotional energy, the collective would disperse, while in the absence of the economic, the social cannot be sustained either. The culture also sustains the social in a more collective sense, as in its absence, the individuals would lose the sense of a collective. The culture may provide an answer to how, but not why, or offer the teleological perspective to the moral, which is rather provided by the meta-norms, where the culture also becomes an instrument of the transcendental goals that the meta-norms, like those of religion, point toward. So, religion, culture, moral agency, socioemotional energy, economic activity, and contractual arrangements, potentially become key elements to sustain the socioeconomic structure of a collective. Each provides an incentive to keep things going both socially and economically.

The sociocultural framework depicted in Fig. 8.3 must remain flexible to adapt to any emerging demands. Change may often require taking a leap of faith, while a sense of insecurity tempts individuals to cling to the known patterns. Faith, therefore, must triumph over fear for the necessary change to happen, both in the social and economic domains. The meta-norms of Islam, for example, take care of this problem by declaring that sustenance, referred to as *rizq*, is promised by God, who will arrange for it, so the focus should be on what is morally necessary, even if it requires letting go of a cultural practice that no longer serves the needs of the community. Likewise, the business also needs to adapt as needed to survive. However, the change needs to be guided by some higher principles, which provide the foundation for the stability of the social order, like keeping the spirit of cooperation, sharing, altruism, or mutual support alive while countering any temptations that may push individuals to do otherwise. Products or services that promote individualistic values and a sense of material competition for the sake of it, therefore, are off the list. That is where religion provides a worldview to put things into perspective while providing a list of what is allowed or encouraged and what isn't.

The multidimensional interdependence, as discussed, also points toward a set of needs that, once met through mutual support, improve interdependence and bonding subsequently. Two broad categories, as noticed, are social needs and economic needs. Social needs may include the need to be cared for, loved, belonged, accepted, valued, and appreciated, while economic needs include financial security to fulfill material needs like shelter, food, transportation, and energy. Further,

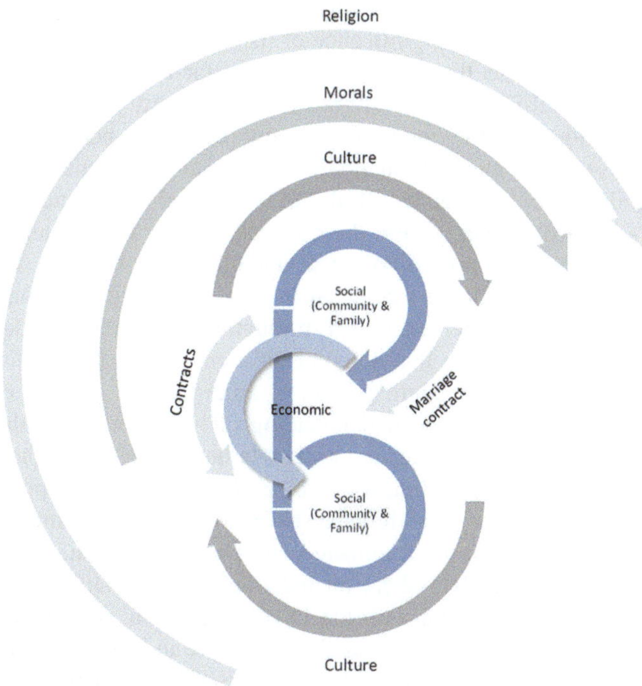

Fig. 8.3 A model for socioeconomic sustainability based on a multidimensional interdependent relationship between moral agents

there is a need for fairness, which involves honoring trust from the other side. And then there is a need to feel secure, which necessitates the idea of an all-powerful Being, or the idea of God, that is capable of providing what one needs when institutions, material resources or human beings fall short, which they eventually do. There is also a need to have a sense of purpose in life and a worldview that helps one make sense of life's difficult experiences. Also, a framework is needed to respond to unfair treatments, conflict resolution, or damage caused unintentionally, to avoid further injustice and prevent any further damage to social cohesion. Even more necessary is a framework where conflicts or injustices are prevented in the first place. Therefore, a structure is needed to organize collective life, but there is also a contrasting need to act on one's ingenious and creative expression. Human needs are also different in different stages of life. The needs of a child cannot be compared with the needs of an adult, while the needs of a sick elderly person cannot be compared with those of a teenager. Likewise, the needs of an expecting mother are different from the needs of a mother-in-law or her husband. The list goes on. The needs can be broadly described as personal, social, sociocultural, economic, structural, and ideological. Individuals have any of these needs at different stages of life, fulfillment of which often requires an appropriate response from the unconstrained moral agents in family and community. Certain stages of one's life make one vulnerable and fully dependent on others, and it is perhaps these moments when the true significance of the social can be appreciated, where individuals fully exercise their moral agency to facilitate those in need. Such capacity of the social was earlier referred to as motherly, the presence of which was extensively found in the communities explored in this book. The role of the economic was seen as a means to facilitate such social environments that take care of the vulnerable whenever needed. Both the family and the businesses run by the family had such a character, where the cultural, structural (formal, contractual), and religious dimensions appear to act as facilitators to navigate various challenges that emerge in the process of balancing the social and the economic, along with the satisfaction of the personal needs through mutual interdependence.

Ideally, all the needs of an individual at different stages of their lives must be understood and addressed. A particular set of arrangements that are employed in a society would be based on an understanding of human needs within the society. Such understanding would depend on how a human being is described by the dominating ideological disposition. A homo-economicus, for example, would have distinct needs. As per this view, humans have evolved from primitive ancestors through intense competition for dominance, survival of the fittest, as they say. This contrasts with the perspective where an individual is seen as having a soul that primarily requires a connection with the Divine. This soul resides inside a body that requires caretakers, particularly at the very start and the very end of its life, or when the body carries a child inside. Both descriptions of who we are would evolve into separate ways of organizing the collective, with distinct social and economic formations. The socioeconomic formations in the modern world, therefore, take a very different route, as compared to those in the communities that are described in this book.

Similar communities exist all over the world. Rather, sufficient evidence suggests that homo sapiens have been living in such communities since the beginning of time (Graeber & Wengrow, 2023; Harari, 2015; Polanyi, 2001). It has been argued that when the self-interest of individuals becomes more important than the interest of the collective, where the economic becomes more important than social, society eventually collapses (Diamond, 2013; Putnam, 2020; Tainter, 1988). Unfortunately, this is very much true for the contemporary globalized order or capitalism, where a small elite often prioritizes their interest over the rest, including non-human lifeforms. The spirit of capitalism when penetrates a community, it colonizes the minds of individuals, subsequently changing their interpersonal dynamics, creating class divisions, changing the nature of relationships between people from socioemotional to rational, often exploitative, and leaving behind many who cannot effectively transform themselves into human resources with required skills or capabilities. The new relationships are predominantly contractual, which often end without remorse, so much so that experts now hint toward the rise of the useless class in the next decade, whose skills would become redundant as they will be heartlessly replaced with artificial intelligence, as mentioned earlier. When the aim is economic, the social is only significant as a dispensable resource in capitalism, with externalities such as social exclusion and alienation.

Instead, for sustaining the social, the social needs to be the aim, while money, or anything that money can buy, should rather be dispensable for the sake of the social. Even better, if the social aims at the moral, which rather aims at a transcendental purpose. The communities that embody such a socioeconomic arrangement have much to teach the rest of the world, but time is not on their side, as their ideological and sociocultural foundations have been significantly shaken by the winds of capitalism, so it is almost an emergency-like situation. A counterstrategy, therefore, is urgently needed.

References

AlAmmar, W. A., Albeesh, F. H., & Khattab, R. Y. (2020). Food and mood: The corresponsive effect. *Current Nutrition Reports, 9*(3), 296–308. https://doi.org/10.1007/s13668-020-00331-3

Alderson, K. (2015). Conflict management and resolution in family-owned businesses. *Journal of Family Business Management, 5*(2), 140–156.

Arregle, J., Hitt, M. A., Sirmon, D., & Very, P. (2007). The development of organizational social capital: Attributes of family firms. *Journal of Management Studies, 44*(1), 73–95.

Astrachan, J. H., & Jaskiewicz, P. (2008). Emotional returns and emotional costs in privately held family businesses: Advancing traditional business valuation. *Family Business Review, 21*(2), 139–149. https://doi.org/10.1111/j.1741-6248.2008.00115.x

Barbera, F., Shi, H. X., Agarwal, A., & Edwards, M. (2020). The family that prays together stays together: Toward a process model of religious value transmission in family firms. *Journal of Business Ethics, 163*(4), 661–673. https://doi.org/10.1007/s10551-019-04382-7

Barnett, T., & Kellermanns, F. W. (2006). Are we family and are we treated as family? Nonfamily employees' perceptions of justice in the family firm. *Entrepreneurship Theory and Practice, 30*(6), 837–854. https://doi.org/10.1111/j.1540-6520.2006.00155.x

Benton, D. (2002). Carbohydrate ingestion, blood glucose and mood. *Neuroscience and Biobehavioral Reviews, 26*(3), 293–308.

Caputo, A., Marzi, G., Pellegrini, M. M., & Rialti, R. (2018). Conflict management in family businesses: A bibliometric analysis and systematic literature review. *International Journal of Conflict Management, 29*(4), 519–542. https://doi.org/10.1108/IJCMA-02-2018-0027

Chaudhary, S., Dhir, A., Ferraris, A., & Bertoldi, B. (2021). Trust and reputation in family businesses: A systematic literature review of past achievements and future promises. *Journal of Business Research, 137*, 143–161. https://doi.org/10.1016/j.jbusres.2021.07.052

Dari-Mattiacci, G., & Fabbri, M. (2023). How institutions shape morality. *The Journal of Law, Economics, and Organization, 39*(1), 160–198. https://doi.org/10.1093/jleo/ewab016

Davies, J. (2019). Preventing and solving issues in family-run businesses. *Nursing and Residential Care, 21*(3), 168–171.

DeFilippis, J. (2001). The myth of social capital in community development. *Housing Policy Debate, 12*(4), 781–806.

Diamond, J. (2013). *Collapse: How societies choose to fail or survive*. Penguin Books Limited.

Falzon, M. A. (2004). *Cosmopolitan connections: The Sindhi diaspora, 1860–2000*. Brill.

Fathallah, R., Sidani, Y., & Khalil, S. (2020). How religion shapes family business ethical behaviors: An institutional logics perspective. *Journal of Business Ethics, 163*(4), 647–659.

Freeman, J., & Engel, J. S. (2007). Models of innovation: Startups and mature corporations. *California Management Review, 50*(1), 94–119. https://doi.org/10.2307/41166418

Freire, P. (2000). *Pedagogy of the oppressed: 30th anniversary edition*. Bloomsbury Academic.

Fukuyama, F. (2011). *The origins of political order: From Prehuman times to the French revolution*. Profile Books Ltd.

Graeber, D., & Wengrow, D. (2023). *The dawn of everything: A new history of humanity*. Picador.

Haidt, J. (2023). Devices and desires: Social media is the major cause of the mental illness epidemic among young women. *New Statesman, 152*(5710–5711), 29.

Harari, Y. N. (2015). *Sapiens: A brief history of humankind*. Harper.

He, Q., Turel, O., & Bechara, A. (2017). Brain anatomy alterations associated with Social Networking Site (SNS) addiction. *Scientific Reports, 7*(1), 45064.

Karra, N., Tracey, P., & Phillips, N. (2006). Altruism and agency in the family firm: Exploring the role of family, kinship, and ethnicity. *Entrepreneurship: Theory and Practice, 30*(6), 861–877.

Kraybill, D. B. (2003). *The riddle of Amish culture*. Johns Hopkins University Press.

Le Breton-Miller, I., Miller, D., & Steier, L. P. (2004). Toward an integrative model of effective FOB succession. *Entrepreneurship Theory and Practice, 28*(4), 305–328.

Levitte, Y. M. (2004). Bonding social capital in entrepreneurial developing communities—Survival networks or barriers? *Journal of Community Development Society, 35*(1), 44–64.

Mitra, S. (2015). From hole in the wall to school in the cloud. In P. Dixon, S. Humble, & C. Counihan (Eds.), *Handbook of international development and education* (pp. 368–376). Edward Elgar Publishing Ltd.

Montag, C., & Diefenbach, S. (2018). Towards homo digitalis: Important research issues for psychology and the neurosciences at the dawn of the internet of things and the digital society. *Sustainability, 10*(2), 415.

Orr, D. W. (2004). *Earth in mind: On education, environment and the human prospect*. Island Press.

Pearson, A. W., Carr, J. C., & Shaw, J. C. (2008). Toward a theory of familiness: A social capital perspective. *Entrepreneurship: Theory and Practice, 32*(6 Spec. Iss.), 949–969.

Perricone, P. J., Earle, J. R., & Taplin, I. M. (2001). Patterns of succession and continuity in family-owned businesses: Study of an ethnic community. *Family Business Review, XIV*(2), 105–122.

Polanyi, K. (2001). *The great transformation: The political and economic origins of our time*. Beacon Press.

Portes, A. (1998). Social capital: Its origins and applications in modern sociology. *Annual Review of Sociology, 24*(1), 1–24.

Poutziouris, P. Z., Steier, L., & Smyrnios, K. X. (2004). Guest editorial: A commentary on family business entrepreneurial. *International Journal of Entrepreneurial Behavior and Research, 10*(1/2), 7–11.

Putnam, R. D. (2020). *Bowling alone: Revised and updated: The collapse and revival of american community*. Simon & Schuster.

Ritzer, G. (2016). The mcdonaldization of society. In E. Mofield & T. Stambaugh (Eds.), *In the mind's eye* (1st ed.). London: Routledge.

Schumacher, E. F. (2010). *Small is beautiful: Economics as if people mattered*. HarperCollins.

Sharma, P., & Irving, P. G. (2005). Four bases of family business successor commitment: Antecedents and consequences. *Entrepreneurship Theory and Practice, 29*(1), 13–33. https://doi.org/10.1111/j.1540-6520.2005.00067.x

Storr, W. (2018). *Selfie: How the west become self-obsessed*. Pan Macmillan.

Tainter, J. A. (1988). *The collapse of complex societies*. Cambridge University Press.

Taylor, C. (1992). *Sources of the self: The making of the modern identity*. Cambridge University Press.

Twenge, J. M., & Campbell, W. K. (2010). *The narcissism epidemic: Living in the age of entitlement*. Atria Books.

Woolcock, M. (1998). Social capital and economic development: Toward a theoretical synthesis and policy framework. *Theory and Society, 27*(2), 151–208.

Zellweger, T. M., Kellermanns, F. W., Chrisman, J. J., & Chua, J. H. (2012). Family control and family firm valuation by family CEOs: The importance of intentions for transgenerational control. *Organization Science, 23*(3), 851–868.

Chapter 9
Conclusion

The book starts by highlighting the problem of alienation caused by the disintegration of pre-modern social reality along with the worldview through which a pre-modern individual would make sense of their existence. This disintegration was caused by the selective instrumentalization of everything, including the social, for amoral economic ends in the modern world. Such instrumentalization became a key design feature of modern institutions as well. This was contrary to the fact that every relationship in a person's life has an underlying a socioemotional dimension, but not every relationship can be economic or transactional. So, when the logic of the economic supersedes, the social is hard to sustain. The social reality that existed in the form of the organic family, tribe, community, and kinship networks, thus found itself to be at odds with the way the capitalist economy organized resources, including manpower, for improving efficiency, and productivity aimed at maximizing profits for the shareholders. The metaphysics of enlightenment allowed such valuation and reorganization of human beings and all other natural resources as per the capitalist instrumentalizing logic. The instrumentalization of humans and social relations led to alienation, a feeling of being used for meaningless ends. Alienation is thus a price that was paid to survive in the market economy. Alienation can be regarded as a modern invention, as it was seldom found in pre-modern, organically organized social reality. Today, it contributes to an epidemic of addiction and often becomes a cause of suicide as well. The presence of these problems at a mass scale, particularly in high-income nations, implies that some basic human needs are not being met, unlike in pre-modern times. However, the organic social reality often allows individuals to feel useful even if they offer no instrumental value to others. This was so because the economy was typically a part of the social order, and the social order was a lot more than the economy itself, which allowed individuals to have a sense of worth beyond their capacity to make money. The economic activity in such a society was organized on social lines, thus serving the needs of the social as well. This is true to some extent in many communities in the world today. This book outlined the example of three communities in Pakistan in this context.

O. Javaid, *Socioeconomic Sustainability Through Moral and Social Capital*, Entrepreneurship and Development in South Asia: Longitudinal Narratives,
https://doi.org/10.1007/978-981-96-8134-1_9

It can be inferred from the discussion in the previous chapters that it is a healthy social environment that can provide an antidote to the problem of alienation. The examples discussed suggest that to sustain the social in a healthy manner, economic activity would serve as a means for social ends, while the social would also facilitate the economic activity, thus sustaining both. The relationship between the economic and the social was operated under the moral framework adhered to by the religiously oriented enterprising communities. The religious beliefs or meta-norms provided the teleological context to the moral framework that prioritized the social over the economic. A bird's eye view of other similar communities around the world, and those that predate the spread of the market society, suggests that they also operated on similar lines. The economic was found to be generally embedded in the social, aligning with Polanyi's thesis of social embeddedness. The book further adds to the thesis that the social is to be embedded in the moral, while the moral needs to be embedded in the meta-norms of a particular belief system. An individual in such communities was(is) typically seen as a person of God, with a duty toward others, for which economic resources would serve as a means, which one has to acquire through ethical economic activity, which would be facilitated through social relationships, that would be sustained through moral conduct. This is in stark contrast to the capitalist meta-norms, where individuals are a resource to be consumed by the capitalist institutions for economic ends, and so are their social relations, even their socioemotional or moral sentiments, which are manipulated in the process of consumption. What is consumed by capitalism is thus hard to sustain.

Therefore, it can be concluded from the discussion in the book that to sustain the social along with the economic, and to allow individuals to have a sense of their existence, the capitalist order must be reversed. This perhaps cannot be done until the meta-norms, a master narrative, a *Weltanschauung*, and the subsequent moral framework, adhered to by a society, undergo a radical change. The perennial questions, like why the universe exists, and why I as an individual exist in this universe, would set the significance of social engagements in contrast to the economic ones. Or if either one of them is a means to the other. A moral framework that aligns with one's purpose in life can thus set the order between the social and economic, that is, which ought to be used for whose ends, or if either of them has to be ignored or not, or if the two need to be managed separately. A moral framework, therefore, which helps align the social and the economic in a meaningful whole, allows the two to go along together, as seen in previous chapters. Religions in general have been offering such a moral framework. So, instead of focusing on either social or economic ends, or both, a religion or belief system often enables its adherents to focus on certain moral ends, which encompass the social and economic, thus eliminating the burden of responsibility of balancing the two. The religious belief system typically saw the economic as a means for the social, and not the other way around, while the social—the act of being kind to others—has been a means to ensure terms with God. The examples discussed in the book thus suggest that turning the economic into a means for the social sustains the social, which then facilitates the economic and thus ensures the socioeconomic sustainability of a community. This is more significant during times when the odds are not in the favor of the community, as people are supposed to be helped even if they cannot return the favor.

A key finding in this context is the ability to exercise moral agency, which is often constrained by too much formalization in an institutionalized world. A person with resources often cannot help others even if they want to, because of the nature of relationships that an institutionalized world creates. When either or both of the two individuals operate as agents of an institution, the extent to which they can facilitate each other is constrained by the responsibilities assigned to them by their employers. So, the degree of social sustainability also largely depends on the degree of institutionalization of a society. However, when individuals are not operating as agents of institutions, but rather independently, they can form interdependent relationships, where commitments are enforced by socioemotional, economic, cultural, religious, contractual, and(or) moral criteria. The interdependent relationships can then potentially ensure socioeconomic sustainability. The meta-norms of the communities in focus put trust in the moral agents who form multiple types of interdependencies among each other. Some of these interdependencies, as discussed, are because of cultural or religious reinforcements, as in the absence of culture and religion, like in post-modern hyper-individualistic cultures, the interdependencies are lesser, therefore, lowering the possibility of sustaining the social. The interdependences then maintain relationships during various stages of the life of an individual with others, or when the community as a whole suffers from a crisis. This makes it critical to ensure the development of moral agents either through the upbringing process at home or through formal education. The role of women in their role as mothers and grandmothers, in particular, was noted as strategically critical in this context.

Some might not be happy to see the endorsement of religion. Common arguments could be that religion promotes intolerance and stifles human creativity. This is perhaps true for certain religious appearing societies in history; however, evidence shows that this might be more because of a sense of insecurity or exploitation of religious dictums to maintain control by a religious elite, as discussed in Chapter 4. However, the entire pre-modern world cannot be painted with the same color, as there are ample examples from Europe and particularly the Muslim world, where both science and technology can be seen as thriving, simply because studying nature to find the signs of God is a directive in both religions. Several notable scholars have explored the development of science and technology during the so-called Dark Ages and the Medieval periods (Falk, 2020; Lindberg, 2013; Numbers, 2009). The same can be said about egalitarianism, a blanket statement cannot be made. Jews, for example, who faced persecution in Europe, survived after finding refuge in the Ottoman Empire, where they are reported to have grown religiously, intellectually, and economically (Finkel, 2007; Lewis, 2013). Many other religious minorities are said to have thrived likewise under Ottoman rule (İnalcık & Quataert, 1994). Cavanaugh (2009) and Armstrong (2014) argue that religion is falsely accused of being violent, which is rather a problem of empires. Empires in the past have misused religion to declare themselves as good, and then claim to fight against their opponents who were declared as evil. Hunger for power, the urge to maintain control over a territory, and the use of violence against a people for that purpose are suggested as the main culprits. In

Pakistan also sectarian violence between the Shia community and the orthodox Sunni has reportedly been an outcome of the exploitative control of peasants by landlords who adhere to the Shia sect (Abou-Zahab, 2017; Ahmar, 2007; Kamran, 2009), but should we blame Shia faith for it?

Many more examples can be cited to make the point that the conflict that appears due to religious differences is primarily due to power differences between two groups, or the urge to take control of a resource, like land, for the expansion of an empire, that leads two groups to be at each other's throats. On the contrary, the groups that have been able to form an interdependent relationship with each other find it difficult to be in conflict due to the cost associated with it. The extreme form of division of labor that prevails today in a complex society, therefore, can allow adherents of different faiths to mutually co-exist. Their relationship can be purely economic, but to survive, they will have to exchange the stuff they produce. This has the propensity to deter conflict, as acknowledged by many notable thinkers (Kant, 2006; Pinker, 2012). The SME sector often requires individuals with specialized skills who may not be found in the community to which the SME owners belong. Several respondents I interviewed admitted that they need the talent to run their firms, which can be found anywhere. Some were even reluctant to hire members of their community who they thought would leave after learning the tricks of the trade to start a business of their own. So, they preferred hiring members of other communities. Their customers can also be anyone from the whole of society. The resulting interdependence with the rest of the society, therefore, naturally keeps them peace-loving. It is needless to mention that a peaceful and stable environment is good for the business. So, it can be argued that entrepreneurial orientation, and the urge to grow, coupled with division of labor, can create a peaceful and harmonious environment of mutual co-existence between a diverse set of populations.

This, however, does not solve the problem of exploitation that may occur due to a power differential, when one community is marginalized and has not been able to develop sufficient skills that can be sold to others, while some groups control a significant amount of resources in a society. This is where it becomes necessary that those in power exercise moral agency and follow their religion's directive to indiscriminately help those in need, in case they adhere to one. Otherwise, unjust exploitative behavior is likely, which eventually would sow the seed of future conflict. The same applies, as discussed earlier, in any relationship with a power differential, even in a very domestic context, which often creates friction between, for example, husbands and wives, in-laws and brides, and even sometimes between siblings or cousins. Often, hyper-independence is suggested as an antidote to exploitative relationships; however, if the problem prevails on a societal scale, even institutionally, then one can potentially land again in an exploitative relationship after escaping from one. The idea of hyper-independence is perhaps oxymoronic even in a society where the division of labor exists, as one eventually has to rely on others for exchange, which one is often unable to do, thus creating the need for a space where one is taken care of by others altruistically. However, altruistic treatment cannot be incentivized into existence, but perhaps can be inspired into the people's hearts. This is where we hit the limits of policymaking, as policymakers generally attempt to incentivize desirable behaviors into existence.

Historically, missionaries have always inspired people toward altruism by walking the talk. Parents instill altruism in their children through demonstration. It is difficult to quantify as well, nor can its benefits be observed in the short term, making it even more difficult for policymakers to demonstrate the 'effectiveness' of their policies and thus secure their careers. To imagine individuals as altruistic also contradicts the worldview of a policymaker with an education in economics, as, from the vantage point of economic theory, individuals are rational and prioritize their material self-interest. All of which makes it difficult for policymakers to promote altruism in a society. However, policymakers can see the economic output generated by the firms owned and started by the entrepreneurs in the enterprising communities, the employment generated, and their philanthropic activities, all of which are sufficiently facilitated by altruistic behavior. Research like the one presented in this book can bring their attention to the qualitative or subjective factors like altruism, moral character that inspires it, and the informal social arrangements where it is practiced, all of which also contribute to strengthening the economic muscle of community entrepreneurs. These factors may also include:

- A typical environment of an extended healthy organic family;
- The role of parents and grandparents, mothers and grandmothers in particular, in the upbringing process to raise psychologically secure, morally empowered individuals, having a sense of purpose;
- A frugal lifestyle, as opposed to the latest consumerist trends;
- A worldview, like that offered by religions, that encourages altruism, instills a sense of security, and provides believers a narrative to help make sense of their existence;
- A culture of cooperation and voluntary sharing within an extended kinship network;
- The use of formal legal structures (like contracts) only when needed by morally conscious individuals without constraining their moral agency; and
- Significance of the informal economic arrangements for exercising moral agency and their subsequent contribution toward building social capital.

I am not the first one to identify the significance of these factors; others have done so across various disciplines. However, further research would be required to understand how precisely these factors play out in religious enterprising communities in Pakistan and the region. The work in this manuscript was based on limited data, much of which was qualitative. It raises many questions, which require further research. These questions include: how to strengthen the process of raising morally conscious individuals with a sense of purpose; what barriers their parents are facing in the process at the moment; how to resolve the differences between the brides and mothers-in-law; how to create the necessary conditions for the required upbringing if that does not exist; how the early educational environment can be transformed in the context of their cultural particularities to develop moral agents, who possess virtues likecooperation and sharing (and wisdom to know where to practice them); instead of competition and self-interest? Further, what can be done to reverse the generation gap that has already been created either due to the attitude of the elders or allegedly due to the modern educational environment or content consumption of digital devices, and how to reverse the antisocial or self-centric behavior where it has been created, if it is possible? To answer questions like these, more insight is needed.

This is where the policymakers can be helpful, that is, to engage the research community to find answers to critical questions and develop precise antidotes to the potential contributors to the disintegration of enterprising communities. The second task policymakers and implementers can engage in is educating the community members about what they need to change and facilitating them in the process. Schumacher (2010) recommends that outsiders must not try to change a community from the inside if the community is not interested in changing as it often fires back, thankfully this does not seem to be the case with the three communities focused in this book, as they identify the challenges at hand and are concerned about it. The challenge for policymakers or researchers would be to gain the trust of the elders or influencers and convince them that the research may provide them with deeper insight into what needs to be done. Engaging the elders and involving them in the research process from the beginning would perhaps be a better way to get their buy-in to the project. After finding the answers to the questions and working out culturally and religiously compatible solutions, a bigger challenge would be their continuous implementation as per the feedback received from all concerned stakeholders. Without a wholehearted buy-in from a significant number of community members, any necessary change may not materialize. The focus should be on education on every level, through every possible medium. Religious places and religious leaders can also play a role, depending on their influence. The lasting impact would perhaps come from transforming the educational environment of school-going children, but it is critical to know what needs to be transformed. Some hints were given in this book in this context in Chapter 8.

The problem described and the course of action suggested are not only relevant for the communities in focus in this book but for everyone who is concerned about the disintegration of the organic social reality and its alienating effects. There are places where the social has been distorted beyond recognition, and there are places where it is just a matter of a generation before any traces of a healthy form of organic social reality may be obliterated. The problem is not only because of the way economic activity is organized, but also the ideological or philosophical justification that legitimizes such an activity, the moral has been hijacked by the economic, and so is the social. Therefore, the likely solution as discussed extensively in this work is not in mere reorganization of the economic, but to reconsider the ideological and (a)moral basis which has allowed the contemporary economic arrangements to spread around the world. The natural in all its forms, be it the organic forms of social reality that humans create or the biosphere, has been disintegrated into bits for the capitalist machines to utilize the parts that appear useful for their amoral goals. This cannot be appreciated anymore when the knowledge of its consequences on the human soul or the soul of the planet has become increasingly obvious. The only choice, perhaps, is to choose against this obliteration and find a path that does the opposite. The amoral has to be replaced with a moral alternative, which comes part and parcel with a master narrative (or meta-norms) that describes who we are, in the context of our place in this universe. Without such a master narrative, a term used by Taylor (2018), the moral becomes a human opinion. Religions already offered such a master narrative in the past, helping the common folks to make sense of their existence by giving them a morally righteous purpose. The common man and the people in power, however, frequently get overpowered by their sense of insecurity or greed, and then use religion to justify their actions. Perhaps awareness about such temptations, coupled with the development of the moral muscle, if made part of the early formal and informal education, may reduce the misuse of any master narratives or moral framework. The development of such awareness and making our moral will stronger than our base desires is perhaps the real challenge of the human story, the answer to which could be found in places where the modern man least expects.

References

Abou-Zahab, M. (2017). The Sunni–Shia conflict in Jhang (Pakistan). In *Lived Islam in South Asia* (pp. 161–174). Routledge.

Ahmar, M. (2007). Sectarian conflicts in Pakistan. *Pakistan Vision, 9*(1), 1–19.

Armstrong, K. (2014). *Fields of blood: Religion and the history of violence*. Random House LLC.

Cavanaugh, W. T. (2009). *The myth of religious violence: Secular ideology and the roots of modern conflict*. Oxford University Press.

Falk, S. (2020). *The light ages: The surprising story of medieval science*. WW Norton & Company.

Finkel, C. (2007). *Osman's dream: The history of the Ottoman Empire*. Hachette UK.

İnalcık, H., & Quataert, D. (1994). *An economic and social history of the Ottoman Empire, 1300–1914*. Cambridge University Press.

Kamran, T. (2009). Contextualizing sectarian militancy in Pakistan: A case study of Jhang. *Journal of Islamic Studies, 20*(1), 55–85.

Kant, I. (2006). Toward perpetual peace: A philosophical sketch. *Toward Perpetual Peace and Other Writings on Politics, Peace, and History, 8*, 360.

Lewis, B. (2013). *The Jews of Islam*. Routledge.

Lindberg, D. C. (2013). Science and the medieval church. In D. C. Lindberg & M. H. Shank (Eds.), *The Cambridge history of science: Volume 2: Medieval science* (Vol. 2, pp. 268–285). Cambridge: Cambridge University Press. https://doi.org/10.1017/CHO9780511974007.012

Numbers, R. L. (2009). *Galileo goes to jail and other myths about science and religion*. London: Harvard University Press.

Pinker, S. (2012). *The better angels of our nature: A history of violence and humanity*. Penguin Books.

Schumacher, E. F. (2010). *Small is beautiful: Economics as if people mattered*. HarperCollins.

Taylor, C. (2018). *A secular age*. Harvard University Press.

Index

O. Javaid, *Socioeconomic Sustainability Through Moral and Social Capital*, Entrepreneurship and Development in South Asia: Longitudinal Narratives,
https://doi.org/10.1007/978-981-96-8134-1

MIX
Papier aus verantwortungsvollen Quellen
Paper from responsible sources
FSC® C105338

If you have any concerns about our products,
you can contact us on
ProductSafety@springernature.com

In case Publisher is established outside the EU,
the EU authorized representative is:
Springer Nature Customer Service Center GmbH
Europaplatz 3, 69115 Heidelberg, Germany

Printed by Libri Plureos GmbH
in Hamburg, Germany